12/14

ON THE ROAD
WITH

janis joplin

ON THE ROAD
WITH
janis joplin

—————

John Byrne Cooke

BERKLEY BOOKS, NEW YORK

THE BERKLEY PUBLISHING GROUP
Published by the Penguin Group
Penguin Group (USA) LLC
375 Hudson Street, New York, New York 10014

USA • Canada • UK • Ireland • Australia • New Zealand • India • South Africa • China

penguin.com

A Penguin Random House Company

This book is an original publication of The Berkley Publishing Group.

ON THE ROAD WITH JANIS JOPLIN

Berkley hardcover ISBN: 978-0-425-27411-8

An application to register this book for cataloging has been submitted to
the Library of Congress.

FIRST EDITION: November 2014

PRINTED IN THE UNITED STATES OF AMERICA

10   9   8   7   6   5   4   3   2   1

Cover and endpaper photographs © John Byrne Cooke.
Cover and endpaper design by Diana Kolsky.
Interior text design by Tiffany Estreicher.

Jacket poster lyrics are from "As Good as You've Been to This World" written by Nick Gravenites.

Most Berkley Books are available at special quantity discounts for bulk purchases
for sales promotions, premiums, fund-raising, or educational use. Special books,
or book excerpts, can also be created to fit specific needs.
For details, write: Special.Markets@us.penguingroup.com.

For Janis

CONTENTS

ACKNOWLEDGMENTS

So MANY PEOPLE have helped in so many ways to bring this book, at long last, into the light of day, that I approach the task of acknowledging them with the certain knowledge that I will forget one or more whose names should be recognized here. I ask your forgiveness at the outset for any omissions, and I promise to rectify them when I can.

Laura and Michael Joplin, Janis's sister and brother, have shepherded Janis's legacy through the years with care and love. They have supported the use of my photographs and films of Janis in many projects, and I am grateful for their support for this one. Jeff Jampol, the manager of Janis's estate, has been similarly supportive; he has preserved and enhanced Janis's legacy through a variety of creative projects and he provided valuable assistance and advice in moving this book along the path to publication.

Candace Lake, my agent and friend for almost four decades, guided the effort to find a home for this book, and provided the vital link that helped us arrive at Anthony Mattero, of Foundry Literary + Media, who expertly planned the final steps that led us to Berkley Books. Their support and friendship is ongoing, and deeply appreciated.

Authors do not choose their editors. I have been very fortunate in the editors who have chosen to work with me, never more so than in the case of my present editor, Denise Silvestro. Her encouragement, advice, and innovative solutions to every vexing question have improved this book in ways I never imagined possible. Denise's assistant, Allison Janice, labored valiantly over the source notes and performed countless other chores without ever making me feel that any other books or authors needed a minute of her time. Managing editor Michelle Kasper kept the book on schedule. She and many others at Berkley Books and Penguin Random House have made me feel very lucky to be with this publisher.

Stacy Kreuzmann Quinn and Nancy Reid, of Acid Test Productions, who published *Janis Joplin: A Performance Diary*, encouraged me to tell my own story of these years and provided helpful suggestions and insights.

Earl Crabb and David Swift scanned research pages and early drafts of this book into my computer before I knew anything about scanning. Earl has contributed so many hours of computer diagnosis, problem-solving and advice over the course of thirty years that I can never adequately repay him, but I will try my best to channel Albert Grossman and pick up the check anytime we break bread together.

Many of Janis's friends and mine, among them many of the people who knew Janis best during her years of national and international touring, contributed their insights and knowledge by agreeing to sit down for recorded conversations with me. Excerpts in the book are credited as "Author interview with," but these were truly conversations that followed wherever the pathways of memory took us, rather than a prepared list of questions, although I had those too. None of these contributors were more consistently helpful than Sam Andrew, of Big Brother and the Holding Company, and Bob Neuwirth. Dave Getz and Peter Albin, the other surviving members of Big Brother, also deserve special mention. Thanks also to Mark Braunstein; Kozmic Blues Band members Brad Campbell, Terry Clements, Snooky Flowers, Richard Kermode, and John Till; Full Tilt Boogie members Richard Bell, Ken

Pearson, and Clark Pierson; and Committee members Alan Myerson (director), Howard Hesseman, Carl Gottlieb, and Garry Goodrow.

I would like to write individual words of thanks to all the others who helped me, but in order that the reader can move along a little sooner to Janis's story, I list them here with my heartfelt thanks to each: Dave Barry, Peter Berg, Barbara Carroll, Ramblin' Jack Elliott, Lyndall Erb, Mimi Fariña, Barry Feinstein, John Fisher, Dave and Vera-Mae Fredrickson, Charlie Frizzell, Ralph J. Gleason, Bennett Glotzer, Bob (Robert E.) Gordon, Allison Caine Gottlieb, Bill Graham, Linda Gravenites, Nick Gravenites, Debbie Green, Sally Grossman, Robert L. Jones, Al Kooper, Jon McIntire, Milan Melvin, Margaret Moore, Seth Morgan, Geoff Muldaur, D. A. Pennebaker and Chris Hegedus, Frazer Pennebaker, Peter Pilafian, Fritz Richmond, Paul Rothchild, Rock Scully, Bob Seidemann, and Mary Works.

Thanks to one and all, and God bless us, every one.

PETER ALBIN, DAVE GETZ, and Sam Andrew continue to perform music together as Big Brother and the Holding Company, and in other combinations. Robert Altman, D. A. Pennebaker, and Bob Seidemann generously contributed photographs that are included in this book. Mary Works's film *The Life and Times of the Red Dog Saloon* beautifully chronicles the origins of the San Francisco rock-and-roll ballroom scene in the midsixties. You can follow their activities and see their work at these websites:

Official Janis Joplin website: janisjoplin.com
Big Brother and the Holding Company: bbhc.com
Robert Altman Photography: altmanphoto.com
Pennebaker-Hegedus Films: phfilms.com
Bob Seidemann Photography: bobseidemann.com
Mary Works: reddogsaloonfilm.com/Red_Dog_Saloon_Film
/Welcome.html

AUTHOR'S NOTE

A FRIEND OF mine likes to say that history is what you remember. Memories are fallible, of course. Our impressions of the past are subjective and selective. They summon up what we want it to be as well as what it was. In preparing to write this story I spoke with many people who experienced the same events I did, and many who were present at times and places where I was not. We all saw the sixties from different perspectives. For many of us, the friendships we formed in those years have proven to be lifelong; we share similar memories of the music and the seemingly unlimited possibilities that characterized the times.

Aided by the recollections of others, this narrative relates my personal experience, focused through my memory and shaped according to my sensibilities. Any errors of fact or interpretation are mine alone.

John Byrne Cooke
Jackson, Wyoming
2014

THE BANDS

BIG BROTHER AND THE HOLDING COMPANY

Janis Joplin—vocals and percussion

Sam Andrew—guitar and vocals*

James Gurley—guitar and vocals

Peter Albin—bass, guitar and vocals

Dave Getz—drums

Road Crew

Big Brother had no road manager until Albert Grossman managed the band.

John Cooke—road manager

Dave Richards—equipment

Mark Braunstein—equipment

George Ostrow—equipment

Management

Chet Helms (1965–1966)

Julius Karpen (1966–1967)

Albert Grossman (1967–)

John Court—Albert's partner
(1967–1968)

Bert Block—Albert's partner
(1968–1969)

---

* "Vocals" is listed for lead vocals only.

THE KOZMIC BLUES BAND

Musicians playing each instrument are listed in the order in which they played with this band.

Janis Joplin—vocals and percussion
Sam Andrew—guitar and vocals
John Till—guitar
Brad Campbell—bass
Roy Markowitz—drums
Lonnie Castille—drums
Maury Baker—drums
Terry Clements—alto saxophone

Snooky Flowers—baritone
    saxophone and vocals
Marcus Doubleday—trumpet
Terry Hensley—trumpet
Luis Gasca—trumpet
Dave Woodward—trumpet
Bill King—organ
Richard Kermode—organ

Road Crew

John Cooke—road manager
    (Dec. 1968–Oct. 1969)
Joe Crowley—road manager
    (Oct.–Dec. 1969)

Mark Braunstein—equipment
George Ostrow—equipment
Vince Mitchell—equipment

Management

Albert Grossman
Bert Block—Albert's partner (–1969)

Bennett Glotzer—Albert's partner
    (1969–)

FULL TILT BOOGIE

There were no changes in personnel during the life of this band.

Janis Joplin—vocals and percussion
John Till—guitar
Brad Campbell—bass

Ken Pearson—organ
Richard Bell—electric piano
Clark Pierson—drums

Road Crew

John Cooke—road manager
George Ostrow—equipment
Vince Mitchell—equipment

Phil Badella—equipment
Joel Kornoelje—equipment

Management

Albert Grossman

Bennett Glotzer

CHAPTER ONE

If You're Going to San Francisco

November 30, 1967

THE 707'S WHEELS touch down at San Francisco International Airport and with few regrets I leave behind the East, where my mother's family has lived since they arrived on the New England coast aboard a vessel that followed in the wake of the *Mayflower*. There they landed and there, for the most part, they stayed, close by the Atlantic shore. In five hours I've covered what it took the emigrants of the nineteenth century's great westward migration months of peril to travel. Like those earlier travelers, I'm casting off the old and hoping to find in California the magic pathway to the rest of my life.

Go west, young man.

In my case, it is Albert Grossman, not Horace Greeley, who points the way.

The southwest wind is roiling the shallow waters off the airport runway, turning them muddy emerald. It has been a cold fall in the East. By comparison, the California air feels springlike as I cross the tarmac to the terminal. The hills that surround the Bay are greened by the rains that return to the coast with autumn. Autumn in the East forces the flora into retreat and quiescence. To an easterner, green hills in November signal rebirth ahead of its time, a resurrection that fills me with hope. The breeze carries the scent of growing things. Mixed with the jet fumes, I can smell salt water, and something more exotic—patchouli oil, maybe, or pot.

Peter Albin greets me at the gate. We have talked on the phone in recent days, to discuss logistics ("My flight gets in at . . ." "I'll pick you up and we'll . . ."). I know Peter by sight because I saw him, back in June, at the Monterey International Pop Festival, standing his ground at stage right as a member of Big Brother and the Holding Company, the band that knocked the audience back on its collective heel. Peter's feet don't move much when he plays the electric bass. His body sways to the beat, sometimes curling over the instrument to wring from it insistent riffs that propel the songs forward, sometimes standing bolt upright, his back arched, shaking the bass so the notes fly from the stage with that much more force.

In the airport, face-to-face, Peter is friendly, open, welcoming. He moves with angular looseness and has a lopsided smile. At twenty-three, he's the youngest in the band. In Cambridge, Massachusetts, where I have lived for the past nine years, Peter's shoulder-length hair would earn him derisive shouts of "Hahvahd fairy!" from the townies, their ducktails rigid with Brylcreem. In SFO, he attracts surreptitious glances from the servicemen emplaning for Vietnam and the businessmen in their suits. It would surprise them to know that Peter is a junior executive, dressed for rock and roll. He is the member of Big Brother who signs the contracts, the one who comes to pick up the guy dispatched from New York by Albert Grossman—creator of Peter, Paul and Mary, manager of Bob Dylan and a host of lesser folk luminaries—to oversee the band on the road. As the music of the counterculture has evolved from folk to folk-rock—the Mamas & the Papas, Simon & Garfunkel, Buffalo Springfield—to full-bore rock and roll, Albert has kept pace.

When Peter's car crests the rise where Highway 101 leaves South San Francisco behind and comes in view of the city proper, I see the white houses dancing up and down the hills and I feel at home. San Francisco is my favorite American city. I have been here often over the years, most recently in June, when I landed at SFO as part of D. A. Pennebaker's film crew, on my way to Monterey for the Pop Festival, fired then, as now, with the sense of moving toward the promise of things to come, ready to do my part to make the promise come true.

I have a family connection to the Bay Area, an uncle who is a professor of botany at UC Berkeley. When I drove across the country for the first time, in the summer after my sophomore year at Harvard, my uncle's Berkeley home was my destination. In recent years, it is music that has brought me often to the cities by the Bay. From the first time I stepped into the Club 47 coffeehouse in Cambridge and heard Joan Baez sing, music has defined my friendships and my life. I discovered bluegrass music and became a member of Cambridge's homegrown bluegrass and old-time band, the Charles River Valley Boys. In the spring of 1963 I drove across the country again, this time with two friends from Cambridge, and we discovered in Berkeley a folk community that was welcoming and familiar.

In the folk music revival, Berkeley and Cambridge were united by enthusiasm for the traditional roots of American music, black and white, and the innovations that creative players could derive from those themes. Some of my Cambridge friends made the journey to California regularly. A few moved here. The kinship forged on the Cambridge-Berkeley axis was based on sharing the music and shunning competition. We believed ourselves to be quietly superior to what we saw as the more commercially oriented pickers in New York and L.A. Our image of the prototypical New York guitar player was a guy who turned toward the wall when he played his hottest licks, so you couldn't see how he did it.

Since that first visit to the Berkeley folk scene in 1963, I have come back whenever I can, to play music and smoke dope and drink Jack

Daniel's Tennessee whiskey and Rainier Ale—Berkeley's preferred boilermaker, known locally as JD and Green Death—and to experience the brilliant, preternaturally focused California days that inspire us to throw some bread and cheese and wine into a backpack and take acid and spend the day somewhere on the coast.

A couple of years ago I moved to California for what I thought would be forever, but it turned out I was chasing the Wrong Girl. This time, I'm here to stay. I have left behind the life of a performing musician in the interest of getting serious about the rest of my life. For now, I will help others devote themselves more fully to their music while I handle the money and logistics. I have exchanged my guitar for an attaché case. It contains itineraries, contracts, and the promise of loud music, late nights, and loose women.

To Peter Albin, I reveal none of the giddy high that the waters of the Bay, the sight of Coit Tower, a glimpse of the Golden Gate Bridge, arouse in me. With Peter, I'm all business. I'm cool. He takes me to a motel on Columbus Avenue, in North Beach. A few years ago, the North Beach coffeehouses were the focus of San Francisco's folk scene, and before that, the home of the Beats. I wonder if any unamplified music survives in the city that has become the wellspring of American rock and roll, but satisfying this curiosity will have to wait. Right now, I've got to pass inspection by my prospective employers. Peter gives me half an hour to come down from thirty thousand feet, then picks me up again and takes me to meet the band.

They rehearse in a third-floor loft in a building they call the Warehouse, close by an off-ramp where the Central Freeway dumps traffic into the city streets. When Peter and I enter the loft, the four other members of the band are sitting at a round oak table by the windows. There's a bed covered with a madras spread, the ubiquitous, versatile fabric by which a generation of bohemian youth is enriching the textile magnates of India. There are amps and instruments and a drum set off to one side, random sticks of furniture, and enough floor space to hold a dance competition. A few oil paintings adorn the walls. They're by the drummer, David Getz, I will learn. David has set his painting aside for a venture into rock and roll.

The space could be any number of artists' lofts where I've been to late-night parties in New York, but, except for the paintings, the art in progress here isn't visible, and the quintet scrutinizing me now is pure San Francisco. This is the moment of truth. The truth is, I'm nervous, which is a condition I customarily conceal beneath a re-served exterior.

I recognize Janis, of course, but Peter is a polite fellow and he introduces her first. It was Janis who took the audience's breath away at Monterey, this Texas white girl who belts the rocking blues like no one else, propelled by one of the founding bands of the San Fran-cisco Sound.

Sam Andrew and James Gurley are the lanky guitar players, sprawled in their chairs with legs askew. Tight-fitting black jeans. Pointy-toed boots. *Long* hair. Way longer than any East Coast beat-nik's. Theirs is down past their shoulders, combed straight like Janis's. I'm six-feet-one-and-a-bit, and I judge that Sam and James, upright, will inhabit the same altitude. Peter is a couple of inches shorter. David is more compact. He falls into the range that eye-witnesses describe as average height. At this meeting he sits squarely on his chair, all his attention on me, just as he sits at his drums on-stage, centered and balanced. David's hair, and Peter's, is a little shorter than Sam's and James's, pageboy haircuts gone to seed.

Janis is watchful. In repose her face is unremarkable, not what you'd call pretty. Only her eyes betray the vitality she releases in per-formance. They are clear and alert, and when the introductions are over it is Janis who speaks first.

"What sign are you?"

"Libra."

"That sounds just," James says. This is a generous reaction and I'm grateful to him, but Janis is looking me up and down with all the distrust appropriate for greeting a newcomer from the East, a road manager imposed on the band by Albert Grossman, the personal manager they barely know and for sure don't fully trust.

Janis shrugs. "I don't care much about Libras one way or the other."

But I'm cool. I take no offense, because they accept me. Cautiously and with reservations, to be sure, but they accept me. I'm a rock-and-roll road manager. When I got off the plane it was only make-believe.

Now it's real.

"I remember Janis took to you right away, man. She thought you were cute."

Sam Andrew

CHAPTER TWO

California Dreamin'

THE POET-NOVELIST ROBERT Penn Warren wrote, "I eat a persimmon and the teeth of a tinker in Tibet are put on edge." He liked to watch the far-reaching ripples of unpredictable cause and effect spread from that crystalline moment when the stone hits the still surface of the pond.

There are times and places where the flow of events becomes focused through an accidental lens—an experience, an event that becomes a turning point in many lives. Our generation is entranced by synchronicity, yet only those most attuned to the flow recognize these confluences for what they are at the time, even when they blunder into them head-on. The Monterey Pop Festival was such a moment for Janis and Big Brother. Their presence at the festival and the effect of their performance were the result of many decisions and turning points, any one of which might have yielded a different result.

For my part, if I hadn't been at the Pop Festival, I wouldn't have become the road manager for Big Brother and the Holding Company. That's as close to fact as you can get in the realm of "what if?"

What if Big Brother hadn't played at Monterey? They might not have signed a management contract with Albert Grossman later that year, maybe never. They might still have achieved the wider renown that launched Janis to even greater fame as the first woman superstar in rock music, for she was a powerful force, probably uncontainable at that point in the evolution of American popular music.

But the alternatives were roads not taken.

We were there, the band and I, borne by ripples set in motion at points far separated in geography and time, and the effect for each of us was life-changing. As a result, I moved from Cambridge to California as the focus of the counterculture shifted from east to west, and I continued to be a participant—in a new capacity—in the music that was pied piper to a decade of innovation and upheaval. For Janis and Big Brother, the attention they gained at the Monterey Pop Festival launched them toward their destiny and summoned the forces that would eventually pull them apart.

At this remove in time, Monterey seems to me the jewel in the crown of the sixties. It was not the largest festival, but the brightest, the most finely formed, where all the benevolent potency that musicians and fans could generate together was made manifest, briefly, like a rainbow, or a ring around the sun, a vision impossible to fix in the physical world, but one whose glow endures in memory, freighted with emotion and meaning.

I'd like to claim that I understood the full significance of the Pop Festival while I was following D. A. Pennebaker around the Monterey County Fairgrounds with a Nagra tape recorder slung from my shoulder, but that would be an abuse of the storyteller's power. Much later, when I traced how the Pop Festival came about, how Big Brother came to be included and how Pennebaker came to film it, I marveled at the winding paths we followed, each strewn with many "What if?" moments, where a different decision, a different opportunity at any step of the way could have changed everything.

The seeds of the landmark gathering were sown by a quartet of would-be rock entrepreneurs from Los Angeles whose names sounded like a promising law firm: Wheeler, Taylor, Pariser and Shapiro. The idea was simple and visionary—corral as many of the reigning pop stars of the moment as could be persuaded to work for a small fraction of their regular fees to play at a three-day festival that would unfold at the county fairgrounds in Monterey sometime in the summer of 1967. Enlist nobody but headliners. Shoot for the stars. Dazzle the music world and reap the harvest.

Things didn't work out quite the way these visionaries planned. They needed one act to commit before the rest, as a bellwether, a stalking horse. Get the bandwagon rolling, they thought, and others will jump on board. They approached the Mamas and the Papas and Simon and Garfunkel, separately.

You want us to play for a small fraction of our regular fee? Who else have you got?

The would-be promoters named a bunch of names tinged with stardust, none of whom had yet pledged themselves to the festival. Forget it, said the Mamas and the Papas and Simon and Garfunkel, separately. The would-be promoters pleaded, and their enthusiasm kindled a spark of light in Papa John Phillips. The Taylor of the firm was Derek Taylor, formerly a tabloid journalist in his native England, more recently the publicist for and a good chum of the Beatles. Taylor was slight and fastidious, whereas Phillips was long and loose. They both had genuine smiles, honest charm, and a way with words. Phillips sensed in Taylor a kindred spirit. I'll tell you what, Phillips said. I'll talk to Paul (Simon) and Art (Garfunkel), and if they say yes we'll say yes.

Already a crucial change had taken place. Instead of the would-be promoters trying to sign up musicians, one of the musicians was talking to other musicians to consider how a new kind of music festival might come to be.

A meeting took place at Jeanette MacDonald's Bel Air mansion, which John and Michelle Phillips had recently purchased, thanks to

John's way with words and harmonies and chord progressions. (A new day had surely dawned when folk-rock stars could buy real estate only movie stars—and a few popular music stars of a very different style—could previously afford.) The main house, a mansion deserving of the name, encouraged everyone to believe that music could build castles in the air.

Attending the summit were John and Michelle and Paul and Art, the would-be promoters, and another quartet—Adler, Melcher, Turetsky and Somer—that in fact included two lawyers. This was, after all, L.A., the land of greed and profit. True, it had welcomed or given birth in recent years not only to the Mamas and the Papas but also to Buffalo Springfield and the Chambers Brothers and the Byrds and the Beach Boys. Hippie chicks with stars in their eyes and love in their hearts flocked to the Sunset Strip, where the promoters and the agents camouflaged themselves with bell-bottoms and hair newly permitted to grow past ears and collars, but the bottom line was still the bottom line.

There was magic in the air at Jeanette MacDonald's castle, and magic carried the day. The musicians decided they absolutely definitely positively would *not* play for a fraction of their usual fees, but they would play for *free*, and from that moment the musicians ran the festival.

Within a few days, the Beach Boys, the Byrds, the Who, the Association, Dionne Warwick, and Buffalo Springfield had added their names to the list of performers, with the Mamas and the Papas and Simon and Garfunkel at the top. Within a week, the festival was christened the Monterey International Pop Festival and it boasted among its board of governors Paul McCartney of the Beatles, Jim McGuinn of the Byrds, Mick Jagger and Andrew Loog Oldham of the Rolling Stones, Brian Wilson of the Beach Boys, John Phillips, Lou Adler—formerly the record producer for Jan and Dean, now producing the Mamas and the Papas—Smokey Robinson, Paul Simon, and Johnny Rivers. An eclectic assortment of talents, heavily inclined toward the L.A. cosmology. The festival would be set up as a nonprofit, with the proceeds to go to causes that benefited popular music, applications to be reviewed by the board.

The momentum began to build, the bandwagon fired up a head of steam, and more talent, from far and near, lined up to climb aboard. The Paul Butterfield Blues Band. Eric Burdon and the Animals. Booker T. and the MGs, Canned Heat, Hugh Masakela, the Electric Flag, Laura Nyro, the Blues Project, the Paupers, Jimi Hendrix. Otis Redding! *Ravi Shankar!* Enough stars, well known and lesser known, to establish a new galaxy and open it up for business.

Okay, what's missing?

The festival directors knew that a bunch of bands with funny names had sprung up in San Francisco in the past couple of years. They knew because Jefferson Airplane already had a hit—"White Rabbit"—whose references to drugs had put a generation of wary parents even more on their guard, and because one of the best-respected music critics of the day was championing the Northern California rockers.

The *San Francisco Chronicle*'s Ralph J. Gleason would not have been out of place in a thirties spy movie by the brothers Warner. He was a between-the-wars character, trench-coated, armed with a sardonic manner, his cigarettes screwed into a short black holder. He looked with amusement on the excesses of the young, and at the same time reveled in the present moment. Gleason had written a jazz column since the day after the Creation. When he blessed a jazz album with liner notes, he bestowed the imprimatur of a recognized authority. He had alarmed his hepcat readers in the early sixties by writing the occasional column about folk music. Joan Baez caught his eye and ear. So did Bob Dylan. Gleason was that rarity among critics, a music lover who dared to applaud new music that he deemed worthy, even if the newcomers were displacing the cherished sounds of his own generation.

Gleason led the way, among the established critics, in recognizing and extolling the unique sound of the San Francisco rock bands. The scene in San Francisco had been percolating for a couple of years, mostly keeping to itself. Bright-eyed kids flocked to the Avalon and the Fillmore, Depression-era ballrooms now levitating to a new beat, where fans gyrated around the dance floors and the bands played the dancers like an instrument. When the energy of the dancers encouraged the songs to run long, the symbiosis offered flashes of enlightenment. There were light shows and acid tests, and the sexual revolution was enlisting eager recruits by the thousand.

The civic authorities, alarmed, resuscitated an archaic bit of municipal code that prohibited dancing at concerts of live music. Gleason lobbied in his column to overturn the code. At his urging, the *Chronicle* editorialized in support of Bill Graham, when the former waiter, actor, and San Francisco Mime Troupe manager applied for a permit to operate the Fillmore Auditorium as a rock-and-roll dance hall. (At the Avalon, a counterculture collective called the Family Dog orchestrated the entertainment.)

When whisperings of the Monterey Pop Festival reached Gleason's ears, he expressed curiosity, then interest. In a twinkling he was invited to join the festival board. Say, fellows, he offered—after hearing what the Los Angelenos had in mind—you really ought to get some of the San Francisco bands. They already planned to invite the Airplane. Gleason suggested more names. Still smiling all around, the members of the board heeded his counsel. But getting the bands with the weird names and the far-out sounds to sign on for the festival was another matter.

The San Francisco bands were like families, and the Haight-Ashbury district of the city, where most of the bands lived, near Golden Gate Park, was their neighborhood. They were clannish, socially radical, wary of the mainstream music business in general and of L.A. in particular. A pilgrimage by John and Michelle Phillips and Lou Adler to the Haight did little to allay the musicians' misgivings. Adler was a smooth type they had seen before and distrusted on sight.

(The fact that he was more than he seemed and would be a guiding force that helped the Pop Festival to fulfill its potential would become apparent only later.) When Paul Simon, soft-spoken and sincere, visited the Haight, that was something else. Derek Taylor won some converts too, just as he had helped to win John Phillips to the idea in the first place.

It was clear to the San Francisco groups that while Adler and company didn't know much about the individual bands, they were aware of the San Francisco scene and they wanted to tap into its energy. Which convinced some of the musicians that the festival would exploit the bands and rip them off. Still, they sensed a not-to-be-missed event in the making. They were as eager as everyone else to hear the Who and Otis Redding and Ravi Shankar. Hey, listen, it might be far out.

The tipping point for the San Francisco bands was that musicians were running the show, and everyone was playing for free.

> "Big Brother and the Holding Company and Janis were on the Pop Festival because I persuaded John Phillips and Lou Adler that they would be a knockout act. They had never heard of them. They wanted three bands from San Francisco, other than the Airplane, which they *had* heard of because the Airplane had recorded for Victor, and had a regional hit going on at that time. And I recommended Big Brother, and the Dead, and Quicksilver."
>
> **Ralph J. Gleason**

Five days before the festival began, Ralph Gleason reported in the *Chronicle* that the San Francisco Sound would be represented at Monterey not only by Jefferson Airplane, but also by the Grateful Dead, Quicksilver Messenger Service, Moby Grape, Country Joe and the Fish, and the Steve Miller Blues Band. And Big Brother and the Holding Company.

With the roster complete, the festival looked like a surefire winner. And just in case the founders' wide-eyed visions came true, the proceedings, from start to finish, would be recorded on film for posterity.

D. A. Pennebaker's role as the Pop Festival's sight-and-sound archivist was even more of a fluke than the bloodless palace coup that put the musicians in charge. And, as it turned out, his presence was the key that unlocked the magic kingdom for Janis Joplin.

The waves of cause and effect that brought Pennebaker to Monterey in June 1967 had begun to spread years before, in the early sixties, when Penny and his partner, Ricky Leacock, made a film in Hungary about the cellist Pablo Casals. Flash-forward to 1965: Bob Dylan and his friend Bob Neuwirth were flipping the channel knob on a hotel TV and chanced to see the Casals film on what was then National Educational Television, not yet PBS. At the same time, a girl named Sara was working in the New York offices of Leacock Pennebaker, Inc. Sara had been impressed by "Daybreak Express," Pennebaker's first film, a five-minute marvel that employed Duke Ellington's eponymous tune as the camera recorded the sunrise journey of a New York subway train from an outer borough to Manhattan. Sara knew Dylan. (She would in time become Sara Dylan.) She thought Bob would like the film. She arranged for him to see it.

When Pennebaker heard that Dylan's manager, Albert Grossman, was interested in making a documentary film about Dylan, Penny presented himself for consideration. Thanks to Sara and "Daybreak Express" and the Casals film, Grossman and Dylan agreed to let Pennebaker film Dylan's upcoming tour of England. Pennebaker asked Bob Altschuler, head of public relations at Columbia Records, Dylan's label, for $5,000 to cover transportation, in exchange for which he offered to give Columbia a 50 percent interest in the movie. Altschuler said thanks but no thanks, demonstrating that 20/20 foresight is often in limited supply. Penny raised the money elsewhere, but he never let Altschuler forget the missed opportunity.

Pennebaker's style of filmmaking is to launch himself into real life, point his camera, and keep shooting. Early on, he found that in a surprisingly short time his subjects stop playing to the camera, more or less, and resume their normal behavior, whatever that might be. There are no staged scenes, no scripted dialogue, no retakes. The films are documentaries, if you understand that they involve going out to document, as best as you can, what's happening, rather than cobbling together a movie from stock footage and staged events and filmed interviews. The French call it *cinéma vérité*. In America, this approach is known as "direct cinema" or "living cinema" or "truth cinema." Penny just goes out and does it. What he gets, he gets. What he misses—because he's eating or sleeping or just because he's tired, for the moment, of lugging the camera around on his shoulder—he misses. Do the subjects ever forget completely that the cameraman and soundman are there? Probably not. Is there truth in what the camera sees, even if the subjects are aware of the camera? You bet your life.

In the spring of 1965, Pennebaker accompanied Bob Dylan on a concert tour of England. He filmed Dylan being funny and cruel, brilliant and petty. He caught the power of one young man alone on a stage, playing his guitar and singing his extraordinary songs to rapt audiences. If Dylan was at any point putting on an act for the camera, he was playing himself as he wanted to be, as he imagined himself to be, which is another way of saying as he really was.

In the spring of 1967, the film, titled *Dont Look Back* (the lack of an apostrophe was intentional), opened in a smattering of art houses. The distribution was about one step higher than what was called a "road show" in the silent era, when a film's producer would book the theaters himself and carry the reels from town to town in a Model T Ford. Limited initial distribution notwithstanding, the film did well and attracted favorable critical notice. Out of the blue, Penny got a call from Bob Rafelson, a TV writer-producer and would-be film director, who, with his partner, Bert Schneider, had created the pop group the Monkees. Rafelson had seen *Dont Look Back*. He wondered if Penny might be interested in filming a pop music festival. Penny was interested. Where's the festival gonna be? In Monterey, California.

At the mention of California, Penny's interest ratcheted up a notch. He had recently seen *The Endless Summer*, a documentary in which director Bruce Brown followed two surfers around the world as they sought the perfect wave. Most people thought of it as a surfing movie, but Penny didn't see it that way at all. His filmmaker's eye perceived the lyrical images as a paean to California—California as a state of mind, California as a new American Dream for the sixties.

Penny knew there had been a film about the Newport, Rhode Island, Jazz Festival, but he hadn't seen it. He was certain no one had made a movie about a pop festival.

Penny flew to Los Angeles, where Rafelson took him to meet John Phillips and Lou Adler. Penny found something about John Phillips intriguing, and Phillips and Adler were intrigued by *Dont Look Back*. They proposed hiring Penny to direct the filming of the Pop Festival, but it was obvious to Penny that neither Phillips nor Adler had the first clue about how to produce a movie. "You need a producer," Penny told them. They were astute enough to agree, and it became Penny's movie.

Back at the offices of Leacock Pennebaker on West 45th Street, Penny began to organize the California expeditionary force. He was going to need a lot of film. He was going to need a lot of cameras. He was going to need a lot of *money*.

Phillips and Adler made a deal with ABC-TV to show the movie. Film arrived at Leacock Pennebaker by the case. Penny spent days and nights in the workshop to see how many cameras he could get up and running in time. The cameras were his design, a modification of a 16-millimeter Auricon, with the two-hundred-foot magazine canted at an angle to the rear so the camera balanced better on the shoulder, and a hand grip added at the front of the housing for stability. They were powered by rechargeable nickel-cadmium battery packs that strapped around the cameraman's waist. Suited up with this outfit for a couple of hours, the effect was like wearing a Colt .45 Peacemaker—when you took it off, you felt naked.

IN THE SPRING of 1967, the siren call of "There's something happening here" is beckoning me. To where, I don't know, but a Harvard degree in Romance languages and literature doesn't provide the road map. Nor, for the first time since I graduated from college, does bluegrass music. I have been playing with the Charles River Valley Boys for almost six years, but the invasion of British rockers that began in 1964 has changed everything, bringing electric music to the forefront. By '67, even for a well-established bluegrass band, folk music gigs are fewer and farther between.

It's my hangout partner and sometimes Cambridge lodger, Bob Neuwirth, who opens the doorway to *what's next* and invites me in. During Dylan's *Dont Look Back* tour of England, Bobby was along for the ride as Dylan's road manager. The next year, following Dylan's electrified set at the 1965 Newport Folk Festival, Neuwirth worked with Pennebaker on a follow-up film of Dylan touring England again, this time with an amplified backup band that within a few years would become known simply as "The Band." The second film is unreleased, but Bobby has kept in touch with Pennebaker. When the Leacock Pennebaker offices begin to hum with preparations for Monterey, Bobby's hip-happening potentiometer goes off the scale. He introduces me to Penny, and Penny hires me onto the crew.

A few days before the Pop Festival, Bobby and I fly to San Francisco. Pennebaker has gone a day ahead of us with the advance guard, to scout the scene and find a cheap motel for the film platoon soon to follow. Bobby and I rent a car at the airport and bushwhack across the peninsula to Highway One, the coast road. As a recent California resident, I'm the designated pilot, and I'm too impatient for the sight of the Pacific Ocean to cruise down 101. We spin the dial of the radio, searching for Procol Harum's "Whiter Shade of Pale," or some AM deejay playing any cut from the Beatles' latest release, *Sgt. Pepper's Lonely Hearts Club Band*. The underground FM stations are playing the whole album in big chunks of uninterrupted awe, but rental cars don't have FM.

In Monterey, Pennebaker is already shooting film. "Here," he says. He hands me a Nagra tape recorder. I like machines and this one is simple. Watch the VU meter. Don't let it pin in the red or we'll get distortion. Try to keep the mike out of the shots. Penny doesn't tell me the Nagra costs thousands of dollars.

Pennebaker and Ricky Leacock's breakthrough technical contri-bution to documentary filmmaking is the light weight and portability of their cameras and tape recorders, so the cameraman doesn't have to be anchored by a tripod, and the sync-pulse generators built into the Nagra tape recorders, which eliminates the need for a wire con-necting the camera to the recorder. At the beginning or end of a shot, the cameraman focuses the camera on the soundman. The soundman pushes a button on the Nagra. A light attached to the Nagra's shoul-der strap flashes, and at the same time a beep goes on the tape. *Et voilà!* In the editing room, you sync the flash of light on the film to the beep on the tape and away you go. In the field, the cameraman and soundman are free to move independently, recording the scene from any angle, and to position the mike close to the sound source, untethered by wires.

Penny and I ramble the grounds. We film Tom Law putting up his tepee and smiling hippies erecting flimsy stalls for what will be-come a sideshow of psychedelia, a midway of far-out fashions and posters and sculpted aromatic candles and hippie gewgaws. We film in the festival office, where John and Michelle Phillips and Lou Adler and a host of assistants perform an intricate ballet from phone to phone. Dionne Warwick can't make it. The Beach Boys? Yes, no, maybe, and in the end, no. Too bad.

The oval fairgrounds arena has roofed tiers of seats flanking the long sides, and the stage fills most of one end. The other end is closed off with a simple board fence to control admissions. The lawn within the arena, built to accommodate horse shows, is covered with orderly rows of folding chairs. For the Pop Festival, seating within the arena is seven thousand plus.

Our film crew badges give us unfettered access to the arena, backstage, everywhere. We film the construction of the stage. When the sound system is hooked up, David Crosby, of the Byrds, tests it by humming into a mike. He smiles. "Oh, groovy. A nice sound system at last."

Elsewhere, the vibes are less jubilant. Monterey police chief Frank Marinello estimates the potential attendance at fifty thousand, and he worries that the Hells Angels may arrive in force. In his mental screening room he is running *The Wild One*, with leather boys Brando and Lee Marvin running amok among the daughters and granddaughters of the Monterey Peninsula's flag-waving Republicans and military families. Nearby Fort Ord is a major training ground for Vietnam-bound troops.

The civic leaders wonder where they are going to get the foodstuffs to feed fifty thousand beatniks and hippies, where all these undesirables will sleep, and, ohmyGod, will they have to defecate while they're here?

The night before the concerts get under way, Pennebaker wangles a dinner invitation from John and Michelle Phillips for himself and his trusty soundman. We arrive with camera and Nagra in hand. Penny is following his instincts, maybe hoping for some behind-the-scenes footage that will illuminate what is about to happen. John and Michelle have rented a house in Monterey to serve as an off-premises retreat during the festival. Outside the windows there are redwoods on a wooded slope that could be in Marin County or the Berkeley Hills. Michelle cooks steaks, makes a salad, sticks some French bread in the oven. The four of us eat, drink wine, and have a lovely time. Penny doesn't shoot a foot of film and I learn one of the ancillary benefits of *cinéma vérité*: Sometimes you just live life with your subjects instead of filming them.

In the course of the evening, there is no hint of the turmoil that Michelle has recently caused within the Mamas and the Papas. Just sixteen when she met John, she is nineteen now. Not yet really mature enough to be a wife or a Mama, she has been testing her wings. Brief affairs with Papa Denny Doherty and the Byrds' Gene Clark threatened her marriage to John and motivated John, Denny, and Mama Cass Elliott (who is carrying a torch for Denny herself) to eject Michelle from the group. They recently performed a four-city tour with Michelle's parts sung by Lou Adler's girlfriend, Jill Gibson, but the fans were loyal to Michelle and the tour went badly. On their return to L.A., John and Denny and Cass took Michelle back. She and John reconciled. Denny, still nursing his wounds, has not yet arrived in Monterey. The group may have to perform without him.

This evening John and Michelle drink their wine and entertain us in a subdued style. It is the calm before whatever the confluence of energies gathered in Monterey is about to release.

On Friday morning, the air throughout the Monterey County Fairgrounds quivers almost audibly with high expectations. The coastal clouds retreat at midday and the sunshine is warm. Everybody's smiling. Ready or not, here we come.

"It's a Mexican standoff, typical of the yawning gulf between L.A. and San Francisco. . . . Paul Simon is the spiritual leader of the festival and most of us get involved because of him. He rises above all the scaly maneuvering and makes us see it from the audience's point of view. . . . The combination of Paul Simon's vision and Derek Taylor's acidic poise convinces us in the end. We do it for the fans and fuck the rest of it. . . . When you walk through the fairgrounds at twilight with the teepees painted with Sioux symbols, people playing guitars, and children and dogs running around the tents, it's worth all the hassles in the world. We've infiltrated the enemy camp and turned it into our own event. . . . We have our peyote-ceremony tents set up just as you walk in the gate."

Rock Scully, Grateful Dead management

CHAPTER THREE

It Happened in Monterey

THE THEME OF the festival is "Music, Love and Flowers." The music is a sure thing. For three days an extraordinary succession of acts will step onto the stage and play for the joy of it. The flowers arrive from Hawaii—eighty thousand orchids, a literal planeload, pink orchids everywhere. The love is speculative. It is a hope. A prayer. You can't ship it in or order it up. Can't buy me love.

The evening performances are sold out before the first ticket holder enters the fairgrounds.

People arrive by the carful, the VW busful, the hand-painted school busful. They come hitchhiking and they come by motorcycle. They come from up and down the coast, from San Francisco and L.A., and from farther afield. One girl has hitchhiked from Champaign, Illinois. Wiping the morning dew off the folding metal chairs in the fairgrounds arena gets her into the show. "How'd you get this job?" Pennebaker asks her, filming all the while. "Do you know somebody?" "No," she says, "I just happened to be lucky, I guess."

The fans have dressed for the occasion pretty much as they dress every day in the Summer of Love. Colors run wild. The range of fashions is broad enough to confound anyone hoping to spot a trend and sell clothes to this crowd next year or next month. Antique clothes and work clothes and formal clothes. Tie-dyes and batiks. Curtains and bedspreads and odd-lot material made into free-flowing shirts and dresses. Hats are much in style. Derby hats and top hats and cowboy hats, berets and Arab fezzes and American Indian headbands and fur hats the Russians wear in winter. Boots too—tall boots and short boots and cowboy boots and hippie boots that zip up the side or the back, and lots of boots with really pointy toes like the English rockers wear. Winkle pickers, the Brits call them. What's a winkle? Something you eat. A very small marine snail. You eat it with your boots?

For the concerts, the Pennebaker film crew will occupy prime vantage points. The festival carpenters have built catwalks at each side of the stage about three feet below its level. The stage has a rectangular thrust that extends out about fifteen feet downstage center. Our catwalks wrap around the front corners of the thrust platform, allowing the cameramen to shoot from several angles.

Thirty feet in front of the stage, in the front rows of seats, Pennebaker places one camera on a tripod. Two more are mounted in the near ends of the permanent, roofed seats on either side of the arena. The others will be shoulder-held, shooting from the catwalks or other vantage points. Pennebaker himself has no fixed position. He will roam, free to shoot from the wings or behind the amps onstage or wherever else the spirit takes him.

The list of cameramen who have come along to film this pop music extravaganza contains some distinguished names. Albert Maysles is on a busman's holiday from *cinéma vérité* filmmaking with his brother David. The Maysleses made *What's Happening! The Beatles in the U.S.A.* a few years ago. Nick Proferes and Jim Desmond are Leacock Pennebaker protégés who have formed their own film company. Ricky Leacock, Penny's partner, is in the front rank of those who pioneered the *vérité* documentary style. He worked with the legendary filmmaker Robert Flaherty on *Louisiana Story*. Before that, Ricky was a combat cameraman in World War II, experience he hopes will not be relevant to surviving the Monterey Pop Festival.

Neuwirth has no camera, no Nagra, no apparent function within the crew—until the music starts. In real life he is an artist, a painter who also plays the guitar and writes songs. His true calling seems to be keeping in tune with the times and being on hand wherever the most memorable events are taking place. At Monterey, Bobby is Pennebaker's aesthetic consultant, the arbiter of hip, the guide for what to shoot and what to ignore. We can't film everybody. We don't have enough film. We have to shoot all the acts in which Lou Adler and John Phillips—the film's co-producers—have a special interest. Beyond that, the choice is ours. Somebody has to make the decisions. Penny has instincts of his own, and when a musical act grabs him, he shoots it. Otherwise he leaves it up to Bob. Bob sometimes consults with me. We rig a red light on a short pole at stage right, on the handrail of our catwalk there, where it can be seen from all the fixed camera positions. When Bobby turns on the light, the cameramen will go into action.

Camping spaces on the fairgrounds and in local campgrounds are full before the Friday evening concert, and the San Francisco bands see a chance to put into practice their music-for-the-people philosophy. In San Francisco they play free concerts and benefits with a frequency that would alarm any profit-minded manager. The Grateful Dead family, spearheaded by co-manager Rock Scully, gets Monterey Peninsula College to open its football field as a temporary campground. More festival pilgrims sack out in the floral pavilion on the fairgrounds, by arrangement with the sponsoring florists. Over the course of the weekend, the Dead and Jefferson Airplane and several other performers play in the pavilion and at the football field for free, to the surprise and delight of the campers.

Everywhere, people are smiling, and we're thinking, Look how *many* of us there are! As the music begins, a gossamer enchantment seems to settle over the fairgrounds.

> "So much of Monterey had *nothing* to do with logistics or planning. The bird just landed there. No rules, no instructions. It also said a lot to me about Northern California. So much of it could *never* have happened anywhere else. . . . It's always an amazing experience for me when I go to something that is *not* my production. I am like the maître d' from the Catskills. . . . Why is it taking so long to move the equipment? You call *this* a hot dog? . . . But Monterey passed the test. In the sense that the majority of the people came there to enjoy themselves, and they did. What prevailed over everything was the meeting of unnamed tribes who didn't even know they were tribes. . . . The looseness of Monterey, I always attributed to Lou Adler. After a while, there was *no* control. But they didn't *need* control because of the audience. They were all already members of the same organization. *Before* they got to the grand meeting of Monterey."
>
> **Bill Graham, rock promoter, Fillmore Auditorium**

My perspective is more San Francisco than L.A. On Friday night, the acts that don't arouse my interest—the Association, Johnny Rivers, Beverley—are the acts, not by coincidence, that Neuwirth and Pennebaker deem not worth filming. The Paupers, a group recently acquired by Albert Grossman, are spirited but unknown. Eric Burdon and the Animals raise the energy a couple of jumps. In performance, their hit version of the folk classic "The House of the Rising Sun" is impressive and moving.

The light show for the evening performances is by Head Lights, from the Fillmore in San Francisco, projected on huge screens behind the performers: bubbles of color pulsating, undulating, overlaid with photos and film clips, a visual supplement to the music that few but the San Francisco ballroom fans have seen before.

By Saturday morning, Chief Marinello is smiling. The feared invasion by the Hells Angels has not materialized and the vibe on the fairgrounds is peaceful, elevated, charged with anticipation of the music yet to come.

In memory, the festival plays like a movie put together by a cheerfully stoned editor. It's a montage of vignettes, each one contributing something singular to the accumulating impression: Simon and Garfunkel singing better than ever . . . Otis Redding, taking obvious pleasure in singing for what he calls "the love crowd," putting his soul into "I've Been Loving You Too Long" . . . Hugh Masakela all but unknown in this gathering, the music jazz, and pretty good jazz at that, the vocals African tribal, the fusion of the two unfamiliar, but we dig it all the same, because it is here and now and part of this scene that is blowing our minds, and because in this context no one can do wrong.

During the concerts, I have no responsibilities. Pennebaker is recording the concert sound from the stage mikes, mixed through the main board. When the act onstage doesn't hold my attention, I stroll the tent-alley bazaar outside the arena, where the incenses and oils give off Middle Eastern aromas. The kaleidoscopic array of tie-dye and batik and beads and face painters is dazzling.

The infectious spirit of the festival draws from one act after another performances that exceed their own expectations, and ours. In the midst of so many successes, the San Francisco bands succeed both individually and as a group. New to most of the crowd, they more than hold their own in this company, validating the recently christened San Francisco Sound. Country Joe MacDonald, on Saturday afternoon, with flower blossoms painted on his cheeks and an antique fireman's hard hat perched on his head, plays an extended rendition of "Section 43," a mesmerizing instrumental. The Fish are in the zone and they bring us with them. Close your eyes and it gets you high without chemical aids.

Jefferson Airplane work their vocal sorcery—Grace Slick, Marty

Balin and Paul Kantner singing alternating leads on "High Flying Bird," Grace and Marty magical in duet on "Today," the band's tonalities and inflections utterly distinctive. After this, we can identify an Airplane song from thirty thousand feet.

The Grateful Dead are down to earth, boogeying, raising some dancers from their seats to vibrate in the aisles, on the grass at the back of the arena, and as far beyond its gates as the sounds carry, but the Dead never fully get up to speed. They're just back from New York and they played in L.A. the night before. Jerry Garcia's guitar has been stolen, he's bummed, the band is tired. But the Dead are the Dead, sui generis, and they add new recruits to the core of San Francisco devotees who are already called Deadheads.

The performance many of us will remember forever comes from Big Brother and the Holding Company. They take the stage on Saturday afternoon, four long-haired guys and Janis Joplin. Their outfits aren't as flamboyant or coordinated as the styles of the L.A. acts. Sam and James are in black jeans and boots and loose-fitting shirts. Peter and David venture more color. Janis wears hippie street clothes, jeans and a top. In San Francisco she's already something of a local legend. She has been singing with Big Brother for just a year, and she has won a reputation as a singer like no other. Beyond the Bay, she is all but unknown.

The short set culminates with Janis's showstopper from the San Francisco ballrooms, Willie Mae "Big Mama" Thornton's "Ball and Chain," which Big Brother has recast in a minor key, the better to evoke the emotion in the lyrics. Their arrangement begins with four ascending notes wrenched from James Gurley's guitar, a momentary Handelian silence, and an intro that shatters all the rules. James plays riffs from an alternative reality, and chords that no one at the Gibson guitar factory ever dreamed. His overture is a wail from another point of view, an assault on the festival's self-satisfied bliss, and it transfixes the audience. Up to now, Big Brother is just another variation on the San Francisco Sound. From this moment, they're Something Else.

James's introduction shrieks to a crescendo and spins off into the ether, leaving only the drums and Peter Albin's bass, slow and low, thumping like a tired heart in labor, as Janis barely whispers the opening lines:

Sittin' down by my window,
Just lookin' out at the rain . . .

She doesn't stay in the soft register for long. Her voice rises, pleads, screams. By the time she hits the first chorus, the audience is mesmerized. Can a white girl sing the blues? Janis's answer is yes, in spades. She matches the intensity of James's guitar while she explores the same outer realms, and . . . she can't . . . but she does. . . . When she really pulls out all the stops she sings *chords*!

In the second row of the audience, in the fenced-off section reserved for performers and VIPs, Mama Cass Elliott gapes openmouthed. When the audience's roar of approval erupts at the end of the song, Cass turns to the guy beside her and exclaims, "Wow. Wow! That's really heavy!"

Backstage, Big Brother is jubilant—but there is trouble brewing, right here in Music City. Big Brother, along with some of the other San Francisco bands, refused permission to be filmed, and Pennebaker is beside himself. Big Brother *has* to be in the movie! Janis's performance will *make* the movie!

The Grateful Dead have also declined to be filmed. So have Moby Grape, but the Bay Area ranks are disunited. Country Joe and the Fish gave permission. So did the Airplane. Julius Karpen, Big Brother's manager, is adamantly against their appearing in the movie. Karpen is a balding, myopic, beatnik businessman who drives a hearse. He is called Green Julius within the San Francisco rock scene because he smokes prodigious amounts of weed. By the account of one insider, Julius refuses to discuss business with anyone who won't first smoke grass with him. He is given to waxing philosophical, and at length, about the state of the world and the unique role of the San Francisco scene in the larger swirl of the cosmos. Like many another eccentric, Julius has found a home in the San Francisco counter-culture. He is deeply suspicious of the music business. The movie is a rip-off, he says. Everybody's playing for free, so why should Phillips and Adler and ABC-TV and whoever else profit from the perfor-mances, while the bands get nothing? Oh, right, proceeds to causes that benefit popular music, whatever that means.

Janis is sympathetic to the anticommercial ethic that pervades the San Francisco music scene. She is devoted to the communal spirit that the bands share, but nothing is more important to her than Big Brother's career. Maybe the fact that the Airplane—the only other San Francisco band that features a chick singer—has agreed to be filmed has something to do with Janis's determination that Big Brother should be in the movie too. She leads the fight against Julius, and a couple of the boys back her. At an impasse among themselves and at odds with their manager, the band casts about for an oracle to show them the auspicious pathway. They turn to Albert Grossman.

Grossman is at Monterey to shepherd two of his acts. The Paupers are Canadian, new talent from north of the border. The Electric Flag is a band recently formed by Mike Bloomfield, the blues guitar vir-tuoso, formerly of the Paul Butterfield Blues Band. Monterey is the Flag's debut performance. Butterfield, of course, is here too, with Elvin Bishop now discharging by himself the lead guitar duties that he has shared with Bloomfield until recently. Grossman knows both Butterfield and Bloomfield from Chicago, where they all got their start in the music business. He was responsible for Butterfield's ac-ceptance in the folk clubs of the early sixties. The Butterfield band is one that other musicians go out of their way to hear. Grossman also manages Peter, Paul and Mary. Hell, he *invented* Peter, Paul and Mary. He noticed that all the folk-pop groups were guys—the Kings-ton Trio, the Brothers Four, the Limelighters, the Chad Mitchell Trio—and it occurred to him that a group with a girl might catch the public's imagination. Grossman tried to interest his friends Bob Gibson and Bob (soon to be Hamilton) Camp, who performed as a duo and sang exceptional harmonies together, in taking on a girl singer to take the harmonies to the next level. Gibson and Camp didn't share his vision, but Peter Yarrow and Noel (soon to be Paul) Stookey, were more open to suggestion, and, together with Mary Travers, they are reaping the rewards.

At the time of the Pop Festival, Grossman's roster of clients also includes the James Cotton Blues Band, Richie Havens, Gordon Lightfoot, Odetta, Ian and Sylvia, and the Band.

The breadth of Grossman's achievements is less important to Janis and Big Brother than the singular fact that he is Bob Dylan's manager and that Dylan has thrived under his care. He encouraged Peter, Paul and Mary to record Dylan's "Blowin' in the Wind," and by so doing accelerated the trio's rise to fame and used their momentum to bring more notice to Dylan, whose name was then becoming known but whom relatively few in the folk music audience had seen or heard. It was not an accident of timing that Peter, Paul and Mary's "Blowin' in the Wind" was rising on the charts in the weeks before the 1963 Newport Folk Festival, where Dylan scored his breakthrough triumph—with a significant boost from Joan Baez, who sang with him in his set and brought him onstage during her Sunday night closer.

Backstage at Monterey, Grossman is the only person who appears unperturbed amid the commotion swirling around Janis and Big Brother. His presence is imposing, in part because of his physical appearance, in part because of his manner. He is portly without being fat. He remains still for long periods of time, but when he moves he moves briskly, in the manner of a slender man. His hair turned gray before he was forty. Half a generation older than most of his clients, his aura can seem parental. When he wants to be overbearing, it's as though your stern grandfather has taken umbrage. John L. Wasser-

man, film critic for the *San Francisco Chronicle*, said in his review of
Dont Look Back that Grossman looked like a Soviet diplomat. Two
years later, Grossman has let his hair grow longer. He wears round
steel-rimmed glasses. They make him look wide-eyed, which is one of
his favorite expressions. Who, me? He resembles no one so much as
the man on the Quaker Oats carton.

Ron Polte, manager of Quicksilver Messenger Service, knows
Grossman from Chicago. At Monterey, he has introduced Grossman to
Big Brother. On Saturday afternoon, Janis approaches Grossman and
asks him to consult with the band about Pennebaker's movie.

By now, John Phillips and Lou Adler have made Big Brother a
tempting offer: If you'll agree to be filmed, we'll put you on again, on
Sunday evening.

Pennebaker has spoken with Albert about Janis's performance,
which blew him away. "Whatever you have to do," Penny said to him,
"I don't care if you have to go in and break a leg. God, we have to film
her! We just have to do it. This is the basis of the whole film."

"Don't worry," Albert said. "I'll fix it for you." And he does.

When Big Brother asks Albert if they should accept the offer to
perform again, if they'll agree to be filmed, he says, Hey, I'd do it. He
doesn't say this just because Penny asked for his help. Albert has no
stake in the movie, no investment yet, either financial or emotional,
in Big Brother's career. He tells them to go for it because he knows
it's the right thing for them to do. If you want wider recognition, he
says, this is the way to get it.

Albert's approval is all the holdouts in Big Brother need. They
consent to be filmed. Janis is elated, and Julius Karpen storms off in
a huff. Adler and Phillips juggle the schedule and make room for Big
Brother on the Sunday evening program.

While this drama plays out in the background, we of the Pennebaker crew are focused on the performances at hand. On Saturday evening, Otis Redding is the highlight, but the Airplane, the

Byrds, Hugh Masakela, and Booker T. and the MGs also work their magic.

On Sunday morning, Chief Marinello sends home half the officers he has mustered to police the festival.

Ravi Shankar is the sole performer on Sunday afternoon. In this gathering where the other performers are mining mother lode veins of rock and roll, R&B, folk, and jazz, the crowd—a scattering of blues and jazz and folk fans among the dominant mass of beatniks and hippies and flower children—accords Shankar the status of guru-for-the-day.

For this performance, I take control of the button that will turn on the red light and signal the cameras to roll. Our tripod cameras have twelve-hundred-foot magazines that run for half an hour without reloading, but the others—the free-roaming cameras on our catwalks alongside the stage—have four-hundred-foot rolls that last just ten minutes. Penny has decided to film Ravi's final raga, which will surely run longer than that. My job is to guess when the tune is within ten minutes of its end, so the shoulder-held cameras can shoot without interruption until it's over.

My qualifications for undertaking this responsibility are late nights in Cambridge that ended up stoned to the gills and zoning out to the recordings of this very same wizard of the sitar, or to Ali Akbar Khan, equally adept master of the sitar's first cousin, the sarod, in the company of my roommate Fritz Richmond, washtub bassist for the Charles River Valley Boys and the Jim Kweskin Jug Band—whose mastery of the washtub approaches Ravi's on the sitar, relatively speaking—and our frequent guest, Bob Neuwirth.

At Monterey, I stroll the arena during Shankar's early pieces, absorbing the music on the move. Ravi feels connected to the audience. He introduces each piece at greater length than is his custom before a Western audience. The crowd is with him all the way. In the front rows of seats reserved for performers, a cluster of musicians—

Mike Bloomfield, Jimi Hendrix, Al Wilson of Canned Heat, Michelle Phillips—listen raptly.

Today the coastal clouds have hung around, and colors glow more brightly in the diffuse light. A plan to have bagsful of the festival's signature pink orchids tossed from a hot-air balloon above the arena has gone awry because of the fog bank, so instead the ushers have placed an orchid on every seat before the concert begins. During Ravi's set, the flowers, threaded through buttonholes, tucked behind ears, held in hands, or woven into long hair, glow like radiant, oversized fireflies that have alighted throughout the audience.

As the final raga begins, I return to the catwalk at the edge of the stage, all my attention on Ravi and his accompanists. I shoot some photos. . . . I wait . . . and wait, through the languid, hypnotic exposition of the opening themes. Almost imperceptibly, the tempo of the music increases, the rhythms of the tabla—the small hand drums played incomparably by Alla Rakha—gaining speed, Ravi effortlessly keeping pace. The tempo becomes insistent . . . and still I wait . . . until I dare not wait any longer. I switch on the red light and the cameras roll, ten minutes of film spooling off at twenty-four frames a second.

The interplay between the sitar and the tabla grows steadily more complex as Ravi initiates the phase where the sitar calls to the tabla and the drums answer—short phrases, simple at first, then more complex, drawing smiles of delight from Alla Rakha, answering smiles from Shankar and from Kamala Chakravarty, who fills out the sound with the mesmeric monotone of the tamboura. Toward the end, the tabla and sitar join together, the players' hands flying over the strings and drumheads in a blur, impossibly fast, until the elation that this music from halfway around the world brings to this arena, this audience, approaches rapture.

The ending brings the crowd to its feet as one with a joyous roar that must be audible in downtown Monterey.

The audience pelts the stage with flowers. Pink orchids pile up at the feet of the musicians. They bow time and again, palms together, beatific, deeply moved by the response. The trio leaves the stage. They are called back. The waves of applause wash the arena. The ovation promises to go on until it's time for the evening concert. In the film, the applause will continue for almost two minutes, which seems like a very long time. Now, in real life, it lasts much longer.

Finally Shankar holds up his arms and the audience quiets. "I want you to know how much I love you all and how happy I am to be loved by you," he says. He picks up a handful of orchids, throws them back into the crowd, bows for the last time, and the grateful people let him go.

It is a singular triumph among many on a triumphant weekend.

I cherish one image, a mental film clip, from Sunday afternoon after Ravi's transcendent set. Strolling the fairgrounds, I see a Monterey motorcycle cop cruising along a roadway, greeted everywhere with smiles and smiling nonstop himself, the whip antenna on the back of the bike waving brightly, pinkly, adorned from bottom to top with skewered orchids.

SUNDAY EVENING IS Big Brother's chance to prove they can repeat their Saturday sensation. For this performance, Janis decks herself out in a gold lamé pantsuit and she sings as if her future depends on it, which it does. This time around, many in the audience know what to expect, but "Ball and Chain" knocks them out all over again and once more they roar their admiration. As Janis leaves the stage, she raises her arms and skips with joy. She knows she nailed it for the cameras.

And still, there is more to come. The Who are straight from two days at the Fillmore. Giddy in their first rush of California gooniness, they turn loose high-volume British rock and roll—"Substitute," "Summertime Blues," and a couple more—and destroy most of their

"The best time of all was Monterey. It was one of the highest points of my life. Those were real flower children. They really were beautiful and gentle and completely open, man. Ain't nothing like that ever gonna happen again."

Janis Joplin

equipment at the end of their last song, "My Generation," shocking some and pissing off the sound crew, who dash onstage to save the microphones, but the band is so off-the-wall, out-of-control, to-hell-with-the-sensible-limits that we just watch, agog, and wait for the stage to be cleaned up before the next act. Being outrageous is part of the countercultural ethic, but our interest in this Götterdämmerung acting out will diminish when we learn it's a regular part of their act. They trash the same amp at every show, and smash up cheap guitars.

And besides, they can't top Jimi Hendrix, who carries *outrageous* to new heights. Pennebaker and I chanced to be on hand for Jimi's sound check this morning, in the empty arena, and we took note that this is a guitar player of exceptional ability. On Sunday night the cameras are on Jimi from the start of his set, but we don't expect another performance that will create a sensation to equal Janis and Big Brother.

Jimi plays the guitar behind his back, over his head, with his teeth. He plays the longest set of the night. He plays B. B. King's "Rock Me Baby," the Beatles' "Sgt. Pepper's Lonely Hearts Club Band," and Dylan's "Like a Rolling Stone." He grabs songs from across the pop spectrum and makes each one his own. He sneaks "Strangers in the Night" into his guitar solo on "Wild Thing" . . . he turns a somersault on the stage without missing a note . . . he makes a little bow before he lays his guitar on the stage, squirts it with lighter fluid, sets it afire, urges the flames higher with his hands, and then, almost regretfully, smashes the guitar and throws the fragments into the audience magnanimously, as a peace offering . . . all of which is easier to understand if you know that Jimi took a bunch of Owsley acid before the performance, the micrograms measured in the thousands, but probably no more than everyone else in the arena ingested collectively.

> "I saw Owsley give him two of his little purple tabs, and I watched Jimi swallow them about half an hour before he went onstage."
>
> **Peter Pilafian, Mamas & Papas road manager**

> "I saw him take, literally, a handful of Owsley tabs. At least four, maybe six. I saw him take it. And then he crumpled up in the corner. And he was wearing—English garb, you know, stuff. Ruffled stuff, psychedelic ruffles. And he looked like a bag of laundry in the corner of the room, and people were taking bets if he could even stand, much less get onstage. . . . And he looked like laundry in the corner of the tent. And when his time came to play, they literally—guys came in and picked him up, and sort of walked him to the stage. And as soon as he got onstage, he transformed into Jimi Hendrix, from a crumpled bunch of laundry into the greatest rock-and-roll guitar player in history."
>
> **Bob Seidemann, San Francisco photographer**

In contrast to the Who's calculated smashup, Jimi's theatrics are spontaneous, fueled by equal doses of LSD and the love made manifest in his music. This is his first American performance since he gigged as an R&B sideman with the Isley Brothers and Little Richard years ago. A few fans might have seen him backing John Hammond, Jr., in a Greenwich Village gig back in the folk days, but here the show is all Jimi. He's making it up as he goes along, and he ends his set in a literal blaze of glory.

To close the evening, and the festival, the Mamas and the Papas float about the stage in floor-length dresses and robes. Denny shows up at the eleventh hour and puts his heart fully into the songs, the group truly reunited and as happy to be on this stage as all the others who have preceded them.

> "I thought that [Monterey] just cut the whole scene wide open. It connected it. It was like opening a gigantic door that suddenly made what was an embryonic West Coast music scene into something of national, cultural prominence. And I thought it sort of put the stamp on the era. I thought it was enormously power-ful. Because it was innocence. It was a window on this land of innocence where sweetness and a certain kind of Tao-like love of poetry and music and friends that was suddenly—the spotlight turned on and it was all there for the country to see, and it made it visible. It didn't last very long."
>
> **Peter Pilafian**

> "My idea of a good festival, the best festival of all time, was Mon-terey."
>
> **Grace Slick**

ON MONDAY MORNING the stragglers melt away into the postpsy-chedelic mists, carrying fragments of the festival's spirit out into the world, while county workers set about raking up the wilting orchids. The dreaded fifty thousand failed to materialize, but Chief Mari-nello figures the three-day crowd at thirty-five thousand, with more than ten thousand able to hear the music coming from the stage at any given moment, including those outside the arena on the fairgrounds.

Janis and Big Brother aren't the only ones who achieve sudden renown at Monterey. Jimi Hendrix becomes an overnight sensation. A measure of how little known he was before Monterey is his third bill-ing, below Jefferson Airplane and the jazz guitarist Gabor Szabo, on the poster—printed before Monterey—for his scheduled appearance at the Fillmore in San Francisco that follows the Pop Festival.

And Otis Redding has brought soul music a giant step closer to the mainstream by knocking the socks off a musical generation that is leavening the pop charts with songs about subjects far beyond teen-age heartbreak.

In the immediate aftermath of the festival, it is Janis who gets the most notice, the biggest boost. The fact that Big Brother was the only act to perform twice gains them an extra measure of attention from the fans and the press. In many of the articles about the Pop Festival that bloom in newspapers and magazines across the land, there's Janis, hair flying, singing her heart out with such conviction that even in a still photograph you can feel her power.

Less noticed, except by some of us who remain connected to Janis through the months and years that follow, is the fortuitous confluence of events that combined here to produce her sudden rise in the popular consciousness. It is not just the fact that a film was being made, but that the filmmaker was Pennebaker, that his reaction to Janis boosted the effort to offer them a second chance, that Penny knew Albert Grossman, and that the need to have Janis in the movie brought Albert and the members of Big Brother to each other's attention in a way that probably contributes to Albert's signing to manage Big Brother before the year is out. So many apparently random ripples flow together to create the perfect wave.

My own presence at the festival is in no way related to Janis's rise to prominence, but if I hadn't been at Monterey, if I hadn't known Bob Neuwirth, who knew Pennebaker, if I hadn't reacted to Janis as everyone who heard her reacted, I wouldn't be able to tell the tale that follows.

In the elevating afterglow, the Monterey Pop Festival reveals itself as something more than the launching pad for new beginnings. It is the culmination of a movement that began when the first inspired soul of the post–World War II generation—inspired by Woody Guthrie, Pete Seeger, the Weavers, Burl Ives, and Josh White, among others—picked up a guitar and strummed out a folk song. In the fifties, teenagers supported the creation of a new kind of pop music. In the sixties, many of those same teens, now in their twenties, are making it. American popular music has become a do-it-yourself enterprise, and it has extended its appeal to a broader demographic. Assembled at Monterey, the leading lights of the new music, in company with their fans, have demonstrated the magnanimous force of music, love and flowers.

As the Pennebaker crew packs up to head for the airport, those who have found Monterey to their liking have got the Leavin' California Blues. I sympathize as best I can, but my exploration of the Summer of Love is just beginning. My bluegrass band, the Charles River Valley Boys, is booked for a California tour.

CHAPTER FOUR

More Pretty Girls Than One

On Monday morning, Ralph Gleason reports in the *San Francisco Chronicle* that Monterey's chief of police, Frank Marinello, now considers hippies his friends. "These people have proved flowers and love are a symbol of what they really believe in," Gleason quotes the chief. The festival's ticket director pays the audience a similar tribute: "I've never seen a crowd like it. These people are polite and patient and gentle."

In his own words, adopting a favorite word of the flower children, Gleason sums up the festival in a glowing review. "The first annual Monterey International Pop Festival this weekend was a beautiful, warm, groovy affair which showed the world a very great deal about the younger generation. In the first place, the music was fine, the staging was excellent and the shows were good. You know they are when the audiences stay until well after 1 a.m. But beyond that, it showed something else very important—you can have 35,000 long-haired, buck-skin and beaded hippies in one place without a hassle. . . . Saturday night was the biggest crowd in the arena in the history of the fairground. . . . So much for an inadequate description of one of the most remarkable scenes in contemporary American history, a giant musical love-in which set a standard of peacefulness and sobriety for the entire country. It was the greatest assembly of contemporary musical talent in history."

Bob Siggins and Joe Val, my fellow Charles River Valley Boys, are due to fly into San Francisco a few days after the Pop Festival. Until then, Pennebaker and Neuwirth and I reconnoiter the San Francisco scene. Penny is sufficiently curious to stick around for a day or two, and Bobby has decided to ride along on the CRVB's California tour. We find a place to crash at a friend's house in Berkeley and set off to scout the Haight-Ashbury.

The Haight is south of the Panhandle, a narrow extension of Golden Gate Park that juts to the east. The great park itself is more than three miles long and half a mile wide, a sylvan retreat that offers informal camping to hundreds of young nomads each night.

Since the first Human Be-In was held in the park in January, the national press has focused a spotlight on San Francisco, sensationalizing the long hair and outlandish clothing, the free love and the acid rock and the drugs, luring a generation that's hungry for new experience. Summer's here, school's out, and the kids are arriving by the thousands.

The park and the Panhandle have been the settings for dozens of free rock concerts since the scene began to percolate a couple of years ago. If these lush green spaces are the playground for the Haight-Ashbury community, the junction of Haight Street and Ashbury Avenue, two blocks off the Panhandle, is the civic center. The streets are as crowded as New York's Fifth Avenue at lunch hour, but here ties and coats are even rarer than beads and tie-dye on the upscale streets of the Big Apple. The kids sit on the stoops of the houses, the fenders of parked cars, the curbstones. They smoke joints and cigarettes, they make out, they play guitars and drums and flutes and instruments contrived of found objects. What do they hope to find here? Drugs and sex, for sure. A place where they can be as

stoned or freaky as they want and nobody will think the worse of
them. Beyond that . . . ?

What Bobby and Penny and I see is what's already changing, but
it's all new to us and we don't perceive the metamorphosis that's under
way. We have been drawn here by the TV news, the pieces in *Time*
and *Newsweek*, the same coverage that brought all these kids, and,
like them, we're digging it for the first time. For the pioneers who
created the upwelling of music, theater, art, and creativity, the erup-
tion of a whole new, gaudy, outrage-the-straights, to-hell-with-limits
lifestyle in San Francisco over the previous two years, this is the beginning of the end. What arose as a community where creative spirits
of many descriptions could live together—young hippies, older beatniks, musicians, potheads, artists—an enclave within the broader
society, removed from the scrutiny of parents and disapproving authorities, has become the focus of the press and the whole damn
country. Among the founders, the exodus has already begun, as residents of the Haight decamp for Marin and Sonoma counties, the East
Bay, and more remote refuges.

We're looking for what lies beneath the hubbub, hoping to find
the genesis of the spirit we felt at Monterey, but we have no one to
guide us, no insider to take us beyond the flow of wandering explor-
ers and runaways. At midweek, we miss Big Brother and the Grateful
Dead playing at a summer solstice celebration in Golden Gate Park
because we're not yet plugged into the rock underground.

A few days later, Penny is airborne for New York and Bobby and
I are southbound with Bob Siggins and Joe Val, heading back to
Monterey and beyond, past Carmel, where I was living just a year
ago, and down the coast to the headlands of Big Sur, where the
Charles River Valley Boys will perform at the country's smallest, best-
kept secret on the festival circuit.

This tour, our first and only venture to California, came about
by accidents as lucky as those that brought me to Monterey with
Pennebaker. Manny Greenhill, our Boston manager, has customarily

booked his artists in the Berkeley Folk Festival, an annual event that has been around even longer than the convocations at Newport. During my year in Carmel, I learned of the much smaller folk festival in Big Sur, also held in midsummer. I knew a few folk music coffeehouses in Berkeley, and the Ash Grove in L.A. has a national reputation equal to that of the Club 47. Could Manny put together enough gigs to make a California tour worthwhile? He could, and he did.

Bob Siggins is a founding member of the CRVB, a Harvard graduate whose postdoctoral studies in neuroscience at Boston University pretty much allow him to set his own schedule. Joe Val is a maestro of the mandolin who plays and sings like Bill Monroe, the father of bluegrass music, with a Boston accent. In his day job, Joe is mild-mannered Joseph Valiante, a typewriter repairman whose boss has belatedly recognized that Joe is his most valuable employee. When the idea for taking the CRVB to California came up, Joe's boss agreed to let him go.

At the helm of the VW bus that is carrying us southward on Highway One is Peter Berg, a Berkeley musician Neuwirth and I have known since the early sixties, when Peter was in a group that played string band music and country songs and some bluegrass of a sort, but they felt it wasn't as refined as bluegrass so they called it crabgrass. The Crabgrass Band featured Toni Brown on guitar and vocals. In the summer of 1967, Toni is better known as half of the Joy of Cooking and our Peter Berg is "the Berkeley Peter Berg," to distinguish him from the San Francisco Peter Berg, who was one of the motivators behind the San Francisco Mime Troupe and the Diggers, and is altogether a different person.

Our Cambridge bass player, Everett Alan Lilly, wasn't able to make the trip. To replace him, we have recruited Peter, who will be the CRVB's first electric bassist.

In a whimsical moment, Peter has decided to assume an alias for his tour with the Charles River Valley Boys. He has a pair of blue jeans that turned purple when they were accidentally washed in hot water with some bright reds. Neuwirth lends him a purple corduroy jacket cut short like a Levi's jacket. Peter comes up with a purple cape and dubs himself Purple Man.

After the intensity of Monterey, the Big Sur Folk Festival is like a weekend at a summer camp for hippies. Big Sur is a place out of time. Access is by the two-lane coast road, California Route 1, from north or south, except when it is washed out by winter rains. It's a second- and third-gear road with a few long straightaways, an invitation to spirited driving. Even in summer, when the flow of tourists makes cruising the coast road at optimal speed unlikely, Big Sur feels remote from what we call civilization.

The audience at this festival is a drop in the bucket compared to Monterey. You can count the fans in the hundreds. They park along Highway One and come trooping down the entrance road to the Esalen Institute, where the festival is held. During the rest of the year, Esalen hosts retreats and workshops featuring a grab bag of current philosophical and humanistic studies aimed at expanding what Aldous Huxley called "human potentialities." Gestalt therapy and transactional analysis are current favorites in the counterculture's explorations of mind and body. Seminars are hosted by resident and guest gurus that have included Fritz Perls, Alan Watts, and Eric Berne. Richard Alpert and Tim Leary have visited Esalen. So have Linus Pauling and B. F. Skinner. Attendees make reservations in advance and pay handsomely to have their consciousness raised. The Folk Festival, in contrast, is the least formal event of the year, a come-one, come-all event that brings a colorful collection of latter-day pilgrims leading kids by the hand and carrying picnic supplies and psychoactives by the bagload. They're mostly locals from a hundred-mile stretch of coastline, joined by a handful of devotees who make the trek from Berkeley and San Francisco and L.A. The daytrippers spread out on the thick lawn below the main building, facing the terraced pool, and it is there on the terrace, with batik banners blowing in the wind and the Pacific Ocean as backdrop, that the celebrations commence.

Joan Baez is the reigning spirit of the festival, the beacon that attracts well- and lesser-known musicians from far afield. Barely a year after I first heard her sing in the Club 47, Joan moved to Carmel. Big Sur has become her hometown folk festival. This year she sings with her sisters, Mimi Fariña and Pauline Marden. Judy Collins makes it a foursome. Al Kooper, who contributed the distinctive organ riff to Dylan's "Like a Rolling Stone," backs up the Baez-Collins quartet on keyboard.

There has been little, if any, bluegrass in Big Sur hitherto, and the change of pace the Charles River Valley Boys provide is warmly welcomed. Bob and Joe and I have been playing together for the better part of five years, briefly interrupted by my recent California sojourn. Bob and Joe are in top form instrumentally, and our three-part vocal harmonies approach sibling symmetry. The audience is surprised to find that our repertoire includes Beatles songs. Last year, the CRVB put out an album on Elektra called *Beatle Country*, a dozen Beatles songs done bluegrass style, recorded in Nashville, the capital of country music. The infusion of bluegrass-country harmonies and rhythms earned Elektra an appreciative letter from Paul McCartney. When I returned to Cambridge from my unrequited quest on the left coast, I learned the Beatles repertoire, and soon I was as happy singing songs by Lennon and McCartney as I am with tunes I learned from Flatt and Scruggs.

Last year I saw the Big Sur festival as an observer; now I'm here as a performer, enjoying the perfect day and the reunion with friends from Carmel. Of these, Mimi is the one I hold most dear. Since I met her as a fifteen-year-old waif at the Baez home in Belmont, Massachusetts, she has blossomed into a rare beauty and a seasoned performer. Five years ago, I introduced Mimi to her husband-to-be, Dick Fariña, in Paris, in the backseat of my brand-new white Volvo, when

Dick was still married to the folksinger Carolyn Hester. Within two years, Dick and Carolyn divorced and Dick married Mimi. Just last year, Dick died on Mimi's twenty-first birthday, which was also the publication date of Dick's novel, *Been Down So Long It Looks Like Up to Me*. At a publication party in Carmel Valley, Dick climbed on the back of a friend's motorcycle for a joyride and never came back. The guy driving the bike survived the crash, but Dick broke his neck.

Even in this out-of-the-way gathering, the pop revolution is represented by ambassadors who have come to make pacts of friendship with the folkies. The Chambers Brothers, who won the hearts of everyone in Cambridge on their first visit to the Club 47, have come up from L.A. Simon and Garfunkel have segued from Monterey Pop to Big Sur. Paul and Art seem to enjoy the low-key gathering and the spectacular setting. Rumor is they're playing for free (the Big Sur festival sure can't afford what they might reasonably ask) just to dig the scene.

Before leaving San Francisco, I borrowed Pennebaker's movie camera. In Big Sur I shoot a little music festival footage of my own. The sight of a professional rig on my shoulder triggers the paranoia of a crew from L.A. who are here to film the festival for TV. They want to rip my film from the camera, but my friend Peter Melchior, Esalen's assistant director, cools them out. Let him alone, he tells them, and they do.

At the end of the afternoon concert, I welcome the opportunity to initiate a foreigner to a pleasant rite of the California lifestyle. The Chambers Brothers' drummer, Brian Keenan, is good-hearted, pink of cheek, and infused with all the modesty of the British Isles, whence he comes. Rock and roll is his life and he's ready for whatever it has to offer—almost. At Big Sur, it's the custom for the musicians to adjourn to the sulfur baths following the afternoon concert. Knowing what lies in store for him, I fall in beside Brian as we move that way when the music is done. Come on, I say, we're all going to the baths.

Before the handful of buildings and cabins perched on this grassy ledge with the coast range at their back and God's own Pacific panorama spread out before them became the Esalen Institute, they were known collectively as Big Sur Hot Springs, for the natural sulfur water that flows from fissures in the coastal cliffs at about 115 degrees Fahrenheit. Down a sloping pathway from the swimming pool and the festival stage are the baths. The building is a rudimentary structure, like many in Big Sur, slapped together out of native timber and set on a concrete foundation, open to the west with only a guardrail between the bathers and a couple-of-hundred-foot drop down the cliff face to the rocks below, which are washed by breakers that roll all the way from Japan.

Brian and I follow a gaggle of musicians down the path: Joan and her sister Mimi, in long colorful dresses, laughing in the midst of Joe, Willy, Lester, and George Chambers. They turn into the doorway of the bathhouse. I usher Brian in ahead of me and he finds himself confronted by a few dozen people of both sexes, every one of them stark bare-assed naked, except for the Baez sisters and Chambers brothers, who are in the process of getting that way.

Brian turns very bright pink.

"Okay, man, listen," I say to him. "Just take your clothes off, right now, and I promise you—I *promise* you—that in ten minutes, you'll forget all about it. Trust me. You only feel self-conscious around naked people when you've got clothes on."

As I speak, I'm removing my own garments as if they're on fire. To the everlasting credit of the olde country, Brian starts to undress. Ten minutes later I see him sitting on the edge of a tub, pink all over, chatting with a naked girl as confidently as if he were in a pub on Carnaby Street.

The CRVB's next gig is at the Jabberwock, a folk music coffeehouse in Berkeley. With or without mind-bending chemicals, Big Sur is an alternative reality where humans and our constructs are humbled by the natural world. Returning from that powerful coastscape to the bustle of Berkeley makes me feel like a time traveler. For my compatriots from the valley of the Charles River, the sudden immersion in the full-blown gooniness of Berserkeley amounts to culture shock.

Bob and Joe regard the goings-on with varying degrees of askance. Bob Siggins dances the Nebraska bop to rock and roll, and you'd never guess he's got a Ph.D. in neuropharmacology unless you chance to pass an offhand remark about serotonin in his presence. He has incorporated Bill Keith's dazzling new style of banjo fingerpicking into his Scruggs picking to produce a sound that is distinctly his own. You can take the banjo out of the country, but it's not gonna sound like city-boy bluegrass so long as Bob is playing the flat-top Gibson Mastertone. His musical tastes go well beyond bluegrass and country, and his bullshit detector tends to peak out in the presence of folk purists who are a little too pure. He's tickled by the Berkeley scene and not above sampling the wares, acoustic or vegetable, but on the whole he prefers to conduct his serious pharmacological experiments in the laboratory.

Joe likes to play the straight man. The unfettered lunacy of the scene is beyond his wildest imaginings, up to now, but he's got a sense of humor. He takes it all in with a twinkle in his eye, as he tries to stay upwind of the smoke.

After our sojourn in Big Sur, Peter Berg is solidly in the CRVB groove. He has decided that the rest of us talk more than enough during our performances, and from here on out, beginning with our three nights at the Jabberwock, he never says a word onstage. In the Summer of Love, nobody blinks at a bluegrass band with a mute electric bass player who resembles a short, purple Superman.

A few days later, we play the opening night of the tenth annual Berkeley Folk Festival. The festival's director, Barry Olivier, is keeping up with the times. Last year, his inclusion of Jefferson Airplane must have been something of a surprise to Pete Seeger and Phil Ochs and the Greenbriar Boys. This year, the Charles River Valley Boys share the opening-night bill with the Reverend Gary Davis, Janis Ian, an oral storyteller, and Kaleidoscope, an electrified band from L.A. that has brought Middle Eastern influences into the psychedelic mix. There's patchouli and pot in the air, and the colorful clothing worn by many in the audience evokes memories of the midway at Monterey.

In the course of the five-day festival, the dazzling guitar work of Doc Watson and the passionate singing of Richie Havens are interspersed with electric explorations and blues that boogie from Crome Syrcus, Red Crayola, the James Cotton Blues Band, and Country Joe and the Fish, which is a Berkeley band. The Steve Miller Blues Band commutes between the folk festival and the Fillmore, where they're playing nights with Chuck Berry and Eric Burdon and the Animals.

The mix of sounds on the Berkeley stages makes visible for me what was groundbreaking about the Pop Festival at Monterey. It was the first festival of the sixties that was *not* organized around acoustic folk music. For almost a decade, since the folk revival kicked into high gear, the model has been festivals with "folk" in the title, from Newport and Indian Neck and Philadelphia to Berkeley and Big Sur, each presenting many of the same artists who travel the summer circuit, featuring English ballads and Scotch-Irish fiddle tunes and American work songs and union songs and songs of the westward migration, a songwriter or two like Dylan, Tim Hardin and Tom Paxton, along with bluegrass and old-time music, and the greatest American form, the blues.

The folk revival scorned pop music. In Cambridge, we put down the commercial folk acts, the guy duos and trios, the brother groups that smoothed out the mountain harmonies and rewrote traditional English and Appalachian ballads so the lines rhymed where the originals didn't. The early rockers got our attention—the Everly Brothers, Jerry Lee Lewis, Little Richard, Chuck Berry, Carl Perkins, and, of course, Elvis—but they were from somewhere else; they weren't *us*, and their music wasn't ours.

Now, with the transition from folk to folk-rock and the rise of the San Francisco bands, pop music has become Us. Janis Joplin's Monterey sensation, "Ball and Chain," is grounded in the twelve-bar blues, but the San Francisco Sound of Big Brother and Quicksilver and the Airplane and the Dead represents a leap that transcends gradual evolution. In logic, a sudden advance based more on intuition, or faith, than logic, is called the inductive leap. In music maybe we can call it the psychedelic leap.

On the Fourth of July, the Charles River Valley Boys follow Country Joe and the Fish and precede Doc Watson in the Berkeley Folk Festival's grand finale, which is held at UC's Greek Theater, up in the hills. The order of performance may be purely serendipitous, or maybe Barry Olivier sees the CRVB's bluegrass-style Beatles tunes as an appropriate bridge between Country Joe's far-out music of the present moment and Doc Watson's traditional roots.

The last whistle stop on our California ramble is L.A., where we play five days at the Ash Grove. Founded in 1958, the same year as the Club 47 in Cambridge, the Ash Grove has served a similar role as a focal point for the folk boom. It feels friendly and familiar, but our L.A. crash pad is a far cry from the funky folkie houses in Berkeley and the rustic cabins of Big Sur.

Purple Man's father and stepmother have a house on the beach in Malibu. Better still, they're out of town. Peter clears it with the folks, and we settle down in a style to which we're quickly accustomed, lulled by the rhythm of the waves and dazzled by the view of the Pacific out the floor-to-ceiling windows. The album of the month is *Sgt. Pepper's Lonely Hearts Club Band* and the grass of the month is a particularly elevating harvest called Ice Bag, so named because it comes packaged in plastic bags intended for ice-dispensing machines. Two hundred bucks a key. Peter's folks' liquor cabinet features Jack Daniel's, which we sip at first, then tap more liberally. (I hope we replaced it.) Evenings after the Ash Grove, we often end up paralyzed on the living room floor by a combination of the two, trying to detect the exact moment when the perpetual chord at the end of "A Day in the Life" finally evaporates in the sound of the surf.

The day we arrive in town, we're driving along the Sunset Strip in Peter's VW bus when Neuwirth suddenly shouts, "Stop! Stop the bus, man! Pull over here!" He has spotted, walking on the sidewalk, a stunning model whose acquaintance he made in New York, back in the spring. The unlikelihood of seeing someone you know walking along the street in L.A. is astronomical, given that nobody in L.A. walks anywhere. In the residential sections of Beverly Hills, a pedestrian is likely to be stopped by the police and questioned as a suspicious character. The Sunset Strip, for a mile or so, is a stroller's sanctuary.

Bobby intercepts Phyllis, their relationship blooms in the California sunshine, and they take over one of the guest rooms in Malibu. Phyllis is cheerful, gorgeous, and very fond of Bobby. He gives her a nickname, Tonto, which she accepts and invites us to use freely. For Bobby, it's an ironic way of admitting that he is modifying, for now, the Lone Ranger's role that he has so carefully refined. I have never seen him so much at ease. Witnessing the flowering romance is one more intoxicant that lightens our Malibu days. For my own part, the ladies of the canyons find the beach house a pleasant place to visit, and I am warmed by their company.

Joe Val declines to share our beachfront idyll, choosing instead to keep himself at a safe remove from the goofy hippies his bluegrass cohorts have become. It's bad enough that Bob Siggins and I took to wearing psychedelic shirts onstage in Berkeley. What gives Joe real concern is that we might get him arrested for being in company with a bunch of potheads. In Cambridge, nobody smokes dope in the Club 47 and Joe finds it fairly easy to distance himself from the illicit practices of his fellow musicians. In Northern California, he was eating and sleeping in the same premises where we indulged our enhanced explorations. Assuring him that the cops can't be bothered busting everybody with a joint in his hand hasn't brought Joe peace of mind. In L.A., Joe looks up a musician friend who has fled the freezing slush of Boston winters for the land of swaying palms. He never sets foot in the Bergs' Malibu house. During our gig at the Ash Grove, Joe sleeps safe and sound, far from the surf and the scent of Ice Bag. Each evening, properly attired in black jeans, dress shirts, vests and string ties, we meet Joe at the Ash Grove and belt out our own mix of breakdowns, heart songs, gospel tunes and Beatles songs.

> "I thought [Joe Val] was a really good steady guy, and a good musician. . . . Either through maturity or good character, he put up with all our craziness with very great equanimity, and didn't give anybody a hard time about being strange. I thought that was absolutely wonderful."
>
> **Peter Berg**

Joe's day job compels him to fly back to Boston before our last night at the Ash Grove. With our straight man homeward bound, we cast off the last restraints we've kept in place out of love and respect for Joe. Chris Darrow, of Kaleidoscope, sits in on mandolin. On the whole, I don't perform bluegrass stoned, not since the night a few years earlier, at the Club 47, when the words to several songs suddenly eluded me midverse. Tonight I cast my fate to the wind. If I forget the words, I'll make up new ones.

Our imaginations, fueled by intoxicants consumed during the Malibu cocktail hour, lead us to a new plane of psychedelic bluegrass. We call on Neuwirth's artistic talent: Before we go onstage, Bob paints our faces. The style is more appropriate to an acid test than the warpaths of the Old West. We announce to the audience that the evening's entertainment will be a bluegrass opera, but it's a narrative only in the most free-associative sense, a tale that Aldous Huxley could follow more easily than Puccini. We introduce each song with a story that's made up on the spot. The next singer picks up the story and carries it forward to introduce the next song. That's the idea, anyway. Along about midevening the narrative threads grow exceedingly thin, but our Ash Grove audience is ready for anything. If by chance anyone recorded the proceedings, please contact me by Galactic Express Priority Overnight.

CHAPTER FIVE

Sittin' on the Dock of the Bay

JANIS AND BIG Brother are frustrated by a feeling of a bright promise delayed. After their spectacular success at Monterey they are touring the same circuit of gigs that has become familiar to them. They play the Avalon, the Fillmore, the California Hall. They play the Straight Theater and Golden Gate Park. They play around the Bay.

In August, their first record album hits the stores, but the record isn't all they hoped it would be and its appearance now is bittersweet. They signed with Mainstream—a small label known mostly for blues and jazz—over a year ago. At the time, the recording contract seemed like confirmation that the group was bound for bigger things, and it had the more important effect of solidifying Janis's connection to the band.

Big Brother was first approached by Bobby Shad, the owner of Mainstream, in the summer of '66. The band had been playing together for eight or nine months, but Janis was a new addition, called up from Texas by her fellow Texan, Chet Helms, who had midwifed the birth of Big Brother and the Holding Company, and who had functioned since its beginnings as the band's manager without portfolio.

Shad was in San Francisco to check out the new rock groups. He expressed interest in recording Big Brother, but he triggered all of Helms's distrust of outsiders from the Music Business, and Chet rebuffed the offer. Chet's out-of-hand dismissal of Shad's interest proved to be the catalyst that led Big Brother to dissolve their informal management arrangement. Chet had established Family Dog Productions within a hippie commune of the same name. It was a catch-as-catch-can organization, very much in the spirit of the times, that managed the Avalon Ballroom and associated events. Big Brother felt their needs were playing second fiddle to Chet's other interests. It was time for someone a little more professional.

Soon after parting from Chet, the band took a monthlong booking at a club in Chicago called Mother Blues, but Janis wasn't sure she would go.

"I have a problem," she wrote to her parents in Port Arthur, Texas. She told them what she had not yet told the boys in the band: She had been approached by a record producer named Paul Rothchild. Paul worked for Elektra Records. He had produced a handful of folk artists including Tom Rush and Tom Paxton. He produced the Butterfield Blues Band. The first record Paul ever produced was the Charles River Valley Boys, but he had no reason to mention this bit of arcana to Janis. In the summer of 1966, Paul had sold Elektra's president, Jac Holzman, on an idea: He would assemble a group of young urban interpreters of the blues, pay their expenses for six months, and see if the effort produced a viable band. Jac came to San Francisco with Paul, they auditioned Janis, and Jac liked what he saw.

Paul gathered several musicians in a living room in Berkeley. Among those present were Al Wilson, who owned every blues record ever pressed and could play most of the songs; Taj Mahal, who had been playing solo, mostly in the East, for several years; and Janis.

> "In San Francisco, Paul Rothchild and I tried to recruit Janis Joplin
> for Elektra . . . she brought her guitars and sang for us at a mutual
> friend's apartment—incredible power, the room was too small
> to hold her, she just about pushed you against the wall."
>
> **Jac Holzman**

They traded songs back and forth for a while, and it was beginning to click. Somebody would say, What about Such-and-Such-a-Blues? Oh, yeah, I know that. And they'd play it. Janis was having a good time, but the Mother Blues gig was looming. She had to decide whether she was going to stick with Big Brother or take a chance that Paul Rothchild's idea would pan out.

Janis wasn't sure she and Big Brother were going to pan out. She had never sung rock and roll before. Except for a raggedy-ass and briefly popular band in Austin, where she just as briefly attended the University of Texas, she'd never sung with a band before at all. She was having to invent a whole new vocal style for San Francisco acid rock, and Big Brother was having to adjust their instrumental style to accommodate her singing. But Janis liked the feeling Big Brother gave her, the power of it, and she loved the interplay between the bands and the dancers in the Avalon and the Fillmore.

In the letter to her parents, Janis expressed another doubt. "I'm not sure yet whether the rest of the band (Big Brother) will, indeed *want to*, work hard enough to be good enough to make it. We're not now I don't think. Oh God, I'm just fraught w/ indecision!"

A month after the Monterey Pop Festival, Janis and the guys in Big Brother had moved to a house in Lagunitas, in Marin County, north of San Francisco. The shift to communal living was intended to strengthen the bonds within the group and make them a true family band in the San Francisco style. One morning when everybody was up and about, Janis told the boys about Paul Rothchild's offer, and she told them she was considering it. Her announcement provoked a shocked response. To Peter and Sam and Dave and James, joining a band was a sacred trust. It wasn't just a business, it was a commitment. You didn't just back out after a couple of months when something that looked like a better offer came along. Peter Albin was the one who reacted most indignantly. He went at Janis hammer and tongs, demanding that she commit to the Chicago gig right then and there.

Taken aback by Peter's onslaught, Janis gave in.

At her next meeting with Paul Rothchild, Janis told him she liked playing with Taj and Al, but she really wanted to play electric music. "Oh, hey," Paul said, "we'll do that too." Janis said, "Well, I've been working with another group of musicians and I want to try that for a while and if that doesn't happen, we'll put this thing back together." She had committed to the Mother Blues gig, but she was still weighing her options. She wrote her parents that she hoped the time in Chicago would give her perspective and help her make a final decision.

In Chicago, Bobby Shad approached the band again, renewing his offer of a record contract. This time there was no Chet to blow him off. Peter and David and Sam and James wanted to go for it. Janis's uncertainty about staying with the band had shaken them all. They recognized that her vocals were a vital addition to the group's unique sound. Some of Big Brother's San Francisco partisans had objected at first to the addition of a chick singer, but as the band's music adapted to embrace Janis, her lead vocals had become the high points of their performances. A record deal would hold the band together, at least for a time.

The boys argued for accepting Shad's offer, and Janis gave her consent. Mainstream wasn't Elektra by a long shot, but the record would be made now, not six months or more down the road, *if* the prospective blues band panned out. A more important consideration for Janis was proving herself to her parents. Growing up in Port Arthur, a Gulf coast oil town, and during her brief stab at college in Austin, she had always felt like a misfit. In San Francisco, she had found a band and a community that welcomed her, that made her feel she belonged. She wanted her parents to approve of her unconventional life. She had written them enthusiastically about Big Brother in her first weeks with the group. Making a record would prove that her contribution to the band was real. It would prove that she could take a job and stick to it.

The relationship with Mainstream was uneasy from the start. The Mainstream engineers couldn't grasp that James Gurley *wanted* the VU meters up in the red on the guitar solos. Distortion had been an essential element of his technique since the early days of '65, when he was known as Weird Jim Gurley and called his music "freak rock," playing an acoustic Martin guitar with a vocal mike taped to it for amplification.

Big Brother's music proved too out there for Bobby Shad. He wouldn't allow the band in the control room during the final mix. Still, for all the hassles, the Mainstream deal and the Mother Blues gig did what the boys hoped they would do—they kept Janis in the group. After Mother Blues, she didn't raise the subject of leaving the band again.

Big Brother recorded some songs at a studio in Chicago, and more, later in the year, in Los Angeles. While they were in L.A., Mainstream put out two songs from the Chicago sessions as a single that sank without a whimper. In May '67, Mainstream issued another single whose A side, "Down on Me," aroused some notice.

All of this was before Monterey. After the band's success at the Pop Festival, Mainstream scrambled to get out an album to capitalize on the publicity.

When the record hits the stores, Janis and the boys feel it's too little, too late. The album has a thin, strangled quality, as if the sound that won over the San Francisco ballroom fans and made such an impression at Monterey had been squeezed through a two-inch car radio speaker. In the months since the Mainstream recording sessions, Big Brother has continued to evolve. The changes Janis and the band have made to adapt her singing and their sound to each other have achieved a synthesis, a unity that isn't present on the Mainstream album. All the same, having a record in the stores a few weeks after Monterey, however much they dislike the sound, helps Big Brother believe that their Pop Festival success wasn't just a onetime thing.

In September, another triumph helps to banish that fear. The band's champion, Ralph Gleason, has arranged for Big Brother to play on a Saturday afternoon blues program at the tenth annual Monterey Jazz Festival. Gleason is producing a TV special on the festival for KQED, San Francisco's educational television outlet. In the world of jazz, Monterey is as much revered by western fans as the jazz festival at Newport is by East Coast devotees.

This time, the audience in Monterey is shy on hippies and long on blacks. As Big Brother begins their first song, the crowd is silent, stunned by the sounds emerging from Janis's Texas-white mouth. After sixteen bars they are on their feet, dancing in the aisles. When the set ends, Big Brother gets a standing ovation.

Janis comes offstage, skipping and happy, bumps into Ralph Gleason, and throws her arms around him. "It was good, huh?" "It was dynamite," the usually sardonic Gleason agrees. "Didja get it okay?" Janis asks. "Whaddya mean get it?" Gleason says. "Julius wouldn't let us film it."

As at the Pop Festival, Julius Karpen reacted to the presence of a film crew with instinctive hostility. Before Big Brother's set at the Jazz Festival, Karpen and Gleason had a shouting match in the festival office, during which Julius expressed his conviction that if Big Brother were in the TV film, someone would steal it and sell it in Australia. This bizarre comment convinced Gleason there was no reasoning with Julius, who proceeded from the office to the backstage control boards of Wally Heider's sound company—there to record the festival performances—where he made Heider shut down the taping system as Janis and the boys went onstage.

This time, there is no chance for a second performance.

In his Monday column in the *Chronicle*, Gleason writes, "Big Brother was really a delight and Miss Joplin is a gas, easily the most exciting singer of her race to appear in a decade or more."

Like Chet Helms's rejection of Bobby Shad's first offer, Julius Karpen's exclusion of Big Brother from the KQED special brings smoldering resentments within the band to full combustion in the days following the Jazz Festival. They have already realized that Julius isn't as big a departure from Chet as they had hoped. He's too local, too focused on the San Francisco scene, not adequately aware of or connected to the wider world of music. Bill Graham won't talk to Julius. If Big Brother wants to play the Fillmore, they have to talk directly to Bill. Janis hasn't gotten along with Julius from the start. They fight like alley cats.

Peter Albin's uncle, a real-estate investor who owns the house in the Haight where Big Brother first rehearsed, asks if the band has ever seen Julius's accounts for the time he has managed the band. They have not. You're giving him a license to rob you blind, Peter's uncle says. He insists the band ask for an accounting. They take his advice, but Julius refuses to open the books, and that's the last straw. The band fires Julius and lets it be known that they are seeking new representation. They talk to their friends. They put out the word.

Big Brother's willingness to dump Julius rises from the confidence they gained from their triumphs at Monterey, first at the Pop Festival and then at the Jazz Festival. The receptions they earned not just from the audiences, white and black, but also from the musicians with whom they shared the stage, including some of the best in the world, has given them the courage to take a leap of faith.

They talk to Bill Graham. He already manages Jefferson Airplane. Can't he manage Big Brother too? Graham knows that realizing Big

Brother's full potential will take more time than he can devote to the task. He recommends that Big Brother talk to Albert Grossman.

> "At that period, there were only two people that Albert really wanted to work with. It was Janis and Jimi Hendrix. He really had the utmost appreciation for both of them, musically."
>
> **Barry Feinstein, photographer,**
> **member of Pennebaker film crew at Monterey**

Grossman has been in Big Brother's thoughts since they sought his guidance at the Monterey Pop Festival. Now Janis asks her San Francisco friends for advice. One of those closest to her is her new roommate, Linda Gravenites. Six months in Lagunitas cured Big Brother of the communal living trip. When the landlady wanted the house back, they returned to the city and moved into individual pads where they have some space and privacy. Linda was one of a few creative women who were making clothes for the San Francisco bands. She had made a couple of shirts for Sam Andrew, and she made Janis's outfit for the Jazz Festival. She had been looking after the Grateful Dead's house while the band was on tour; when they came back Linda asked Janis if she could crash on her couch in the Lyon Street apartment where Janis had settled. Not long after that, they were cleaning up the kitchen together one morning when Janis said, in an offhand kind of way, "I need a mother." And Linda thought, "I could do that. Take care of all the shit she doesn't want to do. Sure. I could do that." So that's Linda's role in Janis's life: roommate and mother, including mother as advisor on the things Janis needs advice about.

Linda knows Albert. She doesn't know him well, but she knows a lot about him from people who are close to him, people who believe in him. Linda's former husband, Nick Gravenites, is a blues singer and songwriter from the mean streets of Chicago, where he was known as Nick the Greek and carried a gun. Nick is tight with Paul Butterfield and Mike Bloomfield. He's one of Albert's inner circle of confidants from the early days.

When Janis asks Linda who she thinks would be the best manager for Big Brother, Linda says, "If you want to stay in San Francisco and play around and have a good time, it really doesn't matter. But if you want to be an international phenomenon, Albert. No question."

Others offer conflicting advice. A New York manager! Are you crazy? The San Francisco paranoia about being ripped off is a formidable obstacle to any kind of business deal with someone who isn't a hippie: Don't go to Monterey, you'll get ripped off. Don't be in the movie, you'll get ripped off. Don't sign a record deal, you'll get ripped off. Don't be on TV, you'll get ripped off. And, hey, don't sign with a New York manager, man, you'll get ripped off for sure.

Well, yes. Somebody might make some money *off you*. But that's the way it works! Somebody makes money off you, and if they're good at what they do, they help you get seen and heard by more people than will ever see and hear you if you scurry for your hole every time the possibility comes up that somebody else will make money off you. Yes, a manager gets a percentage of your earnings, but he only makes money when you make money, and *you make more than he does*.

No one in Big Brother has accepted all of this as gospel yet, but for the band even to consider approaching Albert Grossman to manage them represents a sea change. They have recognized that they need businesspeople, not hippies, to handle the business.

Albert comes to San Francisco. Janis and the boys can't get over the fact that he looks like the guy on the Quaker Oats box. It amuses them, and it kindles in them the first glimmers of affection for this taciturn man who has expanded his influence so surely, so apparently effortlessly, beyond folk music into the realm of rock.

He's funny too. The humor is bone dry, understated, but some of the band members, Janis and Sam in particular, pick up on Albert's wordplay and note the comic spark in his eyes.

The meeting is in Janis's apartment on Lyon Street, between Haight Street and the Panhandle. The living room is furnished in a Beat-Victorian style that is uniquely Janis. Posters and pieces of fabric are hung on the walls and more odd bits of fabric are draped over the furniture and the lamps.

Albert is a past master at Socratic inscrutability. When the guys in the band ask him a question, he asks one in return.

As our manager, what will you do for us?

What do you want?

They tell him, and he listens. His eyebrows are slightly raised behind his round glasses, giving him the expression of a curious owl.

Big Brother is contractually bound to Mainstream. That is something Albert will have to deal with, because they have no intention of recording for Bobby Shad again. Earlier in the year there were feelers from Warner Brothers. Julius fielded them and they went nowhere. More recently, Columbia has expressed interest. At the Monterey Jazz Festival, Columbia's legendary producer, John Hammond, Sr., who signed Bob Dylan to the label, invited Janis and Peter Albin to sit in his private box. Big Brother is ready for a real manager and a real record deal. They want to see the world beyond the San Francisco Bay. They want to find out how far they can go.

Sitting with them in Janis's living room while they lay this out for Albert is Bob Gordon, an attorney who represents Albert on the West Coast and has also represented Big Brother, independently, in some recent matters.

Bob earned his law degree in Berkeley, at Boalt Hall, in the fifties, when the campus was a bastion of peaceful conformity. He is now a partner in a Los Angeles law firm that boasts former California governor Pat Brown on its letterhead. Of those gathered in Janis's living room, Bob is the one who looks most out of place, the only one wearing a tie. He presents the appearance and demeanor of a solid citizen. A square. But beneath the traditional exterior lies a more individualistic spirit. For a time, Bob represented A&M Records. The founders, Herb Alpert and Jerry Moss, set out to establish a company that would be scrupulously fair to musicians and songwriters and represent their interests in a business that was not noted for giving artists—the creative spirits—their due. With the phenomenal success Alpert and his band, the Tijuana Brass, achieved by the midsixties, it seemed to Bob Gordon that Moss and Alpert became focused on making every deal bigger than the last and lost sight of their altruistic ideals, and Bob found himself less interested in working with them.

By then, Bob was traveling often to San Francisco on business and he became fascinated by the growth of the music scene there.

> "I wouldn't say that either Jerry or Herb are really nasty people. They're not. They're really good people, except that they got into a competitive spirit that belied the basis on which the company was formed. And at the same time, I was going to San Francisco and seeing kids working for nothing twenty hours a day, sanding floors and building community facilities, and putting every ounce of their soul into what they were doing, for nothing. And the contrast was so striking to me, that I gradually kind of lost interest in A&M . . . and at the same time I found myself just so pleased with what was going on in San Francisco, and feeling a part of it, and feeling worthwhile."
>
> **Bob Gordon**

Early in 1967, before the Pop Festival, Bob represented Big Brother when they were asked to appear in director Richard Lester's film *Petulia*, starring Julie Christie and George C. Scott, which was shot in San Francisco. Lester had directed the Beatles in *A Hard Day's Night*, so Big Brother jumped at the chance to work with him when he was recruiting bands for *Petulia*. The contract that Warner Brothers, the film's producers, presented to Big Brother would have transferred to Warner Brothers the copyrights of the songs Big Brother performed in the film.

Excuse me, Bob Gordon said, what are you trying to pull here? You don't get the copyright. All you get is a sync license.

The Warner Brothers lawyers smiled and said, Oh, sure, of course, while under their breath they were muttering, Curses, foiled again. Warner Brothers offered union scale for Big Brother's performance in the film. Bob got them more. This negotiation won Bob Gordon a lot of points with the band.

Between the Pop Festival and the Jazz Festival, Julius Karpen called on Bob to accompany him to Columbia Records' annual convention, held in L.A. Julius was invited as Big Brother's manager. He asked Bob to come along to protect his back. They met with Columbia president Clive Davis to discuss Big Brother, but the existence of the Mainstream contract posed an obstacle that was not overcome at the convention.

In the matter of Albert's management contract with Big Brother, Bob has told Albert that Big Brother needs his advice more than Albert does. Bob represents the band, while Albert's New York lawyers can oversee his side of the contract. Big Brother knows all this and they trust Bob to protect their interests.

The band wants an escape clause that will get them out of the management contract if things don't work out. They ask Albert to guarantee that he will make them an outlandish amount of money in the coming year. Name your price, Albert says. The figure the band has in mind is $75,000. Albert smiles his enigmatic smile. "Make it $100,000," he says, and then he has a better idea. "I'll tell you what," he says. "If I don't make you that much money, I won't take my twenty percent. I won't take anything, and you can fire me."

Janis and the boys sign on the dotted line.

CHAPTER SIX

Gonna Lay Down My Old Guitar

ON OUR RETURN to New York after the Pop Festival and the Charles River Valley Boys' cruise through the Summer of Love, Neuwirth and I feel that we have been expelled from the initiates' level of paradise to the midregions of purgatory. The return to the East is a rude reminder that the rest of America hasn't yet received the message that music, love and flowers are here to stay. We cushion the shock of reentry by ensconcing ourselves in the screening room at the offices of Leacock Pennebaker, in the company of friends who still glow in the dark with memories of Monterey, and we let the celluloid images transport us back. They're all there, Paul and Art, John and Michelle and Cass and Denny, Otis and Ravi and Grace. And Janis. On repeated viewings, "Ball and Chain" loses none of its power.

Within a few days, Bob and I are festival-bound again, off to Newport, where the barricades are still manned against amplified music that is too far out for the traditionalists. The Chambers Brothers startle the old guard with their break-out, space-out hit, "Time Has Come Today," but the brothers are fully fledged members of the folk family and the audience welcomes "Time" as a breath of fresh air. Buffalo Springfield's ticket to Newport is "For What It's Worth," which carries the folk tradition of protest into electrified pop music. The rest of this summer's Newport roster is down-the-line folk, old-time, gospel, bluegrass, and blues—Joan Baez, Maybelle Carter, Bill Monroe, Pete Seeger, Judy Collins, the Staple Singers, Grandpa Jones. The wild card this summer is country music star Dave Dudley, whose trucking song "Six Days on the Road" has caught the ear of folkies and rockers alike.

It is pleasant to sit in the sun in Peabody Park and listen to the musicians, uniformly excellent, but it is hard to escape a feeling that Newport has become a something of a backwater. Just two years after Bob Dylan shocked the old folkies by playing an electrified set at Newport, the musical offshoots that took so much inspiration from Dylan's amplified sound have gathered strength and spread across the land. The focus has shifted westward, leaping the heartland to settle on the Pacific shore. Is it possible that Monterey marked not the beginning of the shift, but its completion?

Tonto comes east to join Bobby. We take her up to Cambridge and show her the town. We spend time in Cambridge sitting in outdoor cafés on brick sidewalks and soaking up the summertime vibes. The Club 47's calendar is heavily tilted toward blues of the jumping variety—Howlin' Wolf, the Siegel-Schwall Blues Band, Buddy Guy and Junior Wells—along with the Kweskin Jug Band and the far-roaming Chambers Brothers. Close your eyes, and the sounds from the small stage on Palmer Street could be coming from grander platforms. Just to keep the mix interesting, the Club has booked the jazz pianist Mose Allison for a week. Allison's love of the blues makes him an appropriate bridge between Buddy Guy and Bill Monroe and the Blue Grass Boys.

My schedule with the Charles River Valley Boys isn't enough to keep body and soul together. We play a gig here, play a gig there, but the folk boom is spent. Between bluegrass gigs I spend my time in New York, where Pennebaker is assembling a rough cut of the Monterey footage. Some film work seems like just the thing to take up the slack. Penny and Ricky's office manager hires me in an undefined role. "Don't worry," he says, "we'll find something." I finish a transcription of the *Dont Look Back* sound track, which is to be published as a book. I help put together a photo collage that will become the endpapers. I enlist Neuwirth and a couple of the back-room crew to contribute improvisations for some very off-the-wall radio spots Penny uses to promote the film's New York debut.

Until the small hours of the morning, we're often at Max's Kansas City, a restaurant and bar on Park Avenue South that was formerly renowned, possibly apocryphally, for feeding goldfish to a tankful of piranhas at cocktail hour.

Max's is a steak house. The sign out front announces "Steak, lobster, chick peas." The place is long and narrow, the art on the walls is eclectic, and the banquettes, the tablecloths, the napkins—everything but the white walls—are red. A round table in the back room is the late-night rendezvous for Andy Warhol and his crew from the Factory. In the back room, even the lighting is red. After a few drinks, it's like being in a photographic darkroom with the safelight on.

Max's became a favorite hangout for artists when the owner, Mickey Ruskin, began accepting paintings in payment for bar bills. Soon the visual artists were joined by musicians and actors.

The balance of my life has shifted. After almost ten years of living in Cambridge and visiting New York, I'm spending most of my time in New York and making the run up to Cambridge to play with the CRVB. Neuwirth and I talk about sharing an apartment. We look at pads on the Upper West Side—not yet trendy—where rents are cheap. Three hundred bucks a month for five or six rooms with an eye-of-the-needle glimpse of the Hudson River. Whew. Steep. A full-time job at Leacock Pennebaker fails to materialize and I find it hard to settle into any kind of routine. I've been through the looking glass. I've glimpsed a new dimension. I'm not just hoping for a chance to make another trip to California. I want to live there.

As summer gives way to fall and the first gusts of winter probe the rectilinear ravines of New York City, the idea of becoming a road manager is the furthest thing from my mind—until a day when Neuwirth takes me into a cutting room at the Leacock Pennebaker offices on West 45th Street and informs me, in the kind of undertones usually reserved for conveying nuclear launch codes, that Albert wants to have dinner with me.

I don't have to ask "Albert who?" A couple of months after hitchhiking aboard Bob Dylan's springtime road trip, I was splashing in Albert Grossman's swimming pool in Bearsville, New York, just up the road from Woodstock. The house is the first Albert has ever owned, the first house he has lived in. Growing up in Chicago, he always lived in apartments, and he took to the role of country squire as if to the manor born. (A fondness for the bear image may be why Albert bought property in Bearsville instead of Woodstock. He briefly owned a club in Chicago called the Bear, where he often appeared in a huge fur coat, like the raccoon coats from the '20s, taking on the physical presence of a bear. He will later establish the Bear Café and Bearsville Sound Studios in his adopted hometown.)

The summer of '64 was Albert and his new wife Sally's first summer in the house, and they hosted a revolving-door parade of musicians and friends as lord and lady of the sylvan estate. Dylan was in residence, considering finding a house of his own somewhere nearby, but in no hurry. For a time, when Albert was away on business, Dick and Mimi Fariña house-sat for the Grossmans. Calls went out to Cambridge. Hey, come on over! Paul Rothchild and Neuwirth and I joined Dick and Mimi and Bob and Sara-who-would-eventually-become-Bob's-wife for the summer solstice.

Albert recognizes Cambridge as an important way station on the folk circuit, and he has visited several times. On one occasion he made use of the guest room in the Reservoir Street pad that I shared with Fritz Richmond. A few days after Albert's departure, we received as a thank-you gift the Elektra album *Music of Bulgaria*, whose stunning harmonies graced our late-night listening for a long time to come.

Since traveling with Dylan, Neuwirth has become Albert's confidant. He's not supposed to forewarn me about Albert's invitation, but he wants me to be prepared. Dinner is fine with me, I say. Albert is a convivial host. Bobby tells me there will be more to it. Albert has signed to manage Big Brother and the Holding Company, he says. This gets my attention. And (pause for effect) Albert is looking for a road manager.

It is not Albert's practice to send his musicians out on the road unattended. Not long after Bob Dylan committed himself to Albert's keeping, Albert decided that Bob should have a road manager. In the spring of 1964, Dylan arrived in Cambridge in a Ford station wagon driven by Victor Maimudes. Victor was the first road manager anyone in folk music had ever seen, and we were duly impressed. Jazz bands had road managers. Scruffy folk troubadours got lost driving from New York to Boston and were usually late for their gigs. Not Bob Dylan.

Bob and Victor used Cambridge as their base of operations for the better part of a week. Dylan liked the company of kindred souls, which in those days included many of the folks who lived at the heart of the Cambridge music scene.

Several of us went with Bob and Victor to Providence, Rhode Island, where Bob played at Brown University. We hung out backstage at a concert in Boston. We took another day trip to Amherst, where Bob played UMass, and where we met a student named Henry Fredericks, but we didn't know that was his name because a couple of years earlier he had a dream about Gandhi, and India, and started calling himself Taj Mahal. Taj could definitely play the blues, and more. He had absorbed the folk boom and was finding his own music.

Beaujolais was the drink of choice during these New England rambles. Genuine French Beaujolais for $1.95 a bottle. Victor made sure there were always a few bottles in the car. The Beaujolais went well with pot. Dylan laughed a lot, and he never gave a thought about where he was going or what time he was supposed to be there. Neither did the crew of hangers-on. Victor road-managed all of us. He drove the Ford station wagon, he made sure we got there on time, he got us in backstage at the gigs, and before the gig was over he disappeared briefly to collect the money.

I thought Victor had the coolest job in the world.

By now, in 1967, having a road manager is a mark of success both among the harshly winnowed ranks of folk performers and in the booming electrified free-for-all. With no pool of experienced candidates to draw from, what Albert is looking for is someone who can do the job but doesn't know he can do it. Bobby has assured him I have the requisite potential.

Albert and I dine at Max's Kansas City. I smile at the waitresses and try to make small talk with Albert, which is not easy. He prefers to listen more than he talks. In negotiations, or conversation with those he regards as opponents, silence is his preferred weapon and he wields it without mercy. Reluctant to reveal himself, he is adept at getting others to reveal *them*selves. When an adversary is done delivering his pitch at great length, Albert will nod ever so slightly. He'll say, "Mmm," as if what he heard is worthy of consideration, and he will sit there, waiting for more. His interlocutor, burdened with responsibility for the silence, will step in to fill the void, trip over things he hadn't intended to say, and prostrate himself before the Sphinx.

In congenial company, Albert often uses his natural reticence for humorous effect, capping the conversation of others with a pithy comment that gets the biggest laugh. When I come to know him better, I realize that Albert has turned the natural demeanor of a shy man to his advantage.

With me, Albert has always been friendly, rarely intimidating. Maybe he recognizes me as a fellow member of Shy People Anonymous. I'm not often tongue-tied, but with Albert I don't want to rattle on like an imbecile. I want to say things that interest him, things that make him think well of me. Things that make him laugh. I want to impress him. As a consequence, I'm tongue-tied.

"So, John," Albert says, when a silence grows long. "How would you feel about going on the road?"

He surprises me by saying that he has three groups in need of supervision—the Paul Butterfield Blues Band, the Electric Flag, and Big Brother and the Holding Company. Bobby didn't warn me I'd have to make a choice. Maybe he didn't know. Albert doesn't reveal all his cards, even to his intimates.

I pretend to think it over. Butterfield is from the Chicago blues scene, a long way from the Club 47 in Cambridge. As a white guy playing black music, Butter is a phenomenon. Invited to sit in with Junior Wells at the Blue Flame Lounge, a black club in Chicago where Paul was a regular—kind of a novelty act, like "Watch this white boy play the harp!"—he blew Junior Wells off the stage so thoroughly that Junior put on his hat and coat and left the club. The crowd wouldn't let Paul go, but they let Junior go without a peep. This is Junior Wells, the guy who *defines* the Chicago style of playing harp. Junior didn't come back until the next night, invited Paul to sit in again, and *the same thing happened!* Paul blew him away just like the night before. Junior put on his hat and coat and was out the door.

Paul not only plays blues harp, he can *sing*. He brought the Chicago sound—electrified, contemporary, urban black music—to the white folk fans that have become the core audience for the rock-and-roll explosion. I love Paul's music, but the Butterfield band plays two-week club dates in places like Detroit where I will die of boredom. The urban blues scene isn't my first choice for hanging out.

The Electric Flag is already notorious within Albert's office for some band members' propensity for serious substance abuse. No, thank you. I tell Albert that Big Brother impressed me at Monterey, and I've always liked San Francisco. Yadda, yadda, yadda.

If Albert finds either irony or pleasure in the fact that the son of immigrant Jewish tailors from Riga, Latvia (his mother), and Odessa (his father) is hiring a Harvard-graduate bluegrass singer who is the son of Alistair Cooke to be a rock-and-roll road manager, he keeps his feelings to himself. (Few Americans are aware that my father is the chief American correspondent for the British newspaper *The Guardian*, or that for more than twenty years he has written and broadcast a weekly radio program, *Letter from America*, for the BBC. At this time, he is somewhat known in the United States as a television "personality," a term he loathes, because from 1952 until 1961 he hosted *Omnibus*, a ninety-minute variety program of a type never seen before or since, that ran on Sunday afternoons. In November 1967, *Omnibus* is six years in the past and *Masterpiece Theatre* four years in the future.)

Albert wants me on the West Coast by the first of December. Thanksgiving is just a week away.

By the next day I'm—well, I'm not really having second thoughts; I want to do this gig, but I'm wondering if I can. Neuwirth reassures me: Hey, man, nothing to it.

Yeah, well what do I do?

Simple: get the band to the gig, collect the money, make sure everybody's happy. Bob has one piece of serious advice: Don't be a fan, he cautions. Sometimes you'll have to tell the band what to do. If you're a fan, they won't listen to you. Be the road manager. Don't be the guy who runs to buy them cigarettes. Be the guy who knows all the shit they don't know.

Great, but I don't know all the shit they don't know.

Pretend you do.*

---

*What Bob doesn't tell me, until much later, is that Albert wanted *him* to road-manage Big Brother: "[Albert] tried to get me into it. I said, 'No, Albert, I'm not doing this.' Albert had gone all the way from 'Who the fuck is this guy from California that's come to town to work with Bob [Dylan],' to later trying to get me to be Janis's roadie. I said, 'No, I can't do it, but I know somebody who can.'" (Author interview with Bob Neuwirth, August 13, 1997.)

I fill up on Thanksgiving turkey in Cambridge, play a final gig with the Charles River Valley Boys, spend a few days in New York to see my parents, and on November 30 I catch a cab for JFK.

Just like that, my California visa has fallen into my lap. I don't tell Albert or anyone else that I view this job as temporary employment to carry me through a transitional phase. For now, I'll help Janis and Big Brother do their thing. I'll travel the country, I'll meet new people (including, in my imagination, many fetching young women) and see new possibilities. Somewhere along the way, I'll decide what to do next. Whether I stay in California will depend on what *my* thing eventually reveals itself to be. For now, the road-managing gig is the ideal bridge between my Cambridge past and a future that I hope will not be too far removed from the music and the friends I found in Cambridge.

I resolve to give the job six months, enough to get Big Brother up and running on the national stage.

CHAPTER SEVEN

Hit the Road, Jack

WE'RE ON THE road within a few days of my arrival in California. For the month of December and into the new year, Albert is keeping Big Brother on the West Coast, in the wings, as he prepares to bring them east. He's planning the band's New York debut for midwinter. In the meantime, I'm grateful for a chance to learn the job in high school gyms and war memorial auditoriums up and down the San Joaquin Valley and in the kaleidoscope dance halls of San Francisco.

On December 10, Otis Redding dies in the crash of a chartered plane. Janis takes it especially hard. She first heard Otis perform live just a year ago, at the Fillmore. She and Dave Getz had been to a party in the city where someone spiked a bottle of Cold Duck with LSD. Janis enjoyed acid but took it rarely. On the other hand, she rarely turned down a bottle passed in her direction. When she learned what was in the duck she forced herself to throw up, but the bottle had been liberally medicated and she had already absorbed more than enough to get high. Being Janis, she wasn't about to miss Otis Redding live just because someone had dosed the wine. Acid made her spiritual, contemplative, which was not necessarily how she might have chosen to approach hearing Otis live for the first time, but it turned out just fine. Janis and Dave sat on the floor in front of the stage at the Fillmore, and they *dug* Otis Redding.* The next day, Janis could sing half his riffs. His performance at the Monterey Pop Festival blew her away all over again.

From repeated viewings in Pennebaker's screening room, I know Redding's set by heart. It comforts me to imagine him now in an exclusive group, made up of musicians who have died in plane crashes, that entertains the Heavenly Choir on its days off. Otis sings in harmony with Buddy Holly and Richie Valens and J. P. "the Big Bopper" Richardson, and he gives a soul twist to the country melodies of Patsy Cline and Hawkshaw Hawkins. The backup band is conducted by Glenn Miller.

We play Fresno and Turlock, Merced and Modesto, small cities strung along U.S. 99, which traverses the San Joaquin Valley north-and-south, a strip of macadam that runs through the heart of America's vegetable basket. The kids in the Valley aren't quite sure what's expected of them. Their hair is still short, but they're on the receiving end of prevailing winds from the coast and they've picked up a contact high. The grown-ups have felt the vibe too, and it makes them edgy. Soothing the powers that be is part of my job from the start. We're just a jolly bunch of long-haired musicians, sir—nothing to worry about.

Until my first gig with Big Brother, I've heard the band do only the songs they performed at Monterey, with "Ball and Chain" foremost in memory. Sam Andrew's "Combination of the Two," about the San Francisco dance-hall scene, is in the movie too. The lyrics include a play on "Fillmore" in a line directed to a girl who has caught his eye: "I'd like to feel *you* more, baby."

---

*Sam Andrew and Milan Melvin both also related, in interviews with the author, sharing enjoyable trips with Janis on acid and mescaline.

In the band's concert sets, which run forty-five minutes to an hour, there are songs from many backgrounds. I'm pleased to find a couple of traditional folk songs on the list. Clarence Ashley's 1929 recording of "The Coo-Coo Bird" is on Harry Smith's six-LP *Anthology of American Folk Music*, which was the Rosetta stone to the folk boom. I've heard Ashley perform the song live, at the Club 47 and Newport. More than thirty years after his original recording, he gives it new life each time. Big Brother's version is faster, driving, but it has the right feeling, Janis singing up high, flying with the coo-coo bird. Peter Albin plays lead guitar. The band has combined "The Coo-Coo" with another song, "Oh, Sweet Mary." When the vibe is right, Big Brother's medley can run for a long time, like a Grateful Dead jam.

The band's version of "Easy Rider" is very different from the slower, traditional bluesy version that was a staple of the folk revival. This one swings right along. Janis and James share the lead vocals and James sings a verse that was definitely not in the traditional version (nor is it on the Mainstream album): "I got a woman who walks like a duck; she ain't good-looking but she sure can . . . dance! Easy Rider, don't you deny my name! Oh, no!"

In the mild December of California's Central Valley, the high school and college kids in Big Brother's audiences are getting a dose of traditional American music, turbocharged by the San Francisco renaissance, as well as tunes from unexpected sources beyond the traditional canon.

An eerie song called "All is Loneliness" is unique, unlike anything I have heard before. I am astonished to learn that it was written by Moondog, an anachronistic apparition I have seen on Sixth Avenue in New York. He is very tall, has a long gray beard, carries a spear, and wears homemade clothes and a leather hat with horns that makes him look like a Viking. Finding that Big Brother does a song by this singular character from my hometown makes me feel connected to Janis and the boys in an unexpected way. Like my friends in

Cambridge and Berkeley and New York, Big Brother has gleaned songs from far-ranging sources. Unlike many in the folk revival, they aren't trying to replicate the original forms. With rhythms and vocal harmonies that are distinctly their own, Janis and the boys have brought the older songs beyond folk and folk-rock into the present moment, charging them with new energy and offering them to a wider audience than the folk boom reached even in its largest assemblies.

James Gurley was Big Brother's lead guitarist at the band's creation, and his unique style defined the group's distinctive sound. By the time I join them, Sam has become the co-lead. He and James swap rhythm and solos, and you have to pay close attention to tell who's doing what. The synthesis they have achieved is impressive, because they are in many ways polar opposites. Sam's musical education is rooted in the classical tradition, while James has absorbed his music from the ether. He is unacademic, nonintellectual, and a thinker all the same. Like Sam, James is given to damping down excess cerebral activity with alcohol and drugs.

One of the songs they play together, a real surprise on the set list, for those who recognize the theme, is Sam's arrangement of Grieg's "Hall of the Mountain King," from the Peer Gynt Suite. The original is less than four minutes long, but Big Brother's version explores rambling variations on the theme that never occurred to Grieg.

At most of our shows I get to hear part of the set, but I have other responsibilities when the band is onstage.

Road managing is about logistics, communication, and money. The basics are simple: Get the band to the gig, see that they fulfill their obligations, see that they get paid. Ideally, the musicians can think about nothing but the music, while the travel arrangements and the business are handled so smoothly that they're scarcely aware of it. Keeping the promoter satisfied is part of the job. So is seeing that he holds up his end of the bargain. It's just what Neuwirth said: Get the band to the gig, collect the money, make sure everybody's happy.

Early on the job, I establish as policy another piece of Bob's advice: The road manager does not carry your guitar. You are the musician. You carry your own guitar. When you need cigarettes or booze, you will buy them yourself. "Don't be their gofer," Bob said. "If you're running around getting them cigarettes or a bottle of whiskey, you won't be able to do your job."

The band's equipment travels ahead of us in a beat-up van driven by Big Brother's equipment man, Dave Richards. Dave carries only the stage equipment—the instrument amps and Dave Getz's drums. The promoters provide the PA system. Checking that the PA is adequate is up to Dave. If he runs into an uncooperative promoter or some schmuck who thinks one mike and a fifty-watt amp is enough, Dave calls me and I get to play Bad Cop, but this is rare. Dave has been doing this job for a while. He's got it covered.

When we arrive at the gig, I introduce myself to the promoter and get the band to their dressing room. I check with Dave to make sure he's cool, then scout the layout of the hall. Where's the box office? How many doors are there?

There are two kinds of gigs: flat-rate and percentage. The simplest, from a road manager's point of view, is a flat-rate deal. If the band is getting paid a flat $3,000, the promoter can let the whole town in free and I don't care. He has deposited 50 percent of the fee with Albert's office beforehand. I collect the other half at the gig. A flat-rate gig is an incentive for the promoter to advertise the show effectively and make a bundle. Everything above our guarantee is his. It is to the band's advantage, of course, to share in the profits if they draw a big audience. This is why, from my first days on the job, most of Big Brother's gigs are percentage deals. On a percentage deal, the band gets a guarantee plus a percentage of the gross receipts. For these early gigs under Albert Grossman's management, the guarantee usually ranges from $2,500 to $3,500 against 50 or 60 percent of the gross.

On a percentage deal, I have to know how many tickets the promoter sells and I have to calculate what Big Brother is owed, to make sure the promoter's accounting is accurate. If the tickets are printed for the gig, I want to see the printer's manifest. For roll tickets, I take the starting number on each roll. At the end of the show, I get the end numbers and we assume the promoter sold all the tickets in between, less a reasonable number of comps that he gave away. He's supposed to have a written record of these, plus any comps issued to the band or our guests.

I'm still learning the routine when—Oops! Gotcha! On the seventh or eighth gig I discover a scam.

We're playing a Saturday afternoon concert in the Valley. The promoter—I'll call him Joe Promo—is selling roll tickets, nice little "Admit One" red jobbies just like Saturday afternoon at the movies. Each ticket is numbered. There are two box offices, the better to serve the eager fans. Joe has provided me with the starting numbers from two rolls of tickets, one for each box office. At the doors to the hall, the ticket takers are tossing the tickets into big wastebaskets without tearing them, which is okay—any ticket no longer attached to the roll is sold. Big Brother has attracted a good crowd and the mood is up. The kids are happy, Joe's happy, the band's happy, I'm happy. Until I pick up a handful of tickets from one of the wastebaskets by the entry doors to check the numbers. Egad, Watson, what's this? Some of the tickets are from a roll my starting numbers know nothing about.

I stroll out to the box offices and check the stream of kids coming away from the ticket windows. "Could I see your ticket, please? Thanks." The out-of-sequence tickets are coming from one of the two box offices.

I present the rogue tickets to Joe Promo. He turns red and storms off to talk to the ticket seller. He comes back with a story about his box office guy selling tickets from a third roll under the counter and pocketing the money. This may be true, but it's just as likely that Joe himself was responsible for the scam. It's not my job to determine who is the guilty party. In situations like this, the promoter is guilty until proven innocent.

I spend the first half hour of the concert sorting through the purchased tickets with the help of the ticket takers. I find the highest serial number from the third roll and assume all the tickets up to this number were sold, starting at 0000. Joe Promo accepts my calculations without complaint. For this gig, the tickets from the third roll make the difference between collecting just the other half of our guarantee and going into percentage.

When I send the proceeds to the New York office, I report the scam to Albert so he can decide if he'll do business with Joe Promo in the future. Joe is a two-bit local promoter, but if I were to find a similar rip-off being run by a regional promoter, someone Albert does business with regularly . . . the responsibilities of the job just got bigger.

In San Francisco I am camping in a cream-colored stucco motel a block off Lombard Street in the Marina district until I can find a pad. West of Van Ness Avenue, Lombard is a commercial strip lined with restaurants, motels and businesses. I can get my laundry done or buy a meal within a few minutes' walk of my motel, but it's not a part of town where I want to live for long. I've got a station wagon from Hertz until I get a car, and I start looking for a place to rent on my days off.

My mornings are spent on the phone. Albert's office has supplied me with an itinerary for the coming weeks and contracts for the gigs. I check the flights if we're taking a plane, check the motel reservations, call the promoters. What time is the sound check? What time do the doors open? What time is the show? How long is the show? What time will Big Brother go on? In my spare time, I visit with friends in Berkeley or go to the Fillmore or the Avalon with members of Big Brother. Then I get a revised itinerary from Albert's office with new gigs on it, and I'm back on the phone.

For the Valley gigs, I usually drive the band in the rent-a-station-wagon. Where it's a toss-up between driving and flying, I call the band members to take a poll. Would you rather spend three hours in a car or three hours in airports and airplanes? Albert hired me, but I work for them. The band's income pays my salary, and from the start I involve them in these decisions.

On a street map of San Francisco I chart a course from my motel to the band members' homes in the Haight. The day before we travel I call them to let them know what time I'll pick them up. I build a lot of extra time into the schedule. These are musicians. Their clocks run slower than mine. Sam is congenitally late. I tell him to be ready at eleven. He's the last to be picked up because he lives on Oak Street, east of the Haight. From his house it's a straight shot to the freeway on-ramp. When the rest of us pull up in front of his place at eleven thirty, maybe he's ready. But this is a game two can play. Sam begins to allow for the fact that I arrive later than I tell him.

When someone slows us down, I can get wound up in a hurry. If Sam seems to be deliberately lagging, messing with me on purpose, my style of road managing becomes, shall we say, intense. When a member of the band wanders off in an airport and almost makes us miss a plane, my admonitory rant may turn heads in our direction. I vent my displeasure at volume, but I don't hold a grudge, and I hope the band sees that my aim is to get us where we're going. Just because I handle the plane tickets and drive the car like their parents did when they were children, that doesn't mean they can get away with behaving like children now. They're grown-ups. To their credit, they prove they're grown-ups by viewing my flare-ups with humor, except for the one who's bearing the brunt. In those moments, they take to calling me the Road Nazi, and in time they manage to make it an affectionate nickname.

Sam is the one who incurs my outbursts most often, but I can't stay mad at Sam. He's my first real friend in the band. He has played music since his early teens—jazz and classical, saxophone as well as guitar, all through his years as a student. Intellectual, sensitive, thoughtful, a die-hard romantic where women are concerned, Sam dropped out of graduate studies in linguistics at UC Berkeley to play rock and roll. Linguistics is like the philosophy and physics of language rolled into one discipline. Someone who is attracted to linguistics is someone who enjoys the life of the mind in its rarefied recesses. Sam landed in linguistics after earlier studies in philosophy and English literature. In Big Brother, Sam is in retreat from the life of the mind. It strikes me that he will have to find an outlet for his intellect somewhere along the way, or suffer the consequences of keeping it in confinement.

On our car trips, the band is like a bunch of kids. Are we there yet? I have to pee. Who's got a joint? Can we stop and eat?

Well, yes, because I've planned a meal break. When the timing is right, we like to eat at the Nut Tree restaurant in Vacaville, just off Interstate 80, our route from the Bay Area to Sacramento and the Valley. The Nut Tree has been a California landmark since the twenties. In addition to the restaurant, there is a toy store and a small-scale railroad that gives kids rides from the toy store to the restaurant. Inside the restaurant there's a glassed-in aviary. Big Brother likes the Nut Tree because the restaurant bakes its own bread and features fresh vegetables and fruits on the menu. It's as close as we can get to a health-food restaurant in the Valley.

"Are there sprouts on the salad?" Janis wants to know. Janis is sporadically into healthy food. She fights a tendency to plump up on road fare. The boys eat like farmhands. I pay for the meals out of the road fund, and at first the band is horrified by the size of the tips I leave. We've run the waitress ragged for an hour—"Oh, miss, I asked for my coffee black."

"Can I change my soup for a salad?" (This as she sets the soup on the table.)

"Could you get the chef to cook this steak for another thirty seconds on both sides?"

"Can I get ice cream on that pie?"—and they begrudge her a ten-dollar tip. Ten bucks looks like a lot of money lying there on the table. "Hey," I tell them, "the bill was sixty dollars—ten bucks is fifteen percent rounded up to the nearest dollar." Over time, I raise it toward 20 percent. Let's leave a trail of goodwill behind the hippie musicians, instead of frowns and a muttered "Good riddance." Oh, but we're poor, man. We can't afford it. Bullshit. They think this is 1966 and Chet is still managing them. Persuading them that they aren't as poor as they think they are takes some time.

On one of our early trips to the central valley, I see a touchy side of Janis. East of the Berkeley Hills, we're a band of long-haired hippies invading the Land of the Squares. Outside her hometown environment, Janis can be defensive. Something the waitress says, or something in her attitude, sets Janis off. "You know, you could be more polite to us. Our money's just as good as these other people's," is the gist of her short lecture. Janis's tone manages to combine righteous indignation with the feelings of a child who has been unjustly scolded.

On another occasion, the family in the next booth gawks at us and Janis is quick to get her dander up. "What are you looking at?"

At first, I think Janis is too quick to take offense, but I come to see that in these situations Janis's reaction isn't only personal—she's taking offense for all of us. She is just as quick to jump in if someone else is mistreated. If we're eating at a wayside restaurant in the Valley that doesn't get as many long-distance travelers as the Nut Tree and a couple of young hippies come in, the girl barefoot, both of them bedraggled and out of place, they may not be greeted in the same way the straight people are welcomed. When Janis perceives the slight, she intercedes in their defense. She sides with the underdog. She stands up for what is right. It's not right to treat people badly because they're different. This perception becomes a useful key to my understanding of what makes Janis tick.

> "She was very compassionate. And if she saw someone, an un-
> derdog, being treated badly—and she was totally capable of
> treating an underdog badly herself—but she would always really
> react to that. That would get her back up. Particularly if it were
> a woman. She would come to the defense of that person, very
> strongly. That was an enduring quality in her. She not only had
> that, but she consciously wanted to have it too, to project that
> to people."
>
> **Sam Andrew**

Now THAT THE members of the band are living in individual pads in the city, the only time they're all together and not playing music is when we're driving to a gig in the Valley, heading to SFO to catch a flight, or hanging out backstage at a gig while the opening act is on. They take these opportunities to discuss band business that comes up, anything from the set list to whether to play a benefit for some cause or other, or whether the guys' old ladies can come on road trips. Janis would prefer not, but sometimes, if we're going to be in one place for several days or a week, the old ladies travel with us or fly in separately. Peter is married to Cindy. Dave Getz has an old lady, Nancy Parker. James has an old lady also named Nancy, whom I hear about but rarely see.

Big Brother is a democratic band. Everyone is equal. Everyone has a say, and they say it at length. Janis and Peter and Dave are the most forceful in stating their positions when there's a disagreement within the group. Sam and James are a little more laid-back, but that doesn't mean they don't have opinions. The band's decisions are made by voting. Good thing there are five people. If it were an even number, they'd be deadlocked all the time. Sam and Dave are the most flexible, the most willing to try something new. Peter and James usually resist change. Janis is the swing vote. She's very articulate, and amenable to reason until she makes up her mind. Then her opinion is carved in stone. Until she changes it.

Janis and Peter like to press for a vote early in any discussion. "C'mon, let's vote!" As one who observes the passionate disputes from a dispassionate remove, I see that most of the arguments are about small stuff. On the whole, the band shares a similar outlook on the world and its problems. They're proud to be among the founders of the San Francisco rock scene. They're proud to represent San Francisco and the counterculture at large when we play the straight towns of the San Joaquin Valley and farther afield. They delight in the scene that repeats itself almost daily when we're on the freeways, as we're passed by a big American station wagon with an American flag decal pasted to the window, driven by a crew-cut businessman or ex-military father, and the kids in the rear-facing backseat flash us the peace sign.

After a couple of band arguments leave someone feeling sour for the rest of the day, I begin to stick my two cents into the conversations, initiating what will be an ongoing effort to persuade the band that in a group of five people it's possible to govern by consensus. Voting creates winners and losers. Talking over a problem until everyone's willing to go along with what the majority wants takes a little longer, but it's worth it. It's like singing in harmony, even if it's not your favorite song.

As I begin to get a sense of the band members as distinct individuals, it seems to me all the more remarkable that they have come together in this band they believe in so passionately.

Janis, of course, is one of a kind. Born in Port Arthur, Texas, on the Gulf coast, dropped out of college in Austin, played music, traveled around the country, but never really felt she belonged until June last year, when she came to San Francisco to join Big Brother. There's a vortex of energy churning inside her. It manifests itself in her laughter, in her sometimes rapid shifts of mood, in the way she breaks into a conversation with a rap that nails the issues and states her position in a flurry of fast sentences. Some of the time she's like a chain reaction on the verge of going critical. She is quick, smart, and often funny. She's given to delivering lines with a W. C. Fields accent. So am I—we become dueling W. C. Fieldses.

Janis reads a lot. Her intellect isn't disciplined or academically trained like Sam's; it's wilder, and it fires at will. The breadth and sometimes the depth of her interests is startling. She's got an opinion about everything and states it forcefully, astutely, originally. When she really gets going she can weave her sentences into a stunning cascade of words that overwhelms anyone who disagrees with her, often winding up with a capper, a knockout blow that's so neat it delights her as much as her listeners, and she'll burst into a cackle of laughter at her own achievement. When the discussion settles on a subject that just flat doesn't interest her, she drops out and acts bored until the talk moves on to something else.

Janis and Sam like plays on words, and the others sometimes join the verbal game. Favorites within the band include "Sam and Janis evening" to the tune of "Some Enchanted Evening," and a variation on the band's name: "Big Bother and the Folding Company."

David Getz is an artist, taking time out to be a rock drummer. He showed exceptional talent for art early on. From Cooper Union in New York he was going to Yale, but a friend diverted him to San Francisco, where he attended and taught at the San Francisco Art Institute. He's got a BFA and an MFA. He spent a year in Poland on a Fulbright fellowship. It's an unusual pedigree for a rock-and-roller, but no more unusual than Sam's. Dave forms rock-solid positions on the issues in the band, which he rarely changes, but he is slow to anger. Janis and Peter are far more volatile. When Dave's ire is aroused, he can match them in intensity.

Dave was not Big Brother's first drummer. When he first heard Big Brother, he thought the band was fantastic—except for the drummer. He had met Peter Albin, and every time he saw Peter, he'd say, "I can drum better than that guy with one hand tied behind my back. Why don't you fire that guy and hire me?" Dave's persistence got him a chance on a night when the band was short a drummer, and that gig got him the job.

Peter Albin is more typical of what I expect in a California rocker. He's the group's only folkie. He played folk music in college, then switched to amplified sounds. He's been in half a dozen bands. Maybe this rather bland bio is what allows him to masquerade as the straight member of the group.

> Bob Seidemann, a photographer who knew the members of Big Brother from the early days of the burgeoning arts scene in San Francisco, has a vivid memory of James at this time: "One day Nancy [later James's wife] and I took LSD together and we were going back to my apartment to make love, and as we were walking up Grant Avenue and passed the Coffee Gallery, she looked in and said, 'Just a minute, I'll be right out,' and walked in and came out and said, 'There's something I've gotta take care of. This guy here, rah, rah, rah, James,' and 'I'll see ya later.' Left me on the street. And the guy she walked away from me for was James Gurley. That was my first encounter with James, and he had his head shaved and was calling himself the Arch Fiend of the Universe."
>
> **Bob Seidemann**

Somehow I never learn much about James's origins, or the information evaporates from memory because it doesn't fit the here-and-now that he projects. He's from Detroit, for what it's worth, but James belongs in this time and place. It's impossible to imagine him in khakis and a button-down shirt and a short haircut, looking like the other kids in a 1950s Detroit high school. It's much easier to believe that he appeared fully grown in San Francisco in 1965, hair to his shoulders, with beads and jeans and boots, hung about with American Indian totems, sprung from the earth in Golden Gate Park, or risen, on the half shell, like Botticelli's Venus, from the surf at Ocean Beach, and walking—on the water—to shore. A fanciful picture that becomes only a little skewed when I learn that in the folk days, when he played regularly at Leo Rigler's Coffee Gallery in North Beach, James's head was shaved bald.

James and I share a familiarity with Spanish. I take to calling him Jaime and he calls me Juan. Perfecto Garcia is a prominent brand of premium cigars. James has turned the name into an expression of approval. "Ah," he says, "Perfecto, Garcia," as if he's addressing Jerry, of the Dead.

I COME HOME from the road trips with thousands of dollars in small bills in my briefcase. On Monday morning I separate the bills by denomination and "face" them, sorting them with the portrait right side up. This saves time at the bank, where I turn the cash into a cashier's check that I send to Albert's office along with my gig report. Often I keep back a thousand dollars or so for the road fund, out of which each member of the band draws pocket money of $125 a week and from which I pay our expenses on the road. I've got credit cards from Albert's office for Hertz and Avis, but I pay for our meals and most of our lodging in cash, and I have to account for it all down to the last red cent. Nobody told me part of being a road manager was being a banker and an accountant.

On my days off I look for an apartment and I spend some of my money. My salary is $150 a week. It's more than enough for a single guy to live comfortably, not enough to buy a Porsche.

Since Dick died, Mimi Fariña has moved to San Francisco. She lives on Telegraph Hill. We go out for dinner often when I'm in town. Mimi is an incomparable dinner companion. We dine mostly in North Beach, home ground of the Beats and the folkies. We eat on lower Broadway at Enrico's sidewalk café, where live jazz harks back a short historical hop to the heyday of the Beats, when the café opened, or at Vanessi's restaurant, where the waiters whip up sweet foamy zabaglione in copper bowls right at the table. Mimi goes into gales of laughter at my expression of bliss when I taste the zabaglione. (Time spent laughing with Mimi is added to the span of one's life.) Sometimes we hop a cable car downtown for a fancy meal at a French restaurant.

For the first time in my life I'm feeling flush. On the road, all my expenses are covered—travel, lodging, food. The balance in my checking account rises steadily, offset by the occasional splurge. I feel like the sailor played by the character actor Edgar Buchanan in a World War II movie I saw on late-night TV. Back in Hawaii after a long stretch of sea duty, Buchanan tells the girl he's dancing with that he's got three months of back pay coming. "How are you going to spend all that money, sailor?" she asks suggestively. "Oh," he says, "some on whiskey, some on women, and the rest frivolously."

Recently, Mimi has decided to share the gift of laughter with a wider audience. She has joined the Committee, San Francisco's resident satirical-improvisational comedy revue. The troupe was founded by Alan Myerson and Irene Riordan (later Jessica Myerson), two former members of Second City in Chicago. The company holds forth nightly from the Committee Theater on Broadway, San Francisco's benign imitation of a sin strip, which divides North Beach from Chinatown. Unlike its New York namesake, this Broadway sports no movie palaces. It has restaurants, bars and pool halls, a few topless shows, and, since 1963, the Committee, just to keep everything in perspective.

Many of Mimi's new colleagues lived through the Beat era in America's artsy-intellectual ghettos, and most are connected in one way or another to the San Francisco music scene. One of the actors, Howard Hesseman, emigrated from Oregon to San Francisco for the jazz and lucked into a job taking money at the door for the Coffee Gallery on Grant Avenue in North Beach. It was a jazz and poetry joint at the time, but within a year of Howard's arrival it had become a folk music club. A year after that, in walks a twenty-year-old girl from Texas named Janis Joplin, but she won't sleep with the owner,

Leo Rigler, who exercises his own version of a Hollywood casting couch to audition female singers, so he won't hire her. Besides, she's underage. Unlike the East Coast folk music coffeehouses, the Coffee Gallery serves alcohol, and the legal age is twenty-one. Howard, by now the bartender and night manager, lets Janis play when Leo's in his apartment across the street.

> "I would let her sing at the Coffee Gallery if whoever's set it was would let her sit in, and most of these people were not silly enough to say, 'No, thanks, I'd rather go it on my own.' To play, to sing harmony, to share a stage with somebody who had so much going on was obviously a sort of a gift."
>
> **Howard Hesseman**

That trip was Janis's first real foray beyond her native Texas, and Jack Kerouac was her guide. It was a pilgrimage to the Lourdes of the Beat scene, the city where the brightest lights of the Beat Generation started a renaissance, where Dean Moriarty, the alter ego of Kerouac's pal Neal Cassady, ended up after his travels in *On the Road*. Frisco, Ferlinghetti, City Lights bookstore, the Six Gallery—where Allen Ginsberg premiered "Howl"—this was Janis's destination, but it was the budding folk music scene, less celebrated at the time, where she made connections that would bring her back.

On that first visit, she played and sang on *The Midnight Special*, a broadcast hootenanny put on weekly by radio station KPFA-FM. One of the other performers on that show was a kid named Peter Albin. Peter remembers Janis singing in a Bessie Smith kind of style, and he remembers, vividly, that she was one of the first girls he had seen who didn't wear a bra.

Janis was long gone when Bob Neuwirth and I visited the Coffee Gallery in November 1964, after driving a friend's AC Cobra across the country from Cambridge at a high rate of speed, and it was Howard Hesseman we sat and chatted and drank with. Neuwirth stayed the winter in California and he became a regular on the Coffee Gallery's stage. He sometimes managed to play simultaneous gigs on the same night at the Coffee Gallery and across the Bay at the Cabale, Berkeley's answer to the Club 47, cruising across the Bay Bridge in the Cobra between sets.

After her first exploration of San Francisco, Janis crossed the country to New York, went home to Port Arthur, Texas, briefly, and came back to San Francisco, where she settled for a time and got badly enough strung out on speed that it gave her a real scare and sent her back home to Port Arthur to make a stab at being the good daughter her parents hoped she would be. It was this effort that Chet Helms interrupted by summoning Janis back to California to sing with Big Brother.

As Mimi's friend and Janis's road manager, I am doubly welcome at the Committee Theater. Soon I become a regular, passed through the door with a wave and a smile. (Shades of the Club 47.) Reconnecting with Howard among Mimi's friends at the Committee and learning how the strands of coincidence weave together Cambridge and California, folk and jazz and Janis and Bobby and Mimi, is a minor marvel, akin to the many small-world connections I've experienced in the East Coast folk scene. It helps me see that San Francisco's creative fraternities are parts of an extended family, an amalgam of hippies and beatniks, musicians and actors and artists who share a fellowship like the one I experienced in Cambridge. Here, it's more broadly based, limited only by the line dividing the hip from the square, the freaks from the straights. Within the kinship of the arts, the connections are close and personal, maintained by intercourse both social and sexual.

When Janis learns that I know Mimi and Howard and I'm hanging out at the Committee on our nights off, she takes a new interest in me. Not that she's been indifferent. After her dismissive comment about Libras at our first meeting, I didn't expect a lot of attention from Janis, but of course I was wrong. She's curious about everything new, especially guys, within her orbit. She flirts with me. Coming on to a new man is her way of checking him out. When I see that the flirting is real, I try to deflect her advances without offending her. She knows full well how much power she can exert over a man. I know just as surely that I'll never maintain the authority I need to have as Janis's road manager if I let myself become the latest notch in her spangled belt.

She doesn't push it. Maybe she knows we have to get along as friends if this thing is going to work. Maybe I passed the test.

We're still engaged in this dance when we head to L.A. for two nights at the Whisky a Go Go. From Baghdad by the Bay to Sodom in the Southland.

> "I just remember that when I actually heard her, man, it was stunning. Stunning. Because again, there was all this kind of not-so-much world beat as world bend that Gurley and Sam and Peter and—those cats all, I mean it was such a weird fucking blend of stuff. And a lot of it was familiar to me. . . . It just wasn't R and B and it wasn't electric folk. It was something else going on. And then there was this just flat-out, balls-of-the-universe chick. Just singing her ass off."
>
> **Howard Hesseman**

CHAPTER EIGHT

Hooray for Hollywood

FROM THE SAN Francisco viewpoint, Los Angeles is another planet. An entertaining place to visit, but we wouldn't want to live here.

L.A. is gaudy and commercial. It's tacky. It lacks a neighborhood like the Haight to give cohesiveness to the music scene. The Haight, like Greenwich Village in New York, became a haven for artists and musicians because the rents are cheap. In L.A. the cheap-rent zones are scattered hither and yon—Venice, parts of Santa Monica, certain reaches of West Hollywood and the San Fernando Valley. And, for those with good luck or a little more loot, the canyons in the Hollywood Hills. Laurel Canyon is a favorite, but the roads are all up and down and twisty-turny. There are no sidewalks and no street life. Strictly residential. The street life is on the Sunset Strip, the section of Sunset Boulevard that begins on the western edge of old Hollywood and ends at the eastern border of Beverly Hills.

In the late fifties the Strip got a boost from the TV series *77 Sunset Strip*, when private eyes were pushing Westerns off the tube. More recently it has become the gathering place for the L.A. counterculture. Since the folk-rock scene started hopping in '65, the focus has shifted away from the Ash Grove and the other hangouts of the folk days to the rock clubs on the Strip, where the Whisky a Go Go is the centerpiece, and to the Troubadour, a music club down on Santa Monica Boulevard that bridges the gap between folk and rock.

As we cruise the sun-bathed streets in our air-conditioned band wagon, I urge the guys to be a little less obvious about passing joints around. In satisfying Big Brother's curiosity about me, I have let them know that I was at the center of the dope-smoking folkies in Cambridge. I'm the guy who always had a stash, often Lebanese hash I smuggled home from Paris. Janis and the boys were duly impressed when I told them I took acid for the first time when Tim Leary and Richard Alpert were still employed by Harvard University. (Alpert is now Baba Ram Dass, a countercultural guru, and Leary is, well, he's Tim Leary, famous for advising our generation to "Tune in, turn on, drop out," which has not endeared him to parents or higher authorities. Leary and Alpert were let go by Harvard in 1963 for getting too far out.)

With Big Brother, it's my job to be the straight guy, the one who keeps them out of trouble. I suggest that getting busted for pot is just plain dumb, beside the fact that it would create an unnecessary hassle for all of us—cops, jails, judges, courts, dollars.

Backstage at the Whisky a Go Go, the walls are coated with cannabis resin and no one blinks at the pungent scent of pot in the dressing rooms.

For a rock band emerging on the national scene, playing the Whisky is a rite of passage. It's the proving ground for up-and-coming acts. Big Brother's appearance here is a test run for bigger gigs to come, and a chance to get some notice from the L.A. rock press.

The Whisky has go-go dancers in fringed dresses and white boots in hanging cages. (Try to imagine go-go dancers in the Fillmore or the Avalon.) When I comment on the weirdness of the Southern

California scene, Sam Andrew says he thinks of me as an L.A. kind of guy. The abuse I have to take on this job.

On opening night the house is packed. Musicians from other bands are on hand. So are some representatives of the movie business. They've seen Big Brother in *Petulia* and they're here to check out the further cinematic potential.

On the band's first song, Sam Andrew hits the opening chord and breaks his sixth string, the low E. The loss of tension on the fattest string throws the guitar out of tune. Unwilling to cause the anticlimax of a false start, Sam keeps playing, while trying, with limited luck, to retune the remaining strings. Sam sees this as an attack of Big Brother's curse, a persistent jinx that strikes every time it's important for the band to play well. They beat it at Monterey, twice in a row, and Sam hoped the jinx was gone for good.

The other band members are aware of the discord, but they recover, and the audience is focused on Janis's astonishing vocal power. Janis holds the song together with her total dedication to her singing. On the whole, the set goes well enough, but Janis drinks more than usual in reaction to the disruption.

Drinking onstage is part of an image that Janis likes to cultivate. Often she swigs directly from a bottle of Southern Comfort, her signature booze. From the start, I've worked to moderate this image. In the San Fernando Valley, where our audiences are mostly made up of teenagers and college students, Janis has been willing, most of the time, to drink onstage from a coffee cup instead of her bottle. When we're playing at a college, California law reinforces my pitch: Alcohol can't be sold within a mile of college campuses; inciting the students to drink could get Big Brother banned from college gigs. In San Francisco or L.A., or anywhere Janis feels that the audience is made up of her people, the hip rather than the square, her impulse is to flaunt the bottle. It's an ongoing contest between us, one in which I will have some effect but will never finally win. In part, her onstage behavior is a public image Janis wants to cultivate, but she also maintains that drinking is essential preparation for performing at her best.*

Our Los Angeles lodgings are at the Hollywood Sunset Motel, a seedy hostelry farther east on Sunset, on the long straightaway that crosses Vine Street in the heart of Hollywood. Big Brother found this dump when they were starving musicians. Sticking to it now, doubling up in the small rooms, is a measure of their cautionary view of the music business.

One thing I have established at the outset is that I get a room of my own. The boys can double up if they want to, but I get to have a place where I won't be kept up by a roommate watching TV or coming in late or playing music or talking on the phone. I'm the road manager. I get a room of my own, a phone of my own, peace and quiet of my own. Janis and the boys have accepted this declaration of independence with only token resistance.

This early in the job, I hold off on suggesting an upgrade in accommodation, although I think of L.A. as a place to indulge oneself in lavish style.

In the summer after my first year of college, before I discovered the byways of folk music, I was visiting my uncle's family in Berkeley. I flew down to Los Angeles because my father was there (he and my mother long divorced, he long remarried), and I stayed for two dollars at the Beverly Hills Hotel. Not that you could get a room, any room, at the Beverly Hills for anything close to two dollars. Two bucks wouldn't buy you an hour in an linen closet. We're talking here about

*In an interview early the following year, Janis explained to a reporter her reasons for drinking: "The reason I drink is that it loosens me up while the guys are tuning their instruments. I close my eyes and feel things. If I were a musician, it might be a lot harder to get all that feeling out, but I'm really fortunate because my gig is just feeling things. . . ." (Nat Hentoff, *New York Times*, April 21, 1968, section II, 19.)

the rambling, palm-shaded, pink stucco palace on the western, residential part of Sunset Boulevard that Hollywood movies use as an establishing shot to evoke the glamorous life in La-La Land. The same hotel where Grace Kelly was said to enjoy the company of the cabana boys, before she became a princess.

One of my father's few extravagances is staying in first-class hotels. At the time of our L.A. rendezvous, he had hosted *Omnibus* for several years, and it was still on the air. He was entitled. In L.A., he stayed at the Beverly Hills. When I came to see him, he ordered up a rollaway bed and I slept in his room for an extra two dollars. It's a story he loves to tell: "My son stayed at the Beverly Hills Hotel for two dollars."

The Hollywood Sunset Motel is a place you don't brag about, no matter how little you pay. Which makes the contrast all the more striking when we go out to Bel Air to visit John and Michelle Phillips and see the final cut of Pennebaker's movie, *Monterey Pop*.

The mid-December weather is sunny and warm, all the better for us to admire the umpty-room shack that formerly belonged to Jeanette MacDonald and Nelson Eddy. The luxuriant, rambling gardens and grounds, measured in acres, evoke an earlier era when movie stars were expected to live in a style emulating that of European royalty. The grounds are extensive enough to contain an acid trip, if you don't mind being screamed at by the free-roaming peacocks.

For our weekend in L.A., Dave Richards has brought along a candidate for a position as assistant equipment man. With an East Coast tour coming up in the new year, Dave figures a second guy is justified, and the band approves the idea. Mark Braunstein is barely twenty, with an impressive head of dark hair that stands out in all directions. He met Janis in the Haight, on the street, not long after she joined Big Brother, and they became friends. Mark graduated from working in an all-night doughnut shop to managing equipment for the outfit that put on free concerts in the Panhandle. When Dave Richards suggested it might be a good idea to have two guys handling

Big Brother's equipment when we went east, Janis thought of Mark. This weekend, he is just along for the ride, to check out the scene.

> "Before I was working with the band, I remember going to see Kurosawa films with Janis, at her suggestion. . . . She was always less hedonistic and out of control than other people might see her."
>
> **Mark Braunstein**

Judging by Mark's goggle-eyed reaction to the Phillips mansion, he is in the process of deciding that this is the life for him. (When the weekend is over, he will sign on board our rock-and-roll caravan.)

John and Michelle's success is recent enough that they still have the air of kids in a candy store to find themselves living in Jeanette MacDonald's pad. Not expecting a stern parent to come fetch them home, but still a little wide-eyed at what they've managed to achieve, and working hard to appear blasé about it. The enormous Christmas tree in one of the downstairs rooms is merely in proportion to its surroundings, not ostentatious at all.

John is a gregarious host, while Michelle nods in our direction and after that mostly keeps to herself. To see *Monterey Pop*, we adjourn to a recording studio in the attic—a large attic—that doubles as a screening room, where we raise the cannabis content of the air to a self-sustaining level. Big Brother's lawyer, Bob Gordon, is with us for the screening. He isn't aghast at the goings-on, and I begin to understand that his short hair and proper dress are in the nature of a disguise.

Lights go down in the room, and the screen lights up.

I've seen much of the footage, but not the edited film. For Big Brother, it's all new. Janis's eyes are wide as the scenes unreel—the Mamas & the Papas, Canned Heat, Hugh Masakela. Jefferson Airplane gets two songs in the movie. Janis is waiting to see herself on-screen. Audio from an abbreviated version of Big Brother's

"Combination of the Two" ran under the opening titles, but there was no glimpse of the band.

Fifteen minutes into the film I can barely contain my reaction, but I remain outwardly calm. Inside, I'm exultant. Pennebaker has done it. He has captured the feeling of the Pop Festival, intercutting shots of happy hippies arriving, camping, dancing, and grooving to the music, with song after song from the best performances on the big stage. Papa John is proud as punch because the movie makes the festival look like a brilliant accomplishment, a once-in-a-lifetime event, which it was. But his self-satisfaction can't hold a candle to Big Brother's, once they see "Ball and Chain."

The song begins twenty-five minutes into the film, on the heels of Grace Slick and Marty Balin's lovely duet, "Today." The last chord has barely died away when four ascending notes from James Gurley's guitar kick off the intro to "Ball and Chain." We see Dave Getz first, then Peter Albin. Peter is looking up, mouthing the beats, nodding his head in time with the music. Sam and James are on-screen as James's guitar intro winds toward its peak—and now Janis's face fills the screen in left profile as she sings the first words.

In the studio–cum–screening room, Janis breathes, "Far out."

She cackles when she sees Mama Cass's "Wow! That's really heavy!" reaction at the end of the song. "How'd he get that, man?" Janis wants to know.

How indeed? Pennebaker was onstage, filming Janis, during the Sunday evening performance, and it was also Penny who got the shot of Mama Cass—on Saturday. During Big Brother's first appearance, when he was forbidden to film the band, Penny stood in front of the stage and sneaked a few shots of the audience. In the editing room he spliced Cass's Saturday afternoon response at the end of Sunday evening's "Ball and Chain," and with that simple coda he has managed to include in the film the festival audience's first mind-blown reaction to hearing Janis sing.

After the movie, Janis repairs to the pool table with a bottle, Papa

John, and a couple of the boys. With a pool table and a few companions, Janis can be happy for hours. In San Francisco she used to hang out with a bunch of tough women, all Capricorns, like her. They frequented the pool halls, and Janis won a reputation for wielding a mean stick.

> "She could play the roles that men were playing really well. She knew how important a good pool stick was, in the blues."
>
> **Nick Gravenites**

While the rest of us gravitate to the end of the house that contains the kitchen and pool table, Peter Albin hangs out in the big living room and ends up being the only one to have a conversation with Michelle.

I venture outside to survey the grounds. There's an elegant swimming pool with a flagstone terrace and four guesthouses. Four. Count 'em.

The movie, the mansion, the sunny day—we're in dreamland. For Janis and Big Brother it's a glimpse of what success in the music business can bring. When we return to the funky part of Hollywood, that kind of success is a world away. Janis and the boys are playing music clubs and dance halls and college gyms for $2,500 to $3,500 a night. More when the percentage kicks in, but this kind of bread isn't about to buy any mansions in Bel Air. Still, Albert Grossman is booking the gigs, they've got a road manager, and *Monterey Pop* has reminded them that they're on a roll.

So they're unprepared for the shock that Albert delivers during a weeklong club date at the Golden Bear in Huntington Beach, thirty-five miles south of L.A. The Bear is a folk outpost on the southern coast that has turned to amplified music as the folk boom fades. The night Albert comes to hear the band, James is so stoned that he's almost falling off the stage, and it's obvious to Albert that he's stoned on something stronger than grass and booze.

When Albert agreed to manage Big Brother, he made it clear that he wanted nothing to do with anyone who was involved with hard drugs. "No *shmeez*," he said, using a slang term that none of the guys in Big Brother had heard before. "No what?" they asked. No smack, no skag, no horse. No heroin. The Electric Flag had become a vexation to Albert in that regard. He wanted to acquire no more bands that were road wrecks waiting to happen. There are no junkies in this band, right? Oh, right! Big Brother assured him.

This response was not fully honest. Janis and the boys like to call Big Brother the only "alcodelic" or "psycheholic" band in rock. On the road, alcohol is the drug of choice. They all smoke dope, except for Janis, who says it makes her think too much. They don't perform on acid. Conventional wisdom has it that the Grateful Dead play on acid, which may or may not be true. The Dead are known for dosing others, which is true. Big Brother is more conservative, and more private, about their drug use. Janis got heavily into speed when she lived briefly in San Francisco in the midsixties, on her second visit to the Bay. By the time the band signed with Albert, Janis had acquired more than a passing acquaintance with heroin. With her boyfriend at the time, she was shooting speedballs, a combination of smack and speed.

Sam is a former speed freak as well. He is acquainted with smack but trifles with it rarely. For Sam, the lure of exploring heroin is to follow in the footsteps of musicians he reveres—Charlie Parker and other jazz greats. Because of that association, for Sam it has almost the mystique of Holy Communion about it. Later on, this fascination will get Sam in trouble, but for now he holds it at bay.

Dave Getz and Peter Albin are the only ones who told Albert the truth, the only members of the band who don't have at least a nodding acquaintance with heroin. James was the first in the band to try it, and the most serious about it, well before Albert came along. He's into pills too.

At the Golden Bear, Albert contrives to speak with the other members of the band while James is elsewhere occupied. He suggests to them that James be replaced. Maybe not permanently, but at least for now. The real reason behind Albert's request is that he believes the band will improve musically if James is replaced by another guitar player. Albert hopes that if James takes an enforced leave, Janis and Sam and Peter and Dave will come to realize that the band is better without James, but he keeps these hopes to himself for now. If James cleans himself up he can come back later on, Albert says. Let's give him $10,000 and send him away to think about it.

Albert may not know of James's importance among the creators of the San Francisco Sound. He may not recognize how unusual the dissonance of twin guitars that James and Sam have developed is in the constellation of San Francisco bands and in the wider world of rock. But even if Albert knows these things, it doesn't matter. How a musician is regarded by his community or his contemporaries, however unusual his style, how important his innovations—these things don't affect Albert's opinions. His opinions are his own, and his concern is here and now. He doesn't like James's music and he believes that James's drug use is a danger to the band.

Janis and the boys refuse to consider replacing James, even temporarily. James has been in this band from the beginning, they tell Albert. We're a family. We're going to make it or break it together.*

Albert accepts their refusal stoically. It is his first attempt to influence the band's musical development, but not the last.

It rattles the band's confidence when an L.A. rock critic who hears Big Brother at the Golden Bear puts his opinion of the band in the

---

*Which is not to say that the band members were unaware of James's problems. Dave Getz says flatly that James couldn't drink. "He had one of these alcoholic things, like almost a genetic kind of alcoholism, where he would start to drink and he'd go through a massive personality change, and become almost like catatonic. And then he was drinking and he was doing reds too." (Author interview with David Getz, July 24, 1997.)

headline of his review: "Janis Joplin Too Full of Soul for Holding Company Partners."

WHEN WE'RE DONE at the Golden Bear, Janis flies home to Port Arthur for a Christmas visit with her family. In my stucco motel in San Francisco, I'm a long way from my own family, but I join a Christmas dinner in Berkeley. In the sunny week between Christmas and New Year's the temperature in San Francisco reaches seventy each day, which seems like an unseasonal miracle.

On the weekend, Janis is back in San Francisco and we go into Winterland to wind up 1967 with three nights playing for Bill Graham.

For the first two nights, Chuck Berry is the headliner. Big Brother gets second billing, over Quicksilver Messenger Service. On New Year's Eve, Jefferson Airplane tops the bill, followed by Big Brother, Quicksilver, and Freedom Highway. There will be nonstop music from 9:00 P.M. until 9:00 A.M. the next morning, when Graham and his staff will serve breakfast to the survivors. A ticket to this all-night extravaganza costs six dollars.

Peter Albin arrives backstage on New Year's Eve dressed in a silver lamé jumpsuit. His hair is teased and sprayed into a fright wig that's strung with tiny white Christmas tree lights that wink on and off, powered by a battery pack on his belt. The band has an informal rule that they can't wear anything onstage that they won't wear on the street. To accommodate this custom, Peter walks around the block in his costume before coming into Winterland.

This is nothing, Sam tells me. You should have seen him on Halloween. Peter dressed as a penis. The show was called "Trip or Freak." Peter wrapped himself in a sheath of pink cloth, which he draped over a pith helmet he wore on his head. He tied string around the sheath at his neckline to create the (circumcised) head. He attached two pink balloons, painted with black hair, to his feet. *Et voilà*, a walking erection. He cut eye holes to see through and holes in the sides of the shaft for his arms, and he played in this costume onstage. He's the straight one, mind you, the band's businessman, the one who signs the contracts.

For the Halloween show, Janis dressed as Salome.

This is my first gig for Bill Graham, who has become the dominant force in the local rock scene. The Fillmore and Winterland—bigger than the Fillmore, two blocks away—are his, and his success threatens the survival of the Avalon, where Big Brother was once the de facto house band. Some in the local music community resent Graham's hardheaded style, but he has brought a new professionalism to concert promotion around the Bay and he forces others to meet the standards he sets. Some don't, and some fail.

Graham hires and trains his own security guards. They dress in T-shirts instead of uniform jackets, and they treat the audience like "us" instead of "them." Bill's goal is to create a welcoming environment for the musicians and the audience alike. At the top of the stairs, where the audience enters the hall, there's a box of free apples.

Tonight the dressing rooms are provided with a lavish spread of food and drink for the bands, which creates an almost Rabelaisian atmosphere backstage. Why bother to go onstage and play? The party is here.

I meet Bill early in the evening, before the hall is full, before the music starts. He's a high-intensity New York type that's familiar to me. He has done a lot of business with Albert, and he is evidently pleased that Albert is managing Big Brother. The last thing I want to do is screw up Bill's good relations with Albert, so we both have incentives to get along. Bill can be a charmer when he wants to, and I find myself liking him.

Before midnight, while Big Brother is onstage, Bill takes me to his office and gives me a check. Big Brother gets a flat fee when they play for Bill, so my job is a snap. No percentage to work out, no worries about how many hippies may get into Winterland free. The professionalism of the operation puts me at ease. From what I've heard about Bill and what I learn from my early experiences with him, I figure if he's going to rip off Big Brother, he's going to do it by negotiating a tough deal with Albert, and I trust Albert to handle him.

At the stroke of the new year, I'm pouring Graham's on-the-house champagne in the backstage dressing room for Janis. A few days later, I'm almost fired.

New York, New York

IN THE FIRST week of January I find a second-floor walk-up in North Beach. My pad-to-be is on Powell Street, on the west side of the block that houses Saints Peter and Paul Catholic Church, which presides grandly over Washington Square Park. The rent is $155 a month. It's less than a ten-minute walk to the Committee Theater on Broadway, and handy to the Embarcadero Freeway for quick trips to Berkeley. I tell Signora Andoni, the rental agent, that I'll move in at the end of the week.

How come you didn't look in the Haight? Janis and the boys want to know, but they admit the Haight is changing. It's overrun by runaways and would-be hippies and tour busses full of straight people who stop to gawk in front of the Grateful Dead's house.

I have other reasons to prefer North Beach. I like the Italian grocery stores, full of olive oil and handmade pasta. On Columbus Avenue, a broad thoroughfare that separates Telegraph Hill from Russian Hill, I hear Chinese and Italian spoken within the same block. I like the lingering vibe of the Beats and the beatniks and the proximity to the Committee. I'm a beatnik, not a hippie, and settling here keeps me at a certain remove from the band. It preserves my independence.

Maybe this is what makes the band decide I'm not the right guy for them.

I'm dead asleep in my motel when Albert phones at midmorning. I had a late night, but he's wide-awake on Eastern Time. He's had a call from the band. "They don't think it's working," he says. "Incompatible lifestyles," is the complaint. This jolts me wide-awake. I have had no clue from anyone in Big Brother that they aren't satisfied.

I tell Albert, "I'll call you back."

I phone every member of the band and reach four out of five, Janis and all the guys except James. "Meeting at the Warehouse," I tell them. "Right now." On the way across town I'm feeling betrayed and pissed off. If they've got a problem, how about talking to me before they call Albert?

The possibility of failure hasn't crossed my mind. I might quit this job in six months if I find my own work to do, but I'm damned if I'll lose it because my hair isn't long enough. If they'll just give me a chance, I'll be the best damn road manager anybody ever saw. I like it here. What's more, I like them. They're interesting. In my wildest dreams, I couldn't have come up with five more divergent personalities to stick in a rock-and-roll band, and yet they are truly a band. They're united in the music and they believe in what they're doing.

It occurs to me, as I park the car, that maybe Janis is behind the effort to get rid of me. What if the problem, at least on her part, is my refusal to yield to her sexual advances? Did she instigate the call to Albert as her way of getting back at me for not going to bed with her?

When we're gathered in the rehearsal loft, seated around the table by the window, I ask them what's the problem, as if I haven't a clue. Well, you don't hang out with us, Peter says. This is a family, and you don't feel like one of the family, Janis says with a petulant edge.

This I can deal with. The band is put out because I didn't rent an apartment in the Haight and outfit myself from the hippie clothing stores and I don't drop by their pads on our days off to hang out and smoke dope. I respond with the short speech I rehearsed in my head on the way across town: If you want some long-haired fan to hang out day and night, to smoke dope with you, to fetch cigarettes and carry your guitars, we can hire a grateful hippie to do that for fifty bucks a week. But I've got a job to do.

"Well, what exactly is your job?" The question comes from Dave Getz, and I realize that they truly don't know. They know I drive the rent-a-car and handle the plane tickets and register them at the motels, because they see all that. But they don't see the rest of it, the dozens of phone calls on our days off, and what I do while they're onstage. So I tell them about booking the travel and talking with the promoters beforehand, and I remind them about the gig in the Valley where the third roll of tickets was sold under the counter. My job is to spot that kind of shit, I tell them. I get you to the gig on time, I handle the logistics, I make sure you get paid. I keep the promoter happy. I make sure you don't get ripped off. I try to make it possible for you to think about nothing but the music. While you're onstage, I'm checking the box office and the ticket takers. I check the sound. I talk to the soundman if it needs adjusting. Then I check the doors again.

I'm fighting to save my new job and my new life, but I know it can't sound like fighting or begging. I like getting stoned and hanging out as much as you do, I tell them. But when I'm stoned I can't do the job. I lose my motivation. I remind them that I was a bluegrass musician for six years and made two record albums before Big Brother was formed. I loved the life of a beatnik bluegrass picker, but I gave it up to work for you, I tell them. With you, my job is to be the straight guy who keeps it all together.

I'm just a little older than them and I make it sound like more. By implication, I'm beyond being an adoring fan and hangout partner. I don't tell them how blown away I am by their music and the whole San Francisco trip, how much I like the band and being on the road.

Janis reveals no hint of having a stake in the outcome beyond the concerns that she and the guys have expressed. It's all about their gig and my gig, and what's best for the band. She gives no sign of a hidden agenda.

They hear me out and they don't argue. Fine, they say. We'll try it a little longer.

> "You were very distant. The impression, mine and the band's, especially when you first came on board, you know: patrician, East Coaster, snobbish, removed, no fun. . . . As time went on, everybody saw that you had a good sense of humor, weren't judgmental, especially, were interested in keeping things together on the road, which was what your job was. We all could let our jobs slide a little bit. There was a lot of sloppiness in the musicians' job, a lot of sloppiness in my job, we could get away with a lot. You really couldn't get away with very much in having to keep track of seven or eight or ten people like that. That describes you to an extent, especially when you were working. You gotta get these eight freaks out of there."
>
> **Mark Braunstein**

I have survived the first crisis. And, as it turns out, the only one that ever threatens my employment. I've done it by trusting my instincts about how to handle it, which encourages me to believe that maybe I really am cut out for this job. Back at the motel, I call Albert and tell him everything is under control. I try to sound cool about it, but my relief is my high for the day, and it's probably audible through the cross-country phone line.

I PUT A foam mattress on the bedroom floor at 1856 Powell Street. I build some bookshelves out of bricks and planks; I buy a few pieces of furniture at secondhand stores. I spend a week's pay on a big Scan-

dinavian rug, all dark greens and blues. I buy a compact KLH FM-
stereo record player that packs up into a suitcase, and my new home
is open for business.

I go down to Monterey and buy back the white Volvo sedan I sold
to an architect there two years before. I shipped the car back from
Europe in '62 and later drove it to California in pursuit of the Wrong
Girl. I worked for the Monterey architect as a carpenter while waiting
in vain for her to realize I was the love of her life. Having the Volvo
back now connects my past to the future. It pleases me to think that
by selling the car to the architect when I bailed out of that futile quest
I was stashing it, keeping it in reserve against my eventual return to
the coast. Now I'm back. I've got wheels. I'm a California resident.
I'm ready for the next summer of love.

With the road-managing crisis behind us, Janis and the boys accept
me more fully, and there appear to be no lingering concerns. Janis, in
particular, takes a new interest in me. This isn't renewed flirting to see
if she can lure me into bed. She has learned that the Wrong Girl I was
pursuing a couple of years ago in Carmel is a girl named Kim whom
Janis knows from Haight Street, where Kim's San Francisco lover,
Peggy Caserta, runs a hip clothing store called Mnasidika. This discovery intrigues Janis, because her perception of me up to this point hasn't
included the possibility that I could ever be with a girl like Kim. This
seems to open the door for more curiosity and a new level of friendship.

In Janis's talk about Peggy and Kim, I get an inkling that there
may have been something between Janis and Peggy. There's a gleam
in her eye when she talks about Kim too. Maybe . . . ? Janis doesn't
say anything explicit, but in our conversations among the band
she has revealed in a matter-of-fact way that she has had affairs with
women. She has also made it plain that her active interest is focused
on men. On the road, I haven't seen her light up over a woman the
way she lights up nightly about the wealth of what she likes to call
male "talent" in the audience.

> "There were women who turned her on, but her main focus was
> definitely men."
>
> **Linda Gravenites**

At the heart of Janis's justification for doing whatever feels good, and polite behavior be damned, is her belief that our parents lied to us about pretty much everything and so we have to decide for ourselves what's right and what's wrong. This isn't something she has picked up in San Francisco. It comes from personal conviction that she reveals when she talks about growing up in Texas. As a teenager in Port Arthur in the fifties, she felt the imposition of a concept of propriety that she found stifling. Girls behave a certain way. Nice girls don't get drunk. Nice girls don't have sex. Sex is dangerous. The social strictures included a Southern attitude about Negroes that Janis decided was wrong even before she experienced life beyond her hometown. From her Kerouacian rambles in the early sixties, and all the more since she was accepted by Big Brother and San Francisco itself, she has looked back on the guidelines that were laid down in her youth and she feels that she was deceived. "They lied to us about dope, they lied to us about black people, they lied to us about sex, man, they lied to us about everything," more or less sums it up. Taking drugs, getting drunk, exploring bisexuality and adopting black music as her own is Janis's natural reaction.

In the winter of 1965–1966, when Big Brother was formed, and later, when Chet Helms brought Janis up from Texas to join the band, I was just 120 miles away, in Carmel. I visited the city with Kim. I even went to the Avalon and the Fillmore once or twice. If I had connected to the burgeoning San Francisco scene back then, everything might have turned out differently. But then I might have missed connecting to Pennebaker and Monterey and I wouldn't be here now, road-managing Big Brother.

Maybe everything really does happen the way it's supposed to.

Our worlds overlap again when I learn that Janis has another connection to my Cambridge companions through the Cabale coffeehouse in Berkeley, which was founded by Debbie Green, a girl I've known since we were both in the Putney School, a progressive coed boarding school in Vermont. Debbie was the most beautiful girl in my class. Maybe in the whole school. She was one of the handful of students who got in early on the folk revival and introduced her fellow students, including me, to the folk repertoire. Her guitar playing and her songs were part of my motivation to get a guitar, while I was still at Putney, and to begin learning those songs.

Like me, Debbie was Boston bound after our Putney graduation. She met Joan Baez on opening day at Boston University. Before long they both dropped out and migrated to the nascent folk music scene in Cambridge. It was Debbie who taught Joan to play the guitar beyond the simple strums she already knew, and it was from Debbie that Joan appropriated much of her early repertoire. By the time of Janis's first trip to the Bay Area, Debbie had moved to California, and with two partners she established the Cabale as Berkeley's equivalent to the Club 47.

Janis heard about the Cabale through the grapevine and called up to ask if she could audition. It was Debbie who received Janis when she came by on the appointed afternoon, driving a Vespa motor scooter. Janis strummed the guitar and sang an earthy blues; it took only that much to impress Debbie, who is not easily impressed. Hearing Janis sing blew her away. "Oh, man!" she said. "We've got to find you a band! Of course you can play here, but first we've got to find you a band." When Janis left the Cabale that afternoon, she fired up her Vespa, pulled out into the street, and was hit by a car. Debbie ran out to help her, only to find Janis laughing hysterically. Somehow the driver of the car doesn't figure in the rest of the story. Janis was limping slightly, still laughing, only a little the worse for wear, but she agreed to let Debbie take her to an emergency room to get checked out. Debbie thought having a man along might make it go easier, so she called her boyfriend at the time, who was none other than Bob

Neuwirth. The three of them spent hours in the ER waiting room, and they got along like old friends. Eventually a doctor examined Janis, told her she had a sprained ankle, wrapped it in an Ace bandage, and sent her on her way.

Debbie tried to follow up on the idea of getting Janis booked into the Cabale with a backup band, but Janis was hard to reach by phone, and her rambles took her away from San Francisco before the Cabale could be added to her list of solo venues.

Learning of Janis's connections to Kim and the Committee and Cambridge and Berkeley makes me wonder that we haven't met long before now.

On January 19, 1968, which is Janis's twenty-fifth birthday, Big Brother is playing in Kaleidoscope, a club in L.A. When we arrive that evening, we find that the club's manager has arranged three dozen roses on the stage. There are two dozen more in the dressing room, which I ordered, from the band, a dozen from friends in San Francisco, and another dozen from Peter Tork, of the Monkees. Janis fairly swoons. Conspiring with the boys in Big Brother, I have arranged to have champagne and cake appear after the show. Janis clasps her hands to her heart and sighs and smiles and laughs, and drinks champagne from the bottle.

During Big Brother's stand at Kaleidoscope, Janis doesn't make a brazen play for any of the good-looking guys in the audience, or even comment on the wealth of available talent. Her usual style of coming on to members of the opposite sex is like a man's in a way that vanishingly few women will risk. In a club or bar her eyes scan the room. If she spots a likely prospect she'll lean closer to me or one of the boys and say, with a conspiratorial leer, "Oh, my God, I think I'm in love." Backstage at a gig, she'll show up in the band's dressing room all atwitter and report on her sightings just as a guy would report to his partners in lechery, but this is a *girl* who talks about the pretty *boys* she's seen, and she's reporting to *us*. In displaying her interest in the opposite sex, as in her style of hanging out among friends in bars and pool halls and pretty much anywhere she's comfortable, Janis is one of the guys. Which makes her behavior at Kaleidoscope all the more out of character.

After the gig, Janis doesn't fly back to San Francisco with the rest of us. When she does come home, she takes to her bed for more than a week with what she says is a case of the flu. We have to cancel three days at the Fillmore, which costs Big Brother $8,000.

The reason for Janis's restraint at Kaleidoscope was that she was pregnant at the time and had made plans to go to Mexico following the gig, for an abortion. Janis told her roommate, Linda Gravenites, that the culprit was the drummer from Blue Cheer, a San Francisco psychedelic blues-rock band. The drummer is one of Janis's pretty boys. She goes for pretty boys or mountain men—hunky guys who emerge from the interior fastnesses of Marin and Sonoma counties in flannel shirts and work boots—and not much in between.

At the time, I take Janis's flu at face value.

While she convalesces, during the break from touring, I follow the evening news and two stories that foreshadow great changes to come, both in domestic politics and in the war in Vietnam. On January 30, New York senator Robert F. Kennedy announces that "under no conceivable circumstances" will he follow Oregon senator Eugene McCarthy in challenging President Johnson for the Democratic nomination. McCarthy announced his candidacy back in November, on the day I arrived in San Francisco to take up the job with Big Brother. His focus is to oppose Johnson's Vietnam policy and to urge the United States to find a way to end the conflict.

The second story will dominate the news for weeks. On the same day as Kennedy's announcement, in Vietnam, the National Liberation Front attacks South Vietnamese units in the country's northernmost province, along the border with North Vietnam, and in the Central Highlands. The next morning, they attack Saigon and more than thirty provincial capitals. In the days that follow, the attacks include American bases and over a hundred cities and towns across South Vietnam. Launched on the lunar new year, which the Vietnamese call Tet, the coordinated attacks become known as the Tet Offensive.

For much of 1967, my political awareness was quiescent. The starry-eyed high of the Summer of Love made it easy to believe, briefly, the promise of a new day to come. New York's Easter Be-In in Central Park, held in response to San Francisco's January gathering, followed by the Monterey Pop Festival and the CRVB's California tour and—best of all—finding myself, at the year's end, road manager for Big Brother and the Holding Company, encouraged in me a willful naïveté. During a year in which our troop strength in Vietnam increased by another ninety thousand, I turned a blind eye and a deaf ear to the war and, like many of my contemporaries, embraced a hope that music, love, and flowers could influence American politics and perhaps the world.

Before long Janis is up and around and we're off for another gig in L.A., at the Cheetah this time, and one in San Diego. On our first few plane trips, I tried to keep the band together as we passed through the San Francisco airport to the departure gate, but herding musicians is like trying to herd cats. Now I just tell them the gate number and what time to be there (with a safety margin added), and they show up, which encourages me to believe that musicians can be trained to behave like grown-ups.

Not a moment too soon. When we return to San Francisco from San Diego we have a few days to say good-bye to friends and get serious about packing for two months away from home. The great adventure is at hand: It's time for Big Brother's East Coast debut.

FEB. 16, 1968: **Palestra, Philadelphia**
FEB. 17: **Anderson Theater, NYC**

FEB. 22–24: **Psychedelic Supermarket, Boston**

FEB. 25: **The Reflectory, Rhode Island School of Design, Providence***

The first thing Janis and the boys notice about New York, even before we're out of the airport, is that people here don't make eye contact. In California, people look you in the eye. Often they'll nod or smile in the street. Total strangers. Pretty girls acknowledge a guy's appreciative glance, even if they're with their boyfriends. Pretty girls in New York may risk giving a bunch of long-haired California rockers a fleeting smile, but the ordinary man and woman go on their way heads down against the February winds. I find the avoidance of eye contact disturbing, and I realize that I'm looking at my hometown like an outsider, which raises my spirits.

While we tour the eastern states, New York will be our home base. From here we will sally forth to show the San Francisco colors to the coastal metropolises and the unsuspecting hinterland. Dave Richards and Mark Braunstein have flown Big Brother's stage equipment east. They will rent a truck to drive it from gig to gig.

The band's lodgings in New York are at the Chelsea Hotel on West 23rd Street, renowned for the artistic pursuits of its short- and long-term residents and for being the place where Dylan Thomas died. Next door, and accessible through a door in the Chelsea's lobby, is a restaurant and bar called El Quijote. The cuisine is Spanish, of a sort, but it is the bar that catches Janis's immediate attention. She is delighted that she can enter El Quijote without having to brave the winter weather, and she has her first drink at the bar before she sets foot in her first room at the Chelsea.

I have decided to stay at my mother's Upper East Side apartment,

---

* The listings from Janis's itineraries throughout the book are a majority of the gigs she played, but are not all-inclusive.

which I justify by pointing out how much money it will save the band, but once again I am removing myself from the off-hours action and any whimsical demands the band might put on me at odd times of the day and night. At 325 East 72nd Street, I can cook my own breakfast. As a practical matter, I can make phone calls without being subject to the notorious delays occasioned by the Chelsea's switchboard. All the same, it is a decision I will later regret. A writer of my generation, especially one born in New York, should have some stories to tell about the Chelsea Hotel. I missed a lot by not staying in the Chelsea.

On our first evening in town, Albert takes us all to Max's Kansas City. We step in the door, and the song on the background music is Country Joe McDonald singing "Janis," which he wrote for guess who. The cosmic DJ is on the job.

Like a Broadway show, Big Brother opens out of town, in Philadelphia. The following night, the band's New York debut is underwhelming. It takes place in the Anderson Theater on Second Avenue, in the East Village. The neighborhood is dicey, the theater is kind of a dump, and the promoter is a sleazeball. If Janis and the boys were expecting gleaming limos coming and going and the eyes of the city focused on them, they're disappointed, but they're blown away to find that they've got top billing above B. B. King, who is second on the bill. The opening act is a band nobody's heard of called the Aluminum Dream.

It's an easy gig for me. Three thousand dollars flat, no percentage to figure, not much different, in terms of Big Brother's income, from most of the shows in California. If it were a percentage gig, I wouldn't trust the promoter, a dodgy type named Tony, as far as I could throw him. I would spend the whole evening checking the tickets, watching the door, watching the box office, trying to figure out how he was ripping us off.

As hard as it is to believe, New York City has no established venue for rock-and-roll shows. There's no local equivalent for the Fillmore or the Avalon, no promoter who regularly books the top acts in pop music.

The Anderson gig is on a Saturday. We have to wait for Monday's papers to read the reviews. The only one that matters is in the *New York Times*, and it's enough to warm the hearts of a bunch of San Francisco hippies shivering in the New York winter.

Robert Shelton is New York's Ralph Gleason, responsible for bringing Joan Baez and Bob Dylan into the music pages of the *Times*. Like Gleason, Shelton has graduated to rock music, and like Gleason he unlimbers the superlatives when he hears Janis. "Janis Joplin Is Climbing Fast in the Heady Rock Firmament," proclaims the headline on Shelton's review. He judges Janis "as remarkable a new pop-music talent as has surfaced in years." He calls her "sparky, spunky," and compares her to Aretha and Erma Franklin. "But comparisons wane," Shelton writes, "for there are few voices of such power, flexibility and virtuosity in pop music anywhere. Occasionally, Miss Joplin appeared to be hitting two harmonizing notes." Shelton waxes poetic as he describes Janis's vocal dynamics: "Her voice shouted with ecstasy or anger one minute, trailed off into coquettish curlicues the next. It glided from soprano highs to chesty alto lows."

Janis is in seventh heaven. Nor are the boys disappointed. All too often, print reviews, including those from Monterey, have focused mostly on Janis and mentioned the rest of the band in passing, if at all. Shelton, however, singles out the boys for special praise. The band, he says, "is inventive enough to be worthy of its star. Outstanding were its vocal style, which uses the smear and the yelp to startling effect, and arrangements that embroidered 'The Cuckoo' with modernistic lace and framed 'Summertime' with a pale metallic fugue."*

---

* When I asked Sam Andrew to elucidate what Shelton meant by "smear" and "yelp," Sam explained that "smear" was a vocal glissando—"We did lots of that." He said Big Brother used "many 'yelps,' especially in 'Combination of the Two,' but, really, everywhere. 'Summertime' was all about counterpoint (which includes fugal procedures)," Sam added. (E-mail to the author, April 4, 2010.) Shelton's critique, it seems, was well-informed and right on the money.

With Shelton's review clipped from several copies of the Monday *Times*, we grab a couple of cabs and head uptown to the Black Rock, Columbia's headquarters on Sixth Avenue at 52nd Street, to sign Big Brother's recording contract. Albert closed the deal in November, within weeks of signing Big Brother. Now, in the imposing building that says "CBS" on it in very big letters, in corporate offices twenty-six floors above the streets of New York, Janis and the boys pen their signatures on the contract and it becomes real for them. They are Columbia recording artists.

The advance Albert has negotiated for Big Brother is big news. The Airplane, the Dead, and Country Joe have signed earlier with RCA, Warner Brothers, and Vanguard, respectively, for advances, considered precedent-setting at the time, ranging from $25,000 to $50,000. For Big Brother and the Holding Company, Columbia has shelled out $150,000—of which the band will see not a penny, because it all goes to Bobby Shad to extricate them from their contract with Mainstream, together with an additional $100,000 that will come out of the band's earnings. Shad demanded $250,000 to let Big Brother out of the contract and he is sitting in the catbird seat. Columbia and Big Brother have no choice but to swallow their pride and pay him. Janis and the boys are not happy that Shad has enriched himself at the band's expense, but they're free of Mainstream at last.

Following the signing, Columbia throws a press reception for the band at a restaurant on 57th Street, presided over by president Clive Davis. There's an open bar and lavish hors d'oeuvres. The minions of the Fourth Estate buzz around Janis like flies on honey, ignoring the boys. They feel left out, but 57th Street is a lot flashier than lower Second Avenue and they sense that the next phase of their career is truly launched.

*(Promotional information provided by the band members,
released to the press by Albert B. Grossman Management.)*

MEET
BIG BROTHER AND THE HOLDING COMPANY

Janis Joplin

BORN: January 19, 1943

BIRTH SIGN: Capricorn

PLACE OF BIRTH: Port Arthur, Texas

INSTRUMENTS: Vocals, percussion

BACKGROUND: Dropped in and out of four colleges.
Worked intermittently and collected unemployment.
Sang country music and blues with an Austin, Texas,
bluegrass band. Sang blues in folk clubs and bars
in San Francisco. Joined Big Brother via Chet Helms,
old friend, past manager of Big Brother and now the
head of Family Dog.

MUSICAL INFLUENCES: Bessie Smith and Otis Redding
(The King).

I'M A FAN OF: Otis Redding, Aretha Franklin, Moby
Grape, Electric Flag, Bob Dylan, Mother Earth, Tina
Turner, Jimi Hendrix, Cream, Beatles, Quicksilver,
the Dead.

FUTURE: Buy a bar and settle down.

Sam Andrew

BORN: December 18, 1941

BIRTH SIGN: Sagittarius

PLACE OF BIRTH: Taft, California

BACKGROUND: Started playing guitar at 14. Played in rock and roll bands until 18. Began classical guitar in 1962. Played tenor sax in 1963 in a rock and roll band. Played alto sax in a military band. Played jazz guitar at the Juke Box on Haight Street. Came with Big Brother in the summer of 1965.

MAJOR MUSICAL INFLUENCES: Chuck Berry, Chet Atkins, Webb Pierce, Andres Segovia, King Curtis, B. B. King, Albert Collins and Albert King.

I'M A FAN OF: Janis Joplin, Peter Albin, Dave Getz, James Gurley, Bob Mosley, Paul Butterfield, Mike Bloomfield and Jorma Kaukonen.

FUTURE: ?

James Martin Gurley

BIRTH SIGN: Capricorn

PLACE OF BIRTH: Detroit, Michigan

INSTRUMENTS: Guitar and Kelp horn

BACKGROUND AND INFLUENCES: Been bumming around, picking up on Coleman, Lightnin' Hopkins, Broonzy, Bach, Vivaldi, Lord Buckley, Moondog, Big Sur, Mexico, Zen, Zap, Zonk, the usual.

LIKES: Currently dig all those doing their thing well.

FUTURE: Someday I hope to regain consciousness.

Peter S. Albin

BORN: June 6, 1944

BIRTH SIGN: Gemini

PLACE OF BIRTH: San Francisco

BACKGROUND: Got started in folk music, played bluegrass, old timey music and country blues. Got involved in electric blues and rock and roll during college. Went with Big Brother and the Holding Company in 1965.

MAJOR INFLUENCES: B. B. King, John Lee Hooker, Charlie Poole, Chuck Berry, Flatt and Scruggs, Moondog, Lenny Bruce, Captain Zero, Ali Akbar Khan, Otis Redding, Rolling Stones, Spike Jones, Leonard Bernstein, early Brubeck, Bobby Breen and Charley Mingus.

I'M A FAN OF: Otis Redding, Steve Miller Blues Band, John Chambers, Beatles, B. B. King, Dionne Warwick, Siegel-Schwall, Jefferson Airplane, Grateful Dead, Aretha Franklin and Pat Kilroy.

FUTURE: To continue moving people with music and musical entertainment. Producing and promoting.

David Getz

BORN: Yes

AGE: 28

INSTRUMENTS: Drums, piano, vocal

BACKGROUND: Started playing drums and drawing pictures at age 14. Became freak with no context. Lived in Brooklyn. Started art school (Cooper Union) at 17. Played with jazz groups, but mostly schlock weekend gigs for bread. Mostly painted. Went to Europe in 1959 with Dixieland band. Moved to San Francisco in 1960. Went to Art Institute. Didn't play drums too much. Got B.F.A., M.F.A., and Fulbright Fellowship. Lived in Poland for one year. Stopped painting, started playing drums with numerous Polish jazz groups. Returned to San

Francisco in 1965. Became art teacher and 2nd cook. Painted. Frustrated drummer. Met Peter Albin. Heard Big Brother and had to be the drummer again.

MUSICAL INFLUENCES: Roy Haynes, Max Roach, and lots of jazz drummers. Indian drummers (Sivarman). Rhythm and blues and soul musicians. Everything I've ever heard.

CHAPTER TEN

What a Wonderful Town

WE HAVE TO wait until Thursday to learn that the weekly *Village Voice* also gives the Anderson show a rave. When the *Times* and the *Voice* are in agreement, you've got the bases covered.

I spend my most of my weekdays at Albert's office on East 55th Street, making arrangements for upcoming gigs. "The office" is in a five-story town house between Park and Madison avenues. Albert has the fourth floor and part of the fifth. A genial staffer named Marty shows me a spare desk and phone in the room where he works, and this becomes my work space.

I could leave it to the office's travel agency to book the flights and the motels and the rental cars, but they're making arrangements for half a dozen acts on the road at any given time and they don't always take the comfort of the musicians into account. After we experienced a few unnecessarily trying itineraries out west, I gradually assumed the duties of Big Brother's travel agent. The basics are simple: Don't wake the band earlier than necessary on a travel day, don't book connecting flights when there's a direct flight, and ask the band when there are choices to be made. We have a day off between gigs on the road; do you want to spend the layover in city A or city B? Getting an answer to any question involves consulting with all five members of the band, sometimes more than once. Democracy in action. But they appreciate the consideration, and building a consensus on logistical decisions is becoming easier.

Max's Kansas City becomes our regular watering place. Dave Richards connects to a lovely waitress and the single guys avail themselves of the opportunities among the waitresses and the clientele. The guys who have old ladies at home sometimes behave like single guys on the road. These are the sixties, after all.

Janis is always on the prowl and vocal about it. Her most successful pickup line is "Hiya, honey," delivered with a winsome smile. The ballsy-mama-on-the-town persona is a role she puts on partly to cover her insecurities, and because it's part of who she wants to be. In her quieter moments, talking about men, Janis makes it clear that she's really looking for true love, just like the rest of us.

Janis has been to New York before, in her speed-driven wanderings of the early sixties. She comments on the enduring aspects of New York life that she noticed then—the faster pace, the higher level of adrenaline in the streets. She was pool champ of Eighth Avenue, she tells me with a bravado that lets me know it isn't a serious claim. Trust Janis to have ended up in Hell's Kitchen her first time in New York.

Now she has returned in style, no longer scrabbling for a place to stay. The Chelsea is funky enough to win her approval. She likes the mix of artists, musicians, bohemians and beatniks that make up the long-term residents, but she regards New York as an alien environment.

The boys have their own reservations. At the end of a day on the town, James tells me, "I looked up at the sky and a rock fell in my eye." The "rock" was a gnarly piece of urban grit that grated his cornea until he managed to extricate the offending particle.

"At first, [New York] seemed to have made us all crazy; it was dividing the unity of the band. The first three weeks here, we all got superaggressive, separate, sour. . . . San Francisco's different. I don't mean it's perfect, but the rock bands there didn't start because they wanted to make it. They dug getting stoned and playing for people dancing. Here they want to *make* it. What we've had to do is learn to control success, put it in perspective, and not lose the essence of what we're doing—the music."

Janis Joplin

A week after the Anderson Theater, Big Brother plays at the Psychedelic Supermarket in Boston. The Supermarket is as close as you can get to a San Francisco rock-and-roll ballroom on the East Coast, and it's a reasonable facsimile. Janis and the boys feel more at home here than they did at the Anderson Theater, with its fixed seats. The audience fills the dance floor and Big Brother plays a spirited set, happy to feel something like their hometown connection to the dancers.

The other act on the bill is a new band formed by Al Kooper called Blood, Sweat and Tears. They're not anything like a San Francisco band, but Janis is intrigued by the horn section. Al is trying to use horns in a new way, beyond how horns have traditionally been used by R&B groups.

The contrast between Boston and San Francisco becomes apparent when Dave Richards and Mark Braunstein come in on Saturday to find that a bunch of Big Brother's equipment has been stolen since the end of the Friday night show. We routinely leave equipment in the San Francisco ballrooms, where Bill Graham and the Family Dog provide adequate security. Here, Dave and Marko have to scramble to beg, borrow, and buy enough equipment for us to play on Saturday night.

On Sunday we do a show at the Rhode Island School of Design, in Providence, to an enthusiastic crowd of stoned art students. Janis is delighted. "They're just like hippies!" she says. It's a flat-rate gig, so

I don't have much to do. During the performance I'm standing against the back wall of the student union, checking the sound and digging the set, when I feel a hand on my calf. I look down to see a lovely girl making out with her boyfriend. They're sitting on the floor. Their eyes are closed, their lips are locked, and her hand is running up and down *my* leg! This probably has something to do with why, at the end of the show, I grab a mike, thank the crowd for being a great audience, and announce the address in Cambridge where I'm throwing a party for the band that night. A couple of carloads of adventurous RISD fans take me up on it and arrive to discover that the party is in an iron lung factory.

The summer before my freshman year at Harvard, I worked for my uncle Jack, my mother's brother, in his funky three-story brick factory in a working-class section of North Cambridge. Jack was the family dropout. While his elder sister and two brothers followed in their father's footsteps by attending Radcliffe and Harvard and going on to advanced degrees in the sciences, Jack quit college, started his own business, perfected the modern iron lung, and filed a couple of dozen patents for his inventions of mechanical devices that assisted doctors in caring for their patients, many of them related to breathing. In time, his father, my grandfather, a distinguished epidemiologist and a hard man to please, came to acknowledge that Jack had not wasted his life.

Two years ago, when I retreated to Cambridge from my abortive move to California, I lived in one of two apartments on the top floor of Jack's factory. It became a celebrated party pad. The parties ran late and featured dancing to rock and roll on the hi-fi. With no one else living in the building, we didn't have to worry about the noise bothering the neighbors, but the neighbors must have occasionally marveled at the number of cars coming and going from the parking lot of the J. H. Emerson Company late at night. For revelers who found themselves still there in the morning, there was bottled medical oxygen for a quick pick-me-up.

My sound system is still set up in my living room/bedroom and I haven't yet shipped all my records to San Francisco. I have advertised the party through the Cambridge grapevine and it becomes a major event. Blood, Sweat and Tears are here in force. The Chambers Brothers are in Boston this weekend. Neuwirth has come up from New York. The living room is wall to wall with people dancing while James Gurley makes out on the bed with one of the girls from RISD.

In the back room, Neuwirth sets up a camera and tape recorder he has borrowed from Pennebaker. He isn't sure what he'll use the footage for, but his auteurial juices are bubbling. He calls people into the room, seats them in front of the camera, illuminated by the harsh light of a gooseneck table lamp, and interviews them. Sometimes he directs them in hysterical displays that will startle anyone who sees these shots without having experienced the party. He films Lester Chambers screaming like a banshee.

Before the party sighs to a close, in the wee hours, I am rewarded for inviting the RISD students. How can I put this discreetly? Let's say that I share some private time—elsewhere in the factory—with the girl James was making out with earlier in a manner that both of us find pleasurable. Hail, hail, rock and roll.*

---

* If I knew that the writer Michael Thomas was at the party, I didn't know he was on duty. Six months later, his article about Janis and Big Brother appeared in *Ramparts* magazine. It was a rare nonpolitical article in the radical leftist magazine, and it opened with these images: "John Cooke had a party a couple of months ago in an iron lung factory in Cambridge, Massachusetts. . . . Picture all these people, say a hundred odd, following little red arrows through three floors of hospital supplies, artificial limbs, pleural suction pumps and special rocking beds. . . . It's like sneaking in and out of all the doors you ever saw that say 'Do Not Enter'; you keep looking over your shoulder and you talk in whispers if at all. Finally you come to a door with Spider Man on it, and that's where John Cooke lives when he's in Boston. Inside, there are deviled eggs and chili beans and booze and everybody Jim Kweskin knows in town." ("Janis Joplin, Voodoo Lady of Rock," *Ramparts*, August 10, 1968.)

MAR. 1–2, 1968: **Grande Ballroom, Detroit**

MAR. 8: **Fillmore East, NYC**

MAR. 9: **Dining Hall, Wesleyan University, Middletown, Conn.**

MAR. 15–17: **Electric Factory, Philadelphia**

MAR. 22–24: **Cheetah, Chicago**

APR. 2–7: **Generation, NYC**

On the first weekend in March we play the Grande Ballroom in Detroit. It's a homecoming of sorts for James, who was born in the Motor City. As our plane descends through the clouds on the glide path for Detroit Metro, James is sitting in the row behind me, peering out the window. A break in the clouds offers a glimpse of the city below. James casts a dubious eye on his hometown and reflects on the contrast with New York. "Ah," he says, "from plethora to dearth in forty-five minutes."

The city looks like a war zone. It *was* a war zone last summer, pacified only after more than twelve thousand paratroopers and National Guard troops quelled the rioters. Over the past few years, summertime urban race riots have become steadily more numerous. The outbreak in the Watts district of Los Angeles in August 1965 shocked the nation. The next summer saw more than three dozen riots, mostly in northern cities from Brooklyn and Baltimore to St. Louis and San Francisco. In 1967 more than a hundred cities experienced racial violence. Detroit was the worst. The official tally counted forty people dead, but some say the true toll was much higher. More than five thousand people were left homeless when their homes burned.

As in San Francisco, Detroit's rock-and-roll counterculture sprang up near the ghetto. We drive through the combat zone on the way to the gig. There are bullet holes in the walls.

Big Brother and most of the California bands are less focused politically than my folk music compatriots. The folk scene was far more aware of politics, through its connection to the civil-rights struggle and protest songs about race, injustice, and war. Sam Andrew comments on the evidence of the riots as we pass through the Detroit ghetto, but Janis's immediate concern is knowing that Columbia Records will be recording Big Brother at the Grande Ballroom.

The Grande (the *e* is not silent) is the center of the local rock scene. Once we're inside we feel safer, and pretty much at home. MC5 is the house band, locally celebrated, not yet widely known. The names of the other bands on the bill for our Friday–Saturday gig would look right at home on a Fillmore poster—Tiffany Shade, Pink Peech Mob, and the Family Dump Truck.

The Grande's manager, Russ Gibb, visited San Francisco a couple of years ago and saw a show at the Avalon. The Grande is his effort to create a similar scene in Detroit. In a town with the negative vibes of Motor City, he's done as well as anyone could. Here, far removed from the Golden Gate, Big Brother hopes to conjure up some San Francisco magic.

Recording at the Grande is the band's idea. Albert and Columbia are willing to give it a try. The hall is an open-floor ballroom like the Fillmore and the Avalon. It's a well-intentioned effort that recognizes the band's San Francisco origins and the relationship between musicians and audience that is unique to the city by the Bay.

Parked outside the Grande, a truck contains a rolling recording studio that is connected to the stage by a web of cables. For two nights, record producer John Simon and a Columbia engineer make a first attempt at capturing the band in live performance.

The shows feel good to me. Not as good as some, but okay. On our flight back to New York, Janis has some doubts, but she and the boys hope some of the spontaneity will come through on the tapes.

When Albert listens to the recordings, he finds the results less than impressive. He summons the band to his office. Sam arrives late. "Anybody got a joint?" he asks, figuring to get in tune with the music. "We don't need that right now," Albert says. Sam notices that the other band members, who have already had a preview of Albert's disappointment, are stone-faced. Oh shit, he thinks, this is going to be a psychodrama.

   No one in the band can defend the tapes. To a bunch of dancing fans, many of them stoned out of their gourds, the occasional missed chord or fluffed guitar riff passes unnoticed. A brief disagreement between the bass and the drums about just where the beat is going may not faze the audience, but the reels of tape spinning in the recording truck aren't stoned and they aren't dancing. They hear it all, which is why record producers hold recorded tracks to a higher standard than live performances. A recording has to hold up to repeated listenings, but just one listen to the Grande tapes is enough to persuade Janis and the boys that Albert's harsh verdict is justified. The energy that Big Brother managed to ignite in the Grande doesn't come through on the tape. The mistakes do. All too audible is the fact that the band played as sloppily as at any time in recent memory. Big Brother's Curse strikes again.

> "For years, it was our particular lot not to rise to a given occasion. Every time, when it was really necessary for us to play well, we didn't, and the Grande Ballroom is the case in point. It was probably the worst playing we did in those particular months of playing."
>
> **Sam Andrew**

   Sam is afraid that Albert will fire some of the band members on the spot, but it doesn't come to that. What Albert is looking for is something more than technical competence. It's authenticity, both in presentation and in the emotional content of the music, a unity that is honest and real above all, and at the same time free from obvious technical faults. There is nothing phony or insincere about Big Brother, but the emotional authenticity, the enthusiasm that drives the music, sometimes outstrips the technical abilities of the band, and it's this imbalance that Albert seeks to correct.

To this end, he suggests some radical options. How about if Sam plays bass? (Unsaid, but Sam feels it is implied: because he can't play guitar.) How about if Peter plays guitar? (Which he used to do before he took up the bass, and which he still plays on a couple of songs.) Possible remedies are discussed, hashed over, and ultimately rejected by the band. The only conclusion that comes out of the meeting is a clear understanding that Big Brother had better learn quickly to produce better results in a studio.

That effort commences at once. Between our weekend forays into the heartland, the band works under professional conditions in Columbia's New York studios.

The producer, John Simon, is represented by Albert Grossman, as is Elliot Mazer, who will co-produce the album. Albert has chosen Simon to oversee Big Brother's record for Columbia without consulting the band. Simon produced the hit single "Red Rubber Ball" for the Cyrkle, he has worked with jazzman Charles Lloyd, and he produced and wrote the arrangements for Leonard Cohen's first album.

Simon yields to Big Brother's wish to record "live" in the studio—all playing at the same time in the same room, although this method creates technical difficulties. There is "bleed," each microphone picking up not only the voice or instrument it's placed in front of, but the other voices and instruments as well. This makes it difficult, or impossible, to overdub a given voice or instrument to correct errors and improve a track.

Despite this concession, there is friction between Simon and the band from the outset. John is a musician himself, a pianist and composer, very much of the educated and disciplined school. He shows little curiosity about the colorful band of California eccentrics who have generated such interest since the Monterey Pop Festival. The band members feel that Simon is standoffish, sometimes condescending. Dave Getz finds it impossible to talk to him. Sam doesn't get along with him much better. Janis feels that Simon rebuffs her attempts to strike up a dialogue. Peter Albin is alone in believing

there is potential for a good relationship with Simon, if they stick
with it.

> "I think fundamentally he didn't like Janis. You know, he didn't like
> it that she practiced her riffs. This came out later. He said, 'Blues
> artists don't do that.' I just thought, That's ridiculous. I've heard
> Ray Charles practice a riff a million times. . . . And in his biogra-
> phy he says, 'That was a riff, and I practiced that, and it was a
> good one.' [Simon] just had this mental construct about the band.
> I think he wasn't in sympathy with Janis."
>
> **Sam Andrew**

Since Monterey, Pennebaker has kept an eye out for another
chance to film Janis. He has in mind that he might make a *Dont Look
Back*–style film about her. He expresses interest in filming a recording session. He clears it with Albert, I clear it with the band, and I
serve again as Penny's soundman. What his inquisitive camera perceives is an omen. Just as a microphone captures onstage mistakes
that become glaring in playback, the camera often sees in a scene
what the real-life participants miss. Penny's philosophy of documentary film trusts the ability of the camera's impartial eye to ferret out
the truth. In Columbia's New York Studio E, it perceives that John
Simon is out of sync with these free spirits from San Francisco.

On the day we're filming, Janis arrives after the others. The boys
are jamming on a tune that isn't one of their regular songs, a spontaneous jam. Janis skips around the studio, dancing to the music.
When the tune ends, she says, "You wanna hear how shitty some
people can be?" and she launches into a story about this guy she just
met, the guitar player for the Animals, who are in town. The guy was
busted for dope a while ago in Vancouver, British Columbia, and
was released on bail. He was supposed to fly out this week for his
trial, but the Animals' manager told him not to go. Then, without
telling the guy, they wired to England for another guitar player to

replace him when they fired him, which they did yesterday. And now they want him to play with the band tonight because the new guy isn't here yet!

Janis lays out the whole story in a literal minute. "I've never heard of anyone being treated so shabbily!" she says. "And he's not even mad, and I'm *furious!*" She's righteously incensed, but her delivery of the last line recognizes that it has the potential to be funny. No one laughs.

Throughout Janis's rap, John Simon is leaning on the studio piano, uninvolved. He looks exhausted, or maybe exasperated. Without moving or saying a word, he projects an aura of indifference masking annoyance. When Janis delivers her closing line, he says, "Let's do 'Summertime.'"

"It was very hard to work with John Simon. John Simon was put on us by Albert. Albert just said, 'I've got the producer and this guy's producing this other band, and he's great, he's a genius.' And Albert drew up the whole contract. Albert gave John Simon two-sevenths of the [album] royalties. . . . Janis, I think her attitude was, she was gonna have fun anyway. And she was not gonna suffer as much as John wanted everybody to suffer, as much as he was suffering. And I was suffering as much as he was suffering. I think Peter to a certain extent was. I think James and Sam were getting so loaded that they just sort of created a cloud around themselves so that they were impervious to what John was putting out, the vibe that he was putting out. And I think Janis just— I think Janis kind of picked up on where he was at, and was just intentionally, very consciously, not gonna buy into it, and was just gonna go on with her merry little act. And so I think, to her credit, she may have handled it the best of anybody. And she was a consummate performer. When it came time to go in the studio and sing, Janis knew she could do it. She knew she had the facility to perform under those kind of pressure situations, whereas we didn't."

David Getz

Sam Andrew has arranged the Gershwin classic with guitar ar-
peggios that begin slowly, then ripple nimbly through an introduction that doesn't reveal the identity of the song until Janis opens her
mouth and sings the first word: "Summertime . . ."

James plays in a lower register. Together, the two guitars weave
around Janis's high, breathy rendition to create a wholly original interpretation of the song. Gershwin would have smiled. If there's one
song in Big Brother's repertoire that should engage John Simon and
win his approval, this is it.

The first take is a little ragged. The band listens to it in the control
room, then returns to the studio. They debate whether to continue
working on "Summertime" until it's done, or include another song in
this evening's session. Janis wants to work until "Summertime" is in
the can, however long it takes. The clock on the wall of the studio says
9:30. Dave Getz says let's work on it until twelve and move on to
something else if we haven't got it by then.

Penny moves his camera from one participant in the discussion to
another. I stay out of his way and aim the mike at whoever's talking.
John Simon makes no effort to guide the conversation or get the band
focused on the work at hand. Once again, he's off to one side, discon-
nected, waiting.

The only record producer I've spent much time with in a studio is
Paul Rothchild. He produced the Charles River Valley Boys' first
album when he found out we didn't have one. Paul was working for
a Boston-area record distributor at the time. He came into the Club
47, heard us play, and said he'd like to handle our record. We don't
have a record, we told him. Paul came back a week later and said he'd
like to help us make one. That was the start of his career as a producer. He made our record on his own label and later sold it to Prestige Records in New Jersey as part of a deal that got him a job as
A&R (artists and repertory) man for the label. Before long he moved
on to Jac Holzman's Elektra Records in New York. In short order

Paul produced a string of successful folk albums for Elektra, and he was instrumental in Elektra's decision to become the first folk label to expand into recording electrified music. He has produced the Paul Butterfield Blues Band and the Doors.

In the midsixties, when I was in New York, I would check in with Paul and visit the Elektra studio if he was working with someone interesting. Without giving it much thought, until now, I have absorbed Paul's manner in the studio as the model for how a record producer does his job. He guides the proceedings so gently, most of the time, that it would take a stranger a while to figure out who's running the show. Paul understands musicians and gives them a lot of free rein. He wants them to be comfortable. He laughs with them, smokes pot with them, orders out for burgers with them, but he never lets the musicians forget that they're in the studio to get some work done. However relaxed and gregarious he may be at any given moment, Paul is aware of the job at hand and he is guiding those present toward that goal. He is the captain of the ship.

Paul is not a musician. He can barely carry a tune. But he loves music and he has an uncanny ability to communicate with musicians who run the gamut from highly verbal to effectively mute. Paul can express musical concepts and suggestions so articulately that singer after singer and band after band have produced under his guidance definitive performances of their music, albums that stand up to repeated listening and enhance the artists' reputations. In the studio, everything he does is focused on making the best possible recording with these musicians in this time and place.

I gain new respect for the effectiveness of Paul's methods when I see Janis and the boys working with John Simon. From my viewpoint, this ship is caught in irons, with no one at the helm. Each time I visit the studio, John and the band are struggling. Despite the "live" setup, Janis and the boys find it hard to capture on tape the freewheeling sound and the exhilaration—the magic—that they generate in concert.

> "I always felt that the studio recording was stifling. I just could
> not get off. 'Cause I get off playing to audiences, and there's no-
> body there, you know? It's very cold and calculated."
>
> **Peter Albin**

The work is frustrating and tiring. They need a break, something
to give them a boost, and they get it. A week after the disappointing
weekend in Detroit, Janis and the boys play in New York again, on
the opening night of Bill Graham's Fillmore East.

A few people in New York who care about rock music have urged
Graham to open an operation in the city. Bill has resisted. San Francisco keeps him busy. He doesn't want to fail in his hometown but he
was finally persuaded to come take a look. He saw Big Brother's show
at the Anderson. The drab state of the theater and the indifference of
the promoter to the music was just what it took to knock him off the
fence. Anyone who knew Bill could see the wheels begin to spin:
What this town needs is somebody to do it *right*!

Across Second Avenue from the Anderson is the Village Theater,
formerly a 2,400-seat Loews movie house, and, like the Anderson, a
Yiddish theater before that. A few rock shows have been put on in the
Village Theater, but there was no regular operation. Graham bought
the Village, with Albert Grossman and his new partner, Bert Block,
putting up the capital as silent partners. Bill will run the show. Between Big Brother's February 17 appearance at the Anderson and the
eighth of March, Bill and his crew have completely refurbished the
old movie house and rechristened it Fillmore East. The theater's new
technical director is Chip Monck, a lighting designer who illuminated the Newport Folk Festivals and who has moved into rock show
lighting. Together, Graham and Monck have pulled off a miracle. It's
still a sit-down theater, but it has the welcoming atmosphere, and
some of the ambiance, of the San Francisco ballrooms.

Big Brother headlines the opening night, with Albert King, Tim
Buckley, and a San Francisco–style light show rounding out the bill.

The manager of the Anderson prints counterfeit tickets to Bill's show and gives them away on the street, but he fails in his effort to sabotage the party. The line at Fillmore East stretches around the block.

The show presents the kind of stylistic mix—Tim Buckley's folk rock, Big Brother's acid rock, and Albert King's polished blues—that Graham is known for in San Francisco. Janis and the boys are happy to be working for Graham again in front of an appreciative audience. Big Brother rocks and Janis wows the fans. Among Graham's ushers, clad in an orange jumpsuit, is Robert Mapplethorpe, just twenty-one, already an artist, not yet a photographer, utterly unknown, at this time living in impoverished bohemian bliss in Brooklyn with the equally artistic and unknown Patti Smith. Mapplethorpe came to work looking forward to hearing Tim Buckley, but he returns home late at night to announce to Smith that he has seen someone new, someone who is going to make it big. Her name is Janis Joplin.

Fillmore East's opening night generates a lot of press and more good reviews for Big Brother. *Variety* covers the show, as well as *Billboard*, *Cashbox*, and *Record World*.

Good reviews are always good news, but they are too often a double-edged sword for Big Brother. Once again, the press and the public focus most of their attention on Janis. It's her vocals, her dynamism onstage, that knock everyone out. Once again Robert Shelton proves to be the exception by singling out the band for praise in the *Times*. Mostly, the boys get mixed notices. Some reviewers, and some acquaintances unaware of the San Francisco music scene's philosophy, the ethic embraced by the founding bands, have suggested Janis get better musicians.

Janis is loyal to Big Brother. They took her in and gave her a chance. The performances that won over the San Francisco fans and earned the great reviews at Monterey were all given with Big Brother behind her. And that's the problem. Many observers see Big Brother *behind* her. They don't give Sam's vocals, and Peter's and

James's, and the band's unique sound, due credit for the success Janis and Big Brother have earned.

If enough people tell you how great you are and in the same breath suggest that your fellow band members don't measure up, it's understandable that you may begin to wonder if maybe they're right.

Albert's office has a publicist, Myra Friedman, working full-time on Big Brother for their first eastern tour. Myra is in awe of Janis, and she exacerbates the imbalance by devoting most of her efforts to her. In our first few weeks in New York, Myra arranges for *Glamour*, *New York* magazine, *Eye* magazine, and *Life* to do interviews or photo shoots with Janis. (Janis takes an attentive interest in her press coverage. She fires off salvos of clippings and quotes to her family in Port Arthur, along with effusive letters full of news about her rising reputation.)

Myra's greatest coup is arranging for Janis to be photographed by Richard Avedon for *Vogue*, for a photo section about the happening people in show business. A few years ago, Avedon's fashion photos for *Harper's Bazaar* became so creative that the magazine was read and talked about within the folk music underground. Instead of shooting models looking bored, Avedon photographed them looking happy, being funny, even *moving*. He was a past master of black and white. As innovations in art and music blossomed in the sixties, Avedon took to using psychedelic colors and effects in his spreads. In 1966, Avedon left *Harper's Bazaar* for *Vogue*.

Myra further endears herself to Janis by following up on an idea that Janis has been promoting for a while now: Think of all the publicity she has generated for Southern Comfort. Reporters mention Janis's favorite drink in virtually every piece they write. Shouldn't Southern Comfort give Janis something in return? Myra's efforts produce an offer from Southern Comfort for Janis to visit a fur warehouse in New Jersey and choose whatever she'd like. Janis picks a three-quarter-length coat in Russian lynx and a matching hat that become her signature cold-weather traveling wear, even as she forsakes Southern Comfort in favor of drinks that don't make her friends and drinking companions gag.

A week after the Fillmore East, we're in Philadelphia again for three days at the Electric Factory in Old Town, for a guarantee of $6,000 against 50 percent of the gross over $12,000. Big Brother's take-home is $12,160. In the band's first month in the East, they have made close to $40,000. Albert's guarantee of $100,000 in the first year is beginning to look modest, and Janis and the boys dare to believe there may be some money left over after the debt to Mainstream is paid off.

On the same weekend, the Charles River Valley Boys, with my predecessor, Clay Jackson, now back in the band on guitar and lead vocals, are at the Second Fret coffeehouse, the Philadelphia focus of the folk boom. After Big Brother's show at the Electric Factory, I take them to the Second Fret and I sit in with the CRVB for most of a set. I slip back into the three-part harmonies as easily as putting on a familiar shirt, and this role reversal, with me onstage and Big Brother in the audience, makes more real for my new cohort the fact that their road manager had a life in music before he took up the reins of their traveling circus.

Janis has a bottle in her handbag from which she sips with just the right amount of discretion in the nonalcoholic coffeehouse. She sips liberally, however. When we get back to our hotel, I am in my road manager's role once more as I half support, half carry her through the lobby and up the elevator to her room. It's all part of the job.

The following weekend takes us to Chicago, where Albert Grossman, Paul Butterfield, Mike Bloomfield, and Nick Gravenites got their start in the music business. We make a pilgrimage to the fabled South Side, where the blues clubs still flourish, but the streets are uneasy in the wake of last summer's ghetto riots here, and we don't linger long.

New York, Boston, Philadelphia, Detroit, Chicago—we're not in Fresno anymore, Toto.

Janis and the boys take it all in stride, but there's often a gleam in their eyes. These early weeks of touring the East are exceeding their expectations of what working under Albert's guidance might be like.

Janis's professionalism, and the excitement of bringing her music to new audiences across the eastern and midwestern states, usually keeps her drinking within her customary pattern—just enough before a performance to give her the boost she needs to launch herself onto the stage. Sometimes, when the opening acts run long and Big Brother goes on late, she has trouble maintaining the preperformance edge, but when she steps onstage her adrenaline almost always powers her through.

After the shows, she drinks more, as do the boys, but carrying her into a hotel is the exception rather than the rule. The demands of the job keep my own drinking moderate. At the end of the day, my top priority is getting enough sleep so I can get up and eat breakfast in the morning before it's time to phone the members of the band, room by room, to wake them and give them the time they need, individually adjusted, to get their acts together and be in the lobby when it's time to go.

On the last day of March, we're in New York when Lyndon Johnson goes on prime-time TV to announce a halt to the bombing of North Vietnam above the twentieth parallel, as a gesture he hopes will bring the North Vietnamese and the Vietcong to the negotiating table. At the end of the broadcast, Johnson drops a bombshell of his own when he declares that he will not run for reelection.

Since we came east, I have followed presidential politics with little support from Janis or the boys. At first, Gene McCarthy was given no chance of unseating Lyndon Johnson, but he placed a close second in the recent New Hampshire primary. Encouraged by this sign of Johnson's vulnerability on the issue of Vietnam, and further motivated by the Tet Offensive, whose last battles were only recently concluded, Bobby Kennedy entered the race in mid-March, despite his earlier disavowal of interest. Johnson's bowing out now throws the race wide open.

I go to Max's Kansas City to celebrate by getting exuberantly drunk. If anyone had told me this evening that within a year I would miss Lyndon Johnson, I would have laughed in his face.

Sam and Peter show some interest in Johnson's announcement, but for the most part the band members don't see much hope for meaningful change in the traditional political process.

The next day, they're back in Columbia's Studio E, recording "Misery'n" and "Catch Me Daddy."

On Tuesday, April 2, Big Brother goes into a New York club called Generation for a six-night stand with B. B. King. The club is on West 8th Street, a block from Washington Square Park. Backstage on opening night, Janis receives a delegation from *Jazz & Pop* magazine, who tell her that she has been voted best female pop vocalist of the year in the magazine's annual readers' poll, beating out the soul queen, Aretha Franklin, by fourteen votes out of almost eighteen hundred. "But I've only been singing for a year and a half!" is Janis's astonished reaction. She's not about to turn down the award, but "best female pop vocalist" strikes her as a bit much. "Best chick vocalist," she offers. "How about that?"

On the third day of our gig at Generation, the Reverend Martin Luther King, Jr., is assassinated in Memphis.

CHAPTER ELEVEN

Swing Low, Sweet Chariot

THE NEWS FROM Memphis, where Martin Luther King has been supporting a strike by sanitation workers, breaks shortly after 7:00 P.M. Eastern Time. First reports say King has been shot and was rushed to a hospital. Just over an hour later the word comes that he is dead. As dusk falls, riots break out in cities across the country, including Newark, Detroit, Kansas City, Los Angeles and San Francisco.

In Indianapolis, Bobby Kennedy appears in front of a predominantly black crowd, against the counsel of his advisors. He asks his listeners to pray for the family of Dr. King and for the United States. Some credit the speech for preventing a riot in Indianapolis, and perhaps in other places where Kennedy's words are heard.

Pennebaker has planned to come to Generation to film more of Janis and Big Brother. Before the gig, he is with Bob Neuwirth and his lady, Tonto, who have taken a small apartment on West 46th Street, just a block from the Leacock Pennebaker offices. Penny shoots Kennedy's speech off the TV. When they catch a cab to come to the club, the radio in the taxi is warning people not to go to Broadway or Harlem.

At Generation, Janis and the boys are as stunned as I am. As bands, the San Francisco groups are anarchistic, humanistic, and apolitical, except in the broadest sense. The Grateful Dead won't let anyone use their microphones for sociopolitical harangues. Their position is, "We don't want to be connected with anti-anydamnthing. We're not anti-war, anti-this, anti-that, we're just pro-music, pro-party, pro-getting *down*." Which pretty well sums up Big Brother's attitude, especially Janis's. Privately, the members of Big Brother have feelings and opinions that tend to be a country mile to the left of center. Publicly they promote no message except be true to yourself and get it on, but Dr. King's death affects them all.

At Generation that evening, B. B. King sits on his guitar amp onstage and plays gospel songs, moving some in the audience to tears. A number of musicians have come to the club just to be in the company of other people someplace where there's music. After Big Brother's closing set, there is a spontaneous jam, a kind of informal wake.

At closing time, we're wary of venturing into the streets, but the city is quiet. On Saturday, U.S. troops guard the Capitol Building in Washington, D.C., for the first time since the Civil War.

Rock and roll as usual doesn't feel right, so we plan a more formal observance for Sunday, our last night at Generation. President Johnson has declared it a national day of mourning. I use Albert's client roster as a starting point, connecting through these musicians and the members of Big Brother to others who might be in New York. We invite them to join us in celebrating the life and mourning the loss of the most eloquent advocate for nonviolent civil disobedience since Mahatma Gandhi. I send out and hand out photocopied invitations, and we fill the club. Jimi Hendrix, Buddy Guy, Joni Mitchell, Richie Havens, Al Kooper, Paul Butterfield, and Elvin Bishop are among those who answer the call.

Since Thursday, fifty thousand federal and National Guard troops have been dispatched to some of the one hundred cities where rioting followed Dr. King's death. More than twenty thousand people have been arrested.

APR. 10, 1968: **Anaheim Convention Center, Anaheim, Calif.**

APR. 11–13: **Fillmore and Winterland, San Francisco**

APR. 19: **Selland Arena, Fresno**

APR. 20: **Earl Warren Fairground, Santa Barbara**

APR. 27: **San Bernardino**

On Monday, Janis and the boys and I fly to Los Angeles, where the vitality of springtime in California helps to dispel the pall. We have a gig in Anaheim, followed by a weekend at the Fillmore and Winterland for Bill Graham.

Almost losing my job back in January taught me a lesson. The band knows they need a businessman like Albert for a manager, but they don't want too much of a businessman for a road manager. Keeping some distance to establish my authority may have been necessary at the outset, but I can't be so remote that they feel I'm not one of them. They want to feel that I belong. They want to know that I like them.

I *do* like them. I've been showing it more, hanging out more, feeling more like one of the gang, but I have no indication of how the band feels about me until we're cruising down the Santa Ana Freeway to Anaheim, riding the high of a beautiful spring day, rapping and laughing about who knows what, and out of the blue Dave Getz says, "And yes, John, we love you."

I say, "I love you too," and I mean it. Janis and each of the boys have endeared themselves to me in their own ways. Privately, I've decided that I will stay on until the job stops being fun, or until my own work—whatever it may be—makes itself known to me and requires my full attention. And since I'll be staying—

"By the way," I say, but Peter Albin is ahead of me.

"You want a raise."

"Now that you mention it." We all laugh.

I get a fifty-dollar raise on the spot. Two hundred bucks a week. My starting salary was set by Albert when he hired me. Getting a raise from the band, unanimously approved, solidifies the working relationship, but the validation means more than the money. We wander the planet looking for members of our tribe. Once in a while, if we're lucky, we find them.

On Sunday, April 21, the *New York Times* publishes an article by the jazz critic Nat Hentoff that's based on an interview he did with Janis while we were in New York. "Janis Joplin has exploded the increasingly mandarin categories of rock music by being so intensely, so joyfully herself," Hentoff writes. He mentions Big Brother and the Holding Company only in passing, and quotes Janis extensively. Her answers touch on the recurrent themes she emphasizes when trying to give an accounting of herself to the world at large. "I was treated very badly in Texas," she says. "They don't treat beatniks too good in Texas." Of performing, she says, "When everything is together—the band, me, the audience, it's boss! It's just like magic. I don't think I could ever feel that way about a man."

When Hentoff asks if she considers herself a jazz singer, Janis's answer demonstrates the articulate precision she can bring to bear on subjects that matter to her: "No, I don't feel quite free enough with my phrasing to say I'm a jazz singer. I sing with a more demanding beat, a steady rather than a lilting beat. I don't riff over the band; I try to punctuate the rhythm with my voice."

For the rest of the spring and into the summer we're based at home in San Francisco. In our first weeks back in California we play Chico and Fresno, Santa Barbara and San Bernardino. We're flying more often and driving less. The gigs are farther afield. The venues and the money are bigger than they were last winter.

We are veterans of the road now, and the routine of planes and rental cars, motels and gigs is less stressful in the sunshine of the Golden State. Janis and the boys are happy to be on their home ground. In retrospect, this is our most peaceful period. Despite the busy schedule, it's an idyll, but it's tempered by the urgent need to finish the album for Columbia.

The advance orders for the record are huge. The sales reps are clamoring for it. Everyone from Clive Davis on down is frustrated by the slow progress, and John Simon is feeling the pressure. He takes another stab at live recording, this time in Winterland, days after we return from New York. The results are better than the Grande Ballroom, but the evening doesn't yield any tracks deemed adequate.*

On the last Monday in April, Simon and Big Brother begin a ten-day stint of recording in Columbia's Los Angeles studios, but they fare no better there than they did in New York. The tensions between John Simon and the band, which Pennebaker's camera recorded in the New York sessions, are more apparent than ever. Making a record is hard work, but it's also supposed to be fun. In the L.A. sessions, fun is held effectively at bay. The tension between feeling good about their music onstage and feeling bad about it in the studio wears on the band. The difficulties with Simon affect David and Peter the most, while Sam and James medicate themselves to hold the aggravation at bay.

Janis handles it best. She distances herself from Simon, but when it comes time for her to sing, she steps up the microphone and gives it everything she's got. Her ability to summon a definitive vocal rarely fails her. She lays down a couple of takes and all you have to do is choose between them, weighing the small variations.

------

*Two songs from the April 11–13, 1968, Winterland recordings were issued on posthumous albums: "Bye, Bye Baby" on *Joplin in Concert* (1972) and "Farewell Song" on the album of the same name (1982). "Magic of Love," from the March 1, 1968, recording at the Grande Ballroom in Detroit, is also on *Farewell Song*. It is the only song from those sessions issued to date.

> "Janis was as together in the studio as anyone I have ever worked with, interested in everything and totally committed."
>
> **Elliot Mazer, co-producer,** *Cheap Thrills*

The sessions are interrupted by a day trip to Chico, in the Sacramento Valley, for a gig there, and two days at the Shrine Auditorium in L.A. Following these jobs, Janis and the boys have only a few more days in the studio before we undertake a demanding ten-day schedule that keeps us flying back and forth between the northern and the southern parts of the state.

MAY 1, 1968: **Chico State College, Chico, Calif.**

MAY 3–4: **Shrine Auditorium, Los Angeles**

MAY 10: **Cal-Poly State University, San Luis Obispo**

MAY 11: **Veterans Hall, Santa Rosa**

MAY 12: **San Fernando Valley State College, Northridge**

MAY 15: **Carousel Ballroom, San Francisco (Hells Angels benefit)**

MAY 17: **Freeborn Hall, U.C. Davis**

MAY 18–19: **Northern California Folk Rock Festival, Santa Clara Fairgrounds, San Jose, with the Doors, Jefferson Airplane, Eric Burdon and the Animals, Electric Flag, Country Joe and the Fish, Taj Mahal, and more.**

MAY 19: **Pasadena**

IN LATE MAY, we return to Columbia's Hollywood studios to finish the album. To provide the band with some comfort during our stays in Hollywood, I have found lodgings more upscale than the Hollywood Sunset Motel. Elektra Records has built a West Coast studio on La Cienega Boulevard, and Paul Rothchild is spending a lot of time in Los Angeles. He has found lodging at the Hollywood Landmark Hotel, on Franklin Avenue near Highland, where the plain of the Los Angeles basin rises into the foothills. It's on the edge of a residential neighborhood, above the garish, commercial strips of Sunset and Hollywood boulevards, where the tourists search in vain for movie stars and the hookers troll for tourists.

Calling the Landmark a hotel is stretching it. From the street, it looks like any other two-story stucco motel, but the looks are deceiving. Walk through the lobby, past the registration desk, and through a set of glass doors to the large courtyard, and you see that the arms of the establishment ramble up the hillside, enclosing a pool and a sauna and enough terrace to accommodate a couple of rock-and-roll bands. There are palm trees and other plantings. The units that overlook the courtyard are suites, with living rooms and kitchenettes and balconies. The upstairs suites are spacious and airy, with high ceilings. Only the two-story structure that fronts on Franklin Avenue has ordinary single rooms off a central hallway, and even these have kitchenettes.

Bob Neuwirth has a poolside suite next to Paul's. Before Paul and Bobby found the Landmark, it hosted the occasional jazz band. By the time Big Brother and I check in, it is in the process of becoming a preferred hostelry on the rock-and-roll road. Also in residence at this time is Garry Goodrow, of the Committee, which has opened a second company in a theater on Sunset Strip.

With a reference from Paul to Jack Hagy, the manager, I negotiate us a weekly rate so good that Janis and the boys raise only token objections. Hey, with kitchenettes we can save money on meals, I point out, and this helps to convince them. They've been working hard and they feel that they owe themselves a reward.

Janis opts for a single room in the front building. She says the courtyard suites are too big for her to knock around in all by herself. The boys like the suites and they each have one to themselves. The days of doubling up to save money are history.

Neuwirth is employed by Elektra as—what? It's often hard to find a job description for what Bob is doing at a given moment. At present, he's working with Paul, and Paul has bestowed a title on Bob. He is the "expediter," helping Paul and the Doors make the album that will be called *Waiting for the Sun*. Elektra is paying for Bob's room and board and a rented Ford Mustang. Expediting the Doors involves some babysitting of the band in their off-hours, and of Jim Morrison in particular, with an eye to curbing his drinking. This is an exercise that bears more than a passing resemblance to putting the fox in charge of the chicken coop.

Be that as it may, there's no question that Bob earns his keep. An impasse arises in the studio when Morrison wants to use a banjo on a particular song and the other Doors rebel. Jim wrote "My Wild Love Went Riding" with kind of a Celtic sound in mind. Why he believes that a banjo will help produce a Celtic sound he can't exactly explain, but no one in the group plays a banjo and his bandmates don't want anyone playing on the album except the four genuine Doors. Neuwirth offers an innovative solution. He suggests they do "My Wild Love" a capella, and the idea proves an inspiration. John Densmore, the drummer, makes a *tchhh-tch-tch-tchhhh* vocal sound to approximate brushes on a hi-hat. Ray Manzarek and Robby Krieger clap their hands, along with Neuwirth and Elektra's president, Jac Holzman. Listening to the track, it's hard to believe there are no musical instruments, but it's all done with voices and hands.

On the road, there are a lot of hours when Big Brother has nothing to do while the road manager is working full steam. When the band is recording, it's the other way around. Some road managers round up their bands every day and take them to the studio, but my campaign to get the members of Big Brother to take responsibility for themselves is paying off. In New York, I pointed out that it was silly for me to hail two cabs, ride with them to the studio, and sit there twiddling my thumbs. To their credit, the band agreed. They hailed their own cabs and got to the studio on their own.

In L.A., while Big Brother is contending with John Simon, I keep in touch with the office and up-to-date on the arrangements for future gigs. When my work is done, I try not to feel guilty about splashing in the Landmark pool. I hang out with Bobby and Paul when they're free. In the evenings I often go to see the Committee at the Tiffany Theater on Sunset. For music, there's the Troubadour on Santa Monica Boulevard, which is displacing the Ash Grove as L.A.'s premier folk club by virtue of the fact that the bar has become a favorite late-night hangout for rockers and actors.

Outside their long studio hours, Janis and the boys are alert for recreational opportunities. With our friends from the Committee as the catalyst, a party is organized on short notice for a weekend afternoon. Howard Hesseman and Carl Gottlieb have made the acquaintance of two charming young women who are house-sitting in Calabasas, over in the San Fernando Valley, for the singer John Davidson. This is the upscale part of the valley, where the lots are measured in acres and many residents have horses. Davidson's next-door neighbor on one side is Don Drysdale, the Dodgers' pitcher. Across the street is the movie director Don Siegel, who directed *The Invasion of the Body Snatchers* back in the fifties and is currently working on a film with Clint Eastwood.

The house-sitters, Jackie and Lorene by name, are taken with Howard and Carl, and vice versa. (Howard describes Jackie, with great enthusiasm, as a blond bombshell.) Howard and Carl have spent a few nights in Calabasas. Jackie and Lorene have met some of Howard and Carl's friends and find them fascinating. Why don't we have a party? they say. It's a big house. You can invite your friends.

Howard and Carl discuss this between themselves. Do these girls have any idea what they're letting themselves in for? "Are you sure you want to do this?" they ask the girls. "You really do want to do this?" "Yeah. Invite your friends."

There are many accounts of what happens at the party, on the day itself and long after. It gets under way in midafternoon. Janis is there, and Jim Morrison. That much is clear. Some other members of Big Brother and the Doors and the Committee. Many friends. Lots of people.

There are alcoholic beverages. We all bring some, and a wider selection is available after Jim Morrison smashes the glass door of Davidson's locked liquor cabinet. At some point, Howard's blond bombshell informs him that Morrison has thrown up on the cowhide rug in the rec room.

Janis, meantime, has found the pool table. When Morrison joins the game, the play gets lively. Pool isn't my thing and I'm elsewhere at the time. Music is my thing, but no one has brought instruments to this party, so I'm cruising the house and the grounds for interesting conversations and beguiling women. After the fracas, I get fragmentary accounts. It's like the police detective who interviews ten eyewitnesses to a crime and gets a dozen different stories.

Everyone agrees that Morrison offended Janis. He may have told her she can't sing the blues, which would be a mortal insult. He also did her some physical harm. By Howard's account, Jim took hold of Janis by the hair and pushed her facedown onto a coffee table. Others say the tussle started at the pool table. Either way, Janis ran from the room, crying, and locked herself in a bathroom. When she realized she wasn't seriously injured, the hurt was replaced by outrage. She emerged, found a bottle of whiskey, and tracked down Morrison. She broke the bottle over his head. Some say this happened outside; most agree it was inside. Garry Goodrow's old lady, Annie, insists that Janis threw the bottle across the pool table, while Garry, who was standing right next to Annie at the time, sides with those who say the bottle was in her hand when she hit Morrison with it.

Why would Jim Morrison provoke Janis? He's a bigger star—far bigger at this time. The Doors' first album, released more than a year ago, produced a smash hit single, "Light My Fire." The single and the album both went gold. The Doors' second album, *Strange Days*, is already out and *Waiting for the Sun* is in the wings, while Janis and Big Brother's output to date is limited to the year-old Mainstream album.

Morrison is a phenomenon in his own right, but maybe Janis's news-grabbing rise threatens him. Fuck you, Janis, I'm a bigger fucking star than you are. David Crosby, of the Byrds, has hung out with the drunk Morrison and he has formulated a theory: He thinks Jim is a masochist who gets drunk and stoned and picks a fight so he'll get beat up. If that's what he was after, Janis was ready to oblige.

As the sun lowers in the west, Howard and Carl have to leave because showtime for the Committee's evening performance is approaching. By now, it is abundantly clear to Jackie and Lorene that the proceedings are beyond their, or anyone else's, control. But what are we going to do? they plead with Howard and Carl. Are your friends leaving too?

Hey, it's a party, Howard says. I don't know, but I have to go to work.

Jackie follows them out to the driveway. As Howard and Carl beat their retreat, Jackie sees that the Drysdales are having a barbecue. The ruckus at the Davidson house is of another magnitude altogether, and there's a gaggle of Dodgers fans lined up at the Drysdales' fence, staring at what's unfolding next door.

ON AN AFTERNOON when John Simon doesn't need Janis in the studio, she and I take in a more sedate entertainment, a matinee of *2001: A Space Odyssey* at the Cinerama Dome on Sunset, which has the biggest screen in L.A., maybe the world, at this time. It's our first recreational outing together, just the two of us. We have a late brunch and early drinks at a nearby restaurant-bar before the show. Kahlua and cream instead of coffee, as I recall. At the Cinerama Dome we sit midway in the orchestra, on the aisle. *2001* is widely touted as a don't-miss visual trip, and it lives up to its reputation. When we get to the dazzling light show where the spaceship zooms headlong into the most eye-boggling special effect yet produced on film, a dazed hippie rises from his seat and staggers down the aisle, past Janis and me, his saucer eyes riveted on the careening images. He kneels on the plush red carpet right at the center of the screen, which has got to be eighty feet wide.

The curved Cinerama screen is made of vertical slats hung facing the audience, like a venetian blind set on edge, so the projected image reflects straight out and doesn't lose brightness at the edges. The hippie puts his arms *between* the vertical panels and hugs the screen.

Uh-oh, here comes the usher.

I figure he's going to give the hippie a hard time, but I've underestimated how far the prevailing ethic of the counterculture has spread. The usher puts a gentle hand on the hippie's shoulder and says, "Hey, man, it's only a movie." The hippie smiles beatifically and allows himself to be led back to his seat.

For all the film's visual pyrotechnics, it strikes Janis and me that the characters in the space-travel future are bland, two-dimensional, dull. They're squares. Only the apes in the opening sequence are spontaneous and alive to life's possibilities, most dramatically when they discover the potential of using bones as tools—and weapons.

After the movie, we repair to the same bar, where we agree over another round of drinks that we're living in a period of exploration and discovery with music as part of the motivating force, and we don't want it to lead to a future where the squares will be in charge of space travel.

THE CALIFORNIA PRESIDENTIAL primary takes place on the fourth of June. In the evening, as the returns start to come in, I follow them in my suite at the Landmark. Victory in California will clinch Bobby Kennedy's position as front-runner for the Democratic nomination. It's not that I'm unsympathetic to Gene McCarthy, who was first to challenge Lyndon Johnson back before RFK entered the race, but McCarthy is a one-issue candidate, campaigning against the war in Vietnam. He appeals mainly to the educated middle class and the more moderate elements of the counterculture. Minorities and the poor don't feel that he has any special empathy for their problems, while Kennedy attracts all the factions that supported his brother, and more, including passionate support from the disempowered.

A few weeks ago, Janis and Linda Gravenites saw Kennedy campaign in San Francisco. He was touring the neighborhoods, his route announced in advance. Janis and Linda and Janis's mixed-breed dog, George, moved out of the Haight in April, when we got back from New York. They're on Noe Street now, in Noe Valley, a neighborhood that borders the upper Mission district. When Janis learned that Kennedy's motorcade would pass just a few blocks from their apartment, she suggested they walk over to watch, and they got swept up in a vivid demonstration of Bobby's appeal. Engulfed in the mob of onlookers, they saw Kennedy standing in an open car, held upright by two strong aides to keep him from being pulled from the car by the eager hands that reached out to shake his as the car crept along Castro Street. At one point, Janis and Linda were lifted off their feet as the mob surged forward, but they emerged unharmed. Linda lost her shoes. They were affected by the emotional power of the crowd, and its palpable belief—the *need* to believe—that Kennedy could make a difference.

I have followed Bobby's California campaign. Even on TV, the effect of his presence is a phenomenon. His public appearances produce a quickening of the blood. The pundits think he might even carry Orange County, which is usually so right-wing that the ghost of Joseph Goebbels could be elected sheriff by acclamation. The people mob Bobby everywhere—in Oakland and Watts and in the fields where Cesar Chavez and his United Farm Workers labor. The crowds laugh at his jokes, and their eyes glow with hope. Maybe more hope than should ever be vested in one human being. The loss of Martin Luther King should have taught us that. Now, with King gone, all that hope is looking for somewhere to light, and it has settled on Bobby. We are all fallible, the Kennedys along with the rest of us, but I see in Bobby an awareness of his own fallibility. The self-deprecation that dominates his humor is real, and there's a sadness in his eyes that reveals a new depth of understanding.

South Dakota holds its primary on the same day as California. In one precinct on a Lakota Sioux reservation, Kennedy polls 878 votes against 2 for Johnson, who is still on the ballot because of the requirements of the voting laws, and none for McCarthy.

When I'm confident that Kennedy is headed for a convincing win, I leave the Landmark for the Tiffany Theater on Sunset. The Committee's barbed skepticism is a bracing reality check for anybody who lets himself get starry-eyed over a politician. Tonight I find the comedy elevating and I stay for both shows.

In addition to the familiar routines I know well, the Committee is performing in L.A. one I haven't seen in San Francisco. Here, as in the Committee Theater on Broadway by the Bay, the actors work on a bare stage with a few chairs that get moved around a lot, becoming the seats of a car, chairs in a doctor's waiting room, or whatever else the actors' imaginations conjure up. The back and sides of the stage accommodate six or eight doors through which the actors come and go.

In the piece that's new to me, the actors take a question from the audience, something serious, like "How do I avoid the draft?" or "How do I make peace with my parents?" and they improvise off it. There are two TV sets atop the framework that supports the doors, one at each side of the stage, facing the audience. For this routine only, the TVs are turned on, set to different channels, the sound off. The idea is that they tap into the cosmic synchronicity of events. If something on one of the TV screens strikes the fancy of the actors, they play off it. Often they ignore the TVs, but from the audience's point of view sometimes the juxtaposition of what's happening onstage with the images on TV is hilarious, sometimes it's bizarre, sometimes uncanny. The piece is a long-form improvisational exercise, one of the Committee's more existential routines, and they perform it only in the second show.

The election coverage is over and the networks have returned to late-night programming by the time the sets are turned on. There's a movie on one station and a talk show on the other. It's a little after midnight.

Partway through the piece, one of the networks interrupts the program in progress with a news bulletin. At this time, there are just the three networks and the educational channel and it's the Big Three that cover breaking news. The bulletin is from the Ambassador Hotel in downtown Los Angeles, where Bobby Kennedy's election head-quarters are located. The network reporter is in a large room with an empty podium on the dais in the background. The reporter's face is deadly serious and the people in view behind him, moving hither and yon, appear to be on the edge of panic. A crawl at the bottom of the screen says Robert Kennedy has been shot. . . .

One of the actors turns up the sound on the TV and we begin to piece together the story: McCarthy has conceded. Kennedy con-cluded his victory speech minutes ago and left the room to go through a kitchen pantry. . . . There are reports of shots fired . . . and Kennedy is wounded. . . . The other TV, the silent one, is still beaming out the regular program. Now the second TV goes blank mid-program and then displays a "Special News Bulletin" logo. . . . On comes a familiar news face.

For anyone who lived through John Kennedy's assassination, the report of shots fired at another Kennedy is a bad case of *déjà vu*.

The actors tried at first to play off the news report, but the pace of the routine faltered and it has come to a halt. Actors and audience alike stare at the images. After a while, the actors sit down, some onstage, some in the audience. . . . Kennedy has been taken to a hospital. . . . There is no report on his condition yet, but now we see news footage of the hotel pantry, where TV cameramen were present when the shots were fired. The images of Kennedy lying on the floor, people churning around him, some screaming to get back, give him air, are chilling.

With only fragmentary information, the reporters fill the void as best they can. The TVs replay Kennedy's victory speech, the rallying cry, "And now, on to Chicago!" and the scene in the pantry. The accused shooter is a strange little man, black-haired, black-eyed, glimpsed only briefly among the much larger forms of Rafer Johnson and Roosevelt Grier, two former football players in the Kennedy entourage who tackle the gunman.

In the Tiffany Theater, we watch the reports, audience and actors bound together by a real-life drama that renders the Committee's satires trivial by comparison. People begin to leave the theater by twos and threes, couples and groups first. Those who came by themselves stay longest, because once we go out the door onto the Sunset Strip we will be alone again, with no one to share what we're feeling.

The prospect of returning to the Landmark to watch TV, waiting to see if Kennedy will die, is bleak. If Janis and the boys are out, or if they don't share my reaction to the shooting . . .

I want to be with someone who shares my perspective on everything that makes this election year so fraught: the civil-rights struggle, the sense that the transition from Eisenhower's presidency to Jack Kennedy's really did mark the passing of the torch to a new generation that heeds and represents ours better than the one before, and Vietnam looming above everything else. I want to be with an old friend.

I wish Mimi Fariña were in the Committee's L.A. company, and then I remember that Judy Collins is living in L.A., in a rented house on Mulholland Drive.

I've known Judy since the first time she played at the Club 47 in Cambridge. Judy and the Charles River Valley Boys have appeared together at the Newport Folk Festival and on other stages. Her label is Elektra, which connects us further. Judy and I became friends, and, when the stars were right, occasional lovers.

I phone Judy and she answers. Yes, she says, please come over. Her young son, Clark, has gone to sleep and she would welcome my company for all the same reasons I am feeling.

Through the night there is nothing on the networks except the Kennedy story. Hospital spokesmen give updates that repeat each other. Kennedy's condition is critical. No change, nothing to report. When Judy can't keep her eyes open any longer and retires to her bedroom, I watch the TV in her home office, where there's a daybed, hoping with every replay of Bobby's victory speech that it will end another way—this time he won't go into the hotel pantry, or this time the little guy with the black hair and beady eyes will miss.

Judy has been keeping company with the writer Michael Thomas, whom I've met several times, and that relationship is among the reasons that Judy and I sleep apart on this night. Even so, I wonder later that I, or we, didn't seek mutual comfort in the closeness of sharing a bed, with or without following the reproductive impulse that rises so urgently in the face of death.

At some point during the night I turn off the TV and sleep for a few hours. In the morning, Kennedy's condition is officially unchanged, but the faces of the doctors and the campaign spokesmen who address the news crews at the hospital are grim.

When Jack Kennedy was killed in Dallas, I didn't eat for twenty-four hours. I'm experiencing the same suspension of hunger now. At midmorning I go back to the Landmark to check in with the band. They are not as affected by the shooting as they were by the news about Martin Luther King. Kennedy is a politician. King was a crusader working outside the power structure, which gave him in their eyes a moral stature no politician can attain.

The next morning, we hear the news: In the middle of the night, twenty-five hours after he was shot, Robert Francis Kennedy gave up the ghost.

MUCH LATER, I learn that my father was in Los Angeles, in the Ambassador Hotel, covering the campaign, and witnessed the calamity in the fateful pantry. I wish I had known, and that I could somehow have gotten in touch with him. His reporter's experience of momentous events—from the abdication of Edward VIII through the Second World War and the first Kennedy assassination—might have given me some historical perspective, helped me to take a couple of steps back from the moment, to soften the blow. He was in Los Angeles to report on the California primary for the *Guardian*. His weekly *Letter from America* for the BBC this week, written the day after Kennedy died and recorded the following day, was one of the most moving that he ever wrote. In it, he fixed an image of the chaos in the hotel pantry that is indelible: "There was a head on the floor streaming blood, and somebody put a Kennedy boater under it, and the blood trickled down the sides like chocolate sauce on an iced cake. There were splashes of flashbulbs, and infernal heat, and the button eyes of Ethel Kennedy turned to cinders. She was wrestling or slapping a young man and he was saying 'Listen, lady, I'm hurt, too.' And then she was on her knees cradling him briefly, and in another little pool of light on the greasy floor was a huddle of clothes and staring out of it the face of Bobby Kennedy, like the stone face of a child's effigy on a cathedral tomb."

Joe Jr. didn't make it out of his downed plane, Jack didn't turn his head at the right moment to avoid the fatal shots in Dallas, Bobby took a shortcut through a hotel pantry to bypass the crush of reporters. . . . Isn't it time one of Joe and Rose Kennedy's boys got lucky?

In November 1963, I flew from Boston to Washington to shuffle overnight in a line six people wide and a mile long as it made its way like some sorrowful caterpillar toward the Capitol, where JFK's closed casket lay in state. As I came out the other side and saw the first streaks of dawn in the gray-red sky, the man beside me shook my hand and said, "I'm proud to have walked with you."

I find now that I'm more affected by losing Bobby. Janis and the boys make no objection when I announce that I'm going to New York for a couple of days.

I take a red-eye flight, arrive at dawn, take a taxi to Manhattan and stand in a line of thoughtful and silent people to go through St. Patrick's Cathedral on Fifth Avenue, where the closed casket of the junior senator from New York rests on display.

I recognize Theodore Sorensen alone on the steps of the church, unnoticed by the passersby. Sorensen ghost-wrote JFK's book *Profiles in Courage*, and he wrote speeches for Jack as president. He counseled Bobby against challenging Gene McCarthy in the primaries, but when Bobby announced his candidacy, Sorensen left a lucrative law practice to join the campaign.

The next day, my mother and I watch on television in her apartment on 72nd Street as the train carries Bobby's casket to Washington past the mourners who line the tracks all along the two-hundred-mile route. It's an extraordinary sight—police and military men standing to attention and saluting as the train passes, ordinary citizens silent beside the tracks. Some remove their hats as the train passes. Many are weeping. As in the aftermath of Jack Kennedy's death, and Martin Luther King's, I find that the visible grief of others evokes the strongest emotions in me.

When Bobby is in the ground at Arlington beside Jack, I fly back to L.A. On the evening of my return I go to the Troubadour to hear Joni Mitchell and seek some kindred souls. I find Chip Monck sitting with a tableful of friends. When Joni sings "Both Sides Now," the beauty of her voice and the song penetrate the last of my reserves and I lose it completely, weeping freely, with Chip's arm around my shoulders, until the song is over.

CHAPTER TWELVE

Cheap Thrills

THE ALBUM IS lurching toward completion. Finishing each song is a struggle for the band. In the final days, Janis and Sam and the Columbia engineer spend a marathon thirty-six hours in the studio working on what they hope will be the final mix. A day and a half with no sleep and not much to eat. When they step out onto Sunset Boulevard at last, they feel like time travelers.

John Simon revises the mix in ways that strike the band as bizarre when they hear his proposed version of the album. One song ends abruptly in the middle of a chord, as if it had been cut off by accident. The band pushes for changes. In the contract with Columbia, Albert has secured for Big Brother the right of approval on the album, so their requests are more than just requests. John Simon quits the project. He will insist that his name not appear on the album and, much later, he will regret this decision.

Big Brother works on the mix with co-producer Elliot Mazer, but our time in L.A. is up. We have gigs to play, starting with a long weekend for Bill Graham at the Fillmore and Winterland in San Francisco.

"John Simon and I talked in the last few years. I had several conversations with him on the phone, and he said some interesting
things. He kind of apologized. It was a kind of an apology, in effect, that he really felt he had an attitude. He was specifically
sorry, he said, that he hadn't put his name on the *Cheap Thrills*
album. . . . And he said, 'You know, I really had an attitude about
you guys, and I really regret that now. And I listen to *Cheap Thrills*
now and I think it was better than I thought it was at the time.'"

David Getz

In the five weeks that remain before we return to the East, we're
booked to play ten days in San Francisco and a smattering of gigs
around the Bay. At the end of June we'll play in Denver for the Family Dog, our only trip outside California during two and a half
months of touring the Golden State.

JUNE 13–16, 1968: Fillmore and Winterland, S.F.

JUNE 22–23: Carousel Ballroom

JUNE 24: Burlingame Country Club

JUNE 28–29: Family Dog, Denver

JULY 5: Concord, Calif.

JULY 6: Santa Rosa Fairgrounds

JULY 7: Golden Gate Park, free concert

JULY 12–13: Kaleidoscope, L.A.

JULY 16–18: "Carousel at Fillmore," Fillmore West

The mood in San Francisco this summer is a far cry from the
flower child optimism of a year ago. Music, love, and flowers it ain't.
Within the counterculture, even those who have little political
awareness are affected by the lingering bummer of the two assassi-
nations. Before Martin Luther King was killed, many blacks, especially the young, were turning away from his philosophy of
nonviolence to support the more confrontational tactics advocated by

young militants like Huey Newton, Bobby Seale, and Stokely Carmichael. With King gone, the traditional civil-rights establishment is in disarray. Black power and the Black Panthers are attracting more supporters.

I follow the dramatically redrawn presidential race on the evening news before I venture out on the town or across the Bay to Berserkeley. Most of Bobby Kennedy's supporters are turning to Gene McCarthy, but the energy—the *belief*—isn't there. Gene no longer looks like the man to steal the Democratic nomination from Lyndon Johnson's designated successor, Vice President Hubert Humphrey. McCarthy doesn't seem to have the heart for an all-out fight, and RFK's victories in four out of the five primaries where he challenged McCarthy have revealed the limits of McCarthy's support.

And Humphrey! Humphrey was a tub-thumping liberal in his Senate days, when he was dubbed "the Happy Warrior." He gave a courageous speech on civil rights at the 1948 Democratic convention, but in Lyndon Johnson's service Humphrey has become a waffling toady on Vietnam. Even now that LBJ is a lame duck, Hubert won't speak out against Johnson's policies.

On the Republican side, Richard Nixon, of all people, is cleaning up in the primaries. "You won't have Nixon to kick around anymore," he told the press corps after his failed bid to become governor of California, back in '62. Son of a bitch won't keep a promise.

The prospects are depressing. I watch the news less and visit friends in Berkeley more often. I focus on my job. Our next eastern tour is coming up. There are travel arrangements to be made, gigs to confirm with Janis and the band. Janis doesn't want to sing more than three nights in a row, four at most. It's hard on her voice. She has pleaded with Albert to balance the performance dates with days of rest. Others in the office, those handling the day-to-day business, have a habit of calling to say, "When you're in Buffalo, we can add a gig in Syracuse and another in Albany," and suddenly there are five nights in a row on the itinerary. It has become part of my job to help protect Janis's vocal cords.

Big Brother's long weekend for Bill Graham in mid-June coincides, on the Sunday, with an event the Committee bills as the Second Thelonious Monk Memorial Satirathon, a comedy festival in which the company, including members emeritus and unofficial, recalled from afar, will perform starting at 9:00 P.M., when the summer dusk still glows over the Golden Gate, and continue through the night to daylight at the other end. Paul Rothchild gets wind of the event and persuades Jac Holzman to let him record the audio for a possible LP. Paul recruits Bob Neuwirth to be his—what else—hipness advisor, and enlists me to shoot photos for the album jacket and insert. I've been taking photographs since my father gave me a Kodak Brownie while I was still in grade school, more seriously since I learned to develop and print my own film at the Putney School. My first thematic project was shooting the modern dance class in rehearsals and performance. Girls in leotards were the initial motivation. In Cambridge and at the Newport Folk Festivals I have shot folk musicians young and old. On the road with Big Brother, I've been taking pictures of Janis and the boys.

Big Brother's weekend is something of a marathon itself: Thursday at the Fillmore, Friday and Saturday at Winterland, and back at the Fillmore on Sunday for a benefit for the Matrix, the San Francisco club where Jefferson Airplane got their start and where Big Brother played often, when the developing San Francisco scene was still a local secret. I'm on the job until after Big Brother's Sunday set at the Fillmore, and I spend the rest of the night at the Committee. I shoot enough pictures to get at least one good image of each member of the regular company and most of the guest performers. In the end, Elektra elects not to put out an album, but the Satirathon remains in memory as the kind of onetime San Francisco event that made the late sixties an ongoing celebration of the arts.

When Big Brother receives the final mix of the album from Elliot Mazer, we find that he has spliced to the head of band 1, side A, live sound recorded in March at Winterland, full of kids, the band tuning up, and Bill Graham's voice introducing Big Brother: "Four gentlemen and one great, great broad, Big Brother and the Holding Company." With that, Janis hits the scratcher to kick off "Combination of the Two." It's an effective beginning. Elsewhere, Mazer has mixed in live sound from several sources including Barney's Beanery, a Santa Monica Boulevard restaurant-bar-and-pool-hall where Warner Brothers mogul Jack Warner used to eat in anonymity with his mistress during Hollywood's glamour days. In the glamour days of rock, Barney's is Janis's favorite L.A. hangout.

The results of Mazer's editing and mixing create a credible impression of a "live" album. The band's reactions to the end product are cautiously optimistic, and they're tickled pink by the cover illustration, which is by the underground comic artist R. Crumb.

Big Brother constitutes a self-appointed chapter of the R. Crumb fan club. Initially, Columbia proposed for the album cover a photograph of the five of them in bed in the bedroom of a San Francisco hippie pad. The picture was shot in a photo studio, where Janis and the boys rearranged the prepared props with abandon, creating their own idea of an authentic hippie bedroom before jumping into bed together, all naked. The guys, being guys, are "decent" in the photo, since only their chests are exposed. Janis's chest is also exposed. It's a cheerful image without a hint of sexual innuendo, but Columbia balked at a topless Janis.

The band's counterproposal was asking R. Crumb to do the cover. Crumb is widely known in the counterculture for, among other things, a wonderful multipanel strip illustrating the classic blues line, "Keep on truckin', Mama, truckin' my blues away." For Big Brother's album, Crumb has produced a riotous circular comic strip, the panels spiraling out from the center, where Janis, barefoot in a prison-striped dress, is slogging across a desert under the gaze of a smiling, merciless sun, with a ball and chain attached to her ankle. For this masterpiece, Columbia pays Crumb a pittance, and no royalties.

The album's title is a compromise. Somewhere along the road to fame, the phrase "dope, sex, and cheap thrills" has become Big Brother's unofficial motto. They proposed it for the album title. Columbia was understandably reluctant to plaster an advertisement for dope and sex across the nation's music magazines and about a million record labels, if all goes according to plan. Gingerly, Clive Davis and his execs approved *Cheap Thrills*.

When I see the cover for the first time, I am struck by the lower left-hand panel, which shows James Gurley against a backdrop of purple mountains' majesty. The cartoon James has a single eye centered in his forehead and he's puffing on a joint. A golden halo hovers over his head. It brings to mind a night in New York during the winter tour, when I was well lit at Max's Kansas City. James's name came up in conversation and I felt compelled to phone him in his room at the Chelsea. I woke him from a sound sleep to inform him that he is the son of God. I spent a good deal of time and energy convincing him I was serious in this pronouncement, but James took it calmly, as if I had belatedly recognized what was already an acknowledged fact. Since then, this has become a running joke between us. Now I find that *Crumb sees him the same way!* You mean it wasn't just the booze?

We play the Family Dog in Denver, then fly back to California for a flurry of gigs around the Bay, including a free concert in Golden Gate Park, a weekend at Kaleidoscope in L.A., and three days in the brand-new Fillmore West for Bill Graham, who has recently taken over and rechristened the Carousel ballroom. Two days later, we're eastbound, with an intermediate stop in Salt Lake City. We play an afternoon gig in nearby Ogden, across the street from an amusement park that has an airplane ride where you can actually steer the airplanes, somewhat, as they swing around a pylon at the end of steel cables. After the sound check at the gig, we undergo flight training. Peter Albin and I are the most maniacal of the student pilots. Left rudder and *up* she goes. When we get the hang of it, we can take the planes through dives and climbs that set the support cables thwacking against their bolts.

The day after we arrive in New York, we play the Westbury Music Fair on Long Island, just outside New York, for $3,500 plus 50 percent of the gross over $9,000, the house scaled to a potential gross of no less than $25,000. I am no longer carrying cash home in a brown paper bag.

Albert travels with us for the first time when we fly to San Juan, Puerto Rico, for Columbia Records' annual convention. The Columbia bigwigs have heard *Cheap Thrills* and they are genuinely thrilled. In exactly one week, the album will be in the stores. Scuttlebutt at the convention says it will be huge. Clive Davis divides his time between Big Brother and Blood, Sweat and Tears, doing his best to keep his stars happy.

Albert stays close to Janis, shepherding her through brief chats with important salesmen and head-office apparatchiks. This kind of pressing the flesh is new to her, but she is dazzled by the attention and does her best to smile and be polite. At the convention, more than ever, the forces dividing Janis from the boys are plainly visible. It is Janis that Clive Davis and the Columbia functionaries fawn over, while Sam and James and David and Peter hang out with musicians from the other bands.

Janis is dazzled as well by the performance of Blood, Sweat and Tears at the dinner show on the last night of the convention. The band that Al Kooper founded less than a year ago has bitten the hand that gave it birth. Al has been forced out of the group. He has been replaced by singer David Clayton Thomas. Thomas has a strong voice and he knows how to use it. Behind him, the band is tight. Kooper's influence is still audible, especially in the horn section, which has Janis's full attention. As early as last year, she broached with Big

Brother the idea of adding horns to the band, and maybe a keyboard. Their response was split along the customary lines, Sam and David willing to try, James and Peter opposed.

Big Brother's performance at the Columbia convention is joyously received. It's only average, but they're playing for the choir.

In the fifties, most major record labels shunned rock and roll. Elvis, Jerry Lee Lewis, Roy Orbison and Carl Perkins got their start at Sun Records in Memphis. Elvis became the exception to the rule when RCA bought his contract, but rock and roll was widely denounced as a threat to American teens, a new socioeconomic group with the power to define trends in popular music because in the 1950s, for the first time, they had the money to *buy* popular music. White parents and politicians tried to protect white kids from rock and roll by branding it "jungle music" and other, more blatantly racist terms. These efforts helped rock and roll become the music of young rebellion against the staid conservatism of the Eisenhower years. Now, a decade later, one big label after another is recognizing the potential of rock, and the competition to cash in on the top acts is fierce. At the Columbia convention in Puerto Rico, the suits and ties celebrate their shaggy saviors with the fervor of newly baptized converts.

After the show, in the hotel bar, Janis is bubbly at the prospect of finally having a record that will knock the Mainstream album off the shelves. Irrepressible, full of good cheer, she flirts with Albert. It's her customary testing routine, long postponed in Albert's case, until Janis is sure he won't take it amiss. Her come-on is more subtle than is her custom when sounding out a possible sex partner, but subtlety is not Janis's strong suit. What it comes down to is, Hey, maybe we should go to bed to celebrate. She leaves it up to Albert to decide if the proposition is serious. Albert is both flattered and amused. He flashes his best smile, which shines all the more brightly for being reserved for special occasions. "I couldn't possibly do that," he says. "If it didn't turn out that I was great, you wouldn't respect me in the morning."

Janis cracks up. It's the perfect response, disarming and delighting her at the same time.

The next morning, we're airborne, headed back to the mainland for the Newport Folk Festival, already in progress.

There couldn't be a greater contrast between the intently focused commercialism of the Columbia convention and the vigilant anti-commercialism of Newport. In Cambridge, we scorned the "commercial" folk acts, the guy duos and trios, the brother groups that smoothed out the mountain harmonies and made the songs sound like pop music. Newport has admitted some of the folk-pop groups because they're known to the wider audience. Bring them in with the Kingston Trio and expose them to the authentic stuff. Peter, Paul and Mary are regular fixtures at Newport. They helped boost Dylan's career, and they're Albert's act.

Big Brother and the Holding Company is a different matter. Have the walls of Jericho fallen? Has the nation's premier folk music gathering capitulated to the San Francisco Sound? Not by a long shot. Big Brother is one of just two rock acts on the lengthy list of performers, and the band's appearance has come about more through connections on the folk circuit than because of Janis's sudden prominence. Albert Grossman co-produced the festival in its first year. Since then he hasn't had an organizational role, but he has been present for each festival as the manager of important folk acts. And Albert may not be the only one who urged Newport promoter George Wein to hire Big Brother. Also on the bill this summer is Kenneth Threadgill, a Texas singer and club owner, who hired Janis to play in his Austin filling-station bar back in 1962. Threadgill and Wein have a friend in common, Rod Kennedy, who runs the Longhorn Jazz Festival. Through Kennedy, Threadgill has put in a good word for Janis.

Two years ago, the festival board almost rejected the Lovin' Spoonful for being "too pop," but the Spoonful's founder, John Sebastian, was a stalwart of the Greenwich Village folk scene and his traditional roots were impeccable. He was a soulful harmonica sideman who had played and recorded with many folk performers. Last summer, Buffalo Springfield was admitted to Newport because "For What It's Worth" was a protest song.

As these exceptions suggest, the Folk Mafia—the old-guard folkies on the Newport festival board—are often of two minds. They don't want to compromise the festival's standards just to sell more tickets by putting pop-rock performers on the program. But they like to make money to attract the top rank of folk and traditional performers, and acts like the Spoonful and Buffalo Springfield bring in the kids, no question.

For Janis and Big Brother, the board has a simple rationale that makes the decision easier: The blues have been a mainstay of the festival since its earliest days. This year's Newport program booklet points out that Janis "is considered by many the finest white blues singer today." The board members know that Janis is a devotee of Bessie Smith, but that may not have fully prepared them for "Ball and Chain."

The rest of the program is a typical Newport mix. This year, along with festival stalwarts like Pete Seeger and Theo Bikel, Big Brother shares the bill with Joan Baez, Jean Ritchie, Ramblin' Jack Elliott, Arlo Guthrie (Woody's son), Taj Mahal, Richie Havens, the Kweskin Jug Band, Doc Watson, the Almanac Singers, and Cambridge's Eric von Schmidt, an early mentor of young Bobby Dylan. The urban blues are represented by B. B. King, the Paul Butterfield Blues Band, and the Junior Wells Band with Buddy Guy on lead guitar. Ralph Stanley and the Clinch Mountain Boys are the sole bluegrass act this year. Almost hidden away in the program there are some interesting anomalies: Kaleidoscope, an electrified band from L.A. that's influenced by Middle Eastern music, and Buck Owens, a full-bore country music star.

Newport is a prestige gig, not a lucrative one. Bob Dylan's fee at the '65 festival, where he famously "went electric," was $100. This year, B. B. King is getting $1,000. So is Roy Acuff, a country star of an earlier generation, closely rooted in the Appalachian traditions. Ken Threadgill's band will receive $400, plus travel expenses (they drove from Austin). Big Brother's take is just $250, but the festival is also paying for our rooms at the Viking Hotel downtown, long the preferred lodging for the folk in-crowd, and it's covering our rental car. Add it all up, and Big Brother is paid more than any other act on the program.

Janis and Ken Threadgill have a happy reunion, and Janis reconnects with some acquaintances from the San Francisco ballrooms. In her first year with Big Brother, they played a bill at the Avalon with the Jim Kweskin Jug Band from Cambridge. Geoff Muldaur, the Jug Band's blues vocalist, clarinetist, and washboard rhythm king, is Cambridge's reigning authority on the blues and an exacting critic of blues practitioners, instrumental and vocal. Somewhat to my surprise he has judged Janis's singing worthy.*

At Newport, Janis and Geoff fall in together one evening and pass up a late-evening blues jam in favor of a smaller gathering where Jean Ritchie, one of Janis's earliest influences, is singing informally in one of the big mansions where the festival puts up performers like teenagers at summer camp. Janis sits at Ritchie's feet and listens reverently to her southern Appalachian ballads, and Geoff's respect for Janis ramps up a notch.

Being back at Newport is like a weekend holiday for me. Newport has been a high point of midsummer since my first festival, in 1960. I have only missed one since then, when I was in California chasing the Wrong Girl. This year, I am saddened to learn from my Cambridge friends that the Club 47 closed two months ago because it can

---

*Geoff remembers Janis warmly and speaks of her kindly. "She was heartfelt," is the way he put it to me. "It worked. She didn't ever have these heavyweight musicians or anything with her. It was all about her. So she was out there doing it. It was rock and roll. And it was okay." From Geoff, this is not a backhanded compliment, it's real praise.

no longer afford the kind of acts that made it famous. (The demise of the 47 is a sign of changing times, and a portent for the San Francisco ballrooms.)

I'm walking with Janis backstage on Saturday afternoon when I see an old friend approaching. I intercept her and introduce them.

"Janis, this is Joan. Joanie, Janis."

Neither has the first idea what to say, and for the life of me I can't think of a way to bridge the gap. They are incompatible elements, forces that exist in different realms. If Joan Baez is water, Janis is fire. For Joan, Newport is home. For Janis, it's a continent away from San Francisco, the city that has made her feel truly at home for the first time in her life.

They exchange a few awkward words and Joan moves along, but Joan and Janis have more in common than the discomfiting lack of a common language suggests. Joan was the first superstar of the folk revival. Janis is on her way to becoming the first female superstar in rock. For Joan the first Newport Folk Festival, in 1959, was the same kind of launching pad that Monterey provided for Janis just a year ago, and Albert Grossman played a role in creating those opportunities for each of these uniquely talented women.

In the summer of 1959, when he helped George Wein organize the first Newport Folk Festival, Albert was running the Gate of Horn, a small but influential folk club he had established in Chicago a few years earlier. Wein had founded the Newport Jazz Festival in 1954, and he responded positively to a suggestion by Grossman that they trade on the jazz festival's rising reputation to start an annual folk festival in the same venue.

Through the folk grapevine Albert heard reports about the long-haired girl in Cambridge with the amazing voice. He invited Joan to appear at the Gate of Horn for two weeks in July, before Newport. Joan first declined, then reconsidered and accepted. When Albert heard Joan in person and learned that she had no professional representation, he expressed interest in managing her. Joan didn't fully trust Albert, but she recognized his good qualities as well as the self-interested ones. A rising star at the Gate of Horn was Bob Gibson, a handsome folkie with a self-assured stage manner who played the twelve-string guitar. Joan developed a crush on Gibson. When he asked her to appear at the first Newport Folk Festival as his guest, she said yes. In front of ten thousand folk fans, Joan rose to the occasion in her duets with Gibson. The response of the public and the press to her Newport appearance was a revelation, and on the basis of that experience, Joan committed her life to music.

Albert held out the lure of a recording contract with Columbia Records, but Joan turned down both Columbia and Albert's interest in managing her. Instead, she settled on Boston's Manny Greenhill for management and Maynard Solomon's Vanguard Records in New York as her record company. Greenhill was a lefty of the between-the-wars folk school, a benign man with a pleasantly craggy face whose modest, what-you-see-is-what-you-get personal manner couldn't have been farther removed from Albert's opaque style. Vanguard was a small label, unpretentious, although much respected for its classical recordings, virtually a two-man company, founded by Maynard Solomon and his brother. Manny's and Maynard's laid-back styles suited Joan far better than Albert's grand promises that she could have whatever—or whoever—she wanted in all the world.

For Janis, the decision to go with Albert was less fraught with indecision.

On Saturday evening at Newport, Big Brother does a good job of summoning up the ballroom magic in front of a receptive crowd. The music is strong enough that I want to get to a better vantage point so I can see the band from out front and feel the reactions of the audience. Moving through the backstage compound, I run into Albert. "If you want to know what it's like when the magic works, this is it," I tell him. I'm proud of the band, and glad that Albert is hearing them play well, but Albert is less enthusiastic. "Hey," he says, "it's got to be better than that."

To a greater extent than I have revealed to Janis and the boys, I am a fan of Big Brother and the Holding Company. I want them to succeed, because I believe in their magic. I think Albert is too analytical about the band's music. If he won't open himself to the magic, he'll never get what Big Brother is about. From this brief exchange at Newport, and probably from the general tenor of my reports from the road, Albert knows that I am not an objective judge of the band, that I don't evaluate their performances by the same criteria he applies. Albert doesn't need advice from fans. He wants the opinions of skeptics. In the conversations between him and the members of the band that take place after their performance at Newport, Albert doesn't consult me further.

Soon after Big Brother comes offstage, Peter Albin encounters Albert in one of the tents set up backstage for the performers. Albert shakes his head. "I'd like to say it was a good show, but I don't know, it just wasn't happening."

This is not what Peter wants to hear. Like me, Peter felt the set went well and he's still riding the high. Albert is bringing him down. Peter asks if they can talk about it later. Come to my room tomorrow morning, Albert says.

Sunday is a day of rest before we head back to New York and a month of airplanes, rental cars, and Midwest motels. Peter presents himself at Albert's room in the Viking Hotel at the appointed time. He is ushered in by Sally, Albert's wife. Once they're settled, Albert says, "Something's just not happening. I don't know, I guess maybe it's the San Francisco Sound that I'm just not into, but I'm used to things where the rhythm is really tight and it's all together."

This is Albert's third attempt at encouraging some kind of progress toward solving what he perceives as Big Brother's technical problems, their unevenness, the lack of consistency. The band didn't accept his request that James should be replaced, made at the Golden Bear. They haven't tried switching Sam to the bass and Peter to guitar, as Albert proposed after the recording at the Grande Ballroom. Albert has pointed to what he sees as the shortcomings and he has suggested remedies. At Newport, he speaks to David Getz as well as Peter about the rhythm section, but they offer no alternative solutions.

Within days after we return to New York, Janis calls a band meeting in her room at the Chelsea Hotel and announces that she is leaving Big Brother.

CHAPTER THIRTEEN

Downtown Nowhere

EVEN BEFORE NEWPORT, Janis was facing a decision she couldn't put off for long. In Big Brother, she is one of four vocalists. Sam, Peter, and James each sing lead on one or more of the group's songs. Janis is the lead vocalist, but she shares the spotlight with her bandmates. In the summer of 1968, a year after Monterey, her rising renown offers her a new possibility. It is something she dreamed long before Big Brother, a fantasy then. Now it might be a reality. She can claim center stage for her own, sharing the spotlight with no one.

> "I love those guys more than anybody else in the whole world. They know that. But if I had any serious ideas of myself as a musician, I had to leave. . . . We worked four, six nights a week for two years doing the same tunes, and we'd put everything into them we could. We just used each other up. . . . I wasn't doing anything but standing still and being a success."
>
> **Janis Joplin**

Janis has dreaded telling the boys she has decided to leave the band. She knows her decision will hurt Sam and James and Peter and

Dave. She knows she will be criticized. She knows she might fail. But if she doesn't make the attempt, she will never know if she has what it takes to succeed on her own.

For Sam, Janis's announcement comes as no surprise. Janis told him of her decision before Newport, and she asked him to come with her in the new band she would form. At the meeting in the Chelsea, Sam senses something in her tone that makes him suspect Janis has changed her mind.

Peter takes the news badly, erupting in anger that doesn't mask the fear sparked by the sudden collapse of his world. Dave Getz realizes that this is something he has almost been expecting.

> "I think from Monterey on, early '68 on, we all began to sense that there was the possibility that Janis would quit at some point. . . . Although it was never verbalized, never talked about. No one wanted—it was unthinkable, but I think everybody had it on their minds."
>
> **David Getz**

When the others leave, Sam stays behind, and Janis says, "I don't want you to come with me either, Sam."

"Big Bother and the Folding Company" isn't funny anymore.

Soon after the band meeting, Janis takes me aside and asks me to stay as her road manager when her new band is formed. To me, Janis's reasons are self-evident and inescapable. Staying with Big Brother is easy. Leaving them is much harder. Janis has chosen the more difficult course, the greater challenge.

My choice is easier than hers. Without Janis, there's no certainty that Big Brother will continue to perform.

The band's bookings extend through November. Janis will stay until these obligations have been fulfilled. At first it's awkward, but the routines of the road are familiar. After a while it's possible for

Janis and the boys to continue as before, living in the Now of air-planes, rental cars, hotels, and gigs.

AUG. 2–3, 1968: **Fillmore East**

AUG. 9: **Kiel Auditorium, St. Louis**

AUG. 14: **Indiana Beach, Monticello, Ind.**

AUG. 16–17: **Aragon Ballroom/Cheetah, Chicago**

AUG. 18: **Tyrone Guthrie Theater, Minneapolis**

AUG. 23: **Singer Bowl, Queens, N.Y.**

A few days after Newport, we play the Fillmore East again, this time with the Staple Singers and Ten Years After. As the kids stream into the house, I spy Albert's partner, Bert Block, standing at the back of the hall with a middle-aged guy in a suit. Bert's an old hand in the music business. Tall, slightly stooped, bald on top, with a broad smile, he was a drummer and band leader in the big band era, an agent who had his own booking agency before he joined Albert to replace departing partner John Court. Since Bert came aboard, I've had frequent dealings with him about bookings and the day-to-day details of Big Brother's schedule. "Hey, John!" he calls to me. "Come over here. I want you to meet somebody. John Cooke, Benny Goodman."

I manage a handshake with the guy in the suit and mumble some inanity. What I may know, from seeing *The Benny Goodman Story*, but don't have foremost in mind at this moment, is that in his day Goodman was as much a rebel as the San Francisco rockers of the sixties. He didn't care about the waltzes and foxtrots that were con-sidered respectable for white audiences. Goodman wanted to play what the black bands were playing. He broke the color barrier. He was the first bandleader to have an integrated band. He performed and recorded with black musicians. With Teddy Wilson on piano and Lionel Hampton on vibes, he started a revolution. Now Benny Goodman is in the Fillmore East in a suit and tie, looking like a businessman, because his daughter has the hots for Janis and Big Brother.

Janis sings the gospel song "Down by the Riverside" with Mavis Staples in a duet that brings down the house. After the show, Bert Block escorts Benny Goodman and his daughter backstage. Goodman *fille* meets Janis and gets the thrill of her life. What Goodman *père* thinks of the evening's entertainment is later related by Bert to his wife, Barbara Carroll, a noted jazz pianist and vocalist.* "Janis, in her inimitable obscenity, shocked the pants off Benny Goodman," Barbara told me. "Because Benny was kind of a straightlaced guy, and his daughter was a young girl, and for Benny to hear this in front of his daughter, or for his daughter to hear this—it was all kind of a 'moment to be treasured,' as Bert described it."

We face a spate of gigs in the Midwest before we can look forward to some time in California.

Janis's decision not to take Sam with her doesn't end their friendship. As we travel from city to city he helps her think about her new band. "You know who you should get to go with you?" he says. "Jerry Miller, from Moby Grape. He's one of the finest guitar players I've ever heard. He's got a good sound." After a couple more gigs, Janis tells Sam, "Let's get Jerry Miller and you to come along with me." Sam is back on board, and that's the way it stays.

Sam is a link to the past, to Big Brother, to the band and the city that embraced Janis and made her feel at home. Janis and Sam write songs together and they sing together. This is a connection Janis needs. It's too hard to cut at once all the ties that bind.

Peter and David and James didn't know they almost lost Sam at the outset, so the news that he'll go with Janis comes as an unwelcome aftershock. James, being James, accepts it as part of the cosmic inevitability. Peter and David express degrees of anger and resentment

---

*In the late forties, Carroll's trio worked briefly with Goodman's orchestra.

before the demands of touring and playing together paper over the disruption.

Cheap Thrills is released and it shoots up the charts. It goes gold in three days. The satisfaction Big Brother takes from the album's success is bittersweet.

As WORD OF Janis's defection spreads among Big Brother's fans in San Francisco, the consensus that coalesces is that Janis has betrayed Big Brother. Many see Albert Grossman as a Svengali who has pulled Janis away from the band, motivated by nothing but money.

These facile conclusions overlook Janis's strength of will and Albert's dedication to his artists. Albert understands what Big Brother means to Janis and what she owes them. Three times he tried to reconfigure the band to strengthen the music, but the band rejected each of his suggestions. Like Pennebaker, Albert recognizes that Janis is the incomparable element in the band, and his primary dedication is to her. His discomfort with the status quo has become evident to Janis and the implication is clear, even if he never states it explicitly: So long as she remains with Big Brother, she can't know how far she might go as a singer.

> "See, Albert deals in sensible things. . . . The artist is the magic, you dig? I learned that a long time ago. And it's sensible to realize that without Janis, Big Brother was just another band. It was sensible to think that."
>
> **Nick Gravenites**

And if Albert ever did articulate the choice frankly, his view didn't dictate Janis's decision. The most succinct refutation of Albert as Svengali comes from Sam Andrew, looking back on these events long after the fact. He framed it as a rhetorical question: "Can you imagine anyone making Janis do something she didn't want to do?"*

> "[Albert] doesn't direct me. He just finds out where I want to go, then he helps me get there."
>
> **Janis Joplin**

All the same, when we return to San Francisco before the Labor Day weekend, the boys take some comfort in the condolences offered by their friends.

For a time, my attention is diverted to politics as bad news breaks from the Democratic nominating convention in Chicago. The TV news film of convention delegates being manhandled and of newsmen and hippie demonstrators beaten by Chicago police is shocking. Senator Abraham Ribicoff of Connecticut condemns "Gestapo tactics in the streets of Chicago" from the podium, inciting in Chicago's Mayor Richard Daley a rage that makes him look like a choleric gargoyle. Lip-readers interpret Daley's response to Ribicoff, shouted from the convention floor, as "Fuck you, you Jew son of a bitch! You lousy motherfucker! Go home!" The mayhem dramatizes the divisions within the Democratic party and in the society at large, and it taints the anointing of Vice President Hubert Humphrey as the Democratic nominee.

Three weeks earlier, in Miami Beach, behind a wall of security that kept protesters at bay, the Republicans nominated Richard

---

* Dave Getz agrees with Sam, with qualifications: "I don't think Albert ever said to her specifically, 'I think you should go out as a solo group,' but I think there was probably, in their time together, just a lot of things that indicated to her that he didn't really think that much of the band, and that, given the chance, she should go in a different direction." (Author interview with David Getz, July 24, 1997.)

Nixon on the first ballot. On the evening of his acceptance speech, police and five hundred National Guard troops fought rioters in Miami's black ghetto. They are still called "Negroes" in the summer of 1968, not yet "blacks" consistently in the press. Six miles away, in the convention hall, ringed by barricades and beyond the sound of gunfire and the smell of smoke, Tricky Dick soberly proclaimed, "My fellow Americans, the dark long night for America is about to end." The Republicans' Fortress Miami arrangements and the indiscriminate police violence in Chicago show that the Establishment is digging in for the long haul.

Big Brother's first jobs back in California reaffirm what they have achieved together and encourage them to take the pleasure to be gained from living in the moment. A Labor Day weekend concert at the Palace of Fine Arts is a quintessential San Francisco gig— outdoors, with a view of the Bay, the fans generous in the welcome they accord one of the city's signature bands.

A few days later, I pick up Janis and the boys for a flight to L.A., and a gig that is a milestone in Big Brother's career. Since the Beatles sold out the Hollywood Bowl in 1965, it has become a major rock venue. On the Friday after Labor Day, 1968, Big Brother has top billing, with Iron Butterfly and the Fraternity of Man opening. Playing under the white arch of the historic band shell, looking out over the audience that fills the natural amphitheater, Big Brother plays like a band unified in their music and their mission.

"I always have a sense of history, as you do, John, so visiting the Hollywood Bowl was a big thrill," Sam Andrew wrote. "All of the concerts that had taken place there, classical and otherwise . . . I remember standing in the wings, feeling all that history and seeing all those people and exulting."

Sam Andrew

The next morning, I'm headed for Big Sur and this year's folk festival.

Before the music begins, with the fog lingering along the coast, Mimi Fariña marries Milan Melvin, an announcer for KSAN, the hippest of the underground FM stations in San Francisco. Milan was Janis's lover for a time soon after she joined Big Brother, when he was rooming in North Beach with Carl Gottlieb, of the Committee. Janis's roommate and clothes maker, Linda Gravenites, created Mimi's glorious wedding dress. Mimi visited Linda and Janis's Noe Street apartment to plan and fit the dress. That was where she first met Janis. The connections among my Cambridge friends and the San Francisco community keep revealing themselves.*

The Big Sur festival is a world away from the Hollywood Bowl. For me it's like a family reunion. The Charles River Valley Boys are on the program again, and I resume the role of bluegrass singer and picker as if I never put it aside. At some point in the afternoon concert I am at center stage with Joni Mitchell, Judy Collins, Joan Baez, and the festival's organizer, Nancy Carlen, singing a song whose name will escape me thirty-odd years later when a photo of the moment, snapped by Robert Altman (not the film director but the San Francisco photographer of the same name) appears in *People* magazine. The song may have faded, but not the feeling of being back in Big Sur on a few days' holiday between Big Brother gigs.

The idyll is over too soon. Big Brother plays three days at Fillmore West, and then we are on a plane for L.A. again, this time for an even

---

*Milan was unembarrassed about describing his relationship with Janis: "God almighty, man. That still is the sexual highlight of the sixties for me. I mean, the woman was wild. And experimental, and funny, and energetic. I mean, that was our relationship, really, and when we tried to do anything more than that, like carry on any kind of normal relationship, we were fishing in waters where we didn't have the right bait. I don't know what to say. It was almost entirely sexual." (Author interview with Milan Melvin, October 5, 1997.)

larger bowl—the Rose Bowl in Pasadena, seating capacity upward of ninety thousand, where it is evident that football can still outdraw an all-day rock concert. In the vast arena, the music fans fill only a fraction of the seats.

The event is billed as "An American Music Show." Janis's old flame Country Joe McDonald is here with the Fish. The rest of the acts are an eclectic assortment: Joan Baez, the Everly Brothers, the Byrds, the Junior Wells Band with Buddy Guy, the Mothers of Invention, Buffy Sainte-Marie, Albert King, and Wilson Pickett. Even in this company Big Brother closes the show, another measure of how far they have come in so short a time.

The stage is on the football field, but the audience is confined to the stadium seats, held in check by rows of Pasadena and state police. As ever, a seated audience is a challenge to Janis. She wants to put them in motion. The encore is "Down on Me," the semi-hit single from the Mainstream album. Janis pleads with the cops to turn the kids loose, and she finally boosts the crowd's energy to the level of spontaneous fission. Here they come, through the cops, over the railings and through the fence, an unstoppable wave.

This time Janis gets more than she bargained for. She comes to the edge of the stage to touch a few hands, but that only encourages the fans. By the time the song ends they're all over the stage, surrounding her, touching her, grabbing at her, pulling on her beads and bracelets and her clothes. The police help Janis get into a limousine to take her from the stage to the dressing room. Sam is in the limo with Janis. The fans pile on the car, even on the roof. Sam is afraid the roof may collapse, but it holds. The fans don't care about the members of the band who were left behind, so we follow on foot. We wait in the dressing room for the crowd to disperse before we make our escape.

Now and again, Janis likes to shop. On an expedition to Beverly Hills when we were here in the spring, she ventured into Paraphernalia, a happening boutique that features hip designer Betsey Johnson's fashions. Clad in jeans and a T-shirt, Janis half expected to be tossed out as an undesirable. Instead, the manager recognized her and fell all over her, offering to have anything she wanted made up for her at off-the-rack prices.

After the show at the Rose Bowl, Janis shops in Beverly Hills again, this time accompanied by her attorney. Bob Gordon has a Porsche, and Janis has been in touch with him about finding her a car. He takes Janis to his German car dealer, where they show her a 1965 convertible—a cabriolet in Porsche terminology—that they have cherried out with a hand-rubbed paint job in pearl-gray lacquer. Janis falls in love with the car and within days it is hers.

SEPT. 27: **University of California, Irvine**

SEPT. 28: **San Diego**

SEPT. 29: **Tape *Hollywood Palace* TV show, L.A.**

SEPT. 29: **Long Beach Sports Arena**

During this month in California, Dave Richards decides he's had enough of the road. Dave is confident that Mark Braunstein can take over responsibility for the equipment. Hire another guy and let Marko train him, and you'll be fine, Dave tells the band. He stays on the job until somebody comes up with George Ostrow, a lean, sleepy-looking guy who seems bemused by the band and the job and the road, but he's willing to learn. This transition is managed without my having to take part in it, beyond notifying Albert's office of the change.

Life magazine reviews *Cheap Thrills* in its September 20 issue. The article is headlined "Singer With a Bordello Voice" and focuses most of its attention on Janis.

We tape a show for ABC's *Hollywood Palace*. In a letter home, Janis alerts her family to watch it when it airs.

The work begins in earnest when we fly east in the first days of October.

OCT. 4, 1968: **Public Hall, Cleveland**

OCT. 5: **SUNY, Buffalo, N.Y.**

OCT. 11: **War Memorial Auditorium, Syracuse, N.Y.**

OCT. 13: **Music Hall, Cincinnati**

OCT. 15: **Grande Ballroom, Detroit**

OCT. 18: **Pennsylvania State University, State College**

OCT. 19: **Spectrum, Philadelphia**

OCT. 20: **Alexandria Roller Rink, Alexandria, Va.**

OCT. 25: **Curry Hicks Cage, UMass, Amherst**

OCT. 26: **Worcester Polytechnic Institute, Worcester, Mass.**

Big Brother is accustomed by now to being based in New York during our eastern tours. They even look forward to returning to the city and the Chelsea Hotel after a weekend in Squaresville. At least in New York we move in the counterculture of arts and music.

Another bright spot is John Fisher, our New York limo driver. We found him in the summer, after Newport. John is New York born and raised. He's cheerful and ready for anything. Janis took to him right away, and she quickly staked her claim to the shotgun position, sharing the front seat with John. John has driven Richie Havens and Dylan and the Band, all Albert's clients. Why we didn't learn about John sooner, I don't know, but we've got him now. No more straight limo drivers from companies that would rather be shuttling business executives from one meeting to another. John's company is Love Limousines. The rear windows of his personal limo are tinted mauve. From the backseat, it's like looking out on the world through rose-colored glasses.

Earlier in the year, after our first East Coast tour, Sam Andrew wrote a song that is occasionally added to the set list. It's called "Downtown Nowhere," and it's about the grind of touring, the days when you can't remember what city you're in or where you flew in from that morning. On the fall tour, even I sometimes find myself in Downtown Nowhere. In memory, October and November play in a palette of drab grays.

In Cleveland, a contingent of Hells Angels shows up. They know that Big Brother has played benefits for the Angels in San Francisco. By extension, the local chapter feels connected to the band. By implication, they'd like to get in free. Maybe they can help with security? The hall is packed and Cleveland is kind of a tough town. I talk to the promoter, tell him the Angels are our guests. Janis really gets the kids going and a thin line of Angels across the front of the stage seems like a good idea as Big Brother's set reaches its climax. With us, and with the audience, the Angels are polite, never threatening.

A gig in Cincinnati falls on a Sunday when a film clip of the Beatles is scheduled on the *Smothers Brothers Comedy Hour*. So no one has to miss it, Mark and George set up a TV set on the stage and Big Brother interrupts their set when the Beatles come on. With a mike held next to the TV, the band and the audience catch "Revolution" in between songs by Janis and the boys. After the concert, a delegation from the counterculture invites us to an after-concert party, where everyone in the band but Peter Albin shoots up smack.

NOV. 1–2, 1968: Electric Factory, Philadelphia

NOV. 3–5: Chicago? (Aragon? Cheetah? dates and venue uncertain)

NOV. 8: Warwick, R.I.

NOV. 9: Woolsey Hall, Yale University, New Haven

NOV. 10: White Plains, N.Y.

NOV. 11: Ridge Arena, Braintree, Mass.

NOV. 12: Jersey City

NOV. 14: Hartford, Connecticut

NOV. 15: Assembly Hall, Hunter College, NYC

NOV. 16: SUNY, Stony Brook, Long Island, N.Y.

On November 2, *Cheap Thrills* hits number one on *Cashbox* magazine's album chart. Three days later, Dick Nixon squeaks by Hubert Humphrey to win the presidency by half a million votes, less than one percentage point. I'm still registered in New York, where the black comedian Dick Gregory is the Liberal Party nominee. Unable to persuade myself to vote for Humphrey, I pull the lever for Gregory to register my feeling that a comedian has more integrity than either major candidate. When I see the election results, I realize that if a hundred thousand disenchanted Democrats in the right precincts had bitten the bullet and voted for Humphrey, we wouldn't have Dick Nixon to kick around anymore.

Too late. You go to sleep, you miss your turn.

After the election, the schedule is murderous. Starting on November 8, Big Brother plays eight out of nine nights in a row in small to medium cities along a short stretch of coastal provinces, from Braintree, Massachusetts, to Jersey City. This marathon includes the only gig in New York City on the fall tour, at Hunter College, and ends the next night at the State University of New York out on Long Island. The accretion of gigs happened insidiously, one after another added to what started out as a reasonable schedule, filling in the days off until they were gone. Each time a new gig came up, I checked with the band. For the boys, the string of gigs means more money. Dave, James and Peter are facing the imminent end of their performing income for the foreseeable future. Janis recognizes their need and never puts her foot down to refuse a gig, but the demands of these nine days, capping thirty-some gigs in seven weeks, take their toll. At Hunter College, Janis is exhausted. After the SUNY gig, she falls ill and we are forced to cancel the first two of four gigs on a swing through her home state of Texas, which she has been looking forward to all fall.

NOV. 20, 1968: **Austin Municipal Auditorium, Austin, Texas—**
   CANCELLED

NOV. 21: **Theater of Performing Arts, San Antonio—CANCELLED**

NOV. 24: **Coliseum, Dallas**

NOV. 26: **Denver Auditorium, Denver**

NOV. 29: **Seattle, Wash.**

NOV. 30: **Vancouver, B.C.**

DEC. 1: **Family Dog Benefit, San Francisco**

Most of all, Janis was looking forward to playing in Austin. During her brief experiment with college life at the University of Texas, her fellow students, in an act of callous cruelty, voted her the "ugliest man on campus." Performing there with Big Brother, rubbing her success in their faces, would be her revenge. But it's Austin and San Antonio that are scratched.

After a week of rest, Janis rallies enough to sing in the Houston Music Hall. For this gig, her family, including her younger siblings Laura and Michael, will drive up from Port Arthur. Her mother phones ahead to reserve tickets, but there is no way Janis is going to let her parents pay to see her perform. I arrange comps and reserve a block of front-row seats for the family and some of Janis's Austin friends.

After the concert, the Joplins experience firsthand the enthusiasm of Janis's admirers as they join us in running from the backstage door to the cars when a group of young girls who have been waiting nearby spy Janis and give chase. For Laura and Michael, it's an exciting glimpse of life in rock and roll, but their parents' manner suggests concern that Janis is beyond their control in a world they do not and cannot understand. They share a late supper with her in the hotel restaurant before they pile back into the family car for the ninety-mile drive to Port Arthur.

After a concert in Dallas the next evening, we have a day off before a show in Denver. The band has chosen to spend the extra day in Dallas, for the warmer climate, and the weather cooperates. I drive to Dealey Plaza in the rental car, taking with me the Fuji 8-millimeter movie camera I bought early in our first eastern tour. It is five years almost to the day since President John F. Kennedy's open limousine passed through the small park, and it is the same kind of day, mild and brilliantly clear. I film through the windshield as I drive past the spot where the bullets struck the president, and under the railroad bridge beyond. I double back, park the car, and film the Texas School Book Depository from several angles, zooming in on the window where Lee Harvey Oswald found his vantage point. I go behind the fence atop the grassy knoll, where conspiracy theorists believe a second gunman might have been, and I explore what lies beyond. There's a broad expanse of dirt and gravel and three sets of train tracks. Plenty of space for a gunman to get away and be long gone in the minutes of panic and confusion after the shooting.

There are flowers at a small memorial in the park, wreaths and bouquets. "In Memory of John F. Kennedy and Robert F. Kennedy, 1968," says a handwritten card with some white carnations. A white ribbon laced among an expensive array of red roses says "Lest We Forget."

I return to my car and retrace the motorcade's route, continuing beyond the underpass this time. A sign directs me to Parkland Hospital, where they rushed the mortally wounded president. I film the route to the hospital and from there I find my way to Love Field, Dallas's airport, where Lyndon Johnson took the oath of office in Air Force One before the plane took off to carry JFK in his coffin back to Washington.

AFTER DENVER, A two-day swing through the Northwest includes Vancouver, B.C., the only gig on foreign soil while I'm with Big

Brother. A booking that would have taken us to Hawaii for Janis's last show with the band has fallen through, and so, on December 1, Janis and Big Brother end where they began, in San Francisco, at a benefit for the Family Dog, which brings it full circle back to Chet Helms, who presided over the creation of Big Brother in the first place. This seems fitting, somehow, but it is not a night to celebrate.

CHAPTER FOURTEEN

Memphis, Tennessee

WHILE BIG BROTHER and I are powering through October and November, driven by the imperatives of the schedule, Albert is trying to cobble together Janis's new backup band. He consults Janis, to be sure, but Janis is on the road. He enlists Nick Gravenites and Mike Bloomfield, his old Chicago friends, to propose musicians and help shape the sound.

Nick and Mike are both rooted in the blues. Mike left Paul Butterfield last year to found the Electric Flag, which included Nick as vocalist and songwriter. Mike wanted to create a band that would blend strains of jazz, soul, and blues into a new kind of electrified American music, and he achieved at least part of his vision. The Flag's debut at the Monterey Pop Festival was well received. The group's first album, "A Long Time Comin'," performed well on the charts and got good notices. Mike wrote and the Flag provided the music for Peter Fonda's feature film *The Trip*, about an LSD trip, which everyone I knew who ever took LSD found to be terminally strange and unlike anything they had experienced on acid. The Flag's music got better reviews than the movie and the band seemed to be on its way, but just a year after Monterey, Mike, bedeviled by insomnia and heroin, took his leave. The Flag flapped on for a while without him, but by the time Janis and Big Brother go their separate ways, the Electric Flag is history.

What Mike attempted with the Flag bears a relationship to what Janis wants in her new band. She wants a band with horns and a keyboard that will evoke the soul sound of R&B without imitating it. It's a fine distinction, one that confuses the musicians who are hired to fulfill the vaguely defined vision. Janis and Albert plan to debut the new band in the new year, after two months of rehearsals, but while Janis is still on the road with Big Brother, Albert manages to secure a slot for Janis at the Stax-Volt Christmas show in Memphis on December 21. This is potentially a brilliant stroke. It's the kind of strategic move at which Albert excels. If Janis and her new band can win over the soul music crowd in Memphis, the reviews will validate her change of direction and help jump-start the next phase of her career.

Stax and Volt records are the premier labels of the Memphis sound, and the main competitors, in the world of rhythm and blues, with Detroit's Motown. Otis Redding recorded for Stax. Albert King joined the label in '66. Sam and Dave are turning out one hit after another for the label. Booker T. and the MGs are the house band. Wilson Pickett records at Stax, even though his label is Atlantic.

The Memphis sound is closer to the roots of the blues, more soulful, not as inclined to pander to white tastes as Motown's slicker hits. Funkier. Which is not to say it's any less professionally arranged, performed and recorded. In Memphis, Janis will have her work cut out for her to win over a predominantly black audience that regards the Stax and Volt artists as members of their immediate families.

When Janis awakens in her Noe Street apartment on the morning after her last performance with Big Brother, her next gig—her debut gig with the new, as-yet-unrehearsed band—is less than three weeks away.

Janis and the band rehearse first at Big Brother's Warehouse, which makes poignantly apparent the love Janis and the boys have for each other. As wounded as David and Peter and James are by her departure, they make the Warehouse available. It belongs to Janis and Sam as much as to them. The money they all earned together still pays the rent.

Like the Electric Flag, Albert's Canadian group, the Paupers, has also folded. The bass player, Brad Campbell, is brought in to anchor the rhythm in Janis's new band. On alto saxophone is Terry Clements, an English expatriate who played briefly with the Flag in their declining days and just as briefly with the Buddy Miles Express, a group formed by the Flag's drummer. Terry came to San Francisco early in the rock renaissance, and he is thoroughly assimilated. He looks more like a hippie than anyone else among the recruits, complete with long hair held in place by a bandanna around his head. Since playing with the Flag and Buddy Miles, Terry has had some gigs as a sideman, but he's looking for something more comfortable, more permanent, more familial.

Marcus Doubleday is also plucked from the remnants of the Electric Flag to play trumpet. Marcus is an eastern urban musician, and it's rumored that he has a drug problem.*

The organ man, Bill King, and Roy Markowitz, the drummer, are fresh from New York. King read in the press about Janis leaving Big Brother and took the initiative. He phoned Albert's office and asked to be considered for her new band. The office set up an audition where Bill met Roy, and both of them made the cut. Bill seems out of place in San Francisco, but he's a serious musician and maybe he'll

---

*The rumors were true, as Mark Braunstein became aware. "I think that probably that rehearsal with Marcus Doubleday was the first inkling I had of heroin use. Remembering Marcus Doubleday falling asleep at rehearsal. Nodding out at rehearsal. I was pretty naïve." (Author interview with Mark Braunstein, September 9, 1997.)

shine on the road. Roy is a New Yorker through and through. He's a natural comedian and he takes on the role of the class clown.

Sam Andrew will discharge the lead guitar duties on his own. The idea to add Jerry Miller to the new band didn't pan out. Sam and Janis are my friends, my points of reference in this new aggregation of what strike me as very disparate personalities.

The Warehouse is hard to heat on the rainy December days, and soon the rehearsals move to a synagogue that Bill Graham leases next to the original Fillmore Auditorium. Bill manages the Carlos Santana Blues Band, at this time only locally known. They use the synagogue as a rehearsal space. Through Bill's good offices, Janis's band shares it with Santana for the high-pressure rehearsals to prepare for the Stax-Volt show.

I'm in frequent touch with the office as Albert begins to plan the winter tour in the East. When I stop by the rehearsals, it seems to me that no one knows just what they're supposed to be doing. Without much direction, the musicians are trying to figure out their job descriptions. Mike Bloomfield is here to help with arrangements, but Mike isn't one to crack the whip and focus the band members on the task at hand.

Sam takes on the job of teaching the new guys the songs that Janis wants to keep from the Big Brother repertoire. He offers suggestions about how to fit the horns and the organ into the arrangements, but Sam is uncertain in his new role as Janis's employee and he isn't sure how far he can go in guiding the style of the new group. When it comes to the new songs, he's as much in the dark as the others about how to proceed. What is painfully lacking is a coherent vision of how this band is supposed to sound.

Gone from the tentative playlist are "Coo-Coo/Oh, Sweet Mary" and "Easy Rider." Among the songs the band is working on, there are no obvious connections to traditional roots, black or white, save for the fact that rhythm and blues, like rock and roll, is built on the solid foundation of the twelve-bar blues.

Bill King offers some ideas about the horn lines on the Bee Gees' "To Love Somebody," which Janis wants to include, and he recommends a song that was a staple in his previous band, Eddie Floyd's soul hit, "Raise Your Hand," for her consideration.

Janis herself has no idea how to lead the rehearsals. She can say, "That's it," when she hears something she likes. She may suggest that a song needs a stronger introduction or ending, but mostly she looks to Mike Bloomfield or Nick Gravenites when the tunes aren't coming together.

In Big Brother, during my time with them, Janis was almost always confident and assertive, ever ready to put in her two cents, to argue a point or propose a course of action. In the band that took her on as lead vocalist she rose to become the first among equals, and she was comfortable taking that position when it suited her—about the music or anything else—because she knew Sam, Dave, Peter, and James were there to back her up or take charge when she faltered. Now, among the musicians and helpers recruited to form the backup band she has dreamed of, Janis is passive and uncertain, and there is no one to take up the slack.

She has the smarts and the force of personality to be the bandleader, but at this turning point in her career an old habit from her younger days holds her back. When she was growing up in Port Arthur, her intelligence was appreciated in her home. Her parents instilled in Janis and her siblings, Laura and Michael, respect for literature, art, and music, but these values were not common coin among Janis's Texas contemporaries. In a Gulf coast oil town, displays of intellectual agility were not the surest way to make friends in the public school mainstream. Even among Janis's small group of like-minded friends, being a whip-smart mouthy girl was not always the best strategy for earning peer approval. In San Francisco, there was no lack of cerebral wattage among the founders of the scene, but it has grown too fast for an intellectual tradition to keep pace. The philosophizing of the Beats has been reduced to simple platitudes like

"Go with the flow" and "Let it all hang out." At home and on the road, among promoters, fans, and members of the press, Janis often plays to the level of those around her, not condescendingly, but because she wants to fit in, to be one of the crowd. This habit has become so ingrained that she sometimes undervalues her own exceptional intelligence and the answers it might offer for her current problems.

> "It has to do with a certain self-abnegation. She would put herself down to strong men. She liked men who knew what they were saying, who didn't have a thousand self-doubts about the world and what they were. She liked men who would say things with a lot of conviction and knowledge and power and shit like that. She dug that. She dug powerful aggressive-type men. And she'd put herself down in front of those men, you dig? . . . She really depended on people to do things. People she felt know more than she did. Whether that is true or not is moot."
>
> **Nick Gravenites**

In the new band, Janis is on unfamiliar ground. This is nothing like her life with Big Brother. This is the Music Business.

When rehearsal is over for the day, Janis lets off steam by careening around the city in her Porsche convertible, often with a couple of the new boys crammed into the cockpit, as she shows off her uniquely repainted ride.

While we were on the road in the fall, Dave Richards took Janis's new Porsche into Big Brother's Warehouse, where he labored over it lovingly. Janis asked him for a custom paint job and left the rest up to him. Dave has covered every inch of the L.A. Porsche dealer's pearl-gray paint job with hand-painted images of birds and butterflies and satellites and psychedelic mushrooms and undersea creatures and, along one side, a lovely pastoral landscape. A group portrait of Big Brother and the Holding Company adorns the left front fender.

> "I actually found Janis's Porsche for her. She was in L.A. and called
> me, and said that she wanted to buy a Porsche. . . . I had a
> Porsche, and had frequent dealings with a particular Porsche
> agency in Beverly Hills. They had a Porsche . . . and I went and
> saw it and then told Janis about it. It had seventeen coats of lac-
> quer, kind of oyster lacquer. [The dealer] said it was the best
> paint job they ever did in their lives. And after Dave Richards
> finished his job, Janis went down there and showed them. And I
> never heard the end of it."
>
> **Bob Gordon**

WE FLY TO Memphis two days ahead of the Stax-Volt gig and hold a
final rehearsal at the Stax studios in an old movie theater, where we
are made welcome.

The rehearsal is intense. This gig is no tryout in an out-of-the-way
place. This is Memphis, home of the blues, home of Gus Cannon's
Jug Stompers, home of the Memphis sound. Janis and the band work
on getting three numbers nailed. Eddie Floyd's "Raise Your Hand"
has worked out well and it has become Janis's favorite among the new
songs. The Bee Gees' "To Love Somebody" is ready too. For a finale,
she'll do "Piece of My Heart" or "Ball and Chain." Something old,
something new, something borrowed, something blue.

Friday evening, the night before the show, we're invited to the
home of Stax president Jim Stewart for a cocktail party. Janis and
the band can't wait to see what a cocktail party for the cream of the
Memphis sound is like, and they are not disappointed. The house is
a ranch-style mansion. It's on the edge of town, surrounded by a plot
of woods. Indoors, it is apparent that this is a select gathering. The
partygoers are decked out in their flamboyant finest. Booker T. is
here, and Stax's number one songwriter and producer, Isaac Hayes,
but our gang are even more impressed to meet Steve Cropper and
Donald "Duck" Dunn, the MGs' guitar and bass players, Stax-Volt's
premier sidemen. Janis's guys rub elbows with these musical idols as

they group around the dining room table to snack on shrimp, sandwiches, and chicken livers wrapped in bacon.

The music that Stewart has piped throughout the house keeps the party in a reflective mood; it is from unreleased tapes by Otis Redding. The first anniversary of his death has just passed, and in this setting his absence is still a wound not fully healed.

But Janis is always ready for a party. She drinks, laughs at the jokes, talks about music.

We considered names for the new band in the San Francisco rehearsals, but none of the suggestions won out. The Janis Joplin Revue (boring). Janis and the Joplinaires (funny, but not a serious proposal). Janis Joplin's Pleasure Principle. Janis Joplin and the Sordid Flavors, a play on words that probably originated with Janis or Sam. For the Stax-Volt show, she's billed simply as Janis Joplin. When Janis sees a poster for the show, she's embarrassed to see that her name and photo are larger than those of the soul stars she hopes to win over.

The concert, billed as Stax-Volt's "Yuletide Thing," is at the Mid-South Coliseum, which is known as "The Entertainment Capital of the Mid-South." The coliseum boasts ten thousand seats. The audience is overwhelmingly black, and they are dressed to the nines. The performers are even flashier. Everyone's dressed up except our band and crew. Janis is decked out in a cherry-red pantsuit. She moves with apparent confidence among the other groups backstage, conscious of the attention she attracts from all sides. The other groups have matching outfits, but our band members have no unified style. Here, the eclectic haberdashery of San Francisco musicians doesn't stand out as adventurous. They look like a bunch of guys picked at random off a street located far from Memphis.

The show moves like clockwork. One band leaves the stage and the next group comes out, they plug in, and they play. The changeovers take only a few minutes. Janis is next to last on the program. Mark Braunstein and George Ostrow have worked with the equipment men from the other bands to speed the changeover before Janis comes onstage. The plan that involves the least shuffling of equipment has our band set up in a mirror image of their usual layout. Mark talks to our musicians backstage to prepare them. "Can you guys just get on the stage and play, wherever the amplifiers happen to be, please. Everything's backwards. Can you please just get up there and play? Plug in and play?"

When the time comes, the changeover would be considered fast for a show at Fillmore West, but here it seems to take forever as Janis's guys sort themselves out and adjust this and that and check their tuning. In the Coliseum, the audience is growing restless. Offstage, Janis can't keep still. She bounces around, getting herself worked up. As usual, she has tried to drink enough to give her the elevating boost she wants, staying on the upside of the curve until she's onstage, where her own energy is released and sustains her through the performance. This evening she may have slipped over the top of the rise. "Come on!" she says, under her breath, then louder, until finally the announcement comes that launches her into the light.

The band is ragged, but they're trying. The audience is curious to hear in person this white girl they've heard so much about. They're polite, but this isn't the Monterey Jazz Festival, where black and white Californians rose to celebrate a San Francisco band and their stunning female vocalist. The Memphis audience stay in their seats and the applause is—polite.

There may be a political edge to the audience's indifferent reception. The loss of Martin Luther King and the rise of militant black power has made black Americans more wary of whites, less inclined to welcome white musicians riffing on black sounds. In the folk days we sang "Black and white together," but the new theme is "Say it loud, I'm black and I'm proud!"

When Janis wrings out the final notes of "Ball and Chain," there are no cheers. It's clear that the applause won't warrant an encore. Standing with Janis and the band backstage, I'm about to say, "That's it," when Mark Braunstein comes backstage. He has reached the same conclusion. "No encore," he says. Onstage, the changeover to the final act is already under way.

The winter solstice is the darkest day. That's how it feels for Janis in Memphis, but the solstice also marks a turning toward the light.

IN SAN FRANCISCO, the band members disperse to their respective lodgings. Some go home for Christmas. Janis flies to Texas. There are no further gigs on the calendar. On January 2, the band will report for more rehearsals.

I remove myself to what has become my preferred retreat since I lived in Carmel. Three years ago, I was invited to a picnic in Big Sur for Joan Baez's birthday. We sat on the grass at Esalen and ate and laughed and took in the great reach of the Pacific Ocean. I don't remember if I was introduced to the sulfur baths that day, but that's when I was introduced to Peter Melchior and his wife, Marya. Peter was working in Esalen's kitchen and teaching ceramics workshops. By that summer, when I attended my first Big Sur Folk Festival on the Esalen grounds, Peter had become a friend. He and Marya live north of Esalen's buildings, across a creek that tumbles down a steep gully, in a small house on the edge of an improbably well-kept lawn, across from an improbably substantial home that belongs to the Murphy family, who own all the habitable land on this broad ledge that was hewn from the Coast Range by tectonic shifts the present inhabitants hope not to experience.

Peter is close to some members of the Committee and some of the musicians I know from California and Cambridge in ways that take me years to unravel. He seems to know everyone, and everyone holds him in high regard. In December 1968, I know Peter and Marya well enough to call them and ask if I can come down for Christmas.

I sleep late, as they do, and I rarely look at a clock. The sulfur baths are part of the daily routine. On an evening in the week between Christmas and New Year's there are ten or a dozen people in

Peter and Marya's living room after dinnertime, gathered around the fireplace. As the wine and joints and conversations flow, our thoughts turn to the remote world of politics and war, to this interregnum between the November election and the inauguration of Richard Milhous Nixon, and someone proposes that we throw the *I Ching* to see what it has to say. The question we ask is "What's happening?" The hexagram we get is Po, the Splitting Apart. The implications are unsettling and uncanny: Inferior men are rising to positions of power. It is useless to oppose them. The wise course for the superior man is to remain quiet and take no part, for the condition of the time cannot be corrected by action, only by waiting for the condition to change. Careful reading of the interpretations reveals a glimmer of hope. Evil carries within it the seeds of its own destruction. This too shall pass.

For those with a grounding in folk music, there's an equivalent wisdom: To everything there is a season. Turn, turn, turn.

CHAPTER FIFTEEN

On the Road Again

JANIS AND THE new band start the new year by rehearsing for a solid month. Over the Christmas break, Marcus Doubleday decided to grapple with his drug problem. He is replaced on trumpet by Terry Hensley, whose personal style is similar to Terry Clements's. We now have two longish-haired, California-style horn players named Terry.

After the Stax-Volt gig, nobody sets eyes again on Bill King. He flew from Memphis to New York to spend Christmas with his family. The rumor is that the draft was after him and he split for Canada.

To fill Bill's seat at the Hammond B3 keyboard, Janis takes the band to see an organist who has been recommended to her. Richard Kermode has been in San Francisco only a short time, and he must have arrived from a distant planet, because when Janis phoned him out of the blue, he scarcely seemed to know who she was.

At the club where Janis and the band hear him, Richard isn't playing rock, but he impresses them enough that Janis decides to give him a try. With his shaggy hair and full beard and mustache, Richard bears a resemblance to Lon Chaney, Jr., when he turns into the Wolf Man, but he is a benevolent spirit. He is young, laid-back, a little shy,

> "I had never even heard of Janis Joplin until about a month before
> I joined the band. . . . She called me one day and she said 'I'm Ja-
> nis,' and I said 'Well, yeah, I remember seeing that name on a
> record,' and I was totally unaware of like [Big Brother] and all of
> that, and I said 'Well, it's a gig, and I need a gig so I'll take it.'"
>
> **Richard Kermode**

ready to be everyone's friend, quietly surprised at his good luck in landing this job.

Albert's plans for Janis's first solo tour are taking shape. Even more so than with Big Brother, his approach is cautious. Big Brother had a solid fan base in California when they first came east, and word from the Monterey Pop Festival had aroused intense interest. For the new band, Albert adopts a reverse strategy. He knows it will be tough for Janis to win acceptance on Big Brother's home ground, so there are no warm-up gigs in California, no trial runs to Fresno and Merced. He books an eastern tour, hoping some generous reviews will help persuade San Francisco to give her a chance.

I book airline flights, rental cars, and hotels, and talk with promoters about the gigs. By mid-January, the tour is in place. We'll be in the East for a little over five weeks, from February into March. It's a repeat, but shorter, of Big Brother's winter–spring itinerary the previous year. Once again, we will open out of town.

A gig in Rindge, New Hampshire, is billed as a "sound test." At the Music Hall in Boston we'll do a "preview," as if we're a Broadway show, risking the scrutiny of the Boston critics before braving the Big Apple.

Rindge is only sixty miles from Cambridge, so I book us into a hotel close to Harvard Square, which turns out to be a lucky choice. We get back late from the Rindge gig, and when we wake up the next morning there's a foot of snow on eastern Massachusetts and more falling. By evening the streets are plowed. We get to and from the Music Hall without a problem, and the show goes well enough. The next day's *Boston Globe* headline reads "Howling Storm Cripples the Northeast." There is no overnight review.

The real test is New York, where we're booked for a midweek two-night stand at Fillmore East. Janis is comfortable in any house run by Bill Graham. With the Grateful Dead sharing the bill, it's old home week. The members of the band are pumped to be in New York backing Janis Joplin. They've got the will, if they can find the way to pull it all together.

The opening night is sold out and the press is on hand in force. Not just the newspapers, but *Time* and *Newsweek*, *Life* and *Look*. Janis has the rundown from Myra Friedman, whose responsibility for Janis's publicity at this point is largely a matter of fending off the second-stringers and choosing among the many requests for interviews. In advance of the Fillmore East gig, Myra has been contacted by *60 Minutes*, a new show CBS debuted a few months ago that runs every other week on Tuesday night. It's billed as a newsmagazine program. Three or four long pieces in an hour. They're doing a segment on Fillmore East and they want to include Janis, but Albert isn't about to put this untried band on national television, not until it wins critical acceptance. When *60 Minutes* requests permission to film Janis's performance, Albert says no.

On Tuesday, opening night at Fillmore East, there's a snowstorm that is trifling in the city but more serious upstate. Unwilling to risk getting snowbound on the New York State Thruway, Albert remains in Bearsville, and he isn't here to deal with what we find waiting for us at the gig.

CBS reporter Mike Wallace, the host of the *60 Minutes* show, is on hand with a camera crew. The producer corners me and asks to interview Janis on camera and to let them film the performance. Do you have permission from Albert's office? I ask. He hems and haws and it's clear he doesn't. When I don't have word that the office has approved an interview, I usually ask Janis if she wants to do it. That's the routine for magazine and newspaper reporters. This is television. Janis is impressed that CBS wants to interview her, but wary, which is her customary reaction to surprises. She'd like the publicity, but she's against letting *60 Minutes* film the show and isn't sure about doing an interview.

Myra Friedman is here, and she's not about to countermand Albert. We try repeatedly to reach Albert by phone, to no avail. Bill Graham jumps in on the side of *60 Minutes*. If Janis is eager for the publicity, Bill is rabid. I've never seen him like this. Myra bears the brunt of Bill's initial rants.

When Neuwirth and I join them in Bill's office, Graham outdoes, in volume and histrionics, all previous performances that I've witnessed. He is incredulous at the idea we might actually refuse permission for the CBS crew to film Janis in performance. It's a new band, Bill. The arrangements haven't settled down yet. You don't want Janis looking bad on TV, right? Forget reasoning with him. He's on a tirade. He shouts at Myra, he shouts at Bob Neuwirth when he tries to pour oil on the waters, he shouts at me.

A year ago, Bill's tirades intimidated me. By now, I know that he only screams at people he takes seriously.

My position is simple. If *60 Minutes* wants to film an interview with Janis, we have to get permission from Albert. If they want to film the performance, we have to get permission from Albert, which he has already refused.

Finally, we get through to Albert. He is steadfast against allowing the performance to be filmed. If Janis will do an interview, that's okay. Let her decide.

Janis does the interview after the show when she's exhausted and no longer on the upside of her drinking. She's been drinking heavily tonight, both before the show and after, but the high of performing carried her through. Sitting down in front of a camera and Mike Wallace, Janis does her best and she expresses her opinions in her own

Janis with Autoharp, 1969. On her first visit to San Francisco, in 1963, in addition to playing guitar and singing early blues and folk songs, Janis sang Carter Family songs and accompanied herself on the Autoharp.

D. A. Pennebaker and Albert Maysles in Pennebaker's New York office, May 1967, a month before the Monterey Pop Festival. Maysles was one of several independent filmmakers who joined Pennebaker's crew to film the festival.

D. A. Pennebaker's film crew at the Monterey Pop Festival. Author is standing center with sunglasses, mike in hand; Bob Neuwirth is to his right, cigarette to mouth; D. A. Pennebaker is front row, left; Ricky Leacock is standing, third from the left, camera on shoulder.

Albert Grossman, May 1967. Those who did business with Albert often found him intimidating, but among his friends and clients he could be a benign presence, and often funny.

BIG BROTHER & THE HOLDING COMPANY

PERSONAL MANAGEMENT: ABC/ INC./ALBERT B. GROSSMAN/JOHN COURT/75 E. 55 ST., N.Y.C.

Promotional photo of Big Brother and the Holding Company.

Janis signing Big Brother and the Holding Company's recording contract with Columbia Records in Columbia's New York offices, February 1968. Janis's calm expression belies the excitement she felt on signing with Columbia seven months after Big Brother's triumphant success at the Monterey Pop Festival.

Peter Albin signing the Columbia contract.

The author (center) at the Big Sur Folk Festival in 1968, on a break from touring with Big Brother and the Holding Company. With (from left) Joni Mitchell, Judy Collins, festival director Nancy Carlen, and Joan Baez.

Rock promoter Bill Graham and *San Francisco Chronicle* music critic Ralph J. Gleason, 1967. Gleason was responsible for getting Janis and Big Brother on the bill at the Monterey Pop Festival, and Graham booked the band often at his San Francisco venues and at Fillmore East in New York.

James Gurley, 1968. In Big Brother and the Holding Company, Sam, Peter, and James, as well as Janis, all sang lead vocals. One of the songs James sang often was the traditional blues "Easy Rider."

PHOTO © JOHN BYRNE COOKE

Janis's European tour with the Kozmic Blues Band in April 1969 was a triumph. Here, Janis sings harmony with Sam Andrew as young Germans and American servicemen crowd the stage at a concert in Frankfurt, West Germany.

PHOTO © JOHN BYRNE COOKE

Janis and Sam Andrew in 1969, rehearsing on a California motel patio
before a concert with the Kozmic Blues Band.

Janis and the Kozmic Blues Band on *The Dick Cavett Show*, July 18, 1969.
Very few photos of Janis Joplin and her Kozmic Blues Band exist, partly
because it was difficult to fit everyone in the band into a single photo.

At the end of a song, Janis exults in
the audience's reaction to her concert
with the Kozmic Blues Band in
Frankfurt, West Germany.

original way. She's a professional, but she looks haggard, not at her best. I hope the camera will be kind to her.

My experience with Wallace, whom I have known until now as a newsman, leaves me with a diminished view of him. His interest throughout the evening is getting the interview any way he can, regardless of whether Albert or Janis wants it done. Through all the wrangling, his slicked-down hair budges not a whisker. After this experience at the Fillmore East, I think of Wallace as a self-interested huckster.

Sam Andrew comes off the stage unsure if the new band is going to work out. He doesn't feel the show went well. When he muses aloud along these lines, he gets encouragement from an unexpected quarter. Frank Zappa has come to see the show. Don't worry, Zappa tells Sam, it will come together in time. It takes a while for a large ensemble, Zappa says, but it will come together in time. Sam hopes he's right.

The *New York Times* review the next day is kind and hopeful. "Miss Joplin has never been better," the reviewer writes, and he gives a nod to the band: "Even though her new group sounds as if it were just getting to work together, it still is very good."

With a decent review from the *Times* in hand, a less appreciative piece in the *Washington Post* can be consigned to the trash. What do they know about rock music in D.C.?

FEB. 14, 1969: SUNY, Albany

FEB. 15: University of Vermont, Burlington

FEB. 16: Toronto, Ontario

FEB. 21: Colby College, Waterville, Maine

FEB. 22: Clark University, Worcester, Mass.

FEB. 23: Queens College, Flushing, N.Y.

FEB. 28: University of North Carolina, Chapel Hill

MAR. 1: Duke University, Durham, N.C.

MAR. 7: **Northwestern University, Evanston, Ill.**

MAR. 9: **Toledo, Ohio**

Janis gets a day to rest before we launch into a three-week itinerary that starts off in Albany, Burlington and Toronto, and ends up in North Carolina, Illinois and Ohio. It's the hinterland tour again, except for Toronto. In the year that has passed since Janis traveled these regions with Big Brother, the kids have been growing their hair and buying funny clothes and trying to get hip.

We rent two cars at each airport. I train a couple of the band members as follow-car drivers so we won't lose half the band before we get to the hotel. Here's the drill: Pretend there's a fifty-foot rope between my lead car and the follow car. I know you're back there, so you can follow me closer than you'd follow some stranger in traffic. If you need to stop, flash your headlights.

Terry Clements is one of the better drivers. Sam is fine, but he doesn't really want the responsibility. The proof that I haven't got the follow-car driver adequately trained comes when I blow a front tire on an interstate off-ramp near Albany. My car jumps the curb and careens across the mowed lawn that landscapes the interchange until I can bring it to a stop, but the follow car *never leaves the pavement*. Once it's clear that we're all okay, the guys in the band tease the driver without mercy. You're supposed to *follow* him, man!

Monday to Thursday, most weeks, we're in New York. For the trips to and from the airports, John Fisher brings a second limo.

Not long after the band settles into the Chelsea Hotel, their number is expanded by the arrival of Snooky Flowers. Snooky has been playing sax with Mike Bloomfield and another Butterfield alumnus, Mark Naftalin, since Mike left the Electric Flag. Janis heard Snooky rehearsing with Bloomfield in San Francisco, and Snooky stopped by the synagogue to check out Janis's new band. Until then, he had never heard Janis live, and her singing impressed him. The band did not. He figures he's just the guy to whip them into shape.

In the New York rehearsals, Snooky tries to exert an organizing influence. He has more experience than some of the others, and the ego to run rehearsals the way he thinks they should be run. It helps that he is the sole black member of the group. To Snooky's way of thinking, Janis isn't a rock-and-roll singer; she sings black music. She's got the blues in her white soul, she wants a band with an R&B sound, and it takes a black man to run the band. "This is a horn band," Snooky says. You gotta rehearse a horn band in a particular way. He's a horn man himself, and his big baritone sax gives authority to the horn section that it lacked before.

Nobody else in the group has a better idea how to run rehearsals, so Snooky is able to have some effect. He's full of bluster, and he can talk your ears off when he gets wound up, but he is a gentle soul. He doesn't do drugs and he preaches quietly to those who do, encouraging them to quit. He doesn't see it as a strength that he is thoughtful, and capable of kindness, but these qualities emerge in time.

If Janis would give Snooky her approval in front of the others, he might achieve more, but she is unsure how to handle this group that is so unlike Big Brother. When she tries to exert leadership herself, it often has a disruptive effect. She'll start a rehearsal by saying, "We're not leaving the studio until we get two new songs." The musicians feel this isn't how you approach working out new arrangements. Some are more willing than others to express their competing ideas—Snooky and Terry Clements among them. Some days there is more discussion, and shouting, than cooperative effort.

The constant emphasis on rehearsing—first in San Francisco and now in New York—unsettles the musicians. It is presented as an urgent necessity, which it is, but in a way that conveys doubt that the band will ever be good enough.

After a run up to Waterville, Maine, and Worcester, Massachusetts, we're in New York on the last Sunday in February for a gig at Queens College, in Flushing, so we're on hand to get the Sunday *Times* warm off the presses and read a piece on Janis in the magazine section.

In the past year, Janis has been featured or mentioned in many of the nation's top magazines and newspapers, but making the *New York Times Magazine* is a big deal. The writer is Michael Lydon, a Bay Area freelancer who interviewed Janis in San Francisco before we came east. When he asked her if it isn't a little scary going out with a new band, she said, "Oh yeah, I'm scared. I think, 'Oh, it's so close, can I make it?' If I fail, I'll fail in front of the whole world. If I miss, I'll never have a second chance on nothing. But I gotta risk it. I never hold back, man. I'm always on the outer limits of probability." This is the clincher. It gives the lie to the small-minded theories about why she left Big Brother and who made the decision. It's all in these four words: "I gotta risk it."

We play Northwestern University and get a rave review in the *Chicago Tribune* that acknowledges some criticism of the band in other quarters and refutes it. "Rumors had come from New York, where she debuted her new group a few weeks ago, that the band was not together," the *Tribune*'s critic, Robb Baker, writes. "Either the rumors were wrong, or the band has been working night and day since then. From the first number onward, it was clear the exciting young blues-rock belter from Texas had a tight and beautiful group of musicians behind her that would complement her all the way."

In the recent gigs, there's a noticeable difference in the band that I attribute to Snooky's influence on the rehearsals and his presence in the group. The horn section is more confident, more assertive, and the rest of the band seems to be falling in step behind the brass.

As we tour the boondocks, we become aware of changes in the attitude of our audiences that work against the spirit of celebration Janis tries to encourage. It's the difference between the spirit of the kids who discovered the music on their own and those who are attracted to it because they have heard about the scene and the hippie dope-smoker dropout free-love lifestyle in the music media. Rock concerts aren't celebrations of the counterculture anymore. They have joined the mainstream. In the spring of 1969, many of the kids are coming to the concerts because it's the thing to do, rather than from any real devotion to the performers or the music.

The effect of this evolution encourages neither undivided attention to the show nor a purely spontaneous response. Increasingly, Janis finds the audience's expectations in conflict with her own. Nothing is more important to her than getting an honest response from the crowd, establishing a connection in which she and the fans are equal partners. If the communication is right, if there's a little magic in the air, they'll both get off. But increasingly the kids come expecting to get off every time, and they take less responsibility for helping to make it happen. They want it done *for* them. At the end of Janis's set, the applause sometimes feels less like a celebration than a demand: Give us more.

When Janis feels that the crowd lacks the willingness, the openness, she wants, she fights back in ways that only aggravate the problem. She delivers harangues between songs. Even in conventional theaters with seats, she wants the audience to dance in the aisles. She wants to feel their energy the way she felt it in the Fillmore and the Avalon with Big Brother. With the new band, she's trying to tell the audience how to behave, how to respond to the music, and her outbursts embarrass the band.

A weekend in mid-March is a logistical challenge. On Saturday morning, in New York, Janis and the band rehearse blocking for *The Ed Sullivan Show* at CBS-TV's Studio 50. John Fisher has two cars waiting at the stage door. As soon as we're done, we head to La Guardia and a flight to Detroit for a concert that evening at the University of Michigan in Ann Arbor. So far, so good. The flight is on time.

UM is like a remote province of California. These kids are hip. The UM campus has been a wellspring of student activism since the early '60s and they are *ready* to hear Janis. Big Brother never played here. This is Janis's first time in Ann Arbor, the students' and faculty's first chance to hear her. The reception is tumultuous, and the audience needs little urging to get up and dance. Janis is in her element, grinning, shouting, boogeying to the instrumental breaks. *Okay!* This is how it's supposed to be.

Afterward, we're invited to a party. I am in a celebratory mood, but Janis heads off with a writer from *Playboy* in tow to see an old friend play harp in a black club and I have to get the band up early tomorrow because we have to be back in New York by midday for more blocking and rehearsals at the Ed Sullivan Theater. I head to bed early and urge the boys to do the same. This is something we absolutely must not fuck up. It's *The Ed Sullivan Show* and it's live TV.

The band understands. There is a minimum of griping when I roust everybody at eight fifteen the next morning. Janis was up until the wee hours, but there is no bitching. Her oh-my-God-it's-too-early act is the humorous one, all blowsy and bedraggled, hopping into the shotgun seat on the lead car, ready to go. *We're gonna be on* Ed Sullivan! *Can you dig it?*

The return flight gets us to Newark on time, but . . . there is no John Fisher waiting. We mill about on the sidewalk outside the terminal. . . . Finally John shows up—not in his limo, but coming out of the airport terminal on foot. Somehow he missed us when we trooped past him in the concourse. And now John discovers that he has locked his keys in the limo. Not to worry, he has a magnetic key holder under a fender . . . but all he finds is the magnet; the rivet rusted away and the key box gone. I'm on the verge of hailing taxis for the band when Snooky extracts a wire coat hanger from his clothes bag and jimmies a door lock on the long black Caddy.

We're late getting to the city, but at the Ed Sullivan Theater the rehearsals are running behind schedule and airtime is hours away. Whew. We're going to be okay.

It's hard to overstate the importance of getting booked by Ed Sullivan. Anybody remember the Beatles? Five years ago, they landed in New York on a Friday in February. Two days later, on Sunday, they were on *Ed Sullivan* and they drew the biggest audience the show ever had. From that moment, the Fab Four were stars in America. Of course, they had some advance publicity. "I Want to Hold Your Hand" jumped into the American charts in January, reached number one on February 1, and held the top spot through the Beatles' arrival, the Sullivan show, the month of February and most of March. In Cambridge, our first response was to laugh at the silly name, the "Beatles," but when we heard "I Want to Hold Your Hand," we sat up and took notice. Hey, man, listen to that harmony! Right there . . . I want to hold your *hand*! It's the vocal harmonies I love most about bluegrass music, and the Beatles have taken harmony somewhere *else*.

On the Sullivan show, Janis sings "Maybe," a bluesy, gut-wrenching tune, one of the new songs in her repertoire. The band nails the arrangement and Janis nails the vocal.

Janis knows things about the etiquette of *The Ed Sullivan Show* that I never imagined. When all the acts come onstage at the end of the show, Ed Sullivan takes Janis's hand and he says, "Thank you." Afterward, in John Fisher's limo, on the way to Max's Kansas City, Janis is beside herself. She bounces up and down so hard, the people on the street probably think some horny celebrities are getting it on behind the tinted windows. Did you see? she bubbles. He shook my hand! You ain't nobody if he doesn't shake your hand, daddy! And he did it! He shook my hand!

Janis's elation animates Max's above the usual lively hubbub. The mix of artists, musicians, and free spirits who join the celebration includes Bob Neuwirth, who is often on hand to hang out with us when we're in New York. Andy Warhol is here, and the painter Larry Rivers, a resident at the Chelsea. And where but Max's would you see Tiny Tim and Salvador Dalí in the same room?

The celebratory mood doesn't last for long. The latest edition of *Rolling Stone*, just on the stands, has Paul Nelson's review of the Fillmore East show in February, and it is not a rave. The cover story is titled "Janis: The Judy Garland of Rock?" Nelson didn't like the band or Janis's song list, with the exception of "Work Me, Lord,"

Nick Gravenites's gift to Janis for the new group. As he savages the band, Nelson observes that Janis apparently lacks "the essential self-protective distancing . . . the necessary degree of cynicism needed to survive an all media assault. . . ."

We're on a noon flight for San Francisco the day after the Sullivan show, which only brings Janis closer to the source of the criticism. *Rolling Stone* was founded and is still published in San Francisco. For the rock community, it's the hometown newspaper, and Janis is booked for four days straight at Winterland and Fillmore West.

MAR. 20–23, 1969: Winterland and Fillmore West

MAR. 27: Sacramento

MAR. 28: San Bernardino

MAR. 29: San Diego

The San Francisco audience, like the black audience in Memphis, is curious about the new band, but curiosity isn't going to get Janis to the next level. Ralph Gleason, who got Big Brother on the bills at the Monterey Pop Festival and the Jazz Festival, who has supported and promoted Janis from her first days with the band, writes a scathing review in which he suggests that Janis should go back to Big Brother "if they'll have her." With no influential voices raised in support of the new group, it seems that Gleason reflects the prevailing mood in the city, and the loss of his support wounds Janis deeply.* San Francisco is the only place she has felt she truly belongs. If her adopted hometown rejects her, where can she ever feel at home again?

---

*Although he was ungenerous on this occasion, Gleason wasn't blind to the reasons behind Janis leaving Big Brother. In an interview after her death, he said, "I really dug [Big Brother] together, as a group, but it was perfectly obvious that you couldn't have a partnership, you know, a cooperative group, with everybody as an equal partner, if you had a star. . . . It was perfectly obvious that Janis was gonna leap out of that thing and be a star." (Author interview with Ralph J. Gleason, October 3, 1973.)

> Lots of people don't want their stars to change—they want the same thing that made them fall in love with the artist in the first place. But an artist *has* to change or they stagnate."
>
> **Jon McIntire, Grateful Dead management**

It helps to have something to look forward to. Three days after the Fillmore/Winterland weekend we're packing again for a trio of California gigs—Sacramento, San Bernardino, San Diego—but we won't see the Golden Gate again until the middle of May. While we were in the East, Albert put together a tour of Europe, with concerts booked in Amsterdam, Frankfurt, Paris, Stockholm, Copenhagen, and the Royal Albert Hall in London.

Before we leave our hearts in San Francisco yet again, we acquire our third trumpet player. Terry Hensley has tired of the road, or doesn't think this band is for him, or he's been let go because Snooky doesn't think he can cut it. Whatever the reason, it's a big change. The new man, Luis Gasca, was with Woody Herman's band at the Monterey Jazz Festival in 1967 when Janis and Big Brother played there, and he's no slouch with a horn. He is short in stature but long on experience. He studied for two years at the Berklee College of Music in Boston. He has toured and recorded with Perez Prado, Count Basie, Stan Kenton, and Mongo Santamaria. Luis did all that, and more, before serving for two years in the U.S. Army. He was in and out before Vietnam heated up, and back on the road.

The motley makeup of Janis's band may give Luis a moment's pause, but he's here for one reason: He wants to play with Janis Joplin, and Janis is heading for her first European tour. How can he turn it down?

There is virtually no time for Luis to learn the tunes, but while we were in New York, Albert's office recruited a Harvard-educated musician named Warren to write out the band's arrangements, and Luis can read charts. The California gigs are as good as any in recent memory.

On Monday afternoon, March 30, we're at Los Angeles International Airport. Janis has invited Linda Gravenites along for companionship. We're booked on Scandinavian Airlines, so our foreign experience begins when we board the 707 that will take us nonstop to Copenhagen, where we will change for Stockholm.

CHAPTER SIXTEEN

The Grand Tour

THE GREAT CIRCLE route from Los Angeles to Copenhagen takes us over eastern Canada and the North Atlantic on a path that intersects the Arctic Circle. It's a long flight, with plenty of time to sleep, but it's interrupted, without much explanation before or after, when the captain tells us we're going to make an unscheduled stop in Greenland.

We land after dawn and get off the 707 to stretch our legs. Janis comes down the gangway in her fur coat and a pair of low-heeled golden sandals that would be more appropriate on the Sunset Strip. There are patches of snow and ice on the tarmac and the land around the airport is white, but on the last day of March it's not the land of perpetual winter we might expect. Legend has it that Eric the Red called it Greenland to attract Viking settlement.

The name of this place is Søndre Strømfjord. If there's a town, we can't see it. Outside the terminal there's a signpost with signs that point hither and yon like arrows and give the distances in hours of flight time to places we know well, or will soon: Copenhagen and Los Angeles are near the top. Others point to London, Paris, and

Frankfurt, with New York, Moscow, and Tokyo thrown in for good measure. Only the last two cities will not figure in our travels this year. The names are in English, maybe because the airport began as an American air base built here in 1941. At the top of the signpost, an arrow points to the North Pole, which is closer than all the other destinations, although it is only twenty minutes closer than London, as the jet flies. We are almost seven hours from Los Angeles, just over four to Copenhagen.

We supplement the SAS in-flight service by having breakfast in the terminal. We are never told why this stop was necessary, but now we can say we've been to Greenland.

With the stopover in Greenland and a change of planes in Copenhagen, we arrive at Stockholm—nine hours ahead of L.A.—in the late afternoon, with our internal clocks turned upside down. We find that Swedish hotels have single beds that are built for very tall people. The rooms are equipped with heavy drapes to black out the lingering light of the short summer nights. Sealed off, we manage to get enough sleep to begin the adjustment to a time zone east of Greenwich.

We're in Stockholm to tape a TV show, which functions as our first rehearsal in Europe. It's a studio job, no audience. Because it's on tape, there are retakes to correct glitches. The show will be aired before Janis and the band come back to Stockholm two weeks later for the concert here.

MAR. 31, 1969: **Arrive in Stockholm**

APR. 1: **Stockholm, tape TV show**

APR. 2–10: **London, rehearsals**

APR. 11: **Amsterdam, Concertgebouw**

APR. 12: **Frankfurt**

APR. 14: **Paris, Olympia Théâtre**

APR. 17: **Stockholm**

APR. 19: **Copenhagen, Concert Hall, Tivoli Gardens**

APR. 21: **London, Royal Albert Hall**

Our next stop is London. Here the rehearsals get serious—again. There are nine days before the first concert, in Amsterdam. Warren is on hand with his sheet music. His mandate—from Albert? it's never clear to me—is to help with arrangements and vocal harmonies, as well as committing the music to paper. Snooky doesn't bother to hide his disdain. The fact that Warren is a Harvard-educated black man doesn't impress him. In Snooky's view, the band is playing the music correctly, but he doesn't oppose rehearsing. The band needs the experience playing together as a unit, with Luis in the horn section, until the arrangements are second nature and the songs are tight.

The rehearsal space is the Rolling Stones' rehearsal studio. We don't set eyes on the Stones, but working in their studio is a validation that Janis and the band are playing in the big leagues.

In their off-hours, the musicians split off in twos and threes and become American tourists in London. Where's Carnaby Street? Why do the pubs open and close at random hours? These English girls aren't like the girls in California.

Luis is less wide-eyed than the others. He's been here before, with Woody Herman.

Within the band, Snooky Flowers takes Luis under his wing and the two become a unit—nonhippie, nonwhite—sometimes to the discomfort of Terry Clements, the third man in the horn section. Terry is verbal, analytical, a good musician. Sometimes Terry's British reserve is a barrier to revealing himself to the others, but he's sociable, always ready to step out on the town with a few mates, and he's a dedicated believer in the power of music to change the world.

Janis and Sam have adopted Richard Kermode, and Janis has taken Richard into her bed. He is a lover of convenience; at the gigs, Janis is still on the lookout for pretty boys. Richard evidently accepts his role as her fallback comforter.

A couple of the musicians and I discover an enormous flea market in a building that takes up a city block. Inside, there are scores of shops and stalls in a warren of passages that angle this way and that. I am a sightseer, not a shopper, but this is like a Middle Eastern bazaar, full of things you'd never think to find in England. In one of the stalls I discover an extraordinary woman's belt of finely wrought silver, decorated with rows of tiger claws, that was handmade somewhere on the Asian subcontinent. It is a fixed size. Not adjustable. As I hold it in my hands it comes to me that I should buy it, find the woman it fits, and marry her. The price is less than a week's salary, but my thrifty New England genes kick in, abetted by my Libran nature (we are just, as James Gurley observed, but also indecisive). I decide to think about it until we come back to London for our concert here at the end of the tour.

In Amsterdam we are met at the airport by Knud Thorbjørnsen, the Danish promoter who has booked the gigs on the Continent. Knud is about thirty, soft-spoken and polite. He will travel with us for the next ten days, until we head back to London.

We're here a day ahead of the concert. We have arrived in time to check the band into the hotel and still have some daylight left for a little sightseeing. Knud suggests a walk along the canals, and Janis jumps at the chance. She is ready for a break from the band, so we set out, the three of us, with Knud acting as our guide. In the gathering dusk, Knud calls our attention to illuminated windows on a street fronting a canal, where young women who are less than fully dressed sit in softly lit parlors. The few passersby, mostly solitary men, appraise the women frankly as they stroll past the windows. Some of the women are very attractive.

When Janis spies a man walking toward us, she says, "You guys go on ahead." She slips into a doorway. Knud and I follow instructions. We walk ahead. When the man has passed us, we turn to watch. As the man draws even with her doorway, Janis hails him with a "Hiya, honey."

What is she going to do if the guy goes for it, I'm wondering, but we'll never know. The man keeps on walking. Janis rejoins Knud and me, not really disappointed, but hurt that the guy would dismiss her with only a passing glance.

Arriving at the hotel the next morning from a transatlantic flight is another companion for our grand tour. Bobby Neuwirth had been dispatched by Albert as an extra pair of eyes and ears to report on Janis and the band in Europe. The assignment is nominal. Albert is generous with those he's close to. He may simply have intuited that Bobby would like to come along for the ride. Covering his ticket and his expenses for a few weeks is the kind of thing Albert does for a friend.

In London, Janis and the band rehearsed for eight days straight. No one dared to suggest they should rehearse in Amsterdam on the day of the concert. It's a free day, and the band scatters.

Janis wants to ride the canals in one of the tourist boats. Bobby and I escort her. We get directions from the hotel's concierge and I remember to bring my movie camera. What we don't see from the water, we see later on foot and by taxi.

The Concertgebouw, Amsterdam's philharmonic hall, is a late-nineteenth-century gem. The interior is about 150 feet long under a ceiling 50 feet high. Backstage, the band members are bubbling with stories. Most of them have never been to Europe before. They tell tales of explorations and discoveries, several of them related to the tolerant local attitude toward smoking pot, even in some cafés, and the high visibility of Amsterdam's prostitutes. No one, it seems, found just the right moment to do more than admire the offerings.

The Concertgebouw fills, and in high spirits, Janis and the band take the stage. And something happens. Janis cues the band and *bam!* Tight isn't an adequate description. They're playing like one person wailing on all the instruments. The energy level jumps into high gear and never slacks off. "Raise your hand!" Janis sings. The song is a rouser. Janis is smiling as she sings, which isn't normal for her. Female vocalists in the big band era learned how to sing while smiling all the time like an ad for toothpaste. But Janis is not Rosemary Clooney.

Onstage, her expression reveals what she's putting into a song. She'll sometimes smile between numbers, acknowledging the applause. Here in Amsterdam, she's grinning because she feels what's happening. Finally, the band is together.

"Maybe" is followed by "Summertime." Luis's trumpet takes the high road in Sam's Baroque introduction. I never thought his arrangement could sound as soulful with this band as it did with Big Brother, but tonight it comes close.

Snooky takes the mike from Janis. He gets to sing a song in the show. It's an R&B rocker from Otis Redding called "Can't Turn You Loose," and Snooky makes the most of it. Janis dances with him on this song, to give herself something to do and to keep the audience focused on Snooky. This has become a regular thing, but tonight Janis's dancing is purely spontaneous. She skips around the stage. She shakes her butt. She gets in Snooky's face and the audience loves it.

One song after another, like a train coming down the track, the band keeps on rocking. They give a whole new life to Jerry Ragovoy's "Try (Just a Little Bit Harder)." Sam sings "Combination of the Two." Janis soars on "Piece of My Heart," another of Big Brother's hits, reinforced now by the horn section.

In the middle of the set, Terry Clements has so much fun on a solo that he just keeps going, extending the ride, and the band keeps going with him. Nobody's thinking, Hey, that's not the arrangement. Terry is tripping and the band is on his trip.

Nick Gravenites's "Work Me, Lord" is a showstopper, and the closer. "Ball and Chain" is the encore.

After the concert, backstage, everybody is talking at once and nobody can stop grinning. Sam dares to believe that Frank Zappa was right: Don't worry, it will come together in time.

Neuwirth is impressed. He heard the band in New York, at the Fillmore East. What he hears in Amsterdam is like a different band. During the show he took a seat in the hall and recorded the performance on a small cassette recorder. Even on the machine's tiny speaker, you can hear how good it was.

Has it really come together? Or was tonight's performance a non-recurring phenomenon? Time will tell.

Our next stop is Frankfurt. Knud says it's a happening city. There are big American bases near Frankfurt. The audience will be full of Americans.

For most of us, it's our first time in Germany. Knud has booked a minibus to bring us into the city from the airport. I don't have to drive and I don't have to find the hotel, so I'm free to sightsee. What I see here and there, as we pass through the older parts of the city, are walls that are pockmarked by bullets and shell fragments. As a boy, I saw all the Second World War movies I could drag my father to on Saturday afternoons. Only Westerns held more interest for me. Now I'm on enemy ground. This is where it happened.

The same awareness gives Roy Markowitz some cause for concern, because he's Jewish. It's hard to tell if his worry is genuine or if he's playing it for effect.

Russian troops man the East German border seventy-five miles from Frankfurt. Sam and I share an awareness of the recent history that hangs heavy here—the hot war that produced the Cold War. Twenty-four years later, Germany is still divided and the Soviets rule the Eastern Bloc.

Our hotel is modern and classy. It overlooks the river Main, a tributary of the Rhine. In the afternoon, before the sound check, Bobby and I hang out with Janis and Linda Gravenites in their room. Janis is laid-back, relaxed, saving her energy for the performance. She touches up her nails with an emery board, and we take in the river view from ten floors above the Main.

At the concert hall we are met by a crew from Bavarian television, who will film the concert this evening. They greet us as we get off the minibus and follow us into the dressing room backstage. Janis, as always, plays to the cameras—theirs and mine—while the rest of the band goes about their business.

The concert hall is nothing like the historic Concertgebouw. Frankfurt, like many German cities, was pulverized in the war. Here, as in the parts of London that were heavily bombed, much of the construction is new. The hall has a peculiar low-ceilinged lobby that's washed with flat fluorescent light, but the hall itself is fine, fan-shaped, modern, with good sound. Knud and Bobby and I tour the building to familiarize ourselves with the layout.

When the audience is admitted, there are American military police outside and in the lobby. Not a lot of them; just enough to create a presence. Bobby and I cruise the crowd, admiring the girls. Judging by the bits of conversation we pick up, it's a fair guess that about half the young men in the crowd are American. Some have German dates. Everyone's in civvies, so it's hard to tell.

Janis performs two shows back-to-back. The first is the regular show with the houselights off. Here again, the band is hot, and the audience is even more unrestrained in their admiration than the Dutch. When "Ball and Chain" is over, to quiet the demands of the audience for another encore, we announce that we're going to do an abbreviated second show for the benefit of the Bavarian television crew. You're all welcome to stay, we tell the audience. And they do, almost all of them. Play it again, Sam.

This time the houselights are on. The TV cameramen move in front of the stage and onstage too, maneuvering around Janis and the band without worrying about the sight lines of the audience. The original plan was for Janis to do four songs, which will be enough for the program the TV crew is shooting, but Janis and the band are still on a roll and they don't want to quit after four songs. Let's do "Combination of the Two." Let's do "Work Me, Lord."

What keeps the show going is the enthusiasm of the band and the energy Janis gets back from the audience. This is what she wants every time, singer and audience engaged in a duet, each giving to and receiving from the other. She invites them up on the stage, where they cluster behind the instrument amps, forming a solid arc around Janis and the band. The rest stay out front, on their feet, dancing in front of the stage and in the aisles, and somehow the film crew maneuvers around them.

Janis and the band juggle the song list for variety. This time they do "Ball and Chain" as part of the set and save "Piece of My Heart" for the encore. During "Piece of My Heart," Janis is still holding out her hand, helping more people up on the stage. They're dancing within the arc of the amps now, all over the stage. The group around Janis is mostly young men dancing badly, but she couldn't care less. She's radiating joy.

When the song ends, Janis is in a crush so thick that Bobby Neuwirth and Mark Braunstein push through and create a small circle of sanctuary around her. I'm outside the cluster around Janis, holding my movie camera over my head, hoping I'm getting it. A kid in a T-shirt hands Janis a bouquet of flowers.

How do you top that? Well, we've got three days in Paris, with the concert on day two, at the historic Olympia Théâtre. It's in the Ninth Arrondissement, near the Café de la Paix and just a few blocks from Place de l'Opéra, where I picked up my mail at American Express when I spent two months in Paris on a year off from college.

Edith Piaf made her name at the Olympia. Jacques Brel and Marlene Dietrich sang here. In 1964, the Beatles played the Olympia for eighteen days straight.

Our touring band of rock-and-roll vagabonds adds another member in Paris, where we're joined by Bobby's lady, Tonto. Her modeling career brought her to Paris before Bobby knew her. She speaks fluent French and she has friends in town.

The Olympia is mobbed. It's smaller than the halls in Amsterdam and Frankfurt, more intimate. In size, it's like a decent first-run movie theater in America, with a balcony that wraps around the sides, but the ambiance is definitely continental.

Before the show, I walk around the block, following the line of hopefuls who will not all reach the box office before the show is sold out. I approach a beautiful French girl far down the line. Would you like to see the show?—*le spectacle*, in French, which seems especially appropriate for Janis. *Oui*, she says, tentatively. Come with me. She hesitates, suspecting an ulterior motive on my part. The stage door, *la porte des artistes*, is this way, I tell her. She decides to trust me. I take her inside and find her a seat in a box overlooking the stage. She can't believe her luck. Her name is Nathalie Fontenoy: *un nom tres Français, tres Parisien*.

Janis and the band are on a roll. Once again, the energy is up from the start. During the first couple of numbers I move through the hallways and poke my head in the back of the orchestra, then climb the stairs to listen from the balcony. The Olympia has great acoustics.

I imagine the ghost of Piaf in attendance, listening from a box overlooking the stage (perhaps seated next to Nathalie), a look of astonishment on her face at the sounds Janis produces for the delighted Parisians.

The next day, I rent a car and Bobby and Tonto and I make an excursion to Chartres, an hour west of Paris. We invite Janis to come, but the appeal of driving for an hour to wander around a cathedral and look at the stained glass is difficult to convey to someone who hasn't been there. Janis politely declines. Knud will look after her.

Chartres has been on my schedule since I was taken there by Alex Campbell, the World's Only Scottish Cowboy and a mentor to Ramblin' Jack Elliott in his early visit to England, on my second trip to France. It was the same day I introduced Mimi Baez to Dick Fariña in the backseat of my white Volvo, never dreaming the consequences that would flow from that meeting.

You've never been to Chartres? Alex was shocked. Until then, my embrace of European culture had included paintings and sculpture, public statuary and very old buildings, a millennium of history in the place-names and the landscape, but like Janis, I hadn't imagined the glories of stained glass.

On that first visit I took color slides of the beautiful windows, more than seven hundred years old. This time, I shoot movies, and seeing the windows through the viewfinder now as I film them is even more entrancing.

On our last evening in Paris, at twilight, Bobby and Tonto and Janis and I cruise the boulevards in a Rolls-Royce that belongs to one of Tonto's friends. The municipal government has recently initiated a program of steam-cleaning public buildings to remove a century of soot and grime, and the results are astonishing, especially at night, when the governmental and cultural edifices are lit up. Great structures that were glowering hulks when I was here a few years ago are now golden landmarks, standing out from their surroundings. They absorb the floodlights' glare and reflect it back as if the stone were illuminated from within. As we glide along in the Rolls, the city is like a stage set, on display just for us. This evening, it is truly the city of light.

ALTHOUGH WE ARE far from home, in foreign lands, the tour is less demanding for me than flying out of New York to the American Midwest. Dealing with the band, making sure they know when a sound check is scheduled or what time we're leaving for a concert, making sure they're ready backstage when it's time to go on, is always part of the job. In Europe, there's not much else for me to do. Knud has organized the rest: hotels and transportation. In each country, he smooths our way through immigration and customs. I wear a suit and tie for these formalities. Together we're a couple of respectable businessmen overseeing the musicians, which allays the suspicions of the authorities. We're met at each airport by a minibus or a van. I don't have to drive, I don't have to register the band at the hotels, I don't have to check with the promoters. Knud helps with problems that arise about equipment, hotels, hall managers, and he collects the money for each concert. I go with him to the box office; I stand by his side and oversee the calculations and the payment. We fall into a cooperative routine that makes touring the capital cities of Europe easier for me than Cleveland and Chicago. In France, I speak more French than Knud; in Germany, English is the lingua franca; in Scandinavia, Knud speaks all the languages well enough.

If I have less to do than when we're touring in the U.S., Mark Braunstein and George Ostrow are working harder than ever, and I'm grateful for the professionalism they have developed as a team. Mark and George fly with us, and on arrival they disappear. We have brought only our stage equipment—the instrument amps and the drums. Mark and George get these items onto each plane, collect them at the other end, and set up where we need them, for rehearsals and concerts. An added item for the English and European gigs is a large voltage transformer that enables our band to use their American amps.

Amid the welter of European languages, I find a use for my Spanish in forging a working relationship with Luis Gasca. Luis is a professional, and he is touchy about it. He gets his back up when I try to herd him along like some of the others—the habitual laggards in the band. He responds more cooperatively if I simply ask, "*Listo*, Luis?" Are you ready? "*Siempre listo*, Juan," he replies. Always ready. He helps me refresh my Spanish, and I'm delighted to learn that the coarse English phrase "a stiff prick has no conscience" trips off the tongue like poetry in Spanish: "*Una pinga parada no tiene conciencia.*"

The band is a unit at last, relaxed in its new confidence. After Amsterdam, Frankfurt and Paris, no one worries that everything may fall apart in the next show.

From Paris, we return to Stockholm. Here, as elsewhere in Europe, the concert hall has a bar. This is a source of delight to Janis. Knud introduces us to what he calls "snapps." The Germans say "schnapps," but in Scandinavia, it's "snapps." We arrive at the hall, we make sure the band is settled in their dressing room, and Knud says, "We have a snapps?" Yes, we have a snapps. We have a couple of snapps.

The concert goes well, and in what's now part of their continental routine, several members of the band go out to clubs afterward to drink with local fans eager to show them the town. Carousing to wind down after a gig is part of the musician's life, but I keep to my own routine, which is to get a good night's sleep whenever I can, so I miss my chance to meet the mayor of Stockholm.

Bobby and Tonto and Sam are no sooner settled at a table in a restaurant-nightclub than Bobby—on his way back to the table from the bar—meets the mayor. Come on over and meet Sam Andrew, Bobby says. He's here with Janis to play in your city. The mayor of Stockholm becomes their drinking buddy for the evening.

When they get back to the hotel, they find Janis awake, in a reflective mood. She marvels at how the band has come together since we arrived in Europe, how much they've achieved in a short time. She can hardly believe it. Believe it, Bobby tells her. They go to Bobby and Tonto's room, where Bobby plays Janis and Sam the tape he has recorded at tonight's concert. Janis and the boys are a band. Believe it.

In Copenhagen, they play the elegant Concert Hall at the Tivoli Gardens. The next morning, we say good-bye to Knud Thorbjørnsen. We'd like to take him to London. Hell, we want to take him home to America. He has become our hangout partner, and a friend.

THE ROYAL ALBERT Hall is an august pile of Victorian brick that heard Verdi and Wagner conduct English premieres of their works. Churchill spoke here. In modern times it has become the plum venue for pop musicians. Sinatra, in his day, and the Beatles, it goes without saying. In February of this year, Jimi Hendrix sold out two nights at the hall.

Janis is focused on Bob Dylan's sell-out appearance in 1965, which is chronicled in *Dont Look Back*. She is determined to do the same, and, if possible, to get the British audience out of their seats and dancing in the aisles.

The date of the concert is April 21, four months after the Stax-Volt show in Memphis, half a world away in time and space. Outside the hall, as the hour approaches, scalpers are hawking a few stray tickets, but most of the ticket holders won't part with them for love nor money.

It is rumored that some of the Beatles are here, some of the Stones. Fleetwood Mac is here. Eric Clapton is here for sure. Somebody saw him. God knows who else, if you believe the rumors.

The packed house, pop royalty and commoner alike, doesn't need much urging from Janis to get on their feet and boogie. It's like a replay of the first charmed show in Amsterdam.

Coming offstage after the final encore, Janis is irrepressible. A small handful of British music reporters have gathered backstage, from *Melody Maker* and the *Daily Sketch* and the *Daily Telegraph*. When Janis has changed out of her sweat-soaked garments and put on something fresh, she joins us in the band's dressing room and delivers a paean to what the band achieved tonight.

"Don't you know how happy we must be?" she says. "We really broke through a wall that I didn't think was possible. Like ever since we've been here, like the audiences we've had that have danced, we've always felt, oh, too much, that's really wonderful of them. But every-body said, 'Don't expect that of a British audience. Don't expect them to do nothin', man.' And when they first got up and started dancin', it was just like a big hot *rush*. We just went, 'Oh, *yeah*?' It's like a whole other door opened up, a whole other possibility that had never even occurred to you."

"I figure if you take an audience that have been told what to do all their lives and they're too young or scared . . . If you can get them once, man, get them standing up when they should be sitting down, sweaty when they should be decorous, smile when they should be applauding politely . . . I think you sort of switch on their brain, man, so that makes them say 'Wait a minute, maybe I *can* do anything.' Whooooo! It's life. That's what rock 'n' roll is for, turn that switch on."

Janis Joplin

It's significant that Janis says "we" tonight in London. In interviews with the press she often talks about being onstage, what it means to her, what it feels like, the relationship she tries to establish with the audience, and the subject is the first person singular. It's about her, which is, after all, what the interviewers want. Tonight, at Albert Hall, talking not just about tonight, but looking back on the whole European tour, she's talking about what she and the band have achieved. She feels for the first time that she and they are a unit that she is proud to embrace in the first person plural.

The questions the British journalists ask make it clear that the controversy in the American rock press about Janis leaving Big Brother is unknown to them. These pop critics are getting their first look at Janis, and they like what they see. Like tonight's audience in the Royal Albert Hall, they're dazzled.

It's not really a press conference, though a few flashbulbs pop. Janis shows off the new shoes she bought in Paris and she takes an ostentatious swig of tequila from a bottle we brought to the gig. "Do you prefer it?" a reporter asks. "Is it a better drink?" "I love it!" Janis says. "It tastes terrible, but I love it!" When we weren't drinking snapps with Knud in the concert hall bars, tequila has become the libation of choice on the tour, once Bobby joined us. Finding limes is a bitch on the Continent. The French don't even have a word for limes. They call them *citrons verts*—green lemons. In London too, we have to resort to lemons as chasers. (Reports in the American press have continued to tout Janis's devotion to Southern Comfort, but the reporters aren't paying attention. Even before she left Big Brother, Janis switched her affections to B&B, motivated in part by a desire to adjust her image by drinking something more sophisticated.)

Outside the stage door, there is a secure area where the band's limos are parked during the show. The boys in the band have made their escape in one limo, some of them on foot, but the crush of fans beyond the gate are waiting for a glimpse of Janis. The crowd shows no signs of diminishing, so eventually Bobby and Janis and I and at least six other people cram into the back of the other limo, Janis on Bobby's lap. The driver noses carefully through the crowd and gains the street. "I'm so excited!" Janis exults, but she catches herself. "Dylan didn't ever do that," she says to Bobby. "I'm not cool enough, huh? He didn't ever get—happy. I'm ecstatic and screaming." She waves to a trio of pretty boys peering at the limo's tinted windows. "So long, boys," she says. "Oh, my God." Her eye for a pretty boy is ever vigilant.

As in each of the other cities on the European tour, Janis's first stop after the show is the hotel, where she takes her leave and goes to her room. The purpose of these postconcert retreats is to get high before she sets off for late-night recreation in public. Since we've been on the road with the new band, the routine is more regular, more predictable. If the show went badly, getting high is her consolation. Tonight, as after the other European concerts, it's a reward, a celebration.

The party is in Janis's room. It's a suite, actually. We're in London for four nights and Janis has indulged herself by taking a suite for herself and Linda, where they can entertain royally.

I don't join the party, because I have a date. On our first day back in London I made a beeline for the flea market and the stall where I discovered the tiger-claw belt. The minute we left England I knew I had to have it. But I hesitated, and I lost. The belt is gone. Still there, however, is a blond American named Nancy, tending the stall next door. I struck up an acquaintance with her before, and I renew it now with an invitation to the concert. I can't escort her, but I stop by her seat and say hello before the show, and we've arranged to meet at the hotel afterward.

We entertain ourselves in my room, with drinks and a late supper from room service, and it is well after the event that I learn we almost lost Sam in the early hours of the morning.

In Janis's suite, the presence of old friends from San Francisco fuels the festive feeling. Bob Seidemann is a San Francisco photographer who knew the boys in Big Brother before Janis joined the band. He took the photo of Big Brother, including Janis, that Albert Grossman's office used for publicity. Bob has taken a nude portrait of Janis—the only nude portrait of Janis—with her hands chastely folded over her pubic area, which he has refused to exploit for profit. Also on hand is Stanley Mouse, one of the creators and the foremost practitioner of the psychedelic rock-and-roll poster style that defined the Fillmore and the Avalon ballroom scene and has spread as far and wide as acid rock. Eric Clapton is among the celebrants as well. See!—he really was there.

Seidemann hears Janis's voice announce from the bathroom, "Oh, I really got off. I really got off." A short time later, Seidemann peers into the bathroom and what he sees is Sam, in the bathtub, fully dressed, with a girl clad only in panties sitting astride him. Seidemann takes in the fact that Sam is blue and his eyes are closed. And now Janis and Linda Gravenites are bending over Sam, and Seidemann understands that Sam has OD'd.

Seidemann would do anything to help Sam, but three women are ministering to him and there is something else that needs to be done. Seidemann takes Clapton aside and says, "Eric, get out. A guy in the other room's OD'd." If things go badly, no one wants to read in tomorrow's newspapers that Clapton was at the scene of a drug overdose. Clapton splits, and Seidemann gets to work clearing the suite.

It seems to take forever—fifteen minutes to shove the geeks and yahoos and hangers-on out the door—and when they're gone Seidemann returns to the bathroom, where those who know and care for Sam are apparently trying to keep him cold and awake. Which he isn't yet, but there are flickers of returning consciousness.

There's talk of calling a doctor. Seidemann puts a stop to that. He has been in England long enough to know that nobody calls doctors for OD'ing junkies, because calling doctors means the police will show up as well.

Eventually Sam comes out of it, because of—or in spite of—the efforts of Janis and Linda and the nearly naked girl, whose name is Susie Creamcheese. Of course it is.

CHAPTER SEVENTEEN

Back in the U.S.A.

APR. 25, 1969: **Springfield, Mass.**

APR. 26: **MIT, Cambridge, Mass. (1 P.M.)**

APR. 26: **Brown University, Providence, R.I. (8:30 P.M.)**

APR. 27: **Rochester, N.Y.**

MAY 2: **Onondaga War Memorial Auditorium, Syracuse, N.Y.**

MAY 3: **Cornell University, Ithaca, N.Y.**

MAY 4: **University of New Hampshire, Durham, N.H.**

MAY 9: **Cleveland Convention Center, Cleveland, Ohio**

MAY 10: **Cobo Hall, Detroit**

MAY 11: **Veterans Memorial Music Hall, Columbus, Ohio**

ON APRIL 24 we land in Boston and keep right on following the sun along the Mass Pike to Springfield, where we have twenty-four hours to rest and recuperate before the gig. We are a cosmopolitan crew, fresh from European triumphs. Springfield is a manufacturing city in decline, unworthy of our attention, but Janis and the band deign to play for the younger residents, to give them hope.

The next day we have two shows fifty miles apart. The first is at

MIT in Cambridge, with a 1:00 P.M. start, followed by an evening
show in Providence, at Brown University. This is a bit of a scramble
for Mark and George, no sweat for me and Janis and the band. At
Brown, probably half the audience are RISD students, but this time
no fetching girls fondle me as I check the sound from the back of
the hall.

We're coasting on the European high, but Syracuse, Rochester,
and Cleveland can't hold a candle to Paris, Copenhagen and London.
The cohesion Janis and the band found in Europe begins to dissipate.
Janis repairs to her hotel room each night after the gig, sometimes
with Richard, sometimes alone. Linda Gravenites decided at the last
minute to stay in London to make clothes for the English rockers.
Some of the Rolling Stones were among her potential customers.
Linda's real reason is that she can't bear to be around Janis so long as
Janis is in thrall to heroin.

Back in New York, between gigs, Janis and Sam get word that
Nancy Gurley, James's wife, has died of an overdose. James and
Nancy went camping in Sonoma County. They brought along some
smack to get high in the country. When James woke up in the morning, Nancy was dead at his side. James is being charged with second-
degree murder, because he shot her up. Janis and Sam's reaction to the
news is to score and get high.

Janis's next reaction is to call Bob Gordon to ask his help in finding an attorney to defend James. She will contribute to the legal fees,
and this help will prove decisive in keeping James out of jail.

We fly out of New York to tour the Midwest. This spring, the
hyped-up expectations of the audiences, together with the still-
growing disdain for authority that characterizes the youth "movement" as a whole, increasingly threaten concert security. The kids
want in, whether there are tickets or not, whether they can afford
them or not. Controlling entries at a municipal auditorium is one
thing, but as the weather warms and the concerts move out into
stadiums, parks and racetracks, the temptations to gate-crashers are

often irresistible. If enough frustrated fans want to see a show, it takes more than some snow fence and a few rent-a-cops to keep them out.

For the first time, I'm dealing with security as an essential part of the arrangements for every concert. Janis is now so well known that her appearances bring the threat that the ticketless hordes will try to come over the fence or through the back door. A riot at a Janis Joplin concert means bad publicity for Janis and future loss of income, if promoters become reluctant to book her. It means present loss of income too. Janis's fees this year are almost always based on a guarantee versus a percentage. Every nimble kid who jumps the fence is money lost. If the show is sold out, we couldn't care less, because Janis will be paid based on the sold-out seat count, but even so, gate-crashers create resentment among the paying guests and provoke confrontations with the police and rent-a-cops.

In concert halls and auditoriums, there are ways to protect the stage. Is there an orchestra pit? Can it be open during the performance, creating a waterless moat between the audience and the stage? In outdoor settings, a fenced no-man's-land in front of the stage can help. When we arrive at a gig, I talk with the security staff and police. I tell them we know they're on our side. I tell them our preferred method for dealing with fans who make it onto the stage is to take them through the wings and let them back into the audience if they will go peacefully. If not, out the back door. These kids pay all our salaries; they deserve to be treated with care, even if they make trouble.

When security breaks down and the stage is mobbed, the power cords to the stage monitors often get kicked loose. Janis hates it when she can't hear herself. After a few incidents where equipment is damaged or stolen, or where Janis is assaulted in midsong by an especially ardent fan, she is willing for the most part to do what she can to keep the crowd under control. She still urges the audience to get up and dance, but at the same time she asks them to keep off the stage.

Some of the city cops and rent-a-cops belong to Vice President Spiro Agnew's Silent Majority. To them, the culture of rock and roll and dope-smoking hippies is a symptom of the world gone to the dogs, and nothing will straighten out a faggot hippie quicker than a billy club upside the head. More often, the security men's occasional overreactions are prompted less by repressed fascist rage than by fear. At one show where a few enthusiastic fans gain the stage, I arrive in the wings just in time to stop an aging rent-a-cop, a former police-man, from using his billy club on a cowering kid who is maybe all of seventeen. "Hold it!" I shout, and my voice carries enough authority to freeze the old man. I put myself between him and the kid. The rent-a-cop's hand is shaking as he puts his club back in its belt loop. He has never seen anything like a Janis Joplin show before. He doesn't know what to make of it or what the fans might do if they reach the stage en masse. He is as frightened as the kid.

Aside from a few such adrenaline-provoking moments, life on the road follows the familiar routine. There are good days, bad days, and boring days. Within a couple of weeks after our return, the elevating unity the band experienced in Europe is gone. There are spats among the musicians and times when Janis is pushy or demanding or just plain unpleasant to any and all of them. More often, her commitment to good company and good times gives her enough energy to keep the band, despite its interpersonal and musical problems, from degenerat-ing into a group of strangers with no common bonds.

The band member who requires the most maintenance during the intramural upsets is Luis Gasca. Quick to take offense, his frequent reaction to some real or imagined slight is to throw a fit and threaten to quit the band. I played with Mongo Santamaria, man, I don't need this shit! Each time, I take him aside and talk him down. We have a record coming up, and a summer tour. You want to be on the record, right?

On May 12, we fly from Ohio to San Francisco for five weeks' vacation. Janis and the band, still unnamed, have been on the road for three months straight.

THERE IS A letdown from the routine of being on the road and in the company of others who are working together in the same enterprise, but there are compensations too. In the familiar comfort of my North Beach apartment, I sleep well. Apart from time on the phone to make a few arrangements for the summer tour, I am free, for the moment, from the demands of road managing. I put a bunch of paychecks into the bank. I go to the Committee, I have dinner with Mimi, I visit friends in Berkeley—where I find the city on the verge of something like a revolution. The local hippies have occupied a vacant lot, a rectangle of grass and foliage that's owned by the University of California. The lot is near Telegraph Avenue, the Berkeley equivalent of Haight Street. The hippies have christened the lot People's Park. They have planted trees, created a garden. At night, they gather around campfires. It's a tribal gathering place.

The UC regents are taking a dog-in-the-manger attitude: We're not using it, but you can't either. On my third day home, Berkeley police use shotguns and tear gas to break up a demonstration in support of People's Park. An onlooker is wounded. Governor Ronald Reagan mobilizes the National Guard and gives a bogus justification for cops beating kids. A policeman is only human, Reagan says on TV. If you call him obscene names, he'll sometimes react just as anyone would. *Wrong*, Ronnie. A policeman doesn't get to react just like some right-wing hardhat. A policeman represents the state, and the state represents the law. The state doesn't get to mete out summary beatings in response to verbal abuse. Even if some hippie calls a cop a motherfucking pig, the cop doesn't get to pound on the kid with a truncheon.

Four days later the wounded onlooker dies. When a memorial gathering masses on the UC campus, a helicopter drops tear gas on the crowd while National Guard troops prevent the demonstrators from escaping into the city streets. Seen on the evening news, there's an uncomfortable similarity between the Berkeley footage and the preceding report from Vietnam, where the American troop level is now well over half a million.

The next day, I drive through Berkeley with a friend, filming cops and National Guard troops from my car. It's sunny and warm. Springtime in California. Under normal circumstances, a perfect day to stroll up Telegraph Avenue and through the campus. Today, the massed forces of uniformed men in blue and olive-drab uniforms, the cruising convoys of cop cars and National Guard jeeps, turn the familiar streets into something surreal, like a set for a dystopian movie. On Telegraph Avenue, where hippies sell beads and God's eyes and tie-dyed T-shirts in normal times, I see hanging from a second-story window a sheet that evokes the Soviet Union's brutal suppression of Czechoslovakia's peaceful revolution just a year ago. On the sheet, the occupants have painted, "Welcome to Prague."

For a ninety-minute break from Ronald Reagan's California, I go to see *Monterey Pop*, which has opened in San Francisco while we were away. The film was originally planned as a television special on ABC, but ABC took a look and took a pass, so Pennebaker and the festival organizers decided to release it in theaters. Documentaries rarely do well theatrically, but Penny had success with *Dont Look Back* that he hopes to repeat. At the Presidio Theater, where *Dont Look Back* had a successful run, the audience loves *Monterey Pop*. For me, it brings back memories of the screening in John and Michelle Phillips's Bel Air mansion, when the glow of the Summer of Love was still warm in memory. What strikes me now are the cutaways to the faces in the audience and the people strolling the fairgrounds, so young and bright and open, full of hope and joy. With the traumas of 1968 behind us and the National Guard occupying Berkeley, the idea that music, love, and flowers might truly change the world seems impossibly naïve.

Newsweek is on the stands with Janis on the cover for a story on the rebirth of the blues in pop music. The article does a creditable job of tracing the origins of the blues from the early recordings of Bessie Smith and Robert Johnson to the best current practitioners. It places Janis at the center of a blues revival, in company with B. B. and Albert King, Jimi Hendrix, Muddy Waters, Johnny Winter, and Big Mama Thornton herself, whose "Ball and Chain" was Janis's ticket to fame. The article doesn't mention Big Brother or Janis's new band.

Soon after our return to San Francisco, Mark Braunstein announces that he's quitting. He's had enough of the road. With Big Brother, it was fun. With this band it isn't.

> "I felt the [new band] was constantly trying too hard, was somewhat unnatural, was forced. . . . I never felt that the [new band] was receiving the adoration and communication and warmth from the audience that Big Brother was, because I didn't feel they were putting it out."
>
> **Mark Braunstein**

IN THE MIDDLE of June, we convene in Los Angeles to make a record. Columbia wants an album that demonstrates Janis's new sounds to the fans who made *Cheap Thrills* a bestseller.

George Ostrow is in charge of the equipment now. His new assistant is Vince Mitchell, as long and lean as George, his dark hair often in a ponytail.

We have less than two weeks in the studio before a gig in Denver on the way to another eastern tour. The pressure is on, and we have new drummers to break in, first one, then another. After our final concert of the spring tour, in Columbus, Ohio, Roy Markowitz flew home to New York and decided not to return. In his stead there is Lonnie Castille, a tall, genial guy who lasts about a week, to be replaced by Maury Baker, who is shorter, with longer hair.

The producer Albert has chosen to guide this album is Gabriel Mekler. Mekler arrived in L.A. a few years ago, knowing almost nothing about pop music. He lucked into a job at Lou Adler's Dunhill Records, where he produced Steppenwolf's debut album last year. The story is, he gave the group its name. This short pedigree in music producing arouses the interest of Janis's musicians.

Janis has decided that this time around she is going to get along with her record producer come hell or high water. She sets out to win Gabriel to her side, and she succeeds. From the outset, he is solicitous of her and always listens to what she has to say. It wouldn't be accurate to say they become friends. What Janis is after is a working relationship in which she feels recognized rather than neglected, and she achieves this with Gabriel.

In contrast, he treats the band members as if they don't exist. Snooky feels that Gabriel doesn't have the first clue about black music or the hybrid sound Janis and the band have been working to create. Terry Clements musters his verbal skills to communicate with Gabriel about the horns and the arrangements, but Gabriel doesn't show much interest in what Terry has to say. Terry gets the impression that Gabriel has his own idea about what Janis's new band should have been and isn't willing to deal with what it is.

Sam comes into the sessions ready to do whatever he can to make them work, but Gabriel hardly acknowledges Sam's presence. Maybe he sees Sam as a threat because he comes from Big Brother, where he was Janis's equal.

The musicians are looking for recognition of who they are and what they have accomplished in their time with Janis. They are a backup band, pieced together by Albert and Mike Bloomfield and others, but each musician wants it to be more than that. In Europe, it *was* more than that. In Columbia's L.A. studio, they are salaried sidemen who are being paid less than union scale for the sessions. They are being asked to refine the arrangements, to show Janis at her best, but they have no incentive to take on the added responsibilities.

They resent being treated like hired hands, and the fact that Janis won't stand up for them in the face of Gabriel's dismissive attitude.

Janis reacts to the conflicts by separating herself from the band and retiring into semiseclusion. She no longer turns to Richard Kermode as a fallback lover. On the days when Gabriel doesn't need her, when he's working with the band, she spends much of her time alone. The self-imposed discipline that limited her on the road to a daily hit of smack after a performance isn't needed here. In his off-hours, Sam is still Janis's partner in the covert companionship of heroin. He keeps pace with her, and for the first time he feels that the drug use is getting out of hand.

In the studio, their relationship doesn't exist. At work, Janis and Gabriel are a unit apart from the others. Their mutual dependence produces a song that offers at last a name for the band. The song is called "I Got Dem Ol' Kozmic Blues Again, Mama." (This will be the name of the album.) When we leave L.A., the band will be the Kozmic Blues Band. Later, we'll embrace the name, even enjoy it, but during the recording, the concept of cosmic blues suggests the depth of the musicians' discomfort.

Given the tensions in the studio, I have even less incentive than usual to spend time there. I hang out with my fellow Charles River Valley Boy and Cambridge roommate, Fritz Richmond, who moved to L.A. last year to work at Elektra Records' Los Angeles studios as a sound engineer. He trained with Paul Rothchild, who has since left Elektra to become an independent producer. Fritz remains one of Paul's preferred engineers for Elektra projects, and they share a house in Laurel Canyon. Fritz and I dine often at a restaurant called the Blue Boar, just down La Cienega from the Elektra studios. We discover that the restaurant has a stash of exceptional Puligny Montrachet wine at a very reasonable price. Customarily, gourmands of our generation choose a wine to suit the meal. At the Blue Boar, Fritz and I tailor our meals to suit the wine. We get mellow together, and I confide in him about the changes I'm experiencing on the road. A year ago, it was all new and exciting. Now I wonder how much longer I want to do this job.

Albert arrives in Los Angeles early in the recording. He takes up lodging in his customary room at the Chateau Marmont, a 1920s castle above Sunset where hip movie stars and moguls of the music business stay in L.A.

Albert seeks the opinions of the musicians about how to improve the arrangements and the atmosphere in the studio. He talks with Terry Clements, and even asks if Terry knows a third party, someone outside the band, who might help. He consults with Snooky. He talks with Sam. As he did with Big Brother, Albert is looking for solutions to what he sees as an ongoing problem. Each of the musicians tells him what it was like in Europe. Albert has heard about Europe from Neuwirth too. But these exuberant reports don't change what Albert hears in the studio, where the musical cohesion Janis and the band achieved on the European tour is not in evidence.

It doesn't help that Gabriel and the engineer require multiple takes, sometimes dozens, and that many are necessitated by simple technical mistakes—mikes not on, or not properly placed. When the musicians complain about these things, or ask for a better mix in their earphones, Janis gets bitchy with the band. She feels they're being prima donnas, and she doesn't acknowledge, or doesn't recognize, that the sessions are not being competently run.

Insult is added to the other irritants when Richard Kermode arrives at a session to find someone else sitting at his organ. Without consulting or forewarning the band, Gabriel has hired a studio sideman to play on a certain tune. He does this on other occasions, bringing in outside musicians without giving any advance notice to Janis's band members, and in consequence their resentment grows stronger.

The unsung hero of the sessions is Mike Bloomfield. He spends time in the studio and gives of his expertise selflessly. He helps Sam work out an arrangement for "Little Girl Blue," a Rodgers and Hart classic that Mike and Sam transform as thoroughly as Sam did Gershwin's "Summertime."* Mike plays slide guitar on "One Good Man," a song Janis writes during the session. And when it's all over and done, Mike asks for no credit on the album and will accept none.

> "Every now and then a guitarist will still come up to me and he'll go, 'That wasn't you, that was Mike Bloomfield, right?' And I'll say, 'Yeah.' I don't know why he didn't take the credit. . . . He's playing slide on the album. And I still get asked about that. And so he was like real noble. He was doing all this stuff and he didn't put his name on anywhere. And Gabriel wasn't doing anything and he put his name everywhere."
>
> **Sam Andrew**

The sessions are most difficult for Sam. In Big Brother, he was creatively at the center of the band. He wrote "Call on Me" and "Combination of the Two," two of the band's early signature songs. He co-wrote "I Need a Man to Love" with Janis. Without his lyrical arrangement of "Summertime," that song would never have become so identified with Janis, evoking applause from her audiences, even in Europe, from the first notes of the guitar intro. Overnight, Sam has gone from being Janis's equal partner to a guitar for hire. As the gulf widens between Janis and the band, Sam sides with the musicians.

Their resentments come to a head one evening at the Landmark. The musicians feel they should get a piece of the record, just a few percentage points, to reflect what they have contributed, and so they have a stake in the outcome. They ask for a meeting with Albert and Janis. Beforehand, they talk among themselves and build up a head of steam, but in Janis's room, faced with Albert's sphinxlike presence,

---

* Sam feels that "Little Girl Blue" shows Janis's voice at its best. "Whenever I encounter jazz musicians who are condescending about Janis's vocal ability I play them 'Little Girl Blue.' If they can't hear that, they can't hear." (E-mail from Sam Andrew, January 3, 1999.)

the others lose their nerve. Sam has known Albert longest, and he is the one who has the courage to speak. Give us a couple of percent from the album, he says. "Just give us like one percent. Give us anything that'll reflect sales of the album rather than just like the—"

"Why, man?" Albert asks. "I can go get better guys than any one of you guys, in—session men from Nashville."

"That's true, Albert," Sam says. "But what does that have to do with it? The fact is, we've gone through all these gigs with Janis and we deserve something more than just like session pay." All the musicians have contributed to the arrangements we're using on the album, he says. We've worked to make this a band.

Sam's plea falls on deaf ears. The other musicians remain mute, and meekly retire from Janis's room in defeat.

Not long after this confrontation, on another evening at the Landmark, after Sam and Janis have shot up together in her room, Janis seems agitated, despite the soporific effect of the drug. The cause, and the measure of her discomfort, is evident when she works up the courage to say what's on her mind. It comes out sounding artificially formal, as if Janis were a school principal addressing an incompetent teacher across a wide oak desk. "Your services are no longer required," she says. Sam says nothing. "Don't you want to know why?" she says. He says, "Does it really matter?"

Walking across the patio by the pool, Sam encounters Richard Kermode. "How you doing, Sam?" Richard asks. "Well, pretty good," Sam says. "Janis just fired me."

By now, it's clear to both Sam and Janis that Janis brought Sam with her when she left Big Brother because she was unable to make a complete break from the past. She needed to keep some connection with all that San Francisco and Big Brother meant to her, which was everything. Sam was a friend. He was a songwriter, and he knew how to arrange a song so it supported Janis's vocal. With Sam, Janis had a point of reference amid a host of new uncertainties.

Now, six months into the new band, the dissension in the recording sessions has made painfully apparent that there is no solution to the discomfort Sam's reduced position in this group has created. What Janis doesn't tell Sam is that among the other musicians there is a feeling that replacing him is a necessary step to finding the groove Janis wants, and Albert agrees.

So she lets him go. But not yet. There's a record to finish, and a tour that begins in another week, ready or not. Within a day of firing him, Janis asks Sam if he will stay until she can find a new guitar player. Of course he says yes.

JUNE 27–29, 1969: Denver Pop Festival, Mile High Stadium. Big Mama Thornton, Three Dog Night, Frank Zappa and the Mothers of Invention, Iron Butterfly, Johnny Winter, Tim Buckley, Creedence Clearwater Revival, Joe Cocker, Jimi Hendrix.*

JUNE 30: St. Louis

JULY 1: Edwardsville, Ill.

JULY 2: Des Moines, Iowa

JULY 5: Atlanta International Pop Festival, Atlanta International Raceway, Hampton, Ga. Johnny Winter, Johnny Rivers, Blood, Sweat & Tears, Canned Heat, Spirit, Joe Cocker, Creedence Clearwater Revival, Al Kooper, Paul Butterfield Blues Band, Dave Brubeck, Delaney & Bonnie, Led Zeppelin, Grand Funk Railroad, Chicago Transit Authority, and more.

JULY 8: Tanglewood Music Festival, Mass.

JULY 11: Hampton Beach, N.H.

JULY 12: Yale Bowl, New Haven, Conn.

JULY 18: *The Dick Cavett Show*, NYC

JULY 19: Forest Hills Tennis Stadium, Queens, N.Y.

---

* The many pop festivals produced this year offered fans some extraordinary aggregations of talent, as these listings show.

We play the Denver Pop Festival at Mile High Stadium. On the last day of June we fly to St. Louis. We have three gigs in the Midwest before we get to New York, and we're there for just two nights before we're off to the Atlanta International Pop Festival. Two years after Monterey, everybody is having pop festivals. Festivals in Texas and New Orleans are on the itinerary later in the summer.

The word on Atlanta is good and Bob Neuwirth comes along for the weekend. I bring from New York a would-be girlfriend, a major model who is majorly dazzling, and boy do I not know how to solidify this relationship in the densest weeks of Janis's summer schedule. While I'm trying to entertain her, Janis and Bob Neuwirth and Bonnie Bramlett have their own hangout party backstage, keeping to the shade in the hundred-degree heat. Bonnie is an Illinois girl married to the Mississippi-born Delaney Bramlett. They made an album for Stax Records that got little notice, but they are now with Elektra and the buzz within the business says they're going places.

In Atlanta the huge crowd is peaceful and happy and the festival comes off well. Forty-eight hours later, we're at the Tanglewood Music Festival in Massachusetts, a different scene entirely. Renowned for its summer festival of classical music, Tanglewood has begun presenting pop acts to bring in younger concertgoers. Here in the Berkshires, the fans that mob the place to hear Janis Joplin behave themselves on the elegant grounds of the estate, but even in this verdant, refined setting, the Kozmic Blues Band is not at peace. The bitterness engendered by how the musicians were treated during the recording sessions and the decision to exclude them from participation in the album's expected success have put a lid on how much effort they are willing to devote to their jobs. They have settled into a sullen state of reduced expectations.

At the routine gigs between the big festivals, in response to the band's diminished commitment, Janis drinks before the shows and her singing sometimes has an edge of desperation. Her stage manner becomes histrionic. Despite my requests that she use a coffee mug onstage, she revives her old practice of swigging from a bottle, often flagrantly, to the delight of the audience and the annoyance of the promoters. After the show, back at the hotel, Janis disappears into her room for her nightly fix. I never see her high during the day, but the regularity of the nightly ritual reveals a dependence on heroin that is much greater than when she was flirting with it in the days with Big Brother.

Offstage, Janis is too often on what I call her "star trip," expecting—sometimes demanding—special treatment, dismissing rudely someone she doesn't want to be bothered by, even gentle souls who want only to express their admiration for her. It seems to me that the impulse behind this behavior springs from a need to be acknowledged as someone of value at a time when she doesn't value herself.

> "Janis was like this complete person, but the trouble with being a 'star' is that everybody who met her had this image of who she was already in their minds, so that's what they related to in her and that's what she gave them back. And she lost like seven tenths of herself, I mean who she really was. I mean, she was a very intelligent woman, but you wouldn't know it."
>
> **Linda Gravenites**

I am restless with disappointment and bedeviled by guilt. Janis is losing control, going into a tailspin. I feel that Albert and Bob Neuwirth are the advisors most likely to steer her straight when it comes to addressing her addiction, and I perhaps underestimate my own ability to influence her.

AT THE YALE Bowl in New Haven, we meet a prospective replacement for Sam Andrew. Like Brad Campbell, John Till is a Canadian who shares musical credentials with some others among Albert's artists. He has toured with Ronnie Hawkins, an Arkansas rocker who migrated to Ontario and made his reputation in Canada. A few years ago, alumni from Hawkins's band became backup musicians for Bob Dylan, and have since become the Band.

John Till was impressed by Janis's performance in *Monterey Pop*, which was his first and only view of Janis to date. He is even more impressed by what he sees and hears at the Yale Bowl. It seems to John that Janis has matured as a singer and performer. While she's onstage, he can't take his eyes off her. He came to New Haven to see if he wants the gig. After the show, he's sure he does.

In New York, John rehearses with the band. Ever the perfect gentleman, Sam shows him the arrangements and some of the guitar licks he'll need for "Summertime," "Little Girl Blue," "Piece of My Heart," and other tunes where the guitar lead defines Janis's version of the songs. John is appropriately grateful. He is quiet, modest, unassuming. Like Mike Bloomfield, he lives to play the guitar. He wins Janis's approval, and Albert's.

On the Friday following the Yale Bowl, Janis is scheduled for an appearance on *The Dick Cavett Show*. Until recently Cavett hosted a morning show on ABC. This summer, he's doing an interview show like Johnny Carson's *Tonight Show* on NBC, but Cavett's is in prime time, three nights a week. It's Janis's first network TV appearance since *The Ed Sullivan Show* with Big Brother. For this performance, Sam takes the stage with the band. It is too soon to debut a new guitar player.

Janis sings "To Love Somebody" and joins Cavett on the set. Cavett doesn't sit behind a desk like Carson, but in a chair next to his guest. It's a more intimate format. Janis is relaxed with Cavett, and the banter is spontaneous. When she takes out a cigarette, Cavett says, "May I light your fire, my child?" Janis erupts in laughter and says, "That's my favorite singer. How'd you know?" Cavett doesn't know she broke a bottle over Jim Morrison's head, so he misses the irony.

When Cavett asks if there are male groupies, Janis says, "Not near enough," and gets a laugh, but she gives serious answers to serious questions. When Cavett asks why there are no other "superstar rock ladies" like her, as opposed to singers like Jo Stafford, for instance, Janis suggests that maybe it's not "feminine" to sing the way she does, to dig deep into the music, instead of "floating around on the top like most chick singers do."

Among Cavett's other guests are the Committee, some of them fresh from a vacation in Tangier, Morocco. The jet lag renders the actors goonier than usual, which is suitable preparation for a piece they perform called "The Emotional Symphony." From audience suggestions, an emotion is assigned to each player. A member of the company acts as the conductor, summoning up these emotions—expressed vocally and with body language—from the players in turn, modulating and combining the emotional tones. For this performance, Janis and Cavett are enlisted. Janis is assigned frustration, and Cavett love. It is no great stretch for Janis to summon up frustration at this point in her life. The piece is a great success with the audience, and the Committee actors remember it as a standout performance.

The day after the Cavett show, Janis and Kozmic Blues perform in the tennis stadium at Forest Hills, in Queens. For this performance, there are two guitars in the band, Sam and John Till. It is John's first gig with Kozmic Blues, and Sam's last. The next day, as the Apollo 11 Lunar Module touches down and Neil Armstrong prepares to set foot on the moon, Sam is on a plane for California and I've lost my best friend on the road.

CHAPTER EIGHTEEN

Half a Million Strong

JOHN TILL GETS two gigs to find his footing as Kozmic Blues' guitar player before the most anticipated show of the year.

In this short time, it becomes evident that although Sam is gone, the guitar player is still going to be the guy who is chronically late. John Till's principal means of self-expression is through his music. He is limited in verbal communication not by any fault of intelligence, but because he is a natural-born space case. He exists on a plane slightly removed from the rest of us, and communicating through the ether imposes a burden on him that he is loath to bear for long. As I try to do with any new member of the band, I make him welcome and at the same time impress on him the necessity of being on time, being ready when called, but such imposed organization is out of tune with John's natural rhythm. He never confronts my authority outright, but sometimes he does an end run around me just by standing still.

The Woodstock Music and Art Fair is scheduled for three days in mid-August. It's the most thorough attempt since Monterey to replicate both the aggregation of talent and the counterculture atmosphere that festival achieved, and the list of advertised bands is impressive. On Saturday, when Janis is scheduled, the artists include Canned Heat, Creedence Clearwater Revival, the Grateful Dead, Jefferson Airplane, Mountain, Santana, and the Who.

The festival was originally planned for a site near Woodstock, New York, which has gained prominence on the map of popular music since Bob Dylan moved there in the early sixties. (Dylan moved there because Albert Grossman moved there, but Albert neither receives nor wants the credit.) When Bob Neuwirth and Debbie Green and Paul Rothchild and I visited Dylan at Albert's house in the summer of '64, Woodstock had already acquired a nickname, Hipstock. In 1969, Paul Butterfield, Van Morrison, Geoff and Maria Muldaur, songwriter Tim Hardin, and the Band are among those who live in and around Woodstock and Bearsville.

A proposed site for the concert in Wallkill, near Woodstock, fell through. The promoters promised town authorities no more than fifty thousand people would attend the concerts, but that was enough to scare the bejesus out of the rural New York Staters. The final site is at a farm near White Lake, fifty miles from Woodstock, but the name has cachet and nobody's about to change it.

Janis and I figure this is an event, like Monterey, that we want to be part of from start to—well, maybe not to the last gasp, but for most of the festivities. We plan to arrive on Friday, although Janis won't play until the next day, so we can spend more time at the site to take in the music and the scene.

On the drive up from New York, rental cars in convoy, we hear news reports on the radio that a *lot* of people are heading for the festival. When we get off the New York State Thruway and hit two-lane state roads, we are in the company of these pilgrims, and we become part of something larger than anyone imagined.

The Holiday Inn where I have booked us is a mob scene. Everybody wants rooms. Ours are guaranteed by Albert's office, but even so, a couple of our rooms have been hijacked and some of the

Kozmic Blues musicians have to double up. Bob Neuwirth is part of
our party for the weekend. By the time we get settled, it's late enough
that we give up the idea of going to the site this evening. A wise decision, as it turns out. It rains overnight, turning the festival into a
mudfest.

On Saturday morning, the question is whether we'll get to the site
at all. All the roads are blocked with cars and rumors are rife: The
New York State Thruway is closed; the Canadian border is closed;
Governor Rockefeller is calling out the National Guard. Estimates on
the number of people who have shown up for the festival range from
a quarter to half a million.

The promoters have set up a local office with all the phone lines
they thought they could possibly need, but it's barely enough. When
I get through, I'm told the musicians are being airlifted to the site by
helicopter. The promoters have corralled every chopper in a hundred-
mile radius. Later I'm told two hundred. Being Janis's road manager
gets me no special attention. Bands are being flown to the site based
on the order of performance. The office tells me where the choppers
are landing. Be there by midafternoon with the whole band. We'll get
you in when we can.

There's no way I can reach George Ostrow and Vince Mitchell, so
I take it on faith that they made it to the site with Janis's equipment
before the approaching hordes clogged the roads.

The staging area for the helicopter airlift is idyllic. It's a broad
grassy meadow atop a ridge that affords views of the surrounding
countryside. The day is sunny and warm. Among those awaiting their
turn on Saturday afternoon are familiar faces. In the absence of Linda
Gravenites, Janis's friend Peggy Caserta has come to keep her company for the Woodstock weekend. I have seen Peggy only rarely since
she was my erstwhile girlfriend's lover, and I am unsettled by her
presence. When it comes to hard drugs, Peggy will be a conspirator
with Janis, not a restraining force.

Helicopters of all shapes and sizes come and go. The damp heat of the August day is almost tropical, the clusters of people colorful and patient. When it's our turn, Janis and I squeeze into a little bubble-canopy job, both of us sharing the seat beside the pilot, Janis mostly on my lap. At this point, nothing can surprise El Piloto, not even Janis in her tie-dyed velvet pants suit, clutching three more outfits on hangers. He's been on the job since yesterday and he's seen rock royalty in all their plumage.

The countryside is lush and verdant from summer rains as we fly over farms and lakes and country estates. After about ten minutes, the pilot says, There it is. Where? In the midst of the greenery there is a triangle of brown, a gentle hillside that narrows from a wide arc of ridge down to the apex where the stage is located. The hillside is brown because it's covered with people.

When we land and get to the backstage area, we see that the people are brown because they're covered with mud. The Kozmic Blues Band arrives minutes later in a big chopper that brings Neuwirth and Peggy and half of another band.

There is food and drink backstage for the musicians and crews, tables and chairs under sheltering tents and Port-a-Potties you can use without waiting in line for an hour, like those available to the audience, many of whom bag the lines and avail themselves of the tall grass in the adjoining meadows. From the backstage compound, a footbridge over a farm road provides easy access to the stage.

In the performers' tents, I find old friends. Joan Baez is here, and Manny Greenhill, Joan's manager, who also managed the Charles River Valley Boys. Neuwirth and I have known John Sebastian since he was a sought-after harmonica sideman in the folk days and through his success as the leader and songwriter for the Lovin' Spoonful. At Woodstock, John is here to play as a solo in his tie-dyed blue-jean outfit.

The people who are running the show have been playing catch-up since Richie Havens—another of Albert's musicians—kicked off the music yesterday, holding the stage for more than an hour until another band was ready to play.* Everything is running late. Very late. Chip Monck has been up all night, introducing the acts and giving updates to the crowd on food, bad acid, missing children, and medical emergencies. He's haggard and hoarse, but his awareness that he's part of an historic event keeps him going. We'll get Janis on when we can, Chip promises. If it gets too late, we'll shuffle the order.

I pass the news to Janis and the band, but nobody's uptight. We're here. Look at it! From the stage, the mass of humanity covers the landscape up to the ridge line. The scuttlebutt says this gathering is the fourth-largest city in New York State. From across the country the trickles and streams have coalesced into a flood. They have put up with the mud and the reeking Port-a-Potties and the bad trips and the delays between sets and the interminable announcements—"Laura Sunshine, Bobo is having a bad trip. Please come to the Good Karma refreshment stand"—and they have made it a celebration.

We eat and drink and visit with friends and listen to the music. We wait a long time. Janis tries to pace herself as night falls and the evening grows long, but you can't stave off forever the inevitable effect of alcohol. It's a depressant, a soporific. What drinkers are after is the boost, the sense of shifting into a higher gear, that the first couple of drinks provide. Okay! Ready to boogie! When lethargy starts to take over, have another drink. There, that's better. Keep on rockin'. But the lift doesn't last as long, and there comes a point when more drinking only adds to the narcotic effect. Janis struggles to get herself up for the performance. She paces behind the wall of instrument amps as George and Vince hustle through the changeover. "Come on, come on!" she chants, not so much to the equipment men as herself.

When they take the stage at last, Janis and Kozmic Blues make a

* Accounts differ on the length of Havens's set, which began shortly after 5:00 P.M. Some claim he played for nearly three hours, but more sober souls point out that movie film and still photographs show that the two acts that followed Richie both played in daylight, and that the sun set about 8:00 P.M.

valiant effort. It's an adequate set, not outstanding. Ragged around the edges. Within the band, John Till stands out. At each gig since Sam's departure, John has felt the need to prove himself, to show he's up to the challenge. At Woodstock, he rises to the occasion.

As soon as she comes offstage, Janis wants to go back to the hotel. The choppers quit flying at dusk, but the promoters have somehow managed to set up a ground shuttle service to transport musicians away from the site. I see Janis aboard a car that will take her to the Holiday Inn. Some of the Kozmic Blues guys stick around, others go. You're on your own, I tell them. At noon tomorrow, we leave for the city.

My responsibilities over, I hang out backstage with Bobby. It helps that there's food and coffee. At first light, there is even something approximating breakfast. How the promoters manage it, I can't imagine.

As dawn brightens, we're winding down. You ready to get some sleep? Bob is ready. From the stage there's the sound of an electric guitar raising a paean to the approaching sun. Bob beckons me toward a big station wagon. As I get in, I realize that the sound of the guitar is familiar. It's got to be Jimi Hendrix. And what he's playing is a far-out, joyous, free-form improvisational riff on "The Star-Spangled Banner" that may raise Francis Scott Key from his grave.

In the front seat of the station wagon, beside the driver, are Peter Yarrow, of Peter, Paul and Mary, and his wife, Mary Beth. When we get down the road beyond the reach of Jimi's anthem, Peter begins to hum a different tune. He sings the words softly, meditatively: "Here comes Peter Cottontail, hoppin' down the bunny trail," and even though we're in a car, it seems to me that he sees himself as the hopping bunny, Peter Yarrow the folk troubadour, leaving behind him another landmark musical event of the sixties, moving toward the dawn's early light.

Later that day, Max Yazgur, the farmer who agreed to lease his land to the festival, steps to the center of the stage and addresses the assembled horde: "The important thing that you've proven to the world," he said, "is that . . . half a million young people can get together and have three days of fun and music, and have nothing *but* fun and music, and I—God bless you for it."

"Woodstock, in all its mud and glory, belonged to the sixties, that outrageous, longed for, romanticized, lusted after, tragic, insane, bearded and bejeweled epoch."

Joan Baez

THE SHEER NUMBERS of fans who thronged to the remote location in upstate New York have so dominated the news over the weekend that even my father takes note of the event and reports on it to his British readers in the *Guardian*. "There was a vast relief today," he writes, "in the Governor's mansion, the police departments throughout the State, the public health service, and probably also in the minds of thousands of parents around the country—when a camp-out involving twice the number of forces engaged in the Battle of Gettysburg broke out on the small country town of Bethel, New York, and went home." A report by Bernard Collier, in Monday morning's *Times*, includes a quote from the police chief of Monticello, a nearby town, that echoes uncannily the sentiments of Monterey's Chief Marinello, two years before: "Notwithstanding the personality, the dress, and their ideas, they were and they are the most courteous, considerate, and well-behaved group of kids I have ever been in contact with in twenty-four years of police work."

At Monterey, the audience was made up of jazz and blues hipsters, a younger generation of beatniks and folkies, and the even younger hippie followers of the new California bands. The two years since Monterey have seen the full flowering of sixties rock and the mobilization of an audience for what was formerly the music of the counterculture that goes far beyond hippies and flower children. At Woodstock, the performers include representatives of all the musical sources present at Monterey, along with new bands given rise by the varieties of expression catalyzed by that festival and the still-expanding popularity of the music. "Old" folkies like Richie Havens, Joan Baez, John Sebastian, and Arlo Guthrie take the stage between sets by Monterey veterans—the Dead, the Airplane, Canned Heat, Janis, the Who, Jimi, Ravi—and newer groups that raise the energy in new directions. Sha Na Na brings people to their feet by reviving the doo-wop groups of the fifties. Creedence Clearwater Revival, powered by the songwriting and singing of John Fogerty, shows that there's new life to be drawn from heartfelt, full-bore rock and roll that taps the music's Southern roots. Crosby, Stills, Nash and Young—this is their second gig—galvanize everyone from the folkies to the youngest fans with acoustic guitars and intricate vocal harmonies.

The fans are ready for all of it. They suffer the discomforts with generous tolerance and rejoice in the great gathering of the tribes that is christened Woodstock Nation. For the handful of us who were at Monterey, it is an exhilarating flashback, despite the increase in scale by an order of magnitude. That Woodstock remains a peaceful, benevolent gathering is a testament to the herculean efforts of the promoters—who let hundreds of thousands in free—the good spirits of the audience, and the spontaneous, generous help of businesses, citizens, and services from the surrounding communities of White Lake, Bethel, Monticello, and beyond.

Still, something essential has changed since Monterey. We went there expecting to hear some great music and found that we were part of an Event, a not-to-be-missed happening that made us the envy of those who didn't make it. Two years later, there is a built-in hype attached to any rock festival. Each gathering has to top the last, striving to be the one that's definitively not to be missed. When I remember Monterey, I remember the music above all, one act after another that stood an audience of ten thousand on its collective ear. At Woodstock, in memory, the event overwhelms even the glorious variety of the music.

> "But it was very East Coast, Woodstock. . . . On the East Coast, it was like they were all adversaries calling time out for the day. Whereas on the West Coast, they were all like angels flying around who decided, 'Oh, let's land *here* for a while.' It was an entirely different feel."
>
> **Bill Graham**

It takes a while to sink in, but it becomes clear before long that Woodstock was the capper, the one that no sensible promoters should try to top, or even to equal. The lesson is simple: There can be no more music festivals on this scale. Even well removed from the centers of population, an all-star collection of rock and pop headliners will attract an unmanageable number of fans.

After Woodstock, the return to routine touring is a letdown. My own sense of anticlimax is compounded by the feeling that I can do nothing for Janis until she is ready to help herself. My frustration at being unable to solve her problems, or urge her closer to solving them, makes me push her harder than necessary and I blame myself for adding to her woes.

Even so, before we leave New York for Ohio, Texas and California, I present Janis with another problem: I tell her I have decided to leave the road. I will stay to train a replacement, but after that I'm done.

CHAPTER NINETEEN

Little Girl Blue

AUG. 23, 1969: Convention Hall, Asbury Park, N.J.

AUG. 27: Saratoga Performing Arts Camp, Saratoga Springs, N.Y.

AUG. 29: Blossom Music Festival, Cuyahoga Falls, Ohio

AUG. 30: Texas International Pop Festival, Dallas International
   Speedway. Canned Heat, Chicago Transit Authority, Led
   Zeppelin, B. B. King, Sam & Dave, James Cotton Blues Band,
   Santana, Delaney and Bonnie & Friends, Herbie Mann, and more.

AUG. 31: New Orleans Pop Festival, Baton Rouge International
   Speedway, Prairieville, Louisiana. The Byrds, Canned Heat,
   Chicago Transit Authority, Country Joe & the Fish, Grateful
   Dead, the Youngbloods, and more.

SEPT. 9: Rehearse *Music Scene* TV show, L.A.

SEPT. 11: Tape *Music Scene* TV show, L.A., ABC-TV

SEPT. 19: Rehearse Tom Jones TV show, *This Is Tom Jones*, L.A.

SEPT. 20: Hollywood Bowl

SEPT. 21: Tape Tom Jones TV show, ABC-TV

OCT. 3: Tempe, Ariz.

OCT. 4: San Diego Sports Arena

JOHN TILL HAS been in the band for a month now. He's quiet by nature, so we have no way of knowing that he still harbors doubts about whether we have accepted him and whether he is up to the gig.

After a show at the Blossom Music Festival in Cuyahoga Falls, Ohio, John is in the dumps. He's convinced he played terribly. Later that evening, when John and Richard Kermode leave the motel to get something to eat, they're spotted by two groupies hanging around the front office. John and Richard have seen the girls earlier, at the gig. They are not a dream team. John and Richard have to sprint to escape the determined pursuit. Later, when Richard tells the story to the rest of the band, he says, "Boy, John Till just won't quit." It's an admiring comment, Richard's way of saying that John ran like the wind, but John takes it amiss. He is unnerved by the disparate personal and musical trips in the band and by the musicians' fractious relationship with Janis. He isn't sure who to trust. Somehow, John interprets Richard's remark as a hint that he should quit the band.

From Ohio, we're headed for big pop festivals in Texas and New Orleans. John agonizes during the flight to Dallas. Backstage at the Texas International Pop Festival—an all-day marathon with a dozen top acts—John seeks out Janis. He finds her in one of the small dressing rooms we've been assigned, only marginally larger than portable toilets. He asks her if she wants him to leave.

Like the rest of us, Janis has accepted John as a member of the band, and his self-doubts take her by surprise. "No!" she says. "I want you to come to California with me. You can't leave now, that will really screw things up." She thinks a minute and says, "Have you ever been insane, or anything like that? Is it in your family?" It's John's turn to be taken aback. "No", he says. "Well, I have some experience with that," Janis tells him. "Believe me, it's all in your head."

Somehow this bizarre exchange banishes John's doubts. Hereafter, he remembers this moment as the first time he felt close to Janis. When he tells the story, he says, "She really cooled me out."

Janis saw a need in John, and she met it. This is one of her abilities, part of her better nature. Even amid the uncertainties with Kozmic Blues, she manifests this generosity often enough to win the respect of most members of the band. When she turns on them, going on her star trip, ranting that she deserves better, that they don't give her what she wants, they avoid her as best they can. Her worst outbursts are still reserved for strangers—the waiter who doesn't like longhairs, the curious onlooker at the airport, the reporter who comes on too strong, the audiences who don't get it.* Janis is incapable of loosing her real fury at anyone close to her, not even at the band that can't find the way to become what she can't describe but desperately wants it to be.

This is the persistent problem: Sam's departure and John Till's arrival haven't solved the lack of direction in the music. John brings new life to some of the arrangements, but he is just one of seven electrons orbiting Janis's nucleus in random paths, only occasionally falling into a pattern with the others that permits the energy of the whole to be exerted in a unified way. The Kozmic Blues Band has acquired a stubborn identity all its own, one that endures despite changes in personnel.

Just a year after Janis made the difficult decision to leave Big Brother, she is facing the probability that her new band may be a failure.

ON SEPTEMBER 1, at long last, we fly back to California. Except for a few weeks' vacation in the spring, the Kozmic Blues Band has been

---

*Terry Clements was embarrassed when Janis took out her discomfort on the audience: "She was on a really weird trip with the audience, you know, swearing at them and—you know, she could say some pretty strange things to them sometimes that weren't relative to bringing about a true renaissance of spirit in the world, which I was hoping to be committed to, in that scene." (Author interview with Terry Clements, January 24, 1974.)

on the road since the beginning of February. They have played six concerts in Europe and more than forty in the U.S. outside California, against just seven dates there, including the depressing four-night stand in San Francisco back in March.

With Big Brother, every homecoming felt like a celebration. Now we slip into town like thieves. Some of the musicians have homes in the city or Marin County, north across the Golden Gate Bridge, which has become the preferred destination for rockers abandoning the Haight. Janis retreats into her Noe Street apartment and the company of her closest friends.

The band members get just a week to rest before we fly to L.A. to tape a performance for a new rock-pop TV show called *Music Scene* that will debut later in the month. The concept is that each week the show will feature artists whose songs are at the top of the charts. Columbia has just released the Kozmic Blues album. The expectation is that Janis's appearance will air as the record hits the charts and give it a boost.

Janis and the band rehearse in the ABC studio on a Tuesday and return to tape the show on Thursday. The musical acts will perform in a concert setting, with Janis, as the headliner, scheduled last. She will sing three songs, of which the producers will choose two to air on the show. The opening acts are the comedian Pat Paulsen, folk legend Pete Seeger, and the English bluesman John Mayall, who has recently introduced a quieter, acoustic version of his Bluesbreakers band.

These are the early days of videotape, and the technology is cumbersome. The cameras are larger than 35-millimeter film cameras and awkward to move. It's a convention that they not be seen on-screen, so repositioning the cameras requires a break in the taping.

The taping goes slowly. The Committee actor Carl Gottlieb is writing for the show, so we have a friend in-house. Carl keeps us amused in the green room. He tells us, when we are the only ones in the room, that the director is "a deaf old fart" from New York who's got himself on the show as a co-producer so he can direct when he wants to. The guy has hearing aids in both ears and he's used to directing old-style musical reviews. Tommy Smothers fired this director from the Smothers Brothers TV show, Carl says. He is not exactly up to rock and roll.

Janis paces her drinking through the hours of waiting. We arrived at the studio at three P.M. It's almost eleven when Janis's turn comes at last, but somehow she is raring to go. She and the band take the stage, they plug in, and Janis says, "Are you ready?" From the control room, the old-fart director gives the okay. "Good," Janis says, "'cause I'm only doing this once. One, two, three!" She kicks out her leg, the band launches into the first song, and the cameras barely get tape rolling in time. Janis and the band play three songs in a row with scarcely a moment to draw breath between numbers. The live audience is *alive*. By Carl Gottlieb's account, knowing he has to get it with no retakes gives the director such a boost of adrenaline that he does his best work of the seventeen shows *Music Scene* produces before it is cancelled.

Once again, by pure luck, a break in the schedule makes it possible for me to attend this year's Big Sur Folk Festival. It has become for me an annual ritual of rest and renewal. The connection I feel with old friends among the performers, with the music, with the California coast, reinforce me in my decision to leave the rock-and-roll road.

Joni Mitchell is here again, and she bewitches the Big Sur crowd with a song she has written about Woodstock, the first time she has sung it in public. The irony is that Joni didn't attend the festival because her manager thought keeping a date on *The Dick Cavett Show* was more important. Mitchell's remarkable achievement is that she has not only captured the spirit of Woodstock, based on the account she heard from Graham Nash, her current lover (he's here in Big Sur with Crosby, Stills and Young), and what she saw on television, but she has crystallized the lesson of the gathering: We have got to get ourselves back to the Garden.

At the end of the week it's back to work for Janis and Kozmic Blues. A week after taping *Music Scene*, they report once more to the Los Angeles studios of ABC-TV, this time to tape the singer Tom Jones's weekly show, *This Is Tom Jones*. In the green room, a bar in the corner is doing lively business in midafternoon. Some members of the Committee are on this show too—it's our year to connect with them in TV studios. Janis and I launch into catch-up conversation with the actors. The guys in the band remember them from the Cavett show. The green room is ours, the atmosphere relaxed and lively.

Before long, Jones himself, still getting mileage out of "It's Not Unusual," his big hit of a few years earlier, wanders in with a drink in his hand. He says hello to Janis and soon wanders out again. He seems uncomfortable around beatniks and rockers. He has a small corner of the youth audience, enough to need some top rock acts on his show, but Jones is already edging toward his later position as the darling of the blue-haired set in Las Vegas.

Janis, giving credit where it's due, admires Jones's singing, if not always his choice of material.

> "Tom Jones could've been a real heavyweight in the music biz. I mean he could've really *meant* something in the music biz. He's *that* talented. He sold out the minute they came to him, instead of letting his talent grow."
>
> **Janis Joplin**

Janis will do two songs on the show. The first, a duet with Jones on "Raise Your Hand," presents no problems. The unusual setup has a few members of the audience seated on the floor behind the singers, and the band in front of them. It makes sense when we see how the cameras shoot through the band, toward the singers and the audience beyond. As seen on the studio monitors, it works. Jones and Janis have fun swapping verses and the energy is good.

Janis's second song is the wistful Rodgers and Hart tune "Little Girl Blue." Sam Andrew and Mike Bloomfield's arrangement has caught the interest of Jones's producers. The art director has dressed a corner of the huge soundstage as a garden, complete with a white picket fence and a trellis archway covered with plastic vines and flowers. The idea is to have Janis wander through the garden while she sings, followed by a boom mike. The band will be out of sight behind a gauze scrim.

When the director explains the concept to Janis I expect her to reject it out of hand, which she does, emphatically. She is used to singing mike-in-hand in front of her band and that's that. To my surprise, when she cools down she reconsiders. She agrees to give the plan a try if the stagehands will strip the tacky props from the set so she will sing on an empty stage, backed by the scrim, with a mike on a stand. She wants something to hold on to.

With these conditions met, Janis dutifully runs through the song several times so the director can work out the camera moves. She is intrigued by the novelty of doing a number as a television torch singer, but when we leave the studio after the rehearsal, she wonders aloud if she should call off the experiment.

On the day between the rehearsal and taping of the Jones show, Janis and the Kozmic Blues Band headline at the Hollywood Bowl. Just a year after Big Brother's triumph at the Bowl, this is Janis's first L.A. appearance with Kozmic Blues, and the controversy over the new band has aroused a lot of curiosity. The Bowl is sold out and the stars are right. For Janis and the boys, it is the most satisfying concert since the Albert Hall show. From the first number, the audience is unreservedly enthusiastic. We're all so eager for approval, one good gig makes us giddy with joy.

The next day, the taping of the Tom Jones show goes smoothly.

During "Little Girl Blue," small spots of light float across the scrim behind Janis, like drifting stars. Janis is satisfied with her performance, but she won't rest easy until she has seen it on the air, and the air date is almost three months away.

For this busy weekend in L.A., we have a road manager trainee in tow. Joe Crowley has some experience promoting rock concerts in Seattle but no time on the road. He keeps close by my side and appears to be absorbing the essentials of the job. The show at the Hollywood Bowl is as big as anything Joe will have to cope with on Janis's fall schedule. As he follows me around, I tell him more than he ever wanted to know about being a road manager, with special attention to Janis's problems and peculiarities. Joe is attentive and willing, and I figure he has an even chance of becoming adequate in the job.

On the road for a two-state, three-concert foray in the first week of October, I shadow Joe while he takes on most of the responsibilities, and he acquits himself well.

The last of the three shows, back in San Francisco for Bill Graham, involves nothing like the tensions of Janis's first hometown appearance with Kozmic Blues back in the spring. The local fans know by now that they are getting something very different from Big Brother and they come anyway, if not in such passionate throngs as in the past.

The San Francisco gig is my last day on the job, and my twenty-ninth birthday to boot. During September, Janis has approached me a couple of times to ask if I will stay with her a while longer. She and Albert have decided to call it quits with Kozmic Blues when the booked gigs are completed. "Can't you finish the tour?" she asks. These requests come from the little-girl side of her personality, at her most winsome, hardest to resist because you want to do anything for her. But I manage to resist, and I take some comfort now in knowing that I'm leaving Janis in her hometown, the city she loves. Abandoning her out on the road was unthinkable.

She makes the evening a send-off party for me. When we say good-bye after the show, I ask her to take it easy on Joe Crowley until he has a grip on the job. She gives me a hug and a kiss and she promises to be good. The next day I fly to New York, feeling guilty about leaving Janis while so many uncertainties beset her, but trusting that I have left her in competent, if untried, hands.

I STICK TO my decision to leave Janis because a new prospect beckons. During the summer, I confided in Bob Neuwirth when I was thinking about leaving the road, and he didn't try to dissuade me from quitting. Bob put in a lot of hours talking with Janis in late-night bars while we were in New York this year, and he knows that her problems will persist until she takes responsibility for them.

Bob too is contemplating new horizons. For several years he has been prospecting the New York art scene, deferring his core talent—painting—to experiment with fluorescent light sculptures and other forms of avant art. He has mingled with the Warhol crowd, and squired for a time Warhol's ingenue-of-the-moment, Edie Sedgwick, but he always maintained his autonomy. Bob offered Edie an escape, when she needed it, from the fawning attention of the Warhol Factory group. Among the folk and rock musicians whose company Bobby prefers, Edie was welcomed as his girl and she was treated kindly.

Now, casting about for a project that will fully engage his creative energies, Bob has come up with an idea for an underground movie to be filmed in Paris. His concept is neither a new form of *cinéma vérité* nor a variation on Warhol's often boring, would-be avant-garde filmic exercises. The movie will be a feature film with at least the semblance of a story. We will film in 16-millimeter with Pennebaker's shoulder-held cameras. It will be guerrilla filmmaking, shooting on the run, unimpeded by such formalities as getting permits from the Parisian authorities. We will do everything from writing to filming to dealing with the money and production budgets. All this suits me to a *T.* For two years, I've been shooting Janis and her bands on the fly. I have edited my films, created sound tracks from Janis's recordings, and shown them to the bands in my living room. Bobby's movie sounds like the perfect way to expand my filmmaking skills.

Bob has a title, around which we will shape the film: It will be called *The Fool of Paris*, and the part of the fool, we hope, will be played by Michael J. Pollard, still coasting on his Oscar nomination two years earlier for best supporting actor in *Bonnie and Clyde*. Bobby connected with Michael the same day he saw *Bonnie and Clyde* in New York with Brice Marden, a painter we have known since he was married to Joan Baez's older sister, Pauline. Bob and Brice saw the movie the week it opened. They went to Max's Kansas City afterward for a drink, walked into the place, and there was Michael J. Pollard with his wife, Annie, sitting in a booth. Bob never missed a beat. He went straight over to Michael and said, "We just saw you in the fuckin' movie, man! It's the greatest movie ever made! Blah-blah-blah-blah-blah." Bob hung out with Michael from that day forward.

When I arrive in New York after bidding farewell to Janis and Kozmic Blues, we spend time with Michael and Annie, a gentle beauty, in their West Village apartment. Michael is up for something off the wall, something that will make the powers that be in Hollywood think of casting him in a wider range of parts than replicas of C. W. Moss, driver for Bonnie and Clyde.

Bobby gets a copy of a genuine Hollywood screenplay from a guy named Harry, the son of a labor lawyer who hangs out on the edge of the movie business. Harry wants to break into Hollywood through the back door and create a career for himself that's independent from his father. He'll be our producer.

I read the screenplay to learn the style and the format, and I write a screenplay of sorts for *The Fool of Paris*, more like an extended outline, so we have something on paper to show potential investors.

Meanwhile, Bobby is trolling Wall Street for venture capital. We lunch with young financial types who wish they had the courage to tune in, turn on, and jump into the tail end of the sixties. We offer them a way to do it vicariously, and we have no trouble getting their attention when we mention not only Michael J. Pollard but also Janis Joplin. Bobby has pitched the movie to Janis—and Albert—effectively enough that he has secured a "letter of intent" from Albert, which says if we get financing for *The Fool of Paris*, Janis will take part. We get a similar letter from Michael.

Neither Bobby nor I has ever paid much attention to the national economy, but we get a primer from the Wall Street boys. In the spring of the year, while we were in Europe with the Kozmic Blues Band, the Dow Jones Industrials were flirting with the mythical 1,000 level. In October, the DJIA is around 850. By December it falls below 800. With every slip, the Wall Street playboys grow more cautious. Financial analysts are beginning to use the R-word: recession. While our potential investors wait for the economy to turn around, Bobby and I wind up most of our evenings at Max's Kansas City, praying for an upturn.

Janis's appearance on *This Is Tom Jones* is broadcast on December 4. "Little Girl Blue" is better than I expected. It was almost impossible to hear Janis's voice on the huge ABC soundstage, but on TV she comes across soft and clear. Unseen behind the scrim, John Till adds his own poignant embellishments to the guitar obbligato composed by Sam Andrew and Mike Bloomfield, while Janis puts herself completely into the song. When she gets to the lines, "Oh honey, I know how you feel, I know you feel that you're through / Ah, sit there, count your fingers, my unhappy little girl blue," she embodies painfully, for me, the blue, unhappy, little-girl side of Janis.

While Bobby and I scout the concrete canyons for film funding, Janis and Kozmic Blues are touring the country. In October, Janis finally performs in Austin, at the University of Texas gym. In November, she's in the South and Midwest. On the weekend after the

Tom Jones broadcast, she is in Georgia and Virginia. By great good fortune, these bookings keep Janis from appearing at the Altamont Speedway in California's central valley for a one-day rock festival organized by the Grateful Dead and the Rolling Stones. The bands hope Altamont will be Woodstock West, but the name Altamont becomes infamous as the antithesis of its peaceful forerunners, thanks to a crowd stoned on drugs, Hells Angels stoned on beer and who knows what else, and escalating violence that results in the stabbing death at the hand of an Angel of a whacked-out fan brandishing a pistol. Looking back on the event, Bill Graham will recall, "It was like a concentration camp for a day."

Just a year after their uncertain debut at the Stax-Volt show in Memphis, Janis and the Kozmic Blues Band play their last concert, in Madison Square Garden. When I was a boy, the name had a magic ring for me. The Garden was where I saw the Ringling Brothers and Barnum & Bailey Circus and the World Championship Rodeo, hosted by Gene Autry. Back then, the Garden was at Eighth Avenue and 50th Street, where it had moved in 1925 from its original location on Madison Square, farther downtown. Janis's concert is my first visit to the new Garden, on Eighth Avenue between 31st and 32nd Streets. It opened in this location just last year, following the criminal demo-lition of the great public spaces of Pennsylvania Station.

The new indoor stadium is vast, modern, and sold out. The crowd is liberally sprinkled with celebrities, including New York Jets quar-terback Joe Namath, with whom Janis caroused the night before.*

_____

* This fall, Janis took to using our limo driver, John Fisher, for her personal transpor-tation around the city. On the night before the concert at the Garden, Namath was Janis's guest at her hotel, which was not the Chelsea for this stay. Fisher parked nearby and dozed through the night because Janis had to be somewhere early in the morning. When Janis appeared, she got into the front seat, tossed a football auto-graphed by Namath into John's lap, and informed him cheerfully that Namath was "flabby." (Author interview with John Fisher, November 15, 1997.)

Backstage, Janis gleefully boasts that Broadway Joe couldn't keep up with her hang-out pace. Linda Gravenites is back, she tells me, before I spy Linda backstage. She made me this outfit, Janis says, twirling like a ballerina, and she made the outfit I'm wearing to the party after. Wait until you see it. It's all black and sexy.

You're all white and sexy, I tell her. She laughs, and I realize how much I've missed her.

The band regales me with stories about the fall tour. Joe Crowley is still road-managing the show, but when he's out of earshot the boys in the band tell me that my guarded confidence in Joe was premature. After I left, the self-assurance he manifested while I was showing him the ropes evaporated in the face of the first routinely difficult days he encountered on the road. The unexpected threw him for a loop and he found it hard to relate to the members of the band, who were accustomed to my insistent style. "People expected to be ordered out of bed, and if they weren't they didn't get up," is how Terry Clements puts it.

The band reacted to Joe's lack of aptitude by taking over the driving and many of the other logistical chores, leaving Joe to handle the box office during the concerts. As the musicians tell me about assuming these responsibilities, they try to make it sound like a great burden, but they are obviously proud of themselves.

The decision to disband the group has had a unifying effect on them. This belated coming together, a twilight relaxing of tensions, has helped them achieve their most satisfying musical moments since the European tour. A recent gig in Nashville was a highlight, and they're raring to go out with a bang here in the Garden.

Not present for the swan song is Luis Gasca, who departed a few weeks ago. He is replaced by a trumpet player named Dave Woodward, the fourth to play with Kozmic Blues.

The Butterfield Blues Band opens the show. The Kozmic Blues Band plays a couple of instrumentals on their own, raising the energy before Janis comes onstage. Janis leads the audience in a rousing cheer for the Jets, but Namath hasn't recovered his full vitality and they will lose their game the next day.

Late in her set, Janis sings Bo Diddley's eponymous classic, "Bo Diddley," as a duet with her fellow Texan, Johnny Winter. The song becomes an extended jam when Paul Butterfield joins them onstage, and the response of the audience is ecstatic.

At a postconcert party given by Clive Davis in his penthouse apartment on Central Park West, Janis finally meets another of Columbia's gold-record stars. Like her backstage encounter with Joan Baez at Newport, the meeting with Bob Dylan is the coming together of two fundamentally different life-forms. They shake hands, speak haltingly, fall into an awkward silence, and go their separate ways.

Dylan is in his recluse mode. Once he finds a quiet place to sit he seems to disappear. I am reminded of a scheme he and his first road manager, Victor Maimudes, conceived at a concert on the upswing of Bob's lone-troubadour fame. Besieged by fans outside the stage door, they came up with a fantasy solution: They would enter and leave the shows in an armored personnel carrier, dispensing autographs through a slot in the side. Here, Bob's armor is invisible, but just as effective.

Janis tries to keep on rocking despite the lack of energy at the party, which after all is observing the demise of her band, but it becomes, for her, an early night.

"With the Kozmic Blues Band, nobody gave it a chance, because nobody knew what to expect. Everybody was used to a bunch of little white boys up there playin' some guitars and basses all loud and shit. They weren't used to people playing music. And Janis wasn't a rock-and-roll player, she was singing black music. So we came up with a band that played that kind of music, and it freaked some people out. . . . If they'd of just got out of the fuckin' way and let the band play, we'd of been one of the baddest bands around."

Snooky Flowers

The next day's *Times* is generous in its praise and adds a final review to those that appreciate the Kozmic Blues Band. The critic, Mike Jahn, calls Janis's set "an excellent performance." "When her new band was first heard," he writes, "its main fault was that energy was being sacrificed for precision. . . . That criticism did not apply last night. At the Garden, Miss Joplin's accomplices gave a powerful and spontaneously happy display of brass blues and rock, and she let herself go in a very exciting way."

Janis stays in New York for a few days after the concert, to confer with Albert about her future, and I spend an evening with her in her hotel room. The hotel, One Fifth Avenue, is within shouting distance of Washington Square Park, where Sunday gatherings marked the beginning of the folk boom. This fall, Janis decided she deserves something classier than the Chelsea.

At the Garden and the wrap party, Janis was in her public persona, expecting and prepared for close scrutiny. Here she is unguarded, and I am struck by how much worse she looks than when I left her in October. She is heavier; her face is puffy and her skin is clammy when I hug her hello. We reminisce about our times on the road and explore ideas about the part she might play in *The Fool of Paris*. She tells me she's buying a house in Larkspur, in Marin County. She is excited and happy that Linda Gravenites has returned from London. They plan to move into the Larkspur house before leaving for a holiday in Brazil to check out Carnival in Rio de Janeiro. Her manic mood as she tells me how much she's looking forward to moving into the house and the trip to Rio makes me realize that these things are all that she has to look forward to. For the first time since she joined Big Brother in June 1966, Janis's career prospects are a blank slate. Even when she was touring with Big Brother in the fall of 1968, after she had decided to leave them, she was looking forward to the creating the band of her dreams. National touring was still relatively new to her, she was playing cities and venues that were new and exciting—the Hollywood Bowl, the Rose Bowl, Houston, Dallas—and it was still Big Brother. This fall, since she and Albert decided to give up on the Kozmic Blues Band, she has been repeating a routine she already knows, with no hope for a better to-morrow, a brighter future. Now even the familiar routine of touring is over.

Linda and the house are the only subjects that light Janis up, arousing her characteristic energy. When we turn to something else, she fades. We order drinks from room service. Vodka and Dubonnet on the rocks, a combination Janis is testing. But alcohol alone can't satisfy her. Without much warning she gets out her works and pro-ceeds to shoot up, sitting at the desk. It is the first time I have seen Janis get off, but not the first time I have witnessed the act. I will never forget a scene in Paris, in a cheap Left Bank hotel room, where a very young English junkie needed a fix so badly that he burst into tears when he couldn't find a vein. A friend helped him, then held his head when the English kid gratefully vomited with the first rush. I have a short list of friends lost to heroin. I see the habit as degrading and destructive, the force behind it as insidiously malevolent, but I see it from the outside, with a perspective very different from an addict's.

Janis is not surrounded by innocents. Albert, Bob Neuwirth, my-self, Nick Gravenites, Mike Bloomfield, and others she turns to for advice have pertinent knowledge to draw on. Many of us drink too much, and we underplay the importance of alcohol in Janis's pattern of self-abuse, but no one close to her, except other junkies—after Sam's departure, there was no one in Kozmic Blues or the road crew with hard-drug experience—condones or approves her use of smack. When she asks us for advice, or when we offer it unbidden, we tell her, We love you, we care about you, we'll do whatever we can for you. We want you to quit, but we can't quit for you. You have to do that yourself.

Tonight I watch Janis get off without comment. The hit pleases her but seems to have little effect beyond making her more loquacious about her latest plans. She claims to be full of ideas for a new band that will replace Kozmic Blues, the group that will finally give her what she wants from a backup band, but much of her confidence is generated by the heroin, and underneath the brag talk I see a little girl lost.

As if she can sense my doubts, Janis's rap trails off and she cooks up a second dose. I watch with morbid fascination as she urges the needle home again. This time I remember a friend who died several years earlier. Teddy Bernstein changed in a few months from a fast-fingered New York guitar picker who loved a joint of good grass into a death's-head caricature of his former self who dreamily entreated me to give heroin a try. "It's beautiful, man. It's good for you." A few months later he was dead of an overdose. In a perverse way, remembering the speed of Teddy's decay gives me some hope for Janis. She has been flirting with heroin since I first knew her. This year the affair has become a full-fledged romance, but she doesn't look so bad, compared to Teddy in his final days.

I feel a third presence in the hotel room. Janis's habit's coercive power is so strong, so insidious, it takes on a separate reality. Heroin is an entity in the room and it is possessively jealous of Janis. It demands and cajoles, requiring constant acknowledgment and regular maintenance. For a short time after the monkey is fed, Janis can give me her full attention. Even then she is speaking from within the embrace of the drug. I feel powerless against the invisible presence and I'm afraid Janis may never muster the strength to banish it. For the first time I consider the possibility that she may die before her time and that death may come by her own hand, accidentally or deliberately.

"Heroin has some payoffs. Of course the negative side always begins to outweigh it by so much, but in the beginning, when one first uses heroin, there's a certain kind of freedom that one gets. . . . All of a sudden all the pain and worry and stress is removed. And you're totally relaxed, and you feel good, and you don't have to do anything, you're not tense, and . . . for a performer, for someone as high-strung as Janis, I'm sure for a long time it really had a very positive payoff. Then the debilitating effects start to take over."

David Getz

The awareness makes me too uncomfortable to stay. I've got to get out of here. How can I make my excuses? As it turns out, I don't have to.

The second hit gets Janis off for real. She curls up on the bed like a kitten who has just had a bowl of warm milk. Soon she is over and out. I leave her in the smell of cigarette smoke and alcohol and sweat and patchouli oil and I grab a taxi in the night, glad I left the road when I did, but sad too, because I'm not sure I will want to see Janis again. I love her too much to watch her destroy herself.

It isn't until much later that I remember something she said that evening, between her two hits. She promised me she is going to kick heroin.

Brazilian Interlude:
Manha de Carnival

IN FEBRUARY 1970, Janis and Linda went to Rio de Janeiro for Carnival. Later that year I came into possession of a tape recording of a press conference that took place at the Copacabana Palace Hotel in Rio, where Janis was interviewed by representatives of the local press. On the tape, she sounds like the old Janis from the early days of Big Brother, but without the naïveté. Once again she represents the San Francisco music community as an articulate spokeswoman. She is focused on the future, enjoying a vacation but not seeking a prolonged escape. And she has fallen in love. David Niehaus is an American traveling in Brazil. They met on the Copacabana beach. During the press conference he is by Janis's side.

Janis is disappointed to learn that the official Carnival lasts less than a week and that many of the events can be enjoyed only by tourists and well-to-do Brazilians—those with enough money to buy tickets. She is trying to organize a free concert in a park in Rio with "Carnival lasts all year long" as its theme. She talks of the early days in San Francisco when the rock bands gave free concerts in Golden

Gate Park on Sundays, "and everybody would come and dance, and it was beautiful."

There are no reminders of the wan and lonely girl I left in a New York hotel room only two months before. Janis is at her best, thoroughly comfortable with the press, fielding the questions confidently, revealing something about herself in every answer.

> Q: *Why did you come to Rio?*
> J.J.: Because I saw the movie *Black Orpheus.*

> Q: *Will you come back?*
> J.J.: I'd love to. I don't think I'm gonna leave. (Laughter.)

> Q: *What do you think about Vietnam?*
> J.J.: I think each individual person ought to live the best life they can, to themselves and to other people, and if we did that we wouldn't have any Vietnam. Everybody'd be happy and we'd all be dancing.

> Q: *What do you think about young people dropping out of school?*
> J.J.: Just keep your values straight. Find out what's important to you. Learning how to multiply may not be as important as learning how to communicate.

> Q: *Do you like Brazil?*
> J.J.: I'm really glad I came, because people seem nicer to each other here than in New York. In New York they're very aggressive and here people seem more gentle. I think it's because of the sun.

> Q: *If you weren't a singer, what would you be?*
> J.J. (without hesitation): I'd be a beatnik. I am anyway, only I make more money.

Someone explains to a puzzled Brazilian reporter that "beatnik" is the same as "hippie." Janis overhears and quickly sets him straight: "Beatnik and hippie are different," she says. "Beatniks are older."

Q: *Do you want to have children? If so, how many?*

J.J.: Someday I'd like to have children. Every woman wants to have children. But the most important thing is don't have too many or we're gonna outgrow the world.

Q: *Will your voice last for as long as you'd like?*

J.J.: My voice is better now than it was four years ago. It's getting stronger. And besides, I don't care if I lose my voice. If I lost my voice I'd be something else. I don't want to be a singer for the rest of my life. I'd be a beach bum. I don't care, as long as I'm having a good time.

Before she went to Carnival, Janis had been struggling to kick heroin. Linda Gravenites's vision of the trip was for Janis to experience a great time without dope. But there were lapses, and they cost Janis a great deal. She was using in Brazil. David Niehaus helped Janis get clean while they were together. Linda flew home ahead of Janis to oversee the carpenters working on the house in Larkspur. When David and Janis arrived at the airport in Rio to fly together to San Francisco, David was detained for overstaying his visa in Brazil. Janis went on alone, stopped over in L.A., and scored from her connection there. When David got to Larkspur two days later, Janis was stoned. For him, this was the last straw, and he left.

Later, when Janis spoke of David Niehaus, she described him as the lost love of her life. He was a man outside the usual pattern of her conquests, neither pretty boy nor mountain man, a man she admired, one who might have been able to influence her and guide her in the right direction. David was on his way to Africa when they met in Rio. He wanted to take her to Nepal, to the Himalayas. He was convinced seeing the Himalayas would change Janis's life, but in this hope he may have been projecting his own experience on her. In the end, it wasn't anything Janis and David did together so much as his leaving her that had the greatest, the most beneficial influence on her. The loss of this man who moved her so deeply, her new love, followed by the departure of Linda Gravenites, her longtime roommate, advisor, and best friend, who refused to live any longer in the company of heroin, was what finally forced Janis to confront her addiction and find within herself the strength to bring it under control.

"When I came back from England, she asked me what my attitude toward dope was then. That was the first thing she asked me. I said as long as I think you'll quit sometime, I can stand it. But if I think it's gonna be all the time forever, I can't do it. You know. So, as long as I believe you'll quit, I'll stick around. Otherwise I'm gone. You know, and when she stopped to cop on the way home from Rio after her big quitting . . . I don't know whether she believed me, that I wouldn't stick around for her. Which was one of the reasons, of course, that I left, was for shock value, saying, 'This is what you're doing.'"

Linda Gravenites

CHAPTER TWENTY

The Great Tequila Boogie

THROUGH THE COLD months, the stock market continues its slide. Financial analysts say the U.S. is in a mild depression. Our hopes for *The Fool of Paris* fluctuate with the Dow Jones average. The uncertainty sends risk capital into oil stocks, and Bobby and I are no longer lunching on Wall Street.

In April, the Italian film director Marco Ferreri, little known in America, is in New York. Somehow Bobby makes contact and gets us a meeting. In conversation, Ferreri is like an Italian Albert Grossman—enigmatic, saying little. He has an assistant who translates for him, but it becomes apparent that Ferreri understands English well enough and uses the running translation to give himself more time to think. He offers us $20,000 to finance the film. We've calculated a budget of $100,000 just to get the actors and crew to Paris, shoot the film, develop it, and make a work print. Bobby and I go over the budget line by line and trim it down to $70,000. We present it to Ferreri, but he won't or can't up his offer.

The first warm days of spring bring rumors from California. Janis has moved into her house in Larkspur. We hear she is putting together a new band. We hear she has kicked heroin. We hear she has banished her junkie friends from her house.

Albert calls. He confirms that the rumors are true, and his enthusiasm is palpable. I have never heard him so unrestrained, so optimistic. As he tells me about the new band and Janis's delight in being clean, he reveals the depth of his emotional investment in her well-being.

He asks me to go back on the road with Janis at the end of May, but it is my turn to be cautious. I have known too many reformed junkies to backslide. So long as there's a chance that Bob and I can get our movie airborne, that's what I want to do. I tell Albert, "Probably not." Janis calls to make her own appeal, and I tell her the same thing, but her confidence is so real, her excitement so infectious, I dare to hope she's serious about staying straight.

One evening in mid-May, when I'm too weary from the late-night hanging out to accompany him, Bobby goes to the Village to hear Ramblin' Jack Elliott at the Gaslight. He walks in and finds no one onstage. Jack's on a break. Where's Jack, he asks. Oh, Jack and Kris Kristofferson went around the corner to hear Odetta, the manager tells him.

Kristofferson's is a name that has bubbled through the music underground since last year, when Roger Miller recorded Kris's "Me and Bobby McGee." Ray Price has a hit with another Kristofferson tune, "For the Good Times." But nobody we know has set eyes on Kris until now. Once again, Neuwirth's where-it's-happening radar is zeroed in on the right place at the right time. He finds Ramblin' Jack and Kris at Odetta's gig, and they become a late-night hang-out team, often joined by Michael J. Pollard, that lasts until Jack and Odetta's Village bookings come to an end.

Inspiration strikes Neuwirth one evening midweek. He calls Pennebaker to borrow a camera. Penny's intrigued, so he comes along as cameraman. After the clubs close, Neuwirth takes the crew to the penthouse apartment of a friend of Pollard's where they film *The*

Woody Guthrie Story under Neuwirth's direction. Neuwirth and Pennebaker shoot the life story of the Depression-era songwriter and troubadour, co-founder, with Pete Seeger, of the folk music revival, at night in a penthouse apartment in New York City. How does Bobby come up with these ideas? Sheer audacity, and a creative spark that flares most brightly at unlikely times. Ramblin' Jack plays Woody Guthrie, at whose feet he learned his own troubadour licks. Michael Pollard plays Bob Dylan, who was an acolyte of both Woody's and Ramblin' Jack's in his early days. Kris plays Woody's pal Cisco Houston and Odetta plays Leadbelly. Now that's casting.

When the impromptu movie crew emerges onto the streets in the morning, they find newspaper headlines announcing the Kent State massacre. The day before, at Kent State University in Ohio, National Guardsmen killed four students and wounded nine others who were demonstrating against President Nixon for expanding the Vietnam War into Cambodia.

What am I doing while this is going on? Too tired to come downtown at night? Can't keep up the pace? I have no credible excuse for missing the gathering of talent and energy that launched upon an unsuspecting nation a transcontinental party-hop, bar tour, and roving hootenanny that will become famous enough in its own short life span to be given a name. It is christened the Great Tequila Boogie—by Neuwirth, it should go without saying—and we are not apt to see its like again.

With Bobby in charge there is only one acceptable course: No one will be allowed to abandon ship—the team will continue to the next party, come hell or high water. What matter that the party is a continent away in Janis's house in Larkspur? On very little notice, Ramblin' Jack drives the celebrants to JFK, whence they fly to San Francisco. Bobby's idea is that in addition to hanging out with Janis, they should visit Joan Baez and her sister Mimi. Both would be delighted to see these musical voyagers, but they would be among the least likely to join in imbibing the libation that propels the journey.

Whether Bob, Kris, Michael, and Odetta actually connect with the ladies Bob calls "the Baez brothers" is unclear, but they do visit Janis and so are on hand for a party that will become part of Janis's folklore. For some time a young man named Lyle Tuttle, his own body extensively decorated with indelible artwork he has mostly applied himself, has been introducing some of the leading personalities of West Coast rock and roll to the art of tattoo. Janis has one already, a bracelet on her left wrist, and gets another at the party, a miniature heart located above her real one. It is becoming fashionable, especially among the women, to have small tattoos placed on areas not normally revealed to the casual observer, all the better to delight the favored few. Accounts of how many willing subjects Tuttle actually tattooed at the party differ, but his artistry and the renown of the party contribute to the rising popularity of tattoos among the young that dates from this time.

The party is co-hosted by Lyndall Erb, who has taken Linda Gravenites's place as Janis's roommate. Like Linda, Lyndall designs and makes clothes for the psychedelic era. At the Monterey Pop Festival she sold colorful shirts, one of which I bought and wore during the Charles River Valley Boys' California tour. Lyndall has made clothes for Country Joe and the Fish and for MC5. *Life* magazine has dubbed her "the seamstress to hippiedom." In recent years, Lyndall and Janis have become friends. When Linda left, Janis asked Lyndall to move in.

The Great Tequila Boogie flight crew mingles with a host of Janis's local friends and acquaintances. Ramblin' Jack has made it, after driving across the country in record time. Nick Gravenites is there, and Mike Bloomfield, and Big Brother and their first equipment man, Dave Richards, along with Kozmic Blues equipment men Mark Braunstein and George Ostrow. Also present are the members of Janis's new band, as yet unnamed, with one wife and a girlfriend or two. San Francisco erotic filmmaker Alex de Renzy records the goings-on but the results are hardly arousing. Not enough light, or too much smoke.

There are drawbacks to being descended from a family imbued with the Puritan ethic. I am as desperate as the next guy to get out of New York, but we have set out to produce a movie and if the top man wants to take off on frivolous adventures in the middle of the night, I will prove my mettle by staying on the job and holding down the fort and keeping the home fires burning. The Tequila Boogie is rocking in California and I am marooned in the Big Apple.

Within days of Neuwirth decamping to California, I'm on my way to Washington, D.C., with Larry Poons, a painter friend of Bob's in whose studio we have passed many an hour during the winter, drinking and playing guitars. When we weren't with Michael Pollard and Annie, Larry's place was the other locus of our late-night hanging out.

Larry and I have the same reaction to the shootings at Kent State: Okay, that's it. They're gunning down American students on an American college campus. Fuck 'em. We're going to Washington. Across the country, hundreds of colleges and universities are shut down by a national student strike. Organizers have called for a mass demonstration in Washington on the weekend after the killings.

We drive down in traffic that's a lot heavier southbound toward D.C. than the northbound flow, and we feel that we're part of something big. We stay with Bob Siggins, my fellow Charles River Valley Boy, who has moved to D.C. to practice the art of neuropharmacology for the National Institute of Mental Health. We walk to the Mall on a perfect spring day that has brought out a mostly cheerful crowd of demonstrators. Somewhere in the center of the densest mass there is a stage and a sound system. We hear Judy Collins sing "If I Had a Golden Thread," and a voice that may be Tom Hayden exhorting us: "How can you love the Cambodians, whom you have not seen, if you cannot love the black people in the jails and the ghettos of the United States, whom you have seen?"

Closer at hand, the most popular chant is "One, two, three, four, we don't want your fucking war!" Dozens of demonstrators are frolicking in a knee-deep pool that surrounds a fountain. A couple of girls perched on the shoulders of their boyfriends have gotten topless.

What Larry and I witness is more like a May Day festival than an antiwar demonstration, but the next day, the Sunday papers carry stories of clashes with police and National Guard troops, and of demonstrators smashing windows and overturning cars. Spokesmen for the Nixon administration focus on the violence, and the press doesn't give equal time to the exuberant, peaceful crowd on the Mall.

New York is dull after the energizing weekend. On my own, there's little I can do to further the fortunes of *The Fool of Paris*. I keep up regular appearances at Max's, but when Janis and Bobby call me from the tattoo party and I hear the hullabaloo on the other end of the phone, I regret my overzealous devotion to duty. Bobby tells me to hail a taxi and go directly to JFK. "We'll keep the party going until you get here," he promises. Janis offers to buy me a plane ticket just to come out and meet the band and think about going on the road, but even this isn't enough to get me going.

It takes one more phone call. In the aftermath of the tattoo party, Bobby and Kris and Janis are sitting in Janis's kitchen nursing hangovers. "Boy, I wish we could get John Cooke to go on the road again," Janis says. "You want John Cooke?" Bobby picks up the phone. "I'll get you John Cooke." Janis is better than ever, he tells me, and you've got to hear this band.

I fly into SFO on May 23. The tour will begin six days later, in Gainesville, Florida. I dump my bags in my North Beach apartment, recover my trusty Volvo from Peter Berg's garage in Berkeley, and traverse the graceful span of the San Rafael Bridge at a high rate of speed, determined to make up in the intervening days for the fun I've missed.

When I arrive in Larkspur, I learn that the band has acquired a name. On a recent day when Janis and the boys were winding up rehearsal, Neuwirth and Kristofferson sailed in, already three sheets to the wind, recruiting deck hands for the evening voyage. "Is everybody ready for a full tilt boogie?" Bobby demanded.

Janis lit up like a neon sign. "Full Tilt Boogie!" she cried, and the christening was celebrated with holy water from the agave plant.

By the time I get there, the Boogie has been curtailed, and it's Janis who is cracking the whip. She has banished Bobby and Kris during working hours. When they first arrived in California, they were spreading the good-times gospel of the Great Tequila Boogie around the Bay each day and falling down on Janis's floor each night. Kris's sleeping accommodations soon evolved upward to the comfort of Janis's satin sheets. She persuaded him to remove, at least temporarily, the split-cowhide shirt and pants he has been wearing nonstop since he left New York. He hesitated, briefly, fearing that if he took off his latter-day mountain man's garb, he would fall to the ground while the outfit remained standing, a concern that proved to have some basis in fact.

Each afternoon, after band rehearsal, Bob and Kris would corral Janis and the boys for the evening's rambles. But the drinking, and its effects, were cutting into rehearsal time, and Janis laid down the law: We've got songs to learn, a tour coming up, and I need these guys to stay sober.

Janis's new house is a palatial version of her recent apartments, furnished in a combination of Beatnik Modern and Grand Funk. It is set among old-growth redwoods, where it catches maybe half an hour of sunlight a day in midsummer and exists for the rest of the time in softly filtered light that is gentle on the eyes. I prefer open skies and long vistas, but this nest in the forest primeval perfectly suits Janis's preference to be sheltered from the full glare of day.

The house is full of dogs. Janis's beloved George was let out of her Porsche last year while she was rehearsing with Kozmic Blues in San Francisco, and he vanished. The loss hit Janis hard. To fill the gap, Albert has given her, as a house present, a good-natured malamute mix whose mother was Albert's malamute bitch, and whose father, the story goes, was Bob Dylan's poodle. His name is Butch. Dave Richards has given Janis another puppy, Lyndall has a young dog, and Janis recently acquired a Great Pyrenees and named him Thurber. When a new arrival comes in the door, the canine troop careens through the house for a welcoming inspection. It's a noisy but cheerful domestic ritual.

The garage has been converted into a rehearsal studio that features an antique pool table with a slate top and leather pockets. Janis's two-piece cue, and the set of ivory balls, were a Christmas gift from our New York limo driver, John Fisher. The stick, he told her, once belonged to pool legend Willie Mosconi.

The lamp that hangs over the table has a (genuine) Tiffany shade. A new tape recorder and a rack of tapes stand on a bookshelf in the corner, the source of old and new material to be learned by the Full Tilt kids. On breaks, they can shoot a rack or two.

Janis looks trim and fit, and she is in high spirits as she presents me to the band. Brad Campbell and John Till, the two holdovers from the Kozmic Blues Band, greet me like a long-lost brother. Meeting the three new members, and learning how they all came together, gives me more reasons to believe that Janis's rampant optimism is justified.

In the final days of the Kozmic Blues Band, on a flight to Nashville for the last gig before Madison Square Garden, John Till was feeling low. He had been with the band only five months and it was folding out from under him. He looked up and saw Brad Campbell bouncing down the aisle toward him, all grins, and he wondered what Brad had to be so happy about. Brad sat down next to John. "She wants you and me to come out to California," he said.

Brad and John have spent the winter in San Francisco, living on a retainer, waiting for Janis to put together her next band. The retainer was less than they would have made on the road but more than they would have gotten from unemployment. They did a little freelancing—play a gig here, play a gig there—but nothing regular. One day in the spring, John Till was wandering around North Beach when he ran into Snooky Flowers and a guy he didn't know. "You wanna play guitar tonight?" the guy said.

"Sure," John said.

"Can you get a bass player?"

"How about Brad, man?" Snooky said. "Can you get Brad to play?"

John went off to phone Brad. They spent the afternoon rehearsing in a second-floor loft with Snooky, the other guy, and a drummer named Clark Pierson.

Clark is from Albert Lea, Minnesota. He's an American version of Ringo Starr: It takes a lot to wipe the grin off his face, and he has the same happy-go-lucky basic rhythm. Clark came to California from Chicago with a band that had a recording contract. The record didn't go anywhere, and in the spring of 1970 Clark was living in San Francisco playing music anywhere he could get a job, Polish dances included. He had a small-time agent trying to find him work. One day the agent called up and said, "These people need a drummer for a week. Do you want the job?"

"How much is the pay?"

"Thirty a night."

"Sure."

Clark showed up at the second-floor loft for rehearsal, where he met Brad and John and Snooky's friend. The gig was playing five sets a night in the Galaxy, a topless joint on Broadway. Rumor later has it that Clark was discovered in a strip joint, but he scotches that story: "There's a difference between the strip joints and the topless: Topless is already topless."

One night, along about the middle of the evening, Clark heard a jingle-jangle sound and he saw a long-haired chick come into the club, dressed up in satin and spangles, with small bells tinkling from a sash tied around her waist. She was arm in arm with an older man in a Brooks Brothers shirt and a crewneck sweater and a pair of Levi's turned up at the cuff over a pair of Buster Brown shoes that may never have been polished. His gray hair was tied back in a ponytail and he looked like the man on the Quaker Oats box. "Man," Clark thought to himself, "what a weird couple."

When the song ended, Snooky grabbed the mike. "Ladies and gentlemen, in this club tonight we have one of the finest singers"— racka-racka-racka, giving Janis a glowing introduction. Snooky harbored no grudges about the demise of the Kozmic Blues Band. Albert sat in the spotlight's glare and smiled his best smile. When the set was over, Brad and John went over to talk to Janis and Albert, and after a little while Brad came back to ask Clark if he'd like to audition to play in Janis's new band.

"Well, I ain't got nothing else to do," Clark said. A few days later he went to the house in Larkspur. "We played a couple of tunes and then Janis asked me if I wanted to join the group. Albert is standing there. I can't get used to him. She was real happy when I said, 'Yeah.'"

Besides Brad and John and Clark, there is Richard Bell on electric piano and Ken Pearson on organ. Like Brad and John, they are Canadians. Kenny has played with Jesse Winchester, an American songwriter who removed himself to Canada a couple of years ago, beyond the reach of draft, and made his reputation there. Richard is yet another graduate of Ronnie Hawkins's bands, from which Albert earlier plucked Robbie Robertson, Rick Danko, Richard Manuel, and Garth Hudson to play behind Bob Dylan when Dylan electrified his act.

"Hey, you guys, here's a song I like," Janis will say. She'll play the boys a tape and they'll run through the song to see if it begins to rock. To Big Brother classics like "Ball and Chain" and "Summertime" and "Piece of My Heart," and a few songs from Kozmic Blues, like "Try (Just a Little Bit Harder)," they have added punchy new tunes that will soon become familiar to audiences across the country—"Move Over" and "Half Moon" and "Cry, Baby" and "Get It While You Can."

The band is tight. There is none of the every-man-for-himself wariness that marked the early days of Kozmic Blues. These guys are already a band. They are on Janis's trip and she basks in their selfless support.

In her garage-studio-poolroom, I see something new in Janis. She is running the rehearsals as if she's done it all her life. There is no slack time. Oh, they laugh, and there are jokes, but when Janis counts off a song and kicks a leg to start the beat, the band is right there. She is in charge, with none of the strained authority that marked her occasional attempts to exert leadership with Kozmic Blues. It's clear that the boys already feel they are working with her, not just for her. Unlike the macho-sensitive men in Kozmic Blues, they don't object when Janis calls them "my boys"—they love it. From the stories I hear, Richard and Kenny were sometimes overwhelmed by the level of hanging out that kicked in when the Great Tequila Boogie hit town, but Janis helped them over the rough spots. Now that she has forbidden Bobby and Kris from tempting the band with invitations to play hooky, not even the promise of a full night of rocking can distract Janis from the task at hand: She is getting her act in shape. Put on your dancing shoes, boys, we're going on the road.

The band has already had its local debut. They played a gig at Pepperland, a dance hall in San Rafael, for the Hells Angels, where Janis's act was billed as "Main Squeeze and Janis." Bennett Glotzer, who has been Albert's partner since Albert's relationship with Bert Block ended last year, became close to Janis in the fall, during my hiatus from the road. Bennett was managing Blood, Sweat and Tears when Janis and Big Brother played with them at the Psychedelic Supermarket in Boston and again at the Columbia Records convention in Puerto Rico. Janis has been aware of Bennett since then, and since he joined Albert, he has become someone Janis confides in. Like Albert, Bennett has spent time in California this spring, supporting Janis in preparing for her return to touring. He has been largely responsible for booking the upcoming tour.

Bennett didn't want Janis to do the Pepperland gig. Hells Angels? What are you, crazy? Remember Altamont? Bennett thinks the Angels are sociopaths and thugs. But Janis insisted, and the stories are wild: An Angel (not really an Angel, Peter Albin says—a member of a rival club, maybe a Gypsy Joker; everybody else says he was an Angel) and his motorcycle mama fought Janis for her bottle as she was about to go onstage. Bennett stepped in and got pinned under the melee, which ended when Sweet William, a member of the Angels' San Francisco chapter, stomped the guy on the head and escorted Janis to the stage. During her set, a naked couple tried to make it onstage, in the midst of the music, and an Angel, a real one this time for sure, tossed the naked guy out and let the naked girl stay. Big Brother and the Holding Company, reconstituted since Sam left Kozmic Blues, opened the show, with Nick the Greek Gravenites at the mike, in a friendly battle of the bands. By all reports it was intense like no other gig in memory.

Afterward, when Janis was leaving the hall with Glotzer, she said to him, "Well, Bennett, you were right."

Be that as it may, the Pepperland gig has redounded to Janis's benefit. The reviews, and the word of mouth around the Bay, are favorable. Old prejudices that did so much to alienate Janis from her hometown the year before have evaporated with demise of the Kozmic Blues Band. In the Larkspur house or sashaying into the Trident — the preferred watering hole of the famous and funky in Marin, a hippie rock-and-roll hangout with organic food and tall drinks, stunning waitresses and a view of Sausalito Bay—or whipping across the Golden Gate Bridge in her psychedelic Porsche, Janis is firmly in her element and enjoying every minute.

Even before I absorb the full extent of Janis's rebirth, I want my old job back. But I have delayed accepting the offer long enough that Janis and Albert have taken on a provisional road manager. Stan Rublowsky has some credentials from another wing of the music business—he has toured with the renowned jazz pianist Stan

Kenton—but he seems a trifle out of place in Janis's Marin madhouse. A new age has surely dawned if a guy who has road-managed jazz musicians looks too straight to rock-and-rollers.

Janis feels an obligation to Rublowsky, but she is happy to see me again and tells me so. Finding her so bright-eyed and cocksure, so uncontainably happy, I realize I'll be seriously bummed if I don't get to wrangle this bunch on the road. It's no time to be coy, and I let my enthusiasm show. Janis resolves the dilemma by deciding to take both candidates out for the first couple of weeks. She will decide later which of us to keep. Stan and I agree to do the job together, which should make it easy on both of us. He has already confirmed most of the arrangements for the first weeks of the tour. I look them over and find them in order, which leaves me with little to do by way of work until we are off and sailing. I am out of New York at last, after a long winter of discontent, and glad to be back in California. I'm ready to celebrate. The Great Tequila Boogie, in its final days, provides the vehicle.

Neuwirth and Kristofferson are the sole survivors. Odetta and Michael J. are long gone. Ramblin' Jack has rambled on. Kris and Bobby decamp to my San Francisco apartment when I arrive. They sleep in my living room for the next few days and we put plenty of miles on their rent-a-car and my Volvo, around the Bay, visiting friends, playing music, chasing women, and stopping at assorted bars to refuel.

Kris is a former Rhodes scholar, a former army captain and former chopper pilot in Vietnam, which adds a dimension to his persona as a leather-clad, long-haired songwriter, not a Nashville type at all, but one who has surely got Nashville's attention.

Kris's Bay Area rambles with Neuwirth have already earned him his first booking in L.A., thanks to Ramblin' Jack Elliott. Jack had a gig at the Keystone, a Berkeley music club, where Bobby and Kris joined him on the very evening when Janis and Full Tilt Boogie were debuting at Pepperland. (Like Bennett Glotzer, Neuwirth too was leery of the Angels and what might ensue at a full-on rock-and-roll goonbash fired up by Big Brother and the Holding Company and Janis's new band.)

As Jack tells the story, he invited Bobby to sing a song or two and Neuwirth in turn persuaded Kris to sing. In the club that night was Doug Weston, owner of the Troubadour, in L.A. After hearing Kris, Weston booked him at the Troubadour.

According to Ramblin' Jack, Janis was so pissed at Kris and Bobby for missing the Pepperland gig, she called the Keystone and left a message that was handed to the miscreants as a written note that said, "Thanks a lot. Now I'll know who my friends are."

For the record, tequila is not just another drink. Some component of the agave plant contributes, along with the alcohol, to the elevating result. For many, the effect is psychedelic. Where tequila puts me is out there, especially drinking it day and night with two lunatics who don't know any better. Now and then I suspect that *I* know better, but I try to keep up anyway. It isn't bad, really, once I get used to ordering Bloody Marys for breakfast to calm the tequila willies before I tackle the huevos rancheros. And the truth is, I will remember these days fondly, even though the few scenes I can recall in any detail play like clips from a demented underground movie—

```
EXT. MILL VALLEY HOME—SWIMMING POOL—DUSK

The house belongs to Big Daddy Tom Donahue, a pioneer
of underground FM radio. Tom is not home. The young
men and women in the pool are naked. Donahue's teen-
age son is not sure he should allow these people on
the premises, but he can't imagine how to evict them,
and besides, the naked girls are very attractive.

                                              CUT TO

INT. PEGGY CASERTA'S HOUSE—STINSON BEACH—NIGHT
```

```
The party turns weird when Peggy decides to shoot
herself up. Neuwirth, Kristofferson, and Cooke aban-
don ship.

                                          CUT TO

INT. CARL DUKATZ'S HOUSE—BERKELEY—MORNING

Kris is singing "Sunday Morning Coming Down." It is
morning, but not Sunday. We are coming down but try-
ing to get back up. Carl learns the lead guitar part
as it goes along and Neuwirth finally gets the har-
mony right after weeks of patient instruction from
Kris.

                                         FADE OUT
```

Through it all we avoid serious trouble and get little sleep. On Thursday, May 28, Stan Rublowsky and I pick up Janis and the band and we fly off to Florida. Kris comes with us as far as Atlanta, where he changes planes for Nashville. He has run out of money and I lend him fifty bucks. When he strolls off down the concourse, giving us a parting look at his Western-hero walk, we feel we are losing a member of the family.

It may be the last time Kris has to borrow pocket money. Roger Miller's and Ray Price's recordings of his songs are beginning to pay off. Later in the summer, Kris gets a quarterly royalty payment in five figures that's a boost toward the fame and fortune that will follow. He repays my loan with a check I wish I had framed. For Kris, like Janis, the spring of 1970 marks a turning point toward the good times.

The Great Tequila Boogie is history. Full Tilt Boogie is on the road.

CHAPTER TWENTY-ONE

Full Tilt Boogie

MAY 29, 1970: Gainesville, Fla.

MAY 30: Snider Armory, Jacksonville, Fla.

MAY 31: Miami, Fla.

JUNE 5: Columbus, Ohio

JUNE 6: Indianapolis, Ind.

JUNE 12: Freedom Hall State Fair and Exposition Center, Louisville, Ken.

JUNE 14: Kansas City

JUNE 19–20: College Park,Md.

JUNE 25: *The Dick Cavett Show*

JUNE 26: Schenectady, N.Y.

WE OPEN THE tour in Florida, in the final days of May. Despite her confidence in the new material and the new band, Janis approaches these first concerts as if the judgment to be passed on her were governed by fickle fortune, as if her talent and Full Tilt Boogie might not be enough to recapture what she has lost. To steady her nerves, she drinks before the concerts with only marginally more restraint than she was applying in the final months of touring with Kozmic Blues.

The gig in Miami is our first big show, an all-day outdoor rock festival with Janis as the headliner. We will be flown to the site by helicopter. Our pickup point is a high school football field. The chopper is late. It's a warm day and Janis lies down in the grass to catch forty winks. When the chopper lands, she is sound asleep.

I shake her awake. "Come on, Janis, time to go." She gets up bleary-eyed and blowsy, her hair and feathers in disarray. The alert pilot spots the tequila bottle protruding from her bag. "I can't carry her," he says. "She's intoxicated." No sleazy hippie broad is going to get in his chopper if she's been drinking.

At this very moment there are thousands of passengers airborne over America who have tanked up at the airport bar and had a double on board the plane before lunch, all of them more soused than Janis, but no amount of persuasion on my part or Stan's can convince the Guardian of the Airways to fly the star of the show to the concert site. He'll take the rest of us, he says. Fuck you, we tell him.

We make our way by rent-a-car through crowded streets and unfamiliar byways, but that's what road managers are for, and we've got two. Our combined efforts get us to the festival site just in time for Janis's set. The natives are restless after long hours in the sun with too much beer and too few toilets. The collective mood is, Come on, man, I been sittin' here all day. What else can you show me?

Albert isn't one to pester the road crew with his concerns, but he has given me a message about the opening weekend of the tour: Be cool in Florida, where the local newspapers may remind the fans (and the police) that Janis was busted for obscenity at a concert in Tampa back in November. Reaching an out-of-court settlement on that charge cost her a hefty legal fee.

Before Janis goes onstage, I caution her against doing anything to offend the sensibilities of the Miami constabulary, in case they're looking for an excuse to prove that they are just as vigilant as their Tampa colleagues. Just over a year ago, these same Miami cops busted Jim Morrison for public profanity, indecent exposure, public drunkenness, and incitement to riot when the Doors were here. Morrison's trial is pending.

Not to worry. Janis is a model of superstar decorum. She keeps the tequila bottle out of sight, she holds her tongue between songs, she makes the crowd forget the heat. Full Tilt is on a full boogie, and they bring the show to a rousing finale.

WE SETTLE INTO the One Fifth Avenue hotel in New York and at the end of the week we commence a relatively relaxed, two-gigs-a-weekend schedule. Following his custom, Albert sends us into the heartland to gear up the band on the road before presenting Janis and her new ensemble to the scrutiny of the rock press. In the Midwest, spring feels like summer. We play Columbus, Indianapolis, Louisville, and Kansas City. For the time being we are scrutinized only by David Dalton, a young journalist who will travel with us for several weeks to gather material for a piece on Janis that will appear in *Rolling Stone* too late to affect the initial judgments of her new band.

Janis has warned Dalton at the outset, "I hope you jerkoffs at *Rolling Stone* aren't going to demolish me like you did the last two times," but Dalton isn't here to do a hatchet job. He seems more interested in the multifaceted Janis than the star. He notes with interest that Janis has Nancy Mitford's *Zelda* and Thomas Wolfe's *Look Homeward, Angel* in her carry-on bag.

Albert's prudence is wise but, as it turns out, unnecessary. Any rough edges in the music are smoothed out by Full Tilt's steamroller energy and everyone's good spirits. Janis and the band roll effortlessly through the first weeks of the tour. The Full Tilt boys are neither psycheholic nor alcodelic. Like most musicians, they tend to smoke a little weed or have a few drinks on occasion. The hanging out back in

Marin expanded their concept of what having a few drinks entails, and for the first week or two the boys sometimes overflow their customary limits, but soon enough the postgig partying comes under control.

In Full Tilt, Brad Campbell and John Till seem truly at home for the first time. They are the veterans, and they welcome the newcomers. From the beginning, the five of them form a cohesive unit not only musically but in the off-hours as well, something that never happened in the Kozmic Blues Band. Ken Pearson and Richard Bell give me more laughs than worries. Kenny is like a teddy bear, until he sits down at his organ. Richard is lean, with a dreamy smile that can lure you into mistaking him for a space case, but he's paying attention all the time. He's tied with Brad for best musician in the band, but no one is keeping score and everyone more than pulls his weight. John Till is often late checking out of a motel or getting to the gate in an airport, but he's right there when it's time to go onstage.

Janis's transparent delight in working with these boys makes all the more apparent what was lacking in the Kozmic Blues Band. There is love in some measure in all friendship. For Janis, a professional relationship that doesn't become at least a middling friendship is one that she won't bear for long. In Kozmic Blues, the reserves of love were inadequate. With Full Tilt Boogie, Janis has already created the closeness that's essential to her happiness and success on the road. Nothing will ever be just like Big Brother, but with Full Tilt, it's a family again.

The mood of the tour reminds me of my first months with Big Brother: We are outward bound and the sky's the limit. Even the routine gigs in inconsequential cities lack the tedious aspects that prompted Sam Andrew to write "Downtown Nowhere." This is more like Downtown Everywhere—it's summertime and the living is easy. After Miami, Janis plays no more festivals for a time, as she renews her acquaintance with municipal auditoriums and college gyms.

In Louisville, the audience of four thousand can't occupy a quarter of the seats in the huge Freedom Hall, but Janis revs up enough energy to fill the auditorium. For a time, it seems the security rent-a-cops may overdo their efforts at crowd control. Janis jumps down to dance with the kids in the front row and that gets everyone dancing. By the end of the show, they're on the stage, and the hall manager has the lights on, but the festivities stay just shy of uncontrolled. Janis keeps the energy positive and the crowd in check.

When we have been on the road for two weeks, Stan Rublowsky and I sharing the road manager's duties, neither of us pushing Janis for a decision about which of us to keep, Janis asks me to sit with her on a flight back to New York. She says she wants me to handle the road show for as long as I'm willing to stay. I told her back in California that even if she chooses me I will probably leave her again after the summer tour. I remind her that Stan is willing to stay on the job indefinitely. Janis says what's important is that she and I are friends. We have a history together, shared experience that includes both highs and lows. I tell her if it keeps on being this much fun, I may stay through the fall.

We enjoy our reconfirmed partnership in silence for a time, but I have a bit of business to transact, now that I am officially back on the payroll. I worked with Kozmic Blues for a year without a raise, at $250 a week. I've been on the road now for a couple of weeks with no idea how much I'm being paid. I broach the matter of my salary and Janis doesn't shy away. "How much do you want?"

"How about four hundred a week?"

"All right," she says. This is the first time we have ever discussed the terms of my employment, just the two of us. Janis displays none of the old anxieties about being ripped off or not having enough money, which date back to her first days with Big Brother and complicated many of her dealings with partners and employees in the past.

With that out of the way, Janis reveals a decision that surprises me: "I'm not going to make it with anyone that works for me," she says. It's too hard to keep the intimacy of sleeping with someone balanced with the demands of the employer-employee relationship, she says. I tell her I think keeping some professional distance is a good idea, but I realize she doesn't really need and isn't really seeking my approval. Janis has made this decision from the head, not the heart. She's willing to deny herself the kind of transient romantic attachment with a guy in the band or one of the boys on the road crew that has offered her comfort in the past because she knows it's the smart thing to do, for the greater good of her new band and for her career.

> "Something happened last year and I became a grownup. I always swore I would never become a grownup no matter how old I got, but I think it happened. No sense worrying about it. Just rock on through."
>
> **Janis Joplin**

Seeing the dramatic improvement in Janis's health and her spirits is reward enough for coming back on the road, and I realize that road managing is a valuable resource. It's my safety net. Writing the *Fool of Paris* script, I learned something about how to write screenplays and I want to learn more. Janis's failure with Kozmic Blues made me quit the road. As a result, I may have found my own work. Talk about silver linings. Helping Janis now is a form of payback, a way of saying thanks.

Janis is making decisions about the business side of her career as well. She discusses her investments with Albert, she tells me, and with the office accountant, Sy Rosen, a genial man who helped me get my American Express card. At long last, Janis believes that after the band and the travel expenses have been paid and Albert takes his cut, she will still have enough. More than she ever dreamed when she was just a hopeful hippie on Haight Street.

As Janis opens a book to read, I marvel at what she has accomplished in the six months since we parted in New York. She has brought her formidable intelligence to bear on getting it right this time. She has examined the lessons to be learned from the failure of the Kozmic Blues Band. She took the lead role in assembling Full Tilt Boogie. If she was evading her responsibilities last year, she is embracing full responsibility now, not tentatively, but as if she's been doing it this way all along. There's no more deferring to men she thinks know more than she does, no more waiting for others to solve her problems.

She has cleaned up her act.

Stan Rublowsky departs with no ill will and the road crew takes on its final form for the summer tour. We are hauling our own PA system now, adequate for all but the biggest shows, and we have added two more equipment men to handle the load. George Ostrow and Vince Mitchell are augmented now by Phil Badella and Joel Kornoelje. The four of them are the California hippie wing of our little family. Driving the PA and stage equipment from gig to gig in a truck means that Albert's office has to book the concerts no farther apart than a twelve-hour drive. Three to four hundred miles is about right. George and Vince got the equipment routine down solid with Kozmic Blues, and they come to me only rarely. For the most part, the equipment crew operates on its own and gets the job done.

Besides the equipment truck, George and the boys are in charge of a brand-new, bright red International Travelall, which we immediately dub the Boogie Wagon. Albert's idea is that Janis and I and the Full Tilt boys will use the Boogie Wagon instead of rental cars, thus saving some bucks, but the scheme contains a flaw. After each night's gig the equipment men leave for the next city, driving the equipment truck and the Boogie Wagon. The band and I still have to get to the hotel and from the hotel to the airport. We often arrive at the next destination ahead of the road crew. So we continue to rent a car, which leaves the road crew with a great vehicle at their disposal once they've unloaded the truck into the concert hall. They soon discover that the Boogie Wagon can accommodate a promising number of groupies.

The band is a road manager's dream, almost always willing to follow direction. If I do something that puts somebody's back up, I back off and become the peacemaker. My job is to keep them happy. It doesn't hurt to say so when I have to soothe ruffled feathers.

John Till and Brad Campbell are old hands, accustomed to my style. I have no idea what the new boys make of my role until one morning when Richard Bell breaks out laughing as he watches me get it together to check us out of a hotel. "What are you laughing at?" I want to know, too ready to take offense.

"Nothing. It's great! I never had anyone do all this for me before, is all."

Later on, I learn from the boys that Janis has laid down the law, warning them not to give me a hard time, but Richard's appreciation is spontaneous and genuine. Clark and Kenny second the motion. In a few weeks, we have formed a benevolent cohesion that survives the occasional inevitable dustups on the rock-and-roll road.

Janis and I are comrades in arms. I rarely have to do more than suggest that it would be nice if she could be in the motel lobby in five minutes for her to appear breathless in three, hair and feather boas flying, tripping along in her sashaying run, calling out, "I'm ready, John! I'm ready!" So I'm all the more surprised when she pulls one of her old tricks as the band gathers in the lobby of the Chelsea Hotel to head out of town for a weekend's gigs. (Janis prefers One Fifth Avenue, but it's full up this week.) John Fisher's limo is out front and we're about to leave for La Guardia when Janis presents me with a sloe-eyed pretty boy who has spent the night in her bed. "We've got to drop him off in the East Village," she announces.

In my first weeks with Big Brother, I established it as the Eleventh Commandment that if anyone in the band needed to delay our progress toward a departing flight, that person had better let me know ahead of time. The East Village will take us half an hour out of our way, maybe more, depending on traffic. I always allow extra time to get to airports, but making the detour will cut it pretty fine. I launch into my prerecorded diatribe about no side trips that might make us miss a flight. Halfway through, Janis jumps in with some real heat of her own as the onlookers draw back to a safe distance.

The volume escalates, and suddenly we reach an impasse. Janis sputters for a moment, then says, "I wouldn't take this from anyone but you!"

"Well, I wouldn't do this for anyone but you!" I shoot back.

We stand nose to nose. Janis cracks first. She grins, and we dissolve into laughter. Janis gives the pretty boy ten bucks and tells him to take a cab.

This is the new Janis, who doesn't have to defend her position with the last ounce of her energy. She is more comfortable in herself, more centered. She is the linchpin that holds Full Tilt Boogie together, onstage and off. She is the leader of the band. If the craziness of the road gets to one of the new guys, she lightens the moment with a joke, or says something that helps him cope, much as she cooled out John Till after his first month with the Kozmic Blues Band. Last year, Janis had a clause inserted in her contract rider that required she have a dressing room separate from the band's, to give her some privacy and some distance from the intramural tensions in Kozmic Blues. That provision is still in force, but she spends little time alone now, except to change clothes. The rest of the time she is with the band.

> "She knew what she wanted. She knew ahead of time what you wanted, what you didn't want, or what you thought you wanted. She had herself covered, she had everybody—she tried to cover everybody all the time."
>
> **Clark Pierson**

Shortly before we left California, Janis confided to us that she wanted a nickname, something that suggested a good-time woman. After some discussion it came down to "Rose" or "Pearl," but there is no final decision until we are out on the road. Self-consciously, we try these monikers on for size. It isn't long before Janis decides that "Rose" doesn't suit her and "Pearl" she becomes, the name already taking on an identity separate from the public persona of Janis Joplin. It's a way for her to appear among her friends in human form. It's a private name, an intimate name, used for saying friendly things. We'll say, "Knock 'em dead, Pearl," before a show, or, "You're lookin' good, Pearl," or "Hey, what's the matter, Pearl?" But when the talk is about business, or when communications get strained, as they do on the road, even among family, it's always Janis then, never Pearl.

Later on, when the nickname appears in the press, some people perceive it as a gaudy label associated with Janis's wild outfits and her most outrageous behavior. They'll call out, "Hiya, Pearl!" on the street and Janis will cackle and wave back, loving it in a way, but she loves it most the way it's used among her friends. It's a name that tells her we love her.

IN ONE CONCERT after the next, Janis recaptures her audience without a fight. She controls them confidently, using between-song raps and stories to keep them on her wavelength or to lay a bit of philosophy on them. She has a new introduction to the Jerry Ragovoy tune, "Try (Just a Little Bit Harder)," which she has kept from the Kozmic Blues song list. It's a story whose moral is that if you aren't happy with where you're at, if everyone around you seems to be getting more of the action than you are, you got to try harder. *Wham!* she jams her fist into the air, kicks out one leg, and the band starts the song with a punch that knocks the front row of the audience back ten feet.

That kick gets her into trouble in College Park, Maryland. Mid-song, Janis accentuates a beat with a good hard kick and pulls a muscle deep in her groin. She comes offstage at the end of the set, her face taut with pain. She asks me please to tell the audience that she can't do an encore. The promoter calls an ambulance, and the band and I follow the flashing red lights through the late-night suburban streets at sixty plus to the nearest hospital, where Janis lies on a table in the emergency room for half an hour until a doctor finds time to examine her. He tells her she has pulled a muscle.

She gets a good laugh out of this incident a few days later, on *The Dick Cavett Show,* which is now running five nights a week on ABC's late-night schedule, opposite Johnny Carson. Janis has been invited to appear on other talk shows, but she accepts invitations only from Cavett, because she likes him and because, she says, he's the only talk show host who actually listens to his guests.

"I hear you tore a muscle somewhere near Maryland," Cavett says, once the applause for Janis's opening song has died down.

Janis gives a breathy laugh. "It was a lot closer to home than that, baby." The audience roars.

When Cavett asks her to explain the opening song, "Move Over," which Janis wrote, she says it's the old story about getting a mule to move by holding out a carrot in front of him, dangling from the end of a stick. The woman is the mule, she says, while men are "constantly holding out something more than they can give."

Cavett draws himself up. "I have to defend my entire sex, ladies and gentlemen."

"Go right ahead, honey," Janis says. The audience cracks up.

Cavett has somehow gotten wind of the fact that Janis's Port Arthur high school class is holding its ten-year reunion in August, and Janis is planning to go. "I don't have that many friends in my high school class," Cavett admits. "I don't either," Janis says. Her wistful tone gets her another laugh, but she's serious when she says, "They laughed me out of class, out of town, and out of the state. So I'm goin' home."

Janis holds her own as the next guest joins the conversation. She met Raquel Welch last fall at a party *Life* magazine gave for "the top stars of the sixties." Raquel and Janis hit it off then, and Raquel took Janis to the premiere of *Myra Breckenridge*, a film adaptation of Gore Vidal's novel, in which Raquel co-starred with Mae West, John Huston, Farrah Fawcett, Tom Selleck, and the fastidious film critic Rex Reed, who played a transsexual. When Cavett asks Welch what kind of people come to see a film that many find bizarre, Raquel says she has seen the movie three times and twice the audiences were predominantly homosexual.

"Of course they weren't all homosexual," she adds. "Janis was there."

"Thank you, baby," Janis says with a grin. This gets another big laugh from the audience, as they pick up the reference to Janis's often-alleged bisexuality.

"Can we clear anything else up while we're here?" Cavett asks innocently. As Cavett and Raquel understand and Janis's response makes clear, she prefers to be seen by the public as an enthusiastic heterosexual. Nor is this an evasion. As love objects and sex objects, men are her first choice.

Cavett touches on Janis's winter trip to Rio, but neither mentions the highlight of her summer tour, which is just two days away.

Three venturesome music promoters in Toronto, collectively known as Eaton-Walker Associates, have chartered a Canadian National Railways train that will traverse the continent from east to west. The passengers, an all-star lineup of bands, will give concerts in Montreal, Toronto, Winnipeg, Calgary, and Vancouver. The train, and the tour, is called Festival Express 1970. Like the Monterey Pop Festival, it is envisioned as an annual event. Like Monterey, it will never be repeated.

The passenger list is impressive. In addition to Janis and Full Tilt Boogie, it includes the Grateful Dead, the Band, Delaney and Bonnie and Friends, Tom Rush, the Buddy Guy Blues Band, Ian and Sylvia, Mountain, Traffic, Ten Years After, Seatrain (an act Bennett Glotzer has managed since before he joined Albert), James and the Good Brothers, and more. Janis will get $25,000 for each concert. She will gross $125,000 for a week's work. Two years earlier, it took Big Brother and the Holding Company six months to earn as much.

As the starting date draws near, our imaginations are running wild. Let's resurrect the Great Tequila Boogie and put it on rails. Janis and I call Neuwirth and Kristofferson and I cajole the promoters into reserving them bed space on the train.

Ten days before the start of the tour we learn that the Montreal and Vancouver shows have been cancelled for lack of adequate advance sales. For a time we fear the whole scheme may evaporate like a pipe dream, but the other dates hold firm.

The night before we're due in Toronto, Janis and Full Tilt do a show in Schenectady, New York, near Albany. Because of the last-minute change in the starting point of the train tour, I haven't been able to book a direct flight from Albany to Toronto. The only available flight leaves Albany at eight forty in the morning and involves a plane change in Buffalo, a city I remember mainly for detaining Sam Andrew when he was caught driving without a license after a Big Brother concert. On my birthday. He woke me in the middle of the night to bail him out.

I roll Janis and Full Tilt Boogie out of bed at 7:00 A.M. Bitching and moaning, they straggle aboard the plane. We eat some breakfast in Buffalo between flights, which helps some, but the plane to Toronto is late. By the time we finally land in Canada we are tired and cranky and in no mood for further delays. Hotel rooms await us, and a day off—what's left of it. The band follows me through the Toronto airport like zombies. In their present condition, they would follow me off a cliff.

In this state we approach Canadian customs, notorious throughout the drug underground as being even tougher than their American counterparts. I have warned the band that I will brook no nonsense at customs. No secret stashes, no dumb jokes, nothing that will raise the hackles of officialdom. And it is here that Janis's pride in having kicked heroin manifests itself in an unexpected way.

The smartly uniformed officers take one look at us and decide we warrant closer inspection.

"Step this way, please, and open your luggage."

Like unimaginative civil servants around the globe, the Canadian customs officials judge a book by its cover. Of course the long-haired musicians will be the ones carrying drugs, right? As I was for each border crossing in Europe, I am a model of businesslike rectitude for this one. No suit and tie today, but even the underwear in my suitcase is laid out foursquare and my customs-officer reading material is face-up on top of my clothes—paperback copies of the U.S. Constitution and Thomas Jefferson's *On Democracy*.

"Thank you, sir." I am waved through to await the others.

At the opposite end of the sartorial scale is Janis, who might be Mark Braunstein in drag, dressed up for a costume party. The Full Tilt boys are Ivy League by comparison. The inspecting officers pass them through with a few perfunctory pokes in their bags while a diminutive officer with a solemn, round face begins a thorough search of Janis's luggage. Unaccountably, she seems to welcome his attention.

Her suitcase looks as if she packed by throwing clothes at it from across the room. Her hippie handbag is overflowing with odds and ends scooped up at the last minute during the bleary rush of our early-morning departure.

"Hey, man," Janis says to the small customs officer. "Don't you want to look in here? That's my toilet kit, man, there might be some pills in there."

What the hell is going on? I try to signal Janis to quit goading the inspector so we can get out of here before we all keel over from exhaustion. I'm afraid to do it too openly for fear of arousing more suspicion. Janis takes no notice.

Like a sheep being led to the dipping trough, the officer follows

Janis's direction. He heads straight for the toilet kit and pulls out a bag of powder. My heart skips a beat.

"What is this, *ma'mselle*?"

Janis can scarcely contain herself. "That's douche powder, honey!" she proclaims, loud enough for everyone to hear.

"Ah, *oui, oui, ma'mselle*." The little French-Canadian inspector almost chokes with embarrassment. His complexion explores the scarlet end of the spectrum while he moves on quickly to something safer. But he keeps searching.

I'm pacing up and down, pissed at Janis for delaying us. And then—comes the light. I sit down and prepare myself for a long wait. Belatedly, I begin to enjoy the show.

On Kozmic Blues' tour of Europe, Janis was terrified at every border crossing and customs inspection, knowing that the works and the smack she had stashed on her person could send her directly to jail on a tough rap to beat in foreign courts. But she was unwilling to go without, so she carried a supply everywhere, despite the risks. Now she is taking her revenge on the customs officers of the world, and now I understand the full extent of Janis's joy in her new freedom. The border watchdogs can search all day and never find a thing. Janis is clean. She is as respectable as a symphony conductor. She is proud and she is celebrating.

The boys amuse themselves as best they can. Richard Bell passes the time with a yo-yo. Nothing fancy, just up and down, up and down, grinning as he watches Janis urge the inspector on. John Till wanders around with his cassette recorder slung from his shoulder and earphones on his head, nodding dreamily in time to the music, oblivious to everything else. Clark sits on a bench practicing rhythms. A good drummer is never without his drumsticks and a practice pad.

Every five minutes or so a fat officer walks purposefully through the room muttering under his breath. "Move, move! Goddamn hippies!"

Janis prolongs the game until even the obtuse little customs inspector finally realizes that no one who has anything to hide would behave like this. Janis is still bubbling, joking with the boys as we leave the airport, all the fatigue and hassle of our early start and the Buffalo layover banished. When we are settled in the rent-a-car she says to me, "I had to do it. You understand, don'tcha, honey?"

For once the stern road manager has to give in.

CHAPTER TWENTY-TWO

Riding That Train

THE TORONTO KICKOFF of Festival Express 1970 is a weekend of music, noon to midnight on Saturday and Sunday, but our drawn-out travels keep most of us from the Saturday show. Sunday is a perfect summer day. The concert stadium is in a park on the shore of Lake Ontario. George Ostrow and I and two girls George brought from New York explore the belt of greensward that borders the lake, where sailboats make the most of a light breeze. A tank and an antiaircraft gun and a four-engine bomber mounted on a pylon make up a World War II memorial. We climb on the tank and stroll around the park until the concert starts. We have checked out of our hotel rooms. After the concert, we'll board the train for Winnipeg and the West.

Backstage, Brad Campbell flags me down. Look who's here, he says, and he presents to me none other than Bill King, the Kozmic Blues organ player who played only the Stax-Volt Christmas show before he disappeared. It turns out that when Bill arrived in New York for Christmas with his family after the Memphis gig, the FBI nabbed him for dodging his draft notices and a federal judge gave him a choice: Join the army or go to jail. Bill chose the army. He went through basic training and followed orders for almost a year, until orders came to ship out for Vietnam. At that point Bill, recently married, hitchhiked with his young bride to Canada and settled in Toronto. Bill has a band, Homestead, that opened the concert here today.

Janis greets Bill like a long-lost friend, her irrepressible exuberance in her new life, her new band, and the start of the Festival Express tour pouring out to the organist who knew her briefly in gloomier times. She tells Bill she has quit smack, regales him with accounts of the Full Tilt band and her new material, and even tells him about her Brazilian adventures with Linda Gravenites and David Niehaus, who she still hopes will come back to her.

The energy of the other performers can't match Janis's high spirits, but several groups come close. Like those who were at the Monterey Pop Festival, the bands who have signed up for the cross-country train tour sense that this is the start of something special.

The audience—twenty thousand, they say—seems to feel the same high. Backstage, we hear some talk about fans trying to jump the fences, storm the gates. The word is, they're radical protesters who think the concert should be free.

Janis is receiving a flat fee for each concert. The number of tickets sold and how many kids manage to scale the fence don't affect her pay, so I'm not keeping tabs on security. Later we hear that Jerry Garcia helped arrange a free concert at another park nearby on the lakeshore, where the Dead and the New Riders of the Purple Sage performed, along with Canadian artists Ian and Sylvia and James and the Good Brothers. This diversion draws the protesters from the CNE stadium and apparently pacifies them.

It is past midnight when the last act leaves the stage. In the quiet hours before the short summer night wanes, we are transported to the train, which sits engineless on a siding in the CNR rail yards, and we explore what will be our home for the next five days. I help Janis and the band find their berths in the sleeping cars, but no one is ready to fall into bed. In the middle of the train we discover what will become

the centers of social activity during the journey: a dining car and two
bar cars. Someone points to electrical outlets in the walls of the bar
cars. Is the power up here 110 volts? I think so. Let's try it out.

The road crews have loaded the bands' equipment into the baggage
car. They troop through the train and retrieve some amps, a couple of
drum sets, an electric keyboard, a basic PA with a mike or two, and
before the train begins to roll one bar car is transformed into the
electric-music jam car. Acoustic musicians find a home in the other.

At eight o'clock in the morning, the train pulls out of the yards
and the music falls into the rhythm of the rails. (Neuwirth and Kristofferson are no-shows. They will regret their decision.)

It's a rolling hootenanny. From Toronto to Winnipeg, the music
never stops. At any time of the day or night, you can climb out of your
berth and lurch down the narrow corridors to the bar cars, and you'll
find someone playing. There are brief lulls, but never for long. Someone else picks up a guitar, a drummer finds the beat, and off we go.

I've got my movie camera and my stereo cassette recorder with
me. Somewhere between the lakes and woodlands of Ontario and the
spreading farmland of Manitoba, I set up the cassette recorder in the
electric-music car and record ninety minutes of train music. There are
long instrumental jams, some totally improvised, some based on
known tunes. One of the best, with a trumpet lead, is Hugh Masakela's "Grazing in the Grass," which he played at Monterey, before
it became one of his biggest hits.

The musicians get a joyful workout when Buddy Guy and Bonnie
Bramlett have a blues sing-off, passing the mike back and forth, swapping songs, swapping verses. People moving through the car stop to
listen. In the acoustic car, Janis and Jerry Garcia sing "Careless Love,"
and Jerry and John Marmaduke Dawson of the New Riders wail on
"Wake Up, Little Susie."

When I set aside my movie camera, I borrow a guitar. The Martin
D-18 I played with the Charles River Valley Boys was stolen off a baggage cart in the Chelsea Hotel last year, while Mark and George were

loading Kozmic Blues' equipment into the truck late at night. So far, I haven't replaced it. But there are plenty of guitars. I trade Hank Williams and Jimmie Rodgers songs with Rick Danko of the Band. After I finish one of Hank's lonesome blues, Rick's bandmate Richard Manuel says, "Hey, man, you can't sing like that. You're a road manager." This backhanded compliment from a musician I admire makes my day.

There are other cameras on board, a 16-millimeter film crew hired by the promoters. Cool. Someday we'll relive the trip in a movie theater. When Janis and Marmaduke sing together, Janis motions the cameraman to focus on Marmaduke, so the camera doesn't stay just on her. Give the man his due.

Janis spends most of her waking hours in the acoustic bar car or the dining car, where drinks are also available. By day, the cars are a little brighter than she likes—she prefers cool dark spaces, like her home in the redwoods. On the train, she wears her large round rose-colored sunglasses day and night and it's all the same to her.

The trip gives her a chance to spend time with her old friends from the other San Francisco bands. Her departure from Big Brother, which aroused criticism at the time, is history now, and Kozmic Blues is forgotten. Holding forth with a glass in her hand, Janis is in top form, and she is exuberant in her praise for Full Tilt Boogie.

> "Full Tilt Boogie, from what Janis was telling us—Janis was reporting to Garcia and myself—telling us, I mean she was really turned on about that band. She felt like it was coming back together again. It was like the first band that she'd had that she was happy with, since the early days, and a much better band, at that."
> **Rock Scully**

Whatever other drugs the passengers may consume aboard the train, alcohol fuels the music and the social intercourse. Joints are passed from time to time in the music cars, but most of the smoke that wafts through the train is from tobacco. From the first day out of Toronto, Janis and I buy drinks for Jerry Garcia and encourage him to keep pace with us.

The sleeping compartments seem impossibly small at first encounter. They're completely filled by the bed when it's down. You get out into the corridor, lower the bed, and climb back in. You've got a light, a fan and a little sink. Hmm. Not bad. Lie down and watch the countryside pass by in the Canadian summer dusk, which lingers forever. When you want to shut out the light, pull down the shade, and you're in a comforting cocoon. It's easy to doze when you're lulled by the rhythm of the rails, but it's hard to sleep for long when you're missing the rolling party.

In Winnipeg, the promoters have arranged with the local authorities to make the municipal swimming pool available for the exclusive use of the Festival Express gang before the concert starts at noon. They provide buses. Dozens avail themselves of the offer. The Olympic-sized pool offers a chance to improvise water volleyball or dive off boards and platforms on three ascending levels.

Few of the travelers thought to pack bathing suits. Most swim in their underwear. None get naked, not even the Californians, who have made public nudity commonplace in counterculture environs. The decision to observe this level of decorum disappoints me initially, but I realize it is wise, as is the facility's decision to exclude the curious public while we're splashing about. Long-haired men in Jockey shorts might not occasion scandal, but the women of Festival Express, in their lacy bras and bikini panties, would probably test Winnipegians' sense of propriety.

After the pool, I'm off to the airport. Three of the Full Tilt boys—John Till and Richard and Ken—stayed in Ontario after the Toronto concert to spend a couple of days with their families. I find them in the Winnipeg airport in company with a professional clown in full costume and makeup, who is paid by the provincial government to keep travelers amused.

Another stadium, another sports field. The crowd at this concert is much smaller than Toronto. It's Canada Day, and Pierre Trudeau, the prime minister, is in town to celebrate Manitoba's centennial. Trudeau draws crowds like a rock star. We've got a trainload of rock stars, but this concert is laid-back, a pleasant interlude.

The day is fair and the wind is brisk. Backstage, Janis sits on the grass against a snow fence with Marmaduke. They were keeping company on the train as well. Maybe Janis is experiencing the romance of the rails.

Aboard the train, many of us—musicians and road crew alike—who would normally confine drinking to the evening hours have been drinking during the day. Janis has kept us company. In Winnipeg, she slacks off a little in the afternoon, then has a belt or three as the time to go onstage approaches. The boost she's looking for is harder to feel when it's floating on top of a daylong bender. So she reinforces it.

The result is that Janis performs the show as drunk as she sometimes was with Kozmic Blues. What saves her is that the booze isn't walking hand in hand with heroin, she isn't looking forward to her postconcert fix, and she's got the Full Tilt Boogie Band behind her. She summons her reserves and she is *up* for the show.

Her spoken introduction to "Try (Just a Little Bit Harder)" is longer, as are the improvised raps she inserts in a couple of other songs, pacing the stage, talking to the audience, while the band keeps the groove going, riffing on the tonic chord behind her, until she finally jumps back into the song.

> "The singer is only as good as the band, and this is the first band that really helped me. . . . This band, man, I could be in the middle of a verse and go on a different trip, and they can follow me. They won't go with the arrangement. They go right with *me*, man."
>
> **Janis Joplin**

Given how tight and fine Janis can be with Full Tilt, her rambling raps in Winnipeg seem self-indulgent to me, and I can sense the audience becoming restless when they run long. But when Janis is singing, the band is with her and she's got the crowd.

With most of my road-managing tasks handled by the Festival Express promoters, the concerts are easy for me. They transport us from the concerts to the train and from the train to the concerts. All I have to do is make sure Janis and the boys are ready to go onstage when the time comes.

Onward to Calgary. In the bar cars, the music continues. Life on the train has become the norm. Day and night blend into a continuum. We sleep when we can't stay awake, and wake up to get back on board the party. On the first night out of Winnipeg, I see northern lights in the sky and I haul members of the Grateful Dead to the platforms between the cars to take in the light show, as entrancing as the best of Headlights' efforts at the Fillmore, even without music.

Midday, a rumor sweeps the train: The bar cars are running out of liquor. Given the steady pace of the drinking, no one questions the story. Canadian National Railways no doubt stocked up as they would for a normal passenger run, but this is not a normal passenger run.

I shift into road manager mode and locate Kenny Walker, the Walker in Eaton-Walker Associates. Is there a stop coming up anytime soon? Yes, Kenny says, we'll stop at Saskatoon. Can you get the railroad to give us a car and a driver? He's sure he can.

I need something to collect money in. Fortunately, the women have been shopping in Toronto. What is always on the shopping list when a stylish woman is feeling frisky? Shoes. An empty shoebox is just the thing. I find my old Cambridge friend Tom Rush, another regular at the Club 47, and I enlist him in the cause. We walk the train from one end to the other, soliciting contributions: "Donations for the People's Bar!" In fifteen minutes, we collect over three hundred dollars.

Saskatoon, pearl of the prairie. Cultural hub of Saskatchewan. Chauffeured to a provincial liquor store by an obliging CNR official, Kenny Walker and I and a couple of volunteers who accompany us point at bottles on the shelves and fill cardboard cases. No beer, goddammit, we need booze! We're stumped for how to spend the last thirty dollars until we spot an oversize bottle of Scotch. If it were wine, it would be something more than a magnum, maybe a jeroboam. Is that a display bottle? It's real? We'll take it. And we're done.

Back at the train, eager hands help load the liquor out of the trunk of the car onto the train. And as it turns out, the bar cars aren't running out of booze after all, so we're well provisioned for the final leg of the trip to Calgary.

Late that night, our last on the train, Janis and Marmaduke and Rick Danko and I are among those who launch into a long and loud rendition of "Ain't No More Cane on the Brazos," a Southern chain-gang work song I first learned from Dick Fariña. It's a haunting song, but haunting isn't what we're after tonight. We're into volume and six-part harmony. It's exhilarating at the time, but long afterward, when I see it in the documentary film *Festival Express*, well, let's say it was a rendition best savored in the moment rather than preserved for posterity. You had to be there.

We are not looking forward to our arrival in Calgary. This is too much fun. They can't really take the train away from us, can they? Hey, I know, let's hijack the train! We'll take it to San Francisco! We elaborate the fantasies and eventually retire to our beds, and it may be that a majority of those aboard actually sleep during our last night on the train.

In the morning, hangovers are plentiful as we roll into Calgary. Once the train comes to a stop, the engine is uncoupled and there is no power. The cars soon grow hot on the cloudless day. There is nothing to do but to pack our things and brave the sunshine to grab a taxi and head for the hotel.

> "Everybody was just wiped, and pale. You know. Looked like a bunch of junkies, just falling off the train."
>
> **Clark Pierson**

> "I've never seen Jerry drunk like he got drunk on that train. That goes for Mickey Hart, Bobby Weir.... All of us are seriously hung over, sitting on the railroad tracks, holding our heads."
>
> **Rock Scully**

It's the Fourth of July, but there are no stars and stripes waving in the breeze and there will be no fireworks tonight. Canadians are understandably reluctant to observe the United States' success in casting off the British yoke, a process that for them is still incomplete.

I register Janis and the Full Tilt boys at the hotel and I find messages from the office waiting for me. On the train, we've been out of touch. What I've got on my itinerary is that Janis will play tonight, Saturday, in Calgary, and tomorrow we fly to Seattle for a gig there. After that, we were scheduled for a few days off in San Francisco, but the office has thrown us a curve: They've booked a concert in Honolulu on Wednesday.

I call Janis's room. Lyndall Erb, Janis's new roommate, has flown up to join us for the trip to Seattle and Honolulu, and she's on the job as Janis's guardian.

Janis is trying to catch up on her sleep.

Is she asleep right now?

Well, no.

I ask Janis to make one decision. No sense flying from Seattle to San Francisco on Monday only to get on a plane to Hawaii on Wednesday, right? How about if we take our days off in Hawaii instead? Janis goes for it. I cancel the flight to San Francisco and book us from Seattle to Honolulu. I call the promoter in Honolulu and let him know we'll arrive early, on Monday. Can he adjust our hotel reservations for us? He can.

With the changes made, I join George and the New York ladies for a little sightseeing and window shopping, which becomes actual shopping. I find a pair of genuine smoke-cured buckskin moccasins made by Canadian Indians, with reasonably authentic Plains-style beadwork. Real men shop for footwear too.

Back at the hotel, Janis is up and about, and she and our road crew have hatched an outstanding idea. The equipment guys have bought a model Canadian National Railroad train, with a diesel engine, two passenger cars, and a caboose. They have labeled the cars "Festival Express 1970" and "Bar Car" with press-on letters. They have wired a section of track to a piece of two-by-eight plank about three and a half feet long and wired the train to the track.

They have thought of everything, down to buying two Sharpie markers, in red and black, which Janis is using to letter on the plank, "WITH LOVE," in letters three inches high. Janis's plan is to present the model train to Kenny Walker at tonight's concert, as a gift from the musicians and road crews.

When Janis has finished her lettering, we head for the stadium. The Calgary show began at noon and will run until midnight or beyond. We keep the model train in our dressing room. Between now and when Janis goes on, it becomes my mission to get as many of the musicians and crew as possible to sign the plank before the concert starts, without letting anyone from Eaton-Walker see it. As on the Declaration of Independence, the early signers write large and the latecomers write smaller and find room where they can. The signatures become a network of names that cover the board. A few add grateful sentiments. Someone named Fudge writes "Hugs and Kisses."

The presentation is a great success. When Janis and the Full Tilt Boogie Band are introduced that evening, once the applause dies down, Janis calls Kenny Walker to the mike and holds up the model train on the plank for the audience to see before she gives it to him. Walker is surprised and touched. As he leaves the stage, Janis cues the band and launches into the most exuberant set of the trip. Backstage, someone has spiked the tequila with acid. Talk about a psycheholic high. A couple of the Full Tilt boys got dosed, but they are a band, a bonded unit, and the music hangs together.

Afterward, we're reluctant to leave the stadium. On the train we have become a tribe, united by the singular experience. Tonight we part from our traveling companions. Tomorrow it's back to airplanes and rental cars.

THE SEATTLE GIG is in a big stadium, maybe as many people as the Toronto concert, but Festival Express was something out of the ordinary. From here on, it will take a lot to impress us.

Early in my travels with Big Brother, I discovered, to my surprise, that for coast-to-coast flights the difference between a coach ticket and first class was sometimes as little as twenty dollars. I made the band aware of this bargain and, as their concert fees escalated, Janis and the boys agreed to try traveling in luxury. Once they got a taste of the free drinks, wide seats, and rolled tenderloin roast carved in the aisle by charming flight attendants, they were sold. Now Janis looks forward to any flight long enough that the first-class service is worth the extra cost. She has readily approved giving the Full Tilt kids a treat on the flight from Seattle to Honolulu. The boys are wide-eyed and smiling as we settle into our seats. "Something to drink, sir?" "Now, before we take off? Sure, why not." Cocktails, champagne and wine, and a meal that a decent restaurant could serve without embarrassment, banish the End-of-the-Line Railroad Blues.

The Honolulu promoter greets us on the tarmac with flowered leis in hand. He puts one around Janis's neck and kisses her cheek. He places the next on Lyndall. As he moves toward one of the boys, Janis says, "Aren't you going to kiss her?" and the promoter quickly corrects his oversight. It is such a Janis moment, making sure that no one is slighted.

On an impulse, Janis takes the rest of the leis from the promoter and puts one on each member of the band and crew, her feather boas whipping around her head in the tropical wind. The other passengers take in this ceremony as they come down the steps from the plane. Why is no one offering them a lei? they wonder.

Our accommodations are the Hilton Hawaiian Village on Waikiki Beach. The promoter apologizes in advance. He warns us that we will find the hotel full of "newlyweds and nearly-deads." If "Hawaiian Village" suggests something rustic, like grass huts, we're quickly disabused of this notion. The Hilton looms above the beach, two towers, thirty stories high, and we're lodged on the twenty-eighth floor. Alone, so far as we can tell. We don't see another soul on our floor for the length of our stay. Quarantine the hippies.

> "I had a corner room on the twenty-eighth floor, and there were two French doors on the other side of the room, like at forty-five degree angles to each other, and there was a sign on the wall saying 'Beware of Trade Winds.' I opened one door and saw Waikiki, spread out there for me, and it was calm, and I opened the other door, lamps fell over, bedsheets tore off, the table—everything fell over. It was about a seventy-mile-an-hour wind."
>
> **John Till**

Kenny Pearson collapses on the Hilton's exclusive expanse of sand to recover from the generosity of Continental Airlines' first-class beverage service, only to be prodded awake by two security guys he describes as Samoan Mau Maus, whose attitude is "Get the fuck out of here, dirty hippie." Showing them his Hilton room key doesn't adjust their attitude much, but they leave him alone to bake off his hangover.

Janis would be happier in a funkier hotel where the cabana boys smoked Maui Wowie and responded in kind to her "Hiya, honey," and come-hither smile. But she doesn't complain. Instead, she settles for drinking mai tais in the Hilton's cocktail lounge. She and Lyndall are so engaged the next afternoon when a male guest, closer to nearly-dead than newlywed, approaches them at the bar, his potbelly leading the way, and delivers his opening line: "Hey, how much do you girls want?" This may make up in some measure for the Dutchman's rejection in Amsterdam, but Janis and Lyndall decline the offer.

> "The times that I went out with Full Tilt, we had a great time. She really had a fun time, offstage as well as onstage. I never had felt that way when I'd seen her on the road with other bands."
>
> **Lyndall Erb**

We lie on the beach, bodysurf, and discover a Hawaiian cocktail called piña colada. The concert in Honolulu takes place on the third day of our stay. After the concert, the band and equipment crew will loll about on the beach for two more days, but Janis and I are headed to Austin, Texas, for an event she has been looking forward to all year, a grand jubilee to celebrate the sixtieth birthday of Kenneth Threadgill, the country singer and bar owner Janis has revered since her first days in Austin.

CHAPTER TWENTY-THREE

T for Texas

EARLIER IN THE tour, before we boarded the Festival Express, Janis asked me to come with her to Texas for Threadgill's birthday party. She doesn't want to have to keep track of her ticket and deal with changing planes in Dallas at the crack of dawn, and all the things I handle on the road. She wants me along for companionship as well, a friend from the new life she has made for herself to show around the places where her music began, and because it will impress the shit out of her Austin friends that she's traveling with her own personal road manager. She promises that we'll have a chance to play music with these Austin friends, but even without that assurance I'm already on board.

What I know about Ken Threadgill is that he's a country yodeler who sings the songs of Jimmie Rodgers, the Singing Brakeman, America's Blue Yodeler, which focuses my interest. Rodgers has been my special hero since I found a 78-rpm record of his in the closet of my father's study in New York. "Hobo Bill's Last Ride," the label said. "Solo with guitar." Since then, I have bought and learned a bunch of Rodgers's songs.

For Janis, Threadgill was a mentor and an inspiration. In his Austin gas-station bar and music club, she absorbed the roots of country music and bluegrass. Threadgill motivated her to play the guitar to accompany herself, and among Janis's fondest memories are her early experiences playing in his bar for a couple of bucks and all the beer you could drink.

It's the first time we've traveled together, just the two of us. We leave Honolulu on a red-eye, nonstop to Dallas. After drinks and dinner, we burrow under our first-class blankets against the cool cabin air. We try to watch the movie, a turkey called *Krakatoa: East of Java*. (Never mind that Krakatoa is actually west of Java.) Janis is feeling affectionate. We make out during the movie and we fall asleep with her head on my shoulder.

In Dallas we change planes—it's *very* early—for the hop to Austin, where we're met by Julie Joyce, an old friend of Janis's since her brief stint at the University of Texas. It was Julie who alerted Janis to the date of Threadgill's party and urged her to come. Julie is on the short side, with dark hair and glasses. She looks at Janis in a way that suggests a history between them and uncertainty about how Janis will respond to her now.

With Julie is a friend of hers, a blonde named Margaret. To meet us this early in the morning, they stayed up all night. Margaret is quiet and Julie is drunk. The reunion between Janis and Julie is muted by Julie's intoxication and Janis's exhaustion. Margaret's role becomes evident when we get to the car—she's the one who's sober enough to drive.

Where's the party? Janis wants to know. Threadgill's bar is way too small for the expected crowd. When Janis sang there with a few friends, they packed the place and played to fewer than fifty people. The birthday party, which is billed as the KT Jubilee, is expected to draw five hundred or more. It's being held at an old barn out on the edge of Austin. The Party Barn, it's called, "out by the Y at Oak Hill," Julie says.

That's all we can absorb right now. Margaret and Julie take us to the Holiday Inn, a circular tower by the town lake, where Janis and I gratefully collapse into our rooms and crash for the rest of the day.

Julie and Margaret come back about six in the evening to pick us up, accompanied now by Julie's husband, Chuck—medium height, long hair, comfortable presenting himself as a member of Austin's folkie-hippie community, which is still small at this time. Margaret and the Joyces are on the organizing committee. They've been out to the Party Barn, and there's a hitch in the plans. During the day, a rumor that Janis is in town to attend the Jubilee has run wild. There are several thousand people gathered at the site and more on the way.

Janis wants her appearance at the party be a surprise to Thread-gill, not because she wants to make a splashy entrance but because she doesn't want to steal the spotlight from a man she loves and admires. She's going to borrow a guitar and sing just two songs.

Janis is crushed to hear that the surprise may be blown, but Julie, who is more sober today, says the rumor about Janis's presence is just that, a rumor. No one is sure it's true. Janis takes hope that we can salvage some element of surprise. We discuss our options and come up with a plan. If we arrive at the Party Barn after dark, we can sneak Janis to the stage. So far so good, but it won't be dark for another few hours. What do we do in the meantime? This being the cocktail hour, we hit on the obvious solution and repair to the Holiday Inn's cocktail lounge, which is located on the top floor of the tower, with a sweeping view of Austin and the lake.

On a small stage in one corner of the lounge, a diminutive young man with an electric guitar and a rhythm machine is providing background music. As the waitress delivers our first round of drinks, the singer launches into Kris Kristofferson's "Me and Bobby McGee." Well, "launches" gives the wrong impression. The little guy more like strolls into the song.

At this point in time there is no connection in the public mind between Janis and "Bobby McGee." Even if the little guy recognized

Janis, there's no reason he would think to play this song for her. Bob Neuwirth learned the song last fall and taught it to Janis. She performed it in Nashville in December with Kozmic Blues. The song wasn't on the set list but Janis decided to do it on the spur of the moment, a spontaneous decision that had the best possible outcome: The band found the groove and Janis's first public performance of "Bobby McGee" got a rousing reception in the capital of country music. She played it again at Madison Square Garden in December. Apart from the audiences at these two concerts, and at Janis's shows this summer, the "Bobby McGee" that the public knows is Roger Miller's recording. Kristofferson's first solo album is only now in stores and making few waves. So why does the little guy pick this song to sing in this Holiday Inn on the day when Janis will sing it for Ken Threadgill at his birthday party? Of all the gin joints in all the towns in all the world . . . The cosmic disc jockey is on the job.

When the low-powered rendition comes to an end, Janis leans into the table and confides to us, "That guy can't do that song worth a damn. Wait until you hear me. *I* can do that song."

We time our departure from the Holiday Inn to approach the Party Barn as dusk is deepening. Oak Hill is just beyond the edge of Austin, in the countryside, the rising glow of the capital city behind us.

The mob of Janis-rumor-fans is alert. They peer into every car that approaches the site, and there's no way to keep them from peering into ours. Janis is riding shotgun, her preferred seat. It's too late to get her into the backseat where she could scrunch down to hide.

The car is mobbed, but so long as we keep rolling, we can still make progress. We want to get as close to the stage as possible. It's set up outside the barn, and the pasture is fence-to-fence full of people.

Our only ally is the darkness. Beyond the crush of people around the car—on the car, some of them—no one knows what's happening. When the crowd gets too dense to go any farther, we abandon the car and try to form a protective ring around Janis. Forming a protective ring with four people and trying to keep the mob from grabbing hold of the person in the middle, while simultaneously moving through a crowd as densely packed as rush-hour commuters on the New York subway, is challenging. But I am a New Yorker. I know how to deal with rush-hour crowds. I lead the way, weaving through the crush with Janis holding on to my belt, the others clustered around her.

There is no protected area around the stage, no "backstage," no semblance of a green room. Behind the stage, the crowd is thinner—you can't see the performers from here. We find a small area of sanctuary, a patch of grass, stomped by many feet, where we catch our breath. Chuck has brought a guitar for Janis. Janis is shaken by the intensity of our passage through the throng. Still, she has observed one aspect of the gathering that piques her interest: Look at all the pretty boys, she says, surveying the young men within range.

During our cocktail holding pattern in the Holiday Inn lounge, I had time to observe Julie's friend Margaret and learn a little about her. She's smart and she's funny, and she's good-looking. And smart. For me, smart triples the appeal of good-looking. Margaret graduated from UT Austin in the spring and she's headed for law school in the fall, which impresses me no end. I took a course at Harvard called "The Role of Law in Anglo-American History" that held my interest as few others managed to do. I thought about going to law school. I fantasized becoming a latter-day Clarence Darrow or Oliver Wendell Holmes, but the folk revival seduced me from the halls of academe.

Chuck and Julie huddle with Janis as she tunes up the guitar, which frees me to pay more attention to Margaret. We can't see much from here, so when Margaret says she's going to try to get to the back of the crowd, I tag along.

We circle around to a good vantage point. The PA system, intended for a smaller gathering, is marginal but adequate.

Bands have been playing all day, a lively mix of country-flavored folk and folk-flavored country and just plain good old country music, but Threadgill himself is the main event. When he is introduced, the crowd roars. He sings "T for Texas," Jimmie Rodgers's biggest hit, and his yodel soars above the crowd. I find most performers of Rodgers's songs wanting, but Threadgill does the Blue Yodeler proud.

Between songs in the middle of Threadgill's set, Janis steps out on the stage, provoking an even louder outburst from the crowd. She appears to take Threadgill completely unaware, and he is clearly delighted, grinning from ear to ear.

> "Kenneth was as big a ham as Janis, and the fact that five thousand people showed up instead of five hundred just tickled him to death and it didn't matter why. You know what I mean? It was just a big rock-roaring success. I mean it was everything he had ever hoped for."
>
> **Margaret Moore**

When the applause dies down, Janis places around Threadgill's neck a flowered lei she has brought from Hawaii. "I brought you a nice Hawaiian lei," she says into the mike. Threadgill is tickled by this gesture and embarrassed by the play on words. His affection for Janis is manifest, even from our vantage point at the back of the crowd.

I've got a couple of songs to sing for you, Janis says. She tells the crowd that the songs are by a songwriter named Kris Kristofferson. If you haven't heard of him, you will, she says. She sings "Bobby McGee," and the great crowd gathered in front of the barn in the hot Texas night falls as close to silent as that many people can get.

Janis told the truth when she said she knew how to sing "Bobby McGee." A great singer draws you in and connects you with the emotional content of the song. This ability, this gift, is at the heart of Janis's popularity. She bares her emotions and makes the song her own. With "Bobby McGee," she turns the story around, telling it from a woman's point of view without changing a word, making it even more poignant than Kristofferson's original recording.

Janis follows up with Kris's "Sunday Morning Coming Down." During the song, Margaret and I make our way back to the stage, to be there when Janis comes off.

> "I just remember that she was just awesome. Her version of those two songs was just *real* impressive. I can remember sitting there thinking, Oh, my God, this is really memorable."
>
> **Margaret Moore**

When Janis leaves the stage, her manner is noticeably different than at the end of her own shows. Here, she isn't basking in the ovation as a personal reward. She came here to honor a man she loves and respects, and she is satisfied that she has achieved what she came to do.

Somehow, while Margaret and I were out in the crowd, Janis has managed to pluck a semi-long-haired pretty boy from the mob. She is ready to get out of the crush and take the pretty boy with her. With Chuck and Julie we gather in a bunch and make our way to the car, Janis noticed by all and greeted by some, but our progress is easier now.

Performing at the Jubilee has Janis ready for some late-night rambles in Austin. It's past closing time for public establishments, but we have our own bottle of tequila and it fuels the search for a suitable living room. Our first stop is a house that belongs to a husband-and-wife couple of liberal lawyers who own a music club called the Split Rail, where Threadgill's band has been a fixture and where Margaret first heard him play. The lawyers offer drinks, which we accept, and Janis gets Chuck to let me play his guitar. Janis is in listening mode here, content to let me pick and sing, and she seems pleased by the Texans' appreciative reaction to finding that Janis has a road manager who can hold his own with Ken Threadgill when it comes to singing a Jimmie Rodgers song, as well as a couple by Merle Haggard.

One guitar isn't enough, so we move along to Chuck and Julie's, where we can trade songs back and forth. Janis has more than music on her mind, though, and before long she lets it be known she'd like to head for the Holiday Inn. We bid the Joyces good-bye and navigate to the tower by the lake, where we discharge Janis and her catch of the day. When Margaret and I are alone in the car I take my fate in my hands and ask her to come up to my room. For a drink, I say, holding up the bottle of tequila, which has an inch or so left. This blatant euphemism for what I've really got in mind tickles Margaret's Texas sense of humor. She says yes, and if we catch a few winks sometime before the hazy Texas dawn, they number fewer than forty.

I learn from Margaret that Janis told Julie she had to promise me a chance to play music in order to get me to come with her to Austin. Which wasn't true, but the message Julie got was that this guy's a VIP: If he's not happy, Janis won't be happy. Behind the stage at Threadgill's Jubilee, when I was availing myself of the barbecue and beans and beer laid out for the performers and partygoers, Janis extolled my musical talents to Chuck and Julie and Margaret. As Margaret interpreted the state of things, "I thought it was pretty obvious that she was smitten with you, so I was not looking for attention from you." By now Margaret has figured out that Janis's concern for my welfare stems from friendship, not romance—always a fine line for Janis, but one she has chosen to draw a little more clearly this year.

I would gladly extend my reservation in this particular Holiday Inn indefinitely, trusting room service to keep us fed, but I'm a road manager and Janis has a gig later today in San Diego. When I leave Austin, I'm in love.

After our smooching on the red-eye, and what Margaret told me, I wonder if Janis is maybe a little jealous, but she hasn't forgotten her resolution not to get involved with anyone on her payroll. On our flight to San Diego, she makes a point of letting me know she approves of Margaret. After all, I've had the good sense to fall for a Texas girl.

A week later, Janis receives in the mail a photograph of Kenneth Threadgill leaning against the bar at Threadgill's. On the back, he has written "Threadgill's, 7/15/70, to Janis from Kenneth Threadgill." In the photo, he's wearing a plain white apron and around his neck is the lei that Janis gave him at the Jubilee.

CHAPTER TWENTY-FOUR

That Old Gang of Mine

JULY 11, 1970: Sports Arena, San Diego

JULY 12: Exposition Hall, Santa Clara County Fairgrounds, San Jose

JULY 17: Albuquerque, N.M.

AUG. 1: Forest Hills Tennis Stadium, Queens, N.Y.—RAINED OUT

AUG. 2: Forest Hills Tennis Stadium—played rain date

AUG. 3: *The Dick Cavett Show*, NYC

AUG. 5: Ravinia Park, Highland Park, Ill.

AUG. 6: Peace Festival, Shea Stadium, Queens, N.Y.

AUG. 8: Capitol Theater, Port Chester, N.Y.

AUG. 11: Garden State Arts Center, Holmdel, N.J.

AUG. 12: Harvard Stadium, Cambridge, Mass.

BEFORE JANIS AND I left the Full Tilt boys to bake on the sands of Waikiki, I put George Ostrow and Vince Mitchell in charge of getting everyone on the plane to San Diego. We were in touch once by phone while I was in Austin, but it's a relief to arrive at the San Diego Sports Arena and find everything in place. The Full Tilt band is here, the equipment is set up, everybody's ready to boogie.

The promoter, Jim Pagni, has been running rock concerts in San Diego since Janis and Big Brother played here. He has his act together, so I can devote some of my attention to a task that Albert has given me: The time to record Janis with the Full Tilt Boogie Band is drawing near, and Albert and Janis have chosen Paul Rothchild to produce the record. If—it's a big if—if Paul and Janis agree that they can work together. Janis's failure to form comfortable working relationships with her previous record producers has vexed both Janis and Albert. This time around they want to assure true compatibility—insofar as that's possible—before they set foot in the studio.

When Albert tells me that Paul is in line to produce Janis, I wonder why he didn't think of Paul sooner. I wonder why *I* didn't think of Paul sooner. Paul is an independent producer now. He can work for any label. Albert says Janis thought of it. She remembers Paul from his effort to create a blues band around her and Taj Mahal and Al Wilson back in 1966. She remembers that Paul liked her singing.

Albert is aware of my friendship with Paul. He is asking me to act as an intermediary, to use that friendship to connect, or reconnect, Paul and Janis. He knows I can't determine the outcome, but he hopes I can smooth the way. I told him I'll do whatever I can.

In San Diego, that's not much. The other band on the program is Big Brother and the Holding Company, with Nick Gravenites on lead vocals, so it's a reunion with old friends. Paul gets to hear Janis live with Full Tilt. He likes what he hears, but backstage, before and after, there are too many distractions and not enough time for him to do more than exchange a few words with Janis.

The next day we fly up to San Francisco, and we go straight from the airport to San Jose for an evening concert there with the Joy of Cooking. We've been on the road for more than six weeks. Janis and I are fresh from Austin, where neither of us got enough sleep. Janis wants to get home to her house in Larkspur and sleep the clock around, if that's what it takes to revive her, but even in this condition, powered by Full Tilt Boogie, she musters the energy to put on a first-class show at the Santa Clara County Fairgrounds. "I haven't had so much fun since the first year with Big Brother!" she shouts as she takes the stage.

It's late when we all get home. Paul stays with me in my Powell Street pad. In the morning, we're groggy and Paul is concerned. He's been around Janis for two days and he has no idea if they can communicate on the level that will be necessary if they're going to make a record together.

Paul is convinced that Janis is an even better singer than either the world or she herself knows. His goal is to introduce her to the truly great singer inside her and to get that singer on tape for the first time. To do that, they will have to bond like soulmates. He reveals these concerns over a late breakfast, and the need to help him connect with Janis takes on new meaning for me. This isn't just another job for Paul. He wants to take Janis to the next level.

I'm apprehensive about calling Janis this morning. We had a passing spat about something or other before we left the concert last night, but the minute Janis answers the phone, my worries go out the window. Everything is sunshine and roses. Janis is happy to be home and all is right with the world. Come up to the house anytime, she says. And bring a bottle of rum.

By the time we get ourselves across the Golden Gate to Larkspur, it's afternoon. Janis gives Paul the nickel tour of the house and we go out to the long, narrow deck, where we sit in the filtered light of sunshine peeking through the redwoods. There is a short period of halting conversation as Janis and Paul size each other up. Both prefer to approach the matter at hand obliquely. Nobody's saying, Well, do you think we can work together? but everybody knows why we're here.

Janis, ever the gracious hostess, remembers the bottle of rum we delivered into Lyndall's hands upon arrival. While in Hawaii, Janis learned how to make piña coladas from the bartender at the Hilton on Waikiki, and she is eager to demonstrate this new skill. She disappears into the kitchen and comes back a few minutes later with a

pitcher and four glasses. The drinks go down easily. They're like tropical milk shakes. Nothing to it, Janis says. Pineapple juice and coco-
nut cream and rum whipped up in the blender with ice. She brings
out her Gibson Hummingbird and sings "Bobby McGee" for Paul.
Before long, it's time for another pitcher of piña coladas.

The conversation is rolling nonstop. Nothing about making records, nothing about business. The doorbell rings and Lyndall con-
ducts Shel Silverstein out to the deck. Just dropping by to say howdy.
If we needed another catalyst, beyond the jolly milk shakes, to
move the gathering toward unrestrained merriment, Shel fills the bill.
He writes and draws cartoons for *Playboy*, he's a poet, a composer, a
songwriter—hell, he's got more talents than our favorite jack-of-all-
hipness, Bob Neuwirth. Shel wrote "A Boy Named Sue" for Johnny
Cash, and "The Unicorn," which gave the Irish Rovers their biggest
hit. He's currently working on the music for a film about the Austra-
lian outlaw Ned Kelly, which will star Kris Kristofferson and Waylon
Jennings. (Shel's songs, sung by Waylon, will survive the Hollywood
process, but Kris is replaced by Mick Jagger.)

Shel gets right in the spirit of the piña coladas. He picks up Janis's
guitar and plays a couple of raucous tunes of his own creation, and
we laugh until we ache.

When we run out of rum, we adjourn to Sausalito to drink dinner
at the No Name Bar, where we find ourselves seated next to an excep-
tionally tall fellow who looks as if he may dwell somewhere deep in
the redwoods, emerging only to have a meal and a drink in town on
special occasions. He is clad in leather garments, apparently of his
own making, and he has a few leather hats on his table. Paul asks
him, "Do you make those hats, man?" He says, "Yeah, I make 'em."
"Well, can we see some?" He stands up, which takes a while—he's got
to be seven feet tall—and he goes outside to his car and comes back
with a knapsack full of headgear.

Paul takes an interest in a leather visor that would be great for
playing poker under a bare lightbulb. We're all trying hats on,

including Janis. I'm taken by a kind of a hippie hat with a flat brim and a low crown. If the brim was rolled a little, it might look sort of Western, like those low-crown cowboy hats in Western TV shows from the fifties, which bore no resemblance to anything anyone ever wore in the Old West. I roll the brim, and it promises to hold the roll. I put the hat on, and everybody says, Boy, that looks great. Janis gets the idea that she'll buy it for me. At first I'm reluctant to accept this generous impulse because I'm not sure I can become a hat person. I know I can't accept the gift and never wear it. But Janis has her heart set on buying me this hat and she pays the guy as I examine the hat inside and out. I find no maker's mark, so I say "Hey, man, do you have a pen?" He has just the thing, a Rapidograph with indelible ink. "Put your mark on it," I ask him. "Would you do that?"

He makes his mark, a backward R joined with a frontward B, like a Western brand. His name is Robert Bruce, locally known as Giant Man. When he's done, I pass the pen to Janis. "You can give me the hat, but you gotta sign it."

Janis turns the hat in her hand, figuring out what she wants to write. She sets it on the table and goes to work on the brim behind the crown. She writes carefully, bending over her work, the same way she lettered "WITH LOVE" on the plank that held the model of the Festival Express train. I expect her to write "Love, Janis," or something like that, but when she hands it to me I see that she has written, "To John, with love from Pearl." There's a heart next to "love" and half a dozen x'd kisses after "Pearl."

The next morning, over an even later breakfast than the day before, Paul is thoughtful. He and Janis never did talk business during our hours of carousing. I wonder if he still harbors doubts about his ability to work with her, but he puts my mind to rest.

"John, I learned something wonderful yesterday," he says, dead serious.

"What's that?"

"Janis Joplin is a *very* smart woman."

Paul reveals his delight in this discovery. He is confident that Janis's articulate intelligence will enable them to communicate, and communication is the key: If the lines of communication are open, if they share a common language and skill in expressing it, everything else is possible.

WITH THE CONNECTION to Janis established, Paul sets in motion a campaign he has been planning since Albert first spoke with him about producing Janis's next album. Paul thinks the technology, the engineers, and the union requirements at Columbia Records studios are outmoded. He thinks the whole mind-set at Columbia lags behind where rock recording should be in the 1970s. If he has to work within those limitations, he doesn't believe he can make a record that will sound the way Janis's next album ought to sound.

Paul has a plan, a way to prove to Columbia Records that he's right. Albert supports Paul's idea and they overcome the first hurdle when Columbia president Clive Davis agrees to let Paul record two demos with Janis and Full Tilt, one at Columbia's L.A. studio, where some of *Cheap Thrills* and all of the Kozmic Blues album were recorded, and another at Sunset Sound, the independent studio where Paul wants to record with Janis.

> "Grossman not only said his clients were artists, he believed it, and they, not the manager or the record company, set the artistic and commercial agendas."
>
> **Fred Goodman, *The Mansion on the Hill***

The third week in July, after a gig in Albuquerque, we're in L.A. making the demos. The Hollywood Landmark is full up and we stay at the Tropicana, a motel on Santa Monica Boulevard that's long been a favorite stopping place for musicians and artists of the middling ranks. It's seedier than the Landmark, more exposed. Someone has called it L.A.'s answer to the Chelsea Hotel in New York. Any resemblance is definitely not architectural. The Tropicana is stamped out of the two-story-stucco California mold, but like the Chelsea, the Tropicana has its attractions. It houses Duke's Coffee Shop, which serves the best burgers in Hollywood, and it's just a block or two from Elektra Records' L.A. studio, where I can drop in to visit with Fritz Richmond.

Paul knows that to prove his point he has to make the best possible recording in the Columbia studio. He is convinced that even the best possible recording won't be the kind of sound he wants—and Columbia should want—for Janis. Any trickery, any fudging to make the Columbia demo sound bad, will invalidate the exercise. Janis understands this. When she stands at the mike, she sings as if this is her next record for real.

The members of Full Tilt Boogie, except for Brad Campbell, have very little experience in the studio. It takes time to establish working relationships with each member of a band, to discern their individual modes of communication, more time than Paul has in making these demos. But the Full Tilt boys are good musicians, and above all, they're willing. They hang on Paul's every word and on each take they do their damnedest. Their inexperience will affect both sessions equally, so it doesn't tilt the outcome.

When Janis shows an interest in the technical aspects of the recording, Paul explains what's going on and how it affects the sound. He keeps her involved every step of the way. Even as he makes the crucial demos, Paul is expanding the relationship, laying the foundation for their work together.

When we move from Columbia's studio to Sunset Sound, a Columbia engineer sits in the back of the control room doing nothing, featherbedding. It's part of the deal.

In her downtime, Janis has a reunion with Kris Kristofferson, who is in town. One morning when we gather in the Tropicana parking lot to head for the studio, Janis is fully dressed and ready to go to work, complete with pink and purple feathers in her hair. Kris is barefoot and shirtless, left to lock up her room when he heads out for wherever he's going next.

With the dueling demos in the can, we fly east for a flurry of gigs. We play the tennis stadium at Forest Hills for a crowd of fifteen thousand. Janis appears on *The Dick Cavett Show* again and gives John Fisher's Love Limousine service a big pitch. We play a rock festival in Highland Park, Illinois, north of Chicago. We play a peace festival at Shea Stadium that Peter Yarrow puts together for the twenty-fifth anniversary of the Hiroshima A-bomb. Last year, in the '69 World Series, the Mets lost the first game, then swept the next four, clinching their first world championship on the same field where Janis and Full Tilt Boogie are now rocking and rolling for peace. When it comes to the notion that sports provide appropriate metaphors for every detail of American life, I'm a skeptic, but I like the idea that although Janis failed in her first outing with a new band, she's now on her way to clinching a championship of her own.

We wind up the tour in Cambridge, Mass., for an afternoon show that's part of a series of rock concerts put on in Harvard's football stadium. Warned that rowdy fans have caused problems for the Cambridge police after some of the other shows, Janis suggests before her last song that if the fans have energy to work off when the show is over, they take their boyfriends and girlfriends home and work it off together. The line gets a round of applause and the concert leaves Janis and the fans in high spirits.

When we get back to our Cambridge hotel, I head out on foot with a couple of the Full Tilt boys to eat. As we stroll along the brick sidewalk, four cops get out of a parked patrol car and start toward us. They call out a warning to get off the street. Huh? We're just going to get something to eat. "Fuck off! Get along there!" The cops break into a trot, brandishing their billy clubs. "You fuckin' maggots, get out of here!" They begin to run and so do we, beating a retreat to the hotel. The cops return to their squad car and circle the block, around and around, trying to catch us on the street again. I phone Cambridge police headquarters to request that the cops be called off. I say we're in town with Janis Joplin to perform at Harvard Stadium and the lieutenant on the other end of the line says, "I heard from my officer down there that she incited to riot." I maintain my calm as I tell him she did just the opposite, she told the crowd not to make trouble. "We've had vandalism down in Harvard Square after some of these shows," he says. I say, "Have you had any vandalism, any other problems in Cambridge this evening?" "Well, no," he admits. A while later, the squad car is gone and the streets are safe for long-haired musicians.

THE DAY AFTER the Harvard concert, Janis flies from Boston to Texas for the high school reunion she told Dick Cavett about back in June, but she has no intention of attending the festivities alone. She wants a few friends along for the ride. She has enlisted me, Bob Neuwirth, and John Fisher to make up her cohort.

Janis's idea is for us to rent a limousine in which we will shuttle around Port Arthur in knock-'em-dead style. I have phoned every rental car and limo agency in Houston, but they all say the same thing: You can't rent a limousine without a driver. Janis doesn't want a driver she doesn't know. We've got our own limo driver. So I reserve the biggest sedan we can get, a Chrysler Imperial.

John and Bobby and I fly out of New York and land at Houston a day after Janis. There to meet us is Margaret, my lady from Austin, who I've invited to join us for the weekend.

Before we hit the highway to Port Arthur, we make two stops. The first is at a Western apparel store, where John and Bob buy cowboy hats. Why they think cowboy hats are the thing to wear to a Gulf coast oil town, I'm not sure, but Bobby takes it into his head that we have to have hats, and he insists I buy one for Margaret too. I'm wearing the leather hippie-cowboy hat Janis gave me. Among the Western summer hats the others put on, mine would definitely give a genuine cowboy pause, but we encounter no cowboys in Houston.

The next stop is at a liquor store, for a bottle of tequila. Thus prepared, we head across the flat coastal plains for Port Arthur, for what proves to be a fairly strange weekend.

It begins with Janis's parents taking us out to dinner at their country club. We've brought some semblance of dress-up clothes for the reunion—despite the crumbling of dress codes in the late sixties, Bobby and John and I still travel with sport jackets and ties in our luggage—and we do our best to appear respectable. The Joplins want to please Janis and they are gracious hosts, but they are somewhat ill at ease. With one exception, Janis has always visited Port Arthur alone.* It is easy for parents to treat an adult offspring returning home for a visit as the child she was, but when she arrives with her road manager and limo driver and another friend and confidant from the very different life she has made for herself, it's a way of saying, I'm not your little Janis anymore.

Margaret is the member of our group who handles the dinner best. Her father is an attorney and a Texas legislator. Dressed in a stylish pantsuit, sipping her before-dinner cocktail and chatting with the Joplins, she is totally at ease in a roomful of straight people.

We are all on our best behavior, trying to establish common ground. It seems to me that Janis is a little standoffish with Margaret, which is in contrast to her attitude when we were in Austin last month. I remember Janis's dictum from the Big Brother days: no old ladies on the road. We're not exactly on the road here, but maybe Janis feels I've forgotten that injunction. Did I mention to Janis ahead

---

*Last year, after Kozmic Blues played at the Texas International Pop Festival, Janis brought Snooky Flowers to visit her family in Port Arthur on his way to his hometown of Lake Charles, Louisiana. Snooky was the first black man received as a guest in the Joplin home. During his visit, he took Janis to black music clubs in Port Arthur, where she had never before set foot. (Laura Joplin, *Love, Janis*, 258.)

of time that I was inviting Margaret? I can't remember. I'm sure I didn't ask her permission.

In the course of the dinner, during which we order more drinks than the Joplins think is proper, Janis loosens up and accepts me and Margaret as a couple, and she gives me no further cause for concern.

After dinner, the Joplins and Janis's sister, Laura, go home. Janis takes her accustomed seat, riding shotgun in the big Chrysler, and directs us on the evening adventure she has planned. We are going to visit a landmark of her wayward youth, back when she and her Port Arthur friends would drive across the state line into Louisiana, where you could buy liquor by the drink and it was easy to get served under-age. (In Texas, at this time, liquor is confined to private "clubs," where the club sells setups—glasses with ice and mixer—and the liquor is poured by members from bottles they bring with them, or which are kept for them on the premises. It is an arrangement that keeps Negroes and Mexicans out of the places where white folks drink.)

Freed from the constraints of the family dinner, Janis is in high spirits as we cross the Sabine River into Louisiana, recounting trips she made when she was a pimply, loudmouthed girl in the company of a few other misfits and outcasts.

Our destination is a roadhouse west of Port Charles. It's loud and it's jam-packed, with a rocking country band on a small stage. We're no sooner seated at a table when the band leader calls on Janis to get up and sing a song.

This attention isn't what Janis wants tonight. She wants to be an observer, as if she's watching a movie of her rebellious youth. She wants to re-create within the privacy of our small group what it was like for her ten years ago, so she can take comfort in how far she's come, but that is not going to be possible tonight. People crowd around the table, pushing against us, all trying to talk to Janis at once. It gets so bad, you can't light a cigarette without burning the arm of some asshole who's reaching out toward Janis, trying to get her attention.

"That was when I first realized that, God, these poor people who are famous, the only people who will actually have the nerve to come up and talk to them are people you wouldn't want to talk to. And the nicer people are not gonna bother you."

Margaret Moore

Janis endures about ten minutes of this, then gets up and heads for the restroom in back. She is gone a long time. After a while I ask Margaret to go look for her. Margaret goes off in the same direction, and she too is gone for a long time.

When they return at last, both of them very serious, Margaret suggests we leave. Later, when we have dropped Janis at the Joplin home in Port Arthur and we're back at the motel where Margaret and I and Bobby and John Fisher are staying, Margaret tells me what happened in the women's restroom at the roadhouse. She looked under the stall doors and saw Janis's gold slippers. Margaret went into the adjoining stall and sat down. She said, "Janis, we were worried about you." There was a pause, and then Janis said, "You just don't know what it's like." And Janis told Margaret how she just wanted to show her friends the roadhouse and have a good time, and how hard it is sometimes to be the constant object of attention when you just want to be yourself. She talked about her life on the road, and how unhappy or lonely she was too much of the time. Margaret was half-afraid of this woman she didn't hardly know, whose life she couldn't imagine, who was just five years older than her twenty-two years but seemed so much older at this moment. Margaret pointed out that Janis had people around her who obviously loved her. Janis knew that was true, but what she was feeling at the moment was, You can't possibly understand how hard it is to be me.

For this one evening, Janis wanted to be a normal person out with her friends. When she found she couldn't, she slipped into a well of despair.

In the morning, the bayou blues brought on by our Louisiana

excursion are forgotten. Arriving at the Joplins' house for breakfast, we find Janis's parents leaving for the wedding of a friend's daughter and Janis in the kitchen melting pounds of butter to make hollandaise sauce for eggs Benedict. When I pull out my movie camera to record her culinary skills on film, Janis turns into Julia Child, smiling and talking a blue streak to the camera as she demonstrates her technique. Never mind that I'm shooting silent film. Janis is putting on a show. With an assist from Laura and Margaret, eggs Benedict for six appears on the table. Throughout the process, Janis is the bubbly hostess, giving no sign that the previous evening was anything less than a happy memory. As the perfect complement for eggs Benedict, she has selected Texas-brewed Pearl beer, served ice cold, in the bottle.

When breakfast is over and the kitchen cleaned up—Janis is the good daughter and we are her dutiful guests—it's time to head off to the first event of the Port Arthur High School reunion. Which is, after all, the reason we're here. On the way to the downtown hotel where the reunion events are scheduled, Janis makes a show of pointing out places where people treated her badly. "They wouldn't *talk* to me, man! That's what they thought of me."

This is where it comes from, the behavior that is so familiar to me, the quickness to take offense at any slight, the insistence that she is as good as anyone else, that she deserves respect. Her parents tried to instill in her a sense of propriety that Janis found too confining, but it was among her own contemporaries, the majority who were more accepting of the narrow, conformist views of the 1950s, that the triggers for Janis's defensiveness were put in place. Her inquisitive intelligence saw the hypocrisy in conforming to get along, and she just wouldn't hold her tongue.

The reunion opens with a get-acquainted gathering in a featureless, windowless convention meeting room. Everyone is wearing adhesive name stickers and if they're not talking to each other, they're taking photographs with Instamatics.

Janis is dressed in a long skirt with broad vertical stripes in different colors and a short-sleeved black blouse. She has on a floppy black hat with a bunch of white carnations tied with a ribbon and pinned to one side. For Janis, this is a conservative outfit. In the reunion crowd you can spot her across the room.

Part of our role, as Janis's entourage, is to be her defensive perimeter in public places. Unexpectedly, coming on the heels of our experience in the Louisiana roadhouse, her classmates at the cocktail mixer show no more interest in Janis than in each other. Janis stays close to us at first, but she looks around as if expecting—wanting—someone she hasn't set eyes on since high school to come over and say hello.

In Michael Lydon's article for the *New York Times Magazine* the year before, Lydon asked Janis about Port Arthur and she told him, "Man, those people hurt me. It makes me happy to know I'm making it and they're back there, plumbers just like they were." Home for the reunion, Janis is finding that confronting the actuality of the people she left behind is not as uplifting as contemplating it from afar.

Most of her classmates look older than Janis, older than Bobby and John and me. It's not just how they look, but how they act. There is something in their attitude. It's as if the last time they had fun was in high school and they don't expect to have fun ever again. Except for one young couple with a two-year-old boy in the mother's arms who would look right in place in Golden Gate Park, Janis's contemporaries seem to have accepted, in their late twenties, that what follows high school is middle age.

Janis becomes more venturesome. She moves through the crowd, doesn't find anyone she wants to talk to, and says let's go get a drink. Three male classmates have latched onto her during her foray. They tag along when we head out into the heat of the day to find the nearest "membership club." From the way these three hang on Janis's every word, and the looks they give each other, it's obvious that they're only interested in Janis because she's a rock star. I wonder why she's wasting her time with them until I realize that these bozos are the types she has come to Port Arthur to impress. They're the ones who made fun of her in school, who didn't understand her, who made her miserable, and who gravitate to her now because she has escaped in such a spectacular way the small-town life they're stuck in. She has come home to take her revenge, but it isn't as satisfying as she thought, and after a couple of bar stops we leave the three hangers-on standing in the street when we head back to Janis's house and our motel to get ready for the reunion dinner that evening.

Before the dinner, there is a press conference. Members of the local press have asked for a chance to interview Janis. The reunion committee has set up a table in one corner of the windowless conference room, with bright lights to facilitate photography. Here, for a short time, Janis is in her element, despite some questions that summon painful memories.

Q: *What do you remember most about Port Arthur?*
J.J.: (Laughs, hesitates) Ah, no comment.

Q: *What do you think young people are looking for today?*
J.J.: Sincerity, and a good time. . . . I think they're looking for people not to lie to them.

Q: *Will you come back more often now?*
J.J.: Oh, I can't say, because you see I live in San Francisco, and you can't get any looser than that.

Q: *Did you entertain in high school, when you were back here in high school?*
J.J.: Only when I walked down the aisle. (Laughter.) No, I was a painter, and sort of a recluse in high school. I've changed.

Q: *What happened?*
J.J.: I got liberated. No, I started to sing, and singing makes you

ON THE ROAD WITH JANIS JOPLIN   353

want to come out, whereas painting, I feel, really keeps you inside.

Q: *How were you different from your schoolmates?*
J.J.: I don't know. Why don't you ask them?

Asked about the nickname "Pearl," which has been widely reported in recent weeks, Janis sets the record straight: "That name was not supposed to reach the press. . . . That name's a private name for my friends to call me so they won't have to call me Janis Joplin."

The reunion dinner is a step down from the rubber-chicken circuit much bemoaned by campaigning politicians. The roast beef is cooked to the consistency of shoe leather. We load up on salad and vegetables instead. As Bob Neuwirth makes his way back to our table, his selection draws some taunts from Janis's classmates. "What's the matter, you don't eat meat? You like that rabbit food?"

There are some halfhearted speeches, and a few tales of high-school pranks. We figure we can't leave until it's over, and so Janis is on hand to receive the prize for having come the longest distance to get to the reunion. They give her a bald tire. At least it's painted gold.

It's meant to be funny, but it makes Janis feel the way she felt too often when she was in school with these same people.

On her first day back in Port Arthur, Janis and Laura met with the reunion committee at their request, at one of her classmate's homes. "What do you want?" they asked Janis. Being polite, Janis said, "Oh, nothing." Of course she wanted something, an acknowledgment of her presence and how far she had come, both literally and figuratively, to get there. She doesn't want it to be all about her, but a moment of recognition would be nice. If the committee had an ounce of imagination among them, they would have organized some gesture, something to make her feel welcome without being fawning. But they took Janis too literally, and the bald tire is all she gets.

Dancing is scheduled after the drab dinner, but we are seeking livelier entertainment. Jerry Lee Lewis is playing at a roadhouse out toward Beaumont. A bottle of tequila and some rock and roll by the Killer will lift our spirits. We are ever optimistic.

The roadhouse has a box office, where you pay to see the show. Janis announces, "I'm Janis Joplin," but that doesn't get us in. Informed we'll have to pay like everybody else, Janis pulls out the cash and slaps it down and in we go.*

This is a genuine Texas roadhouse with an unlikely name, the Pelican Club. Smoky and rowdy and drunk from wall to wall. Jerry Lee is onstage, shouting out the rocking blues and making the piano ring. Now and again he hollers instructions to the young bass player.

This is not the first time Janis has set eyes on the bass player. When we played Louisville, Kentucky, back in June, we had a day off after Janis's Friday night concert. On Saturday, Janis and Clark Pierson and David Dalton went to see a big country show starring Jerry Lee and George Jones at the civic auditorium. Backstage, Janis made a blatant play for the bass player, who might be all of seventeen, embarrassing him no end.

Bound to continue her quest tonight, Janis leads the way backstage at the Pelican Club when Jerry Lee and the band take a break. The atmosphere in the cramped, sweaty band room is not festive. There are two or three guys in the room who are not members of the band. They're the heavies. Whatever the details of their role, they are here as muscle. Somebody is counting out money on a small table, and that's part of the heavies' job, to guard the money. One of the guys has a pistol stuck in the back of his waistband.

Lewis himself does not smile, does not react to our group entering his domain, except to follow Janis with a cold stare. In Louisville, he wasn't exactly welcoming. Here, he's downright hostile.

---

*Normally, when I was escorting Janis, I would pay for everything from food and drink to transportation and entertainment. In this instance she paid for all of us out of her own pocket.

> "And I remember Janis was kind of tinkly and giggly and she walked up to Jerry Lee Lewis, who I thought behaved like an absolute prick from the get-go. I mean he was not gracious about anybody being there, and I immediately thought, This is not good. We really shouldn't be back here. This does not feel right. The reception was not friendly."
>
> **Margaret Moore**

Janis is oblivious to the signs. She waves a Hiya, honey, at the young bass player and leads Laura over to meet Jerry Lee. "Hey, Jerry Lee," she says, "this is my hometown, and I want you to meet my little sister, Laura. Isn't she pretty?" Jerry Lee looks at Laura and he's quiet for a long moment, and then he says, "Not really."

And Janis goes straight for Jerry Lee and clips him a flailing smack upside the head and without a second's hesitation, he slaps her right back. Bobby and I grab her, and she's cursing Jerry Lee, calling him a motherfucker and he's responding in kind. Margaret and Laura are out the door and the rest of us aren't far behind. Out to the parking lot and into the car, and so much for the Pelican Club.

> "And she was foul-mouthin' him, 'Yeah, motherfucker, whatever you say, motherfucker,' so like he said, 'Don't talk to me like a man or I'll treat you like a man.' Just two south Texas rednecks going at each other, man."
>
> **Bob Neuwirth**

We were in the back room longer than that, and maybe Janis took a few minutes to chat up the bass player, who, it turns out, is Jerry Lee's son, but that's the way it plays back in memory, both later that night and long after the event.

All in all, not as much fun as Ken Threadgill's birthday party. Yet despite Janis's disappointment that she hasn't gained the satisfaction she was hoping for from her reunion weekend, the next morning, when Bobby and John Fisher and Margaret and I hug her good-bye before we hit the road for the Houston airport, she seems to be centered and calm, as if her not-so-triumphant return to the scene, and the company, of her adolescent difficulties has helped her put at least some of the lingering resentments behind her.

Janis is looking ahead, and she has much to look forward to. She will stay with her family for a few more days before she flies home to San Francisco for two weeks' vacation. After that, we go to L.A. to begin recording with Paul Rothchild. Before the reunion, while we were touring in the East, we got word that Paul played the July demos for Albert and Clive Davis and the Columbia executives in a blind hearing. Nobody knew which demo was made in which studio. Sunset Sound won hands down.

CHAPTER TWENTY-FIVE

A Woman Left Lonely

As soon as Paul Rothchild returns to Los Angeles from his trip to the Bay Area in July, he puts out the word to songwriters and music publishers that he will be producing Janis's next album and she needs material.

Songs arrive by the bucketload, on cassettes and demo discs and reel-to-reel tapes. With help from his housemate and sometimes engineer, Fritz Richmond, Paul goes through the material, looking for anything that might appeal to Janis. A representative of MCA Publishing, with a misguided sense of initiative, shows up at Paul and Fritz's house on Ridpath Drive at eight thirty one morning, barges through the big wooden gate, jangling the bell that's wired to it, and knocks on the door of the house. When Paul mumbles, "Who is it?" from the bedroom, where he is a couple of hours away from his usual rising time, the guy calls out, "I'm from MCA. You might have heard of us." To which Paul replies, "Get the fuck out of here!" No songs from MCA are considered for the album.

At the upper end of professionalism is the Motown representative, who calls for an appointment and arrives at the house on the dot, with reel tapes, discs, and his own cassette player that he plugs into the stereo. He has lyric and lead sheets and he has Paul's and Fritz's full attention throughout his presentation.

Another question on which Paul enlists Fritz's expertise is how best to record Janis's exceptional voice. They talk about different types of mikes they've used for recording different singers, and they hit on the idea of using an RCA ribbon mike, an old-fashioned mike from between the wars that produces a very mellow sound. By capturing Janis's voice, which is anything but mellow, with the RCA mike, Paul may get a more manageable signal to work with.

Janis and Full Tilt Boogie arrive in L.A. before Labor Day and settle into the Landmark Hotel for what could be two months of recording. Janis has driven down from the Bay Area in her Porsche. George Ostrow has decided he's put in enough time on the road. Vince Mitchell and Phil Badella are handling the equipment for these sessions. They have brought the Boogie Wagon, which will be the band's taxi.

In the first week, Janis and Paul Rothchild settle into a routine. Janis drives up to Paul and Fritz's house in Laurel Canyon around eleven in the morning. Paul makes a pot of coffee and they listen to the songs he and Fritz have selected, to see what Janis likes and to decide which song they will work on in the studio that day.

Paul schedules the sessions at Sunset Sound on musicians' hours. Work begins sometime after midday and ends in time for a late supper and drinks at Barney's Beanery. At the end of each day's work, Paul tells Janis and the band when to show up the next day. It's less than a mile from the Landmark Hotel to Sunset Sound. Sometimes the band members walk. Sometimes I shuttle someone in my car. Often Phil or Vince or one of the Full Tilt boys drives the Boogie Wagon.

On some days Paul needs just Janis in the studio, or just the band, but Janis likes to have the band on hand when she's laying down vocal tracks. (The RCA ribbon mike proves to be just the thing, and Janis sings into the forty-year-old mike throughout the sessions.)

As Paul develops his working relationship with Janis, he is also getting to know each member of the band, which for him is an essential part of the producer's job.* He learns how to talk with them. He teaches them the difference between playing in live performance and playing in the studio. When they have questions or suggestions, Paul listens. He makes them feel like an important part of the process.

> "Rothchild is . . . a little bit above the musicians. You know, he just seemed to know how to relate to each musician. And get their ideas in, but also not put anybody down or—you know, he just kept it so fucking comfortable. . . . If I were to ever make another record again, he'd be the first person I would call."
>
> **Brad Campbell**

I spend more time in the studio than I did with Big Brother or Kozmic Blues, because this time it's fun.

Late one afternoon I come back to the Landmark to find Janis sitting by the pool. She's on a chaise on the shady side, looking alone and serious—maybe blue? She's thinking hard. I can almost hear the wheels spinning. I sit beside her. "What's happening, Pearl?" She shakes her head. "Boy, that guy," she says.

"What guy?"

"Rothchild."

I feel a chill. If Janis has decided Paul isn't the right producer,

---

* "I have to get to know the people, the artist in particular. And when you're dealing with a band I have to get to know each and every person to find out what their language is. Once I know what their language is I can speak to them about their music in their language. I love verbal communication, mostly because it's so difficult." (Author interview with Paul Rothchild, March 19, 1974.)

we're in deep shit. "What about him?" Janis shakes her head, still doesn't look at me. "He's really something." She starts to talk now—the serious Janis, explaining something that's important to her—and my fear gives way to a rush of relief as she tells me how much she's learning from Paul, how well it's going. For the first time, she's experiencing recording—the long hours spent in the studio—as a high in itself, rather than a trial to be endured. She never dreamed the relationship between a singer and a producer could be like this.

Paul has been talking to her about how she uses her voice, onstage and in the studio. He has helped her understand that different techniques are required, but he isn't telling her to put anything less than her full commitment into a song. This is something Janis will never do, and Paul's not asking her to do it. He's asking her to explore the different voices she has at her command, the different parts of her range, to experiment with modulating her vocal power and considering more critically when to use it at full force.

Janis talks about these things with something close to a sense of wonder. Paul has opened doors to possibilities she didn't know existed. Maybe she doesn't have to blow her voice out within a few years. She likes to joke that when she loses her voice she'll buy a bar in Marin County and settle down. This is what she has always expected, but maybe it doesn't have to be that way.

I remember what Paul said to me in San Francisco, about wanting to introduce Janis to the truly great singer inside her. Paul is proceeding at his own pace, in his own way, and from everything Janis tells me the plan is on track.

"You know what he told me?" Janis says, and now she's got that little-girl-who-got-an-A-on-her-homework look. "He said I'm the only woman he's ever met who could be a record producer." She's proud, and well she should be. If Paul said that, he meant it.

During breaks in the recording and over the occasional meals and drinks we share, I get Paul's side of the story. He says that working with Janis is going better than he dared hope. His experience with lead singers is that they are self-indulgent children who show up at the studio late, sometimes drunk or stoned, and sometimes you have to send out search parties to find them in a bar or in bed with a groupie. Not Janis. She always shows up within half an hour of the appointed time, which for a rock singer is on the dot. She never gives less than everything she's got, and she always lets her affection show for the boys in the band, which puffs them up with pride and makes them redouble their efforts to please her.

Paul is impressed by Janis's capacity for storing information and using it. In the studio, she often sits beside him in the control room while the band is recording. Whenever she expresses curiosity about some aspect of the recording procedure, Paul fills her up with as much information as she wants. That she takes an interest in the technical aspects of recording adds another dimension to his respect for her, while the center of his focus remains her voice. Since the start of the sessions he has become convinced that Janis has yet to develop her full range. He tells me of a conversation they had recently. Paul asked her, "Come on, Pearl, what do you really sing like?" And she said, "I'll show you." What happened next pleased him no end. "She sang me stuff out of the church choir. Like she used to sing back in the church choir, when she was a teenager, a young teenager. And I heard this pure, straight, white voice. Clean, clear, no vibrato, no fur, no broken glass and rusty razor blades, just 'Ahhhh,' soprano. And I said, 'Right, you can sing, fantastic.'" For Paul, the revelation that Janis has this voice has far-reaching implications for her career, and for his. Paul is never less than self-interested. He knows his work with Janis can benefit his reputation in both the short and the long term. But the long-term benefits will only be realized if he can help Janis develop in a way that is best for her long-term prospects as well.*

---

*Recalling this conversation later, Paul explained his goal: "I was pointing out to her that that voice was her salvation and it was towards that voice that she had to evolve her next voice. You know, a good singer—a singer's voice goes through evolution,

Paul and Janis have been spending time together outside the studio too—not just having drinks or a meal after work, but talking about cars and driving their Porsches along Mulholland Drive, the twisty road that winds along the crest of the Hollywood Hills, at a high rate of speed.

Paul is an automotive enthusiast. When I first knew him in Cambridge, he drove an Alfa Romeo convertible. His present car is a Porsche 911S. The way Janis drives tells him she understands her own Porsche as a finely tuned machine. She doesn't share his interest in the detailed workings of the internal combustion engine, but she understands the coordination of the engine, the gears and the steering. "She drives like a man," he says, and from Paul there is no greater compliment. (He is something of a chauvinist, in these times that are still more than a little chauvinistic.) Paul knew beforehand that Janis is a very emotional person. That's where the music comes from. But she also understands machines. She can examine and analyze and articulate abstract concepts and things in the physical world. Right brain, left brain, both up and running. In a woman or a man, this is a rare combination.

In a few weeks, Paul has become one of the handful of intimates with whom Janis will drop the tough-woman-of-the-streets style she

_____

and develops. They all do. And she should start working towards a pure sound. Because she can't—she couldn't do the 'Ball and Chain' Janis Joplin at age forty. It would be ludicrous, right? And these are things we discussed, and she loved this because it was talk about real direction, what she should do with her vocal career and her future, and what to aim for. . . . To me it was as if my entire career was pointed at working at that record—working on that record and working with Janis. And when Janis and I would sit down and talk about the future, I would be saying things to her like, 'Now, you see, Janis, you don't quite get it. When you're fifty-five I want you to be making your best records. With me. And here's how we'll do it.' You know, 'Here's the thirty-year plan.'" (Author interview with Paul Rothchild, March 19, 1974.)

assimilated in San Francisco. He perceived at once how we use her "Pearl" nickname. Paul uses it as we do, and Janis accepts it. She is willing to reveal herself to him, her hopes and fears, the little girl as well as the woman who is not so tough as she pretends.

She trusts him.

Yet all of this positive energy gives rise to a paradox. Janis's commitment to the work, her excitement at the possibilities she sees opening before her, make her off-hours even harder to bear than usual. She has always complained about the downtime during recording. She gets bored. She doesn't like Hollywood. She'd rather be home in the Bay Area, close to her friends. Here, she's got no one to call when she gets lonely. It seems especially unfair now because she has a boyfriend, a new love, and he's only in L.A. on the weekends. What is she supposed to do the rest of the time?

Seth Morgan was at the tattoo party in Janis's house back in the spring. He's a student at UC Berkeley. He's a rich kid hiding his privilege under a biker-punk veneer. He rides a Harley, has coke in his pocket, drinks Wild Turkey, and enjoys flouting convention with the best of them.

In the summer, after we got back from Hawaii and Ken Threadgill's birthday party and before we headed out for the gigs in the East, Janis and Seth reconnected. She was attracted by his insolence. He doesn't give a shit that she's Janis Joplin. He is neither a pretty boy nor a mountain man. He's not David Niehaus, but neither is he a return to her old pattern. The pretty boy/mountain man dichotomy represents two extremes in Janis, neither of which is the place where she should settle down. The pretty boys are lapdogs. They fawn over her, give her pleasure, and tell her how great she is. With them, she can do no wrong. The mountain men counterbalance the pretty boys. They're big, they're strong, they won't take any of her bullshit, but they're not often equipped to give her the comfort, and the counsel, she needs. For these things, Janis turns to her oldest friends in the San

Francisco community, the ones who knew her before she was famous. Linda Gravenites, her surrogate mother. The boys in Big Brother. And a few others. Whether Seth Morgan can earn a place in this select circle remains to be seen.

With Seth, Janis falls for the punk and comes to love the inner man. She finds that beneath the bad-boy exterior there is a perceptive intellect. They connect through the drinking and the brag talk and, to their mutual surprise, they discover that they like quiet times together too. They find that they enjoy each other's company as much, maybe even more, if they don't go out drinking. They spend mornings reading the newspaper over breakfast on the deck and talking about the news. Seth is surprised to learn that Janis reads the whole front section of the paper every day, that she is aware of current events, that she reads books—Thomas Wolfe, Herman Hesse.*

They talk about books and ideas and the doings of the world. They drive around the countryside, see a movie, have dinner out with just a glass or two of wine and go home early. When they do go out for a rocking good time with Janis's Bay Area or music business friends, Seth notices that Janis never displays to others the current-events and intellectual interests she has revealed to him.

When Janis returned to the Bay Area in August, after her high school reunion, she and Seth talked of marriage. They considered how they might make a life together that won't be subservient to Janis's performing career.

Seth made it clear from the outset that when the two of them are together they are separate from her professional life. Like David Nie-

_____

*Committee member Carl Gottlieb recalls similar mornings at the San Francisco apartment he shared with Milan Melvin in 1967, when Milan and Janis were lovers, when he and Milan would make breakfast for Janis and Carl's girlfriend and they would read the newspaper and discuss politics and news of the world. (Author interview with Carl Gottlieb, August 7, 1997.)

haus, Seth is not from the music world and, like Niehaus, Seth is not about to be drawn into Janis's scene as a hanger-on.

A visit to L.A. early in the recording reinforces this conviction. At the Landmark, or sitting in the control room to watch a recording session, Seth feels like a fifth wheel. He is close to finishing his degree at Berkeley and he doesn't want to blow it. He comes down most weekends and he tries to time his visits when Janis will have a day off.

> "I felt very out of place down at the Landmark and in recording sessions; I just didn't belong there, as much as she wanted me down there."
>
> **Seth Morgan**

This arrangement doesn't satisfy Janis. Her head can understand Seth's reasons for keeping a distance, but her heart wants him *here*, and without him she is lonely.

In Seth's absence, Janis receives another visitor. One day when the band and I are making waves in the Landmark pool, Peggy Caserta comes to the gate of the chain-link fence that encloses the pool, with Janis close behind. They're going out to dinner and they stop by to say hello. Peggy was banished from Janis's house in the spring, along with the rest of Janis's druggie friends. So far as I know, Peggy hasn't been welcome in Larkspur since then. The unease I felt when Peggy was with Janis at Woodstock returns.

On September 18, Jimi Hendrix dies in London of a drug over-dose—his girlfriend's sleeping pills, apparently, too many taken ac-cidentally, because he didn't know how strong they were. As with any death like this there's a shadow of suspicion that it might be acciden-tally on purpose.

Is this what triggers Janis to put aside her caution and her pride in controlling her most dangerous habit? When Janis and Sam Andrew heard Nancy Gurley was dead from an OD, their first reaction was to get high. Is it before the news of Jimi's death, or after, that I find Janis by the pool on another evening? What I see in her face this time gives me a chill. Like Sam, Janis can't hide the telltale signs when she's on smack. Her eyes say "I'm stoned" like a flashing neon sign. The pupils are sharp and cold, and there's a gossamer mask over her face that cloaks her emotions. She retreats inside, hiding, hoping you won't notice what's so plain to see. But I see it, and she sees my disappointment. It's just for now, she says. Drinking to moderate her boredom affects her performance in the studio. A little smack helps her maintain the high she needs for the long hours, the take after take of the same song. This is her excuse.

I've heard this rationale before. The junkie logic doesn't convince me for a New York minute, but you can't tell anybody what to do. You can only tell her how you feel. I tell Janis how happy I've been since she quit. I tell her how it makes me feel to see her high. I tell her I love her.

Most days, Janis displays the same energy she's had all summer. And she is planning for the future. She's serious enough about marrying Seth Morgan to consult Bob Gordon about a prenuptial agreement. This is simple prudence, but it also reflects Janis's lingering fear of being ripped off. Whether she inquires about the extent of Seth's resources isn't something I think to ask at the time. It's possible that his exceed hers. He's an heir to the Ivory Soap fortune. Be that as it may, Bob Gordon recommends and draws up an agreement that will exempt Janis's income from being considered part of community property under California law.

The recording doesn't stop on weekends. The schedule may get a little lighter, but the pressure from Columbia to get the album done is humming in the background.

Since I played music aboard the Festival Express and in Austin with Janis after Threadgill's Jubilee, I've been feeling it's time to find myself a new guitar to replace the one that was stolen last year out of the Chelsea Hotel. I've put out the word among my friends in L.A., and someone tells me that a music store in Huntington Beach has a prewar D-18 ("prewar," talking about Martin guitars, means made before the Second World War). I hop in the Volvo. Down 101 to the 110 to the 405 to Huntington Beach. The guy at the store says no, we haven't had any used Martins in a while, but I think there's a store in Hollywood that's got one. He makes the call. Yup, he's got a D-18. Back up the 405 to the 110 to the 101, and I end up, two hours after I set out, on Sunset Boulevard less than ten blocks from the Landmark. But the trip is worth it. The D-18 is five years old. It's been cracked and repaired. But when I strum an E chord, I know it's a winner.

There's a range of tonal qualities in top-quality acoustic guitars, Martins as much as any other brand. The tone depends on the wood, the age, how much the guitar has been played, and other, intangible factors that make every guitar different. When you pick up a guitar for the first time and play a chord, the first impression can be decisive— good, bad or indifferent. On this Martin, the E chord rings like bells, and I trust my first impression. I shell out three hundred dollars and I take it back to the Landmark. It was worth running down to Huntington Beach and back to get this guitar.

A few days later, on Sunday, I'm in my room in the afternoon, talking with an old friend from Cambridge, Dave Barry. Dave is a talented guitar and piano player and he has taken up songwriting since he's been living in L.A. He has written a song he wants Janis to hear and he has talked to her about it. He plays it for me on my new Martin. He was supposed to meet Janis at the Troubadour last night, but she lingered at Barney's Beanery and they missed connecting. Dave has come to the Landmark today hoping to see Janis before she goes to the studio. We've tried her room, but got no answer.

The phone rings. It's Paul Rothchild, calling from the studio. Janis was supposed to be there an hour ago. It's not like her to be late. Paul tried her room and got the same result I did. I tell him I'll have a look around.

Before we leave my room, the phone rings again. This time it's Seth. He's flying down to Burbank this afternoon. He can't reach Janis. She's supposed to meet him at the airport or send someone to get him.

Around the pool and the patio there is no sign of Janis. We run into Vince Mitchell and Phil Badella. The Full Tilt boys took the Boogie Wagon to the studio. Can they hitch a ride with me? I figure we might as well go to the studio and see if Janis shows up there.

The four of us pile into my Volvo in the Landmark's underground garage. When I pull out onto the short driveway that curves past the Landmark's entrance, I see that Janis's Porsche is parked there. Above the Porsche, there's a light in Janis's window.

Janis, as is her custom, has taken a single room with a kitchenette in the front building, down the hallway from the hotel lobby. Why she would pick a room overlooking Franklin Avenue, with the morning and afternoon rush-hour traffic, instead of on the back side, facing the courtyard and the pool, is beyond me, but it's her choice.

It is a little past sunset, only just dark enough now that Janis might turn on a light in the south-facing room. Maybe she was out somewhere and got back to the hotel in the last few minutes. Maybe she forgot she's supposed to be at the studio.

I back up into the garage so the car isn't blocking the driveway. Wait here, I tell the guys.

As I pass through the lobby, I stop at the desk and get a key to Janis's room from Jack Hagy, the manager. A couple of times since we've been here, I've gone to her room to get something she forgot and wants down at the studio. I can't say just why I get the key now. I think Janis is in her room, so why do I need it? What if she's in the shower? Some such idea may pass through my head, but mostly I'm saving time. If I knock and she doesn't answer I'll have to come back for the key.

When I open the door to room 105, there's no one there. That's the feeling I have even as I see Janis lying on the floor beside the bed. Before I touch the unnatural flesh I know that this is only the vessel. The spirit has departed.

CHAPTER TWENTY-SIX

Cry, Baby

I HAVE NO frame of reference for this. It's like a scene from a Raymond Chandler novel: a body found in a Los Angeles hotel room. Seeing it this way helps to remove it one step from being real. I have no doubt that it's real, but it helps, and I can accept the paradox.

Janis is lying in an awkward position, her head and shoulder wedged against the bed and the bedside table. In her hand, there are four dollar bills and two quarters. On the side table, there's a pack of Marlboros.

The story is obvious to an interested observer: She got change for a five, bought cigarettes for fifty cents from the machine in the lobby, came back to the room, sat down, and keeled over before she could light one. She was sitting on the bed and pitched over sideways. There's dried blood on her face where her head struck the corner of the bedside table.

Janis has added a few touches to personalize the place—scarves draped over the lamps to soften the light. Nothing is in disarray, nothing out of the ordinary. The bed is made.

There's no reason to think this is a crime scene, but that isn't my call. I know the rules. Don't disturb anything. Using the sides of my fingers against the edge of the drawer pull, I open the top drawer of the bureau. Right there, in the first place I think to look, in plain view, there's a hypodermic needle and a spoon. Her works. I close the drawer. Nothing in the other drawers but clothes.

I stand still for a few moments, aware of my breathing, aware of the sound of cars passing on Franklin Avenue, of the silence in the room, the emptiness. In this moment, I am the only one who knows. I don't want to carry this weight alone. I feel an urgency that I need to resist. It's up to me to put the knowledge out into the world, but this is something I have to do very carefully.

I leave the room, lock the door behind me. I keep the key. I go down to the garage by the back stairs so I won't pass through the lobby. I get in the Volvo and start the engine. Without saying a word, I park in the same place where the car was parked when Vince and Phil and Dave and I came down to the garage. Before I knew. The boys think this is strange, and it is. I turn off the engine and I tell them Janis is dead.

I want someone else to see her and the room exactly as I have seen them, so I ask Vince Mitchell to come upstairs with me. Dave Barry asks if he can come too. He's writing freelance articles these days, and this is private. I don't want Dave the writer to see Janis as she is now. I don't want him to write about her like this. Sorry, I say.

Vince and I go into the room. He looks around, takes it all in. Maybe I was hoping it would be different, the room normal, Janis gone, or there to welcome us. With Vince, I confirm the reality. We leave, and again I make sure the door is locked.

I tell Vince and Phil and Dave that I have to plan as best I can how to tell the people who were important to Janis so they will hear it from me, before the news gets out. For a short time it will be possible to control it, but only for a very short time. We'll have to notify the police, and the coroner. Once the authorities know, there will be no stopping it.

We go to my room and I call Bob Gordon first. He's home from work at the Beverly Hills law firm where he is a partner. He's in the shower, his wife, Gail, says. She'll have him call me back. I can't sit by the phone and wait for it to ring. I have other calls to make. I tell Gail I have to speak with Bob now. She doesn't pick up the fraught undercurrents in my voice and finally I have to say it's a matter of life and death. Just death, really, but the clichéd phrase comes more naturally. Bob comes on the phone—I picture him dripping wet with a towel wrapped around his waist, because he's not the kind of person who would come to the phone naked. I tell him, and I feel just a little better. Sharing the awful knowledge helps, minutely. I wait while he struggles to recover his composure.

Bob shifts into lawyer mode. He says he'll notify the police. He'll come to the hotel and call them from here, so he'll be here when they arrive. That gives us a little time.

I phone Albert next, in Bearsville. "Oh, no," he says, and all the breath goes out of him. Janis's parents are next on the list I'm making in my head. It's past seven in L.A., after nine P.M. in Texas. Will Albert call her parents? He's uncertain, fearful, rattled to the core. I've never heard him so—disrupted. Would you mind doing it? he asks. What can I say? No? I say I will. But I can't put off telling Paul and the boys in the band for long, and I can't give them this news over the phone. When Bob Gordon gets to the hotel, I'll go to the studio, but I'll call Janis's parents before I leave. Albert agrees to the order of events I'm making up as I talk. I get the feeling he'll agree to anything I say right now. He's not going to help me plan how to do this. For now, Albert is incapable of handling anything beyond his grief.

Bob Gordon makes record time from Brentwood to the Landmark in his Porsche. I take him to Janis's room. We look, I show him the works, we leave. Together, we tell Jack Hagy, the manager. Bob has called his brother-in-law, a doctor, who arrives minutes after Bob. I give Janis's room key to Bob and leave them to deal with the police.

From this point forward, the news is going to get out and no one will be able to control it. My need to get to the studio, to be with Paul and the Full Tilt boys, is visceral, like hunger, but I promised Albert I would call Janis's parents.

I would like to put off this call forever. I wake Janis's father out of a sound sleep in Port Arthur and I give him a few moments to shake off the cobwebs. Then I say, "There is no easy way to say this, so I'll just say it. Janis is dead." Seth Joplin's first reaction is the same as Albert's. "Oh, no." He makes the same sound Albert made as his breath leaves him, taking with it a measure of his life.

Bennett Glotzer has been in L.A. for the past couple of weeks. He and Janis were in touch often during the summer tour. He has spent time in the studio, had drinks and meals with Janis. I call his hotel. He's not there. In these days, you leave messages with the hotel operator, so I leave a message that reveals nothing amiss, asking him to come to the Landmark.

Phil and Vince have kept close to me. We're bonded in shock, staving off our own grief. They will come with me to the studio. Dave Barry knows he doesn't belong in this coterie of Janis's intimates, so he takes his leave. When he's gone, I can't remember if I cautioned him again about keeping the knowledge to himself. The only way I can hold myself together is to focus on one thing at a time. Right now, getting to the studio is the urgent necessity.

I park in the little lot behind Sunset Sound. Phil and Vince and I come in through the back door. When we enter the studio I see the smiles, the excitement in the eyes, the pride in the work they're doing, and I don't want to say the words that will wipe all that away, because I know the bright, clean, unscarred feelings Paul and the Full Tilt boys have at this moment about the album, and about Janis, will never return.

I take Paul into the hall and I tell him first. Janis is dead. Paul staggers and reaches out to steady himself against the wall. I tell him what little I know. When he recovers sufficiently, Paul asks Phil Macy, the engineer, to step out of the control room so I can tell the band in private. While the boys are absorbing the shock, Paul tells Macy we're quitting work early.

We go in caravan to the Landmark—my Volvo, Paul's Porsche, and the Boogie Wagon.

The police have arrived, and men from the county coroner's office. They are considerate and discreet.

Seth Morgan has taken a cab from the airport. He looks stunned and lost.

Bennett Glotzer is here. I tell him I found Janis's works and left them where they were. Should I have taken them? "Are you fucking crazy?" he says. "That's a felony. You're disturbing evidence." Bennett was with Janis last night after work, he says. They had a couple of drinks at Barney's Beanery. Janis had only two because she had to record the next day. He took note of her restraint.

By now the news is out, racing through the grapevine like a jolt of bad acid. The notion that I could contain it even for an hour or two was a fantasy. Everyone who knows finds the knowledge unbearable and has to share it.

The time remaining to reach Janis's closest friends, and ours, before they hear it by radio or television or telephone is very short. Who have I forgotten? Everyone. I should have called the boys in Big Brother, Sam Andrew first of all, but my need to get to the studio postponed that thought. My phone rings and it's Lyndall, Janis's roommate. She's alone in the house in Larkspur, crying, distraught, almost incoherent. I try to calm her and fail. I tell her I'll send someone to be with her. I call Peter Berg in Berkeley. He knows Lyndall, and yes, he'll drive across the Bay to keep her company.

From now on, it's all damage control. I'm on the phone nonstop. People come in and out of the room. When it gets late enough, when the rest of the country is past midnight and the phone lines fall silent, we huddle together in one of the big suites, anesthetized by alcohol and sorrow. Somewhere before dawn there are a few hours of fitful sleep.

On Monday morning, the phone in my suite rings and rings.

There is no call waiting, no voice mail; you get a busy signal or the phone rings and I answer. The people who get through have won an electronic roulette. John Phillips is one. I haven't seen him since Big Brother and I saw *Monterey Pop* at John and Michelle's mansion in Bel Air. John is genuinely wounded by the news and concerned for those who were close to Janis. He knows there is nothing he can do, but he offers all the same and his sincerity comforts me. My father calls. I haven't thought to phone my parents, so they read the news in the *New York Times*. I phone my mother.

Today is my thirtieth birthday.

At some point I talk with Jack Hagy, the manager. He tells me that early Sunday morning, about one A.M., Janis said hello to the night clerk as she passed through the lobby on the way to her room. She returned a short time later to get change for the cigarette machine. This confirms the story the change and the cigarettes told me. Some things are just as they appear to be.

Albert is on the first plane from New York. I have never seen him so stricken. He is bereft. Lyndall flew down last night.

Kris Kristofferson was at the Big Sur Folk Festival, held in the fall this year. He got back to L.A. late yesterday, as the news was breaking. Today he's at the Landmark.

The gathering this evening is a select group, the core of intimates who have known and worked with Janis. Kris, the band, Paul, Seth, Lyndall, Albert, Bennett, a few more. Linda Gravenites is here. She hasn't seen Janis since she moved out of the house in Larkspur after Janis got back from Rio. The day before Janis died, Linda had a sudden impulse to come to L.A. She flew down, connected with a mutual friend of hers and Janis's, and was making plans to come to the Landmark yesterday to see Janis when she heard that Janis had died.

I have brought my movie projector to L.A., and my editing setup, so I can work on my films while I'm here. I set up my projector and show the movies of Janis and Big Brother, Janis and Kozmic Blues. There she is, alive and well, giving it everything she's got.

Later on, my new guitar is in play. Shared music offers solace.

In a quiet moment, Seth Morgan is riven with guilt. He knew Janis was using, even before we came to L.A. During the summer, she dabbled. After all, she had quit, hadn't she? She was clean for months. Which proved she could do it. So why not give herself a little reward when she felt like it? The paradoxical circularity of an addict's reasoning is self-fulfilling. A couple of weeks ago Janis called Seth and begged him to make her stop. I can't do this for you, he said. She begged him to spend more time in L.A. If only, he says. . . .

This prompts my own hindsight. If only I had done more, been a better friend . . . Paul Rothchild puts a quick end to this line of self-indulgence. "We're all guilty, John," he says.

We console ourselves by clinging together and doing the things that have to be done, as friends continue to arrive.

Bob Neuwirth was in Nashville when he got the news, visiting Norman Blake, a flat-picker and multi-instrumentalist who is a member of the band on Johnny Cash's network TV show. When Bob came into the Blakes' kitchen on Monday morning, Norman's wife, Nancy, was making biscuits. She said, "Bobby, I have some terrible news for you." She heard it on the radio.

Bob arrives in L.A. on Tuesday.

I take a phone call from Dr. Thomas Noguchi, the Los Angeles County coroner. Noguchi became nationally known when he performed the autopsy on Bobby Kennedy two years ago. Noguchi is speaking with as many of Janis's friends and associates as he can reach, assembling a "psychological profile." I answer his questions and add to his list of essential names. He is a dispassionate investigator, looking for any indication that Janis might deliberately have taken her own life, and finds none. His verdict will be death by accidental overdose.

Janis's family arrives from Texas. Mrs. Joplin's sister lives in L.A. The family holds a service to which none of us is invited. Albert and Bennett Glotzer are permitted to attend, but no one else from the musical side of Janis's life, the part that meant more to her than anything else. We are the people who killed their daughter. We represent San Francisco, where Janis's nonconformist outlook made her welcome, where she was no longer the outcast, the misunderstood. Where her talent made her a local phenomenon, then a star. In the Joplins' eyes, we are the world of rock and roll that destroyed her. This is the feeling I project on them, but I may be unfair. Later, Bennett tells me the Joplins blamed no one but themselves.

In any event, we will have a memorial of our own. Bob Gordon tells me that Janis left $2,500 in her will for her friends to have a wake. That's the word she used, and she intended the liveliest kind of wake. She wanted her friends to have a party and drink to her memory. She signed the updated will on Friday.* Bob had also prepared the premarital agreement that would protect Janis's copyrights and royalties. Janis took a copy with her for Seth to sign.

When and where the wake will be is up to us. It will be in the Bay Area, that much is sure. The organizing will fall to Bob Gordon and me, but right now we have a more pressing concern.

For two days we have been avoiding the crucial question—is there an album? Is there enough music on tape, in the can, to make a record? No one is sure, not even Paul Rothchild.

Paul makes a cut-and-paste assemblage of what's on tape. He works for two days and a night. On Thursday, we sit down in the control room at Sunset Sound to listen to what there is. Albert is here, and Bennett, the Full Tilt boys, Lyndall, and Kris Kristofferson. Like Kris, Carl Gottlieb, of the Committee, and his wife, Allison, were at the Big Sur Folk Festival, heard the news Sunday night when they got home. They were part of the Monday evening group at the Landmark, and they are here now.

---

*In an earlier will, when she had few assets, Janis left everything to her brother, Michael. Bob Gordon suggested, and Janis agreed, that the will be revised now to divide her estate equally among her parents and siblings.

Tomorrow is John Lennon's birthday. Some folks have been going around L.A. getting local and visiting musicians to record "Happy Birthday" for a tape that will be sent to Lennon. The first song Paul plays for us at Sunset Sound is Janis and Full Tilt's contribution, which we recorded a couple of days before Janis died, all of us singing along behind Janis. It is raucous and joyful. We hold the final "happy birthday to youuuuuuu," and Janis says, "Happy birthday from Janis and Full Tilt Boogie! Happy birthday, Johnny!" (Did anyone else ever call Lennon "Johnny"?) Janis breaks into her cackling laugh, and we think it's over . . . but then Richard Bell plays the opening riff of the Roy Rogers–Dale Evans theme song, "Happy Trails." His keyboard establishes the Western motif: "dum-da-dum-dum, dum-da-dum-dum," and Janis sings, "Happy trails to you, until we meet again. . . ." in her high, pure soprano.

There are few dry eyes in the control room, but Janis's good spirits are so audible, so irrepressible, that it's healing too. By playing this first, Paul has managed to lighten the mood. It's even possible to smile.

Paul thinks we have three quarters of an album. The vocal tracks are the critical element. Whatever exists on tape—that's it. There are some final vocals and some work vocals. On Saturday, the band laid down the instrumental track for a song Nick Gravenites wrote for Janis, called "Buried Alive in the Blues." Janis was to record the vocal for the first time on Sunday.

We hear songs that are complete, solid, ready to go. We hear Janis sing over instrumental scratch tracks. We hear polished instrumental tracks and scratch vocals.

When Janis's version of "Me and Bobby McGee" comes over the speakers, Kris can bear only the first verse before he leaves the control room, the studio, and the building. I follow him into the parking lot, but he is inconsolable. He goes off into the Hollywood dusk and we don't see him again.

Janis's recording of "Bobby McGee" might have signaled the introduction of a new element in her music. The Byrds' *Sweetheart of the Rodeo* album and Dylan's *Nashville Skyline* have brought country music influences into latter-day rock. Would Janis have recorded more country songs after "Bobby McGee"? I remember her line in the Austin Holiday Inn, in response to the little guy in the bar who couldn't sing "Bobby McGee"—"Wait until you hear me. I can do that song." Can a Texas girl sing a country song? You bet she can. The thought of Janis expanding her fan base to include hard-core country music fans is enough to make me smile.

Today in the studio, when we have heard everything there is, we're convinced there is enough to make a record. Even Albert is optimistic, but Paul doesn't want our expectations, our need, to run away with us. For this to be *the* album, Janis's last and best album, it will take a lot of work. It's possible, Paul says, but it will take a lot of work.

Albert gives Paul free rein. Albert will deal with Clive Davis. And so the decision is made. We have to finish this album. We seize on this goal. Not doing it is unthinkable. Without this record, the world will never hear Janis with Full Tilt Boogie, never feel her joy and pride in this band and the new material she sang across the U.S. and Canada this summer. The spirit Janis reveals in the music is proof that she had recovered from the failure of the Kozmic Blues Band, that her best years lay ahead of her.

The work begins the next day, but it is not a return to the previous routine. It is a new routine, with the task at hand taking precedence over anything else. Our waking hours are in the studio. There is no late-night hanging out, no going to the Troubadour. We eat to sustain our bodies, have a drink or a beer or a glass of wine to sustain the spirit. We're removed from normal space and time. In the windowless studio, hearing Janis's voice from the speakers as the band builds a new track under a vocal brings her back to life. She is with us.

"Everybody continued to make that record with just a little bit more love than they did before, so the mood was one of—how can you name that mood? It was almost monastic zeal, and it became just that. It was like a little monastery."

Paul Rothchild

Paul is the executor of Janis's musical legacy. His focus is total. Every day he develops techniques for things he has never had to do before. On several of the songs, the vocal track that goes on the record, that sounds as if Janis were inside your stereo speakers and singing for you alone, is assembled phrase by phrase from as many as half a dozen work vocals.

"Cry, Baby," one of three Jerry Ragovoy tunes Janis performed with Full Tilt, was one of the test songs they recorded at the July demo session in Columbia's Hollywood studio. At the time, the band was inexperienced, unsure of themselves. At Sunset Sound, the boys have laid down a much stronger track—a great band track, in Paul's view—but it's in a different key and the tempos don't match. Janis has done a work vocal to the new track, but her July vocal is better, no contest. So Paul and the boys make a new band track from scratch, in the original key. As the band plays to Janis's July vocal, they hear in their headphones Clark Pierson's drum track from that session, to set the tempo. When the rest of the instruments are recorded, Paul removes the old drum track and Clark records a new one.

Watching the process, it seems simple enough, until Paul explains that he has never done anything like this before. It's not something you would ever need to do, so long as you have a living singer. What you normally do is overdub instruments and vocals to fill the holes, get rid of mistakes, improve the tracks, until the song is a seamless whole that embodies a definitive performance by the vocalist and the band. Here, Paul and Full Tilt achieve the same result by underdubbing. "Cry, Baby" is seamless.

"It was amazing to watch Paul operate. A total professional. He was really on top of it, and with his experience, pulled it all together with seeming ease. . . . As tough as it was for Paul, after Janis's death the album took on extra special meaning to him, and he pursued it till [it was] complete and released."

John Till

Finishing the album takes ten straight days of work. In the end, the overdubbing, the underdubbing, the cross-cutting from one fragment of usable track to another, the task that seemed all but impossible in the beginning, produce what this was meant to be from the beginning, Janis's best album.*

"That album's a miracle."

Bob Neuwirth

There are eight songs. Two were finished before Janis died—final band tracks, final vocals. Paul and Phil Macy have assembled six vocals piece by piece, with newly recorded band tracks.

"Buried Alive in the Blues" will be on the album as an instrumental.

The tenth track is Janis's a capella rendition of "Mercedes Benz," a song Janis and Bob Neuwirth wrote together around the poet Michael McClure's line, "Lord, won't you buy me a Mercedes Benz." At Sunset Sound, Janis sang it one day on the spur of the moment, and it was captured by the safety tape, a quarter-inch tape left running during the sessions lest a good riff or a good idea be otherwise lost.

---

* In recognition of Full Tilt's achievement in finishing the record, and all the joy they gave Janis, Bob Gordon proposes to her family that the band should receive a small percentage from sales of the album. Like Sam Andrew's effort to get something for the Kozmic Blues musicians from that album, this one fails.

Janis and Paul had planned to expand the song into something more elaborate, but the simple a capella recording seems perfect now, capped by Janis's happy "That's it," at the end, followed by her cackling laugh.

The next day, Clark Pierson and I leave the Landmark in my white Volvo late in the afternoon. We get as far as Santa Barbara, where we spend the night with a bottle of mezcal and a friend of mine from the folk days in Berkeley. Nan O'Byrne is a Texan who has found a home in Santa Barbara. In the early sixties, in Berkeley, with her fellow Texan and hangout partner Suzy West, the two of them defined for me the archetype of Texas women at their best—smart, funny, independent, able to be friends with men, able to keep them in line without putting them down, able to encourage them, admire them, love them, without ever allowing a man to condescend to them in any way—a model that fit Janis perfectly.

EACH DAY AT the Landmark, before we all went to the studio to finish the record, I have been on the telephone organizing Janis's wake. We have settled on the Lion's Share, a music club in San Anselmo, Marin County. The only night we can book the club, which has a schedule laid out for weeks in advance, is on a Monday, when the Lion's Share is usually dark.

On Monday, October 26, three weeks and a day after Janis died, the wake is attended by her old San Francisco friends, by new friends from the tours and the music world beyond the Bay, by all the members of Big Brother and Full Tilt Boogie and most of Kozmic Blues. We have invited Janis's parents, but they choose to stay home. Janis's sister, Laura Lee, flies out from Texas. Laura is twenty-one now and makes her own decisions. I am her road manager for the evening, but that doesn't stop her from getting drunk enough to do Janis proud.

Albert is even quieter than usual. He assumes no role in the festivities. He doesn't preside at a table or serve as a focus around which others gather, as he often does in other settings. Neither is he simply an observer. He needs to be here in this time and place. He is present.

Albert astonishes Linda Gravenites by asking her to dance. I have never seen Albert dance before. I have never *imagined* Albert dancing. Out on the floor, shuffling in time with the music, he looks pleased with himself, and it occurs to me that he wants to please Janis by dancing at her wake.

Big Brother plays, with Nick Gravenites at the mike and, for a song or two, with James Gurley's son, Hongo, on drums, in his public debut. Hongo is about five, on his way to becoming a serious drummer.

David Cohen, Country Joe's keyboard player, quiets the room when he plays "Janis," a song Joe wrote about her, commemorating their time together.

The music continues into the night, members of Quicksilver and the Dead and Big Brother and other musicians forming onstage combinations that are unique to this time and place. Yet despite the music and the open bar that Janis has funded, and other intoxicants privately ingested, the party never achieves the energy level or the buoyant feeling of a ripping good time that Janis wanted it to be, for the simple reason that she isn't here. Her absence creates a gap, a void that prevents this gathering of friends from achieving critical mass.

AFTER THE WAKE, I find ways to fill every moment, to keep *doing* so I don't have to stop and simply *be*. In November I fly east and spend Thanksgiving at Albert's house in Bearsville. He has taken in the Full Tilt boys, giving them a place to shelter from the world until they feel whole again. I am glad for them, and fail to recognize the same need in myself.

Finally, in mid-December, I drive down to Big Sur, where I went two years earlier to recover from the calamities of 1968, where we threw the *I Ching* in the interregnum between Johnson and Nixon, and as Janis turned from Big Brother to seek her independent path. A week, I say, maybe more. Peter and Marya Melchior take me in for as long as I need to stay.

On the isolated coast, the days are quiet. I have read somewhere that alternating hot and cold baths were once a prescribed remedy for schizophrenia. I'm not feeling clinically imbalanced, but I feel the need for a regimen to pacify my spirit, so I walk to the baths each day, and when I've soaked long enough in the hot sulfur waters I emerge from the tub and play a stream of cold water from a hose over my steaming body. I lean on the wooden railing and absorb the vast peace of the Pacific Ocean.

A book of Greek myths on Peter and Marya's shelves offers to remove me by a couple of millennia from the memories of recent events. Instead, I find Janis in the archetype. A footnote suggests that "tragic flaw" is not the best interpretation of the Greek *hamartia*, which might be better translated as a mistake, a misstep, an error in judgment. The tragedies affect us because the protagonists of the myths—men and women of exceptional abilities and achievements—come to *unjustified* bad ends. Their downfall is a reversal of fortune. If the hero's flaw were ordained by the gods, if his bad end were inevitable, if there were no more to the outcome than predestination, his fate would not engage our emotions effectively. And that is the purpose of the myths—so Aristotle wrote—to engage our emotions and to offer catharsis. In tragedy, the hero does not deserve his misfortune; his suffering is out of proportion to his offense. We feel the inequity.

The paradigm fits Janis as if it were drawn from her life alone. She perceived a longer-lasting future than she had formerly imagined, in which she could continue to exercise her exceptional abilities. Her musical potential was greater than ever. She showed that she could overcome her predilection for self-indulgence, and she experienced the exaltation of that achievement. She had learned a measure of self-discipline, but she hadn't yet fully embraced caution and restraint among her hard-earned truths. She believed she could flirt with her addiction. At a time when her fortunes were on the rise, she made a misstep, and she fell. The outcome was out of proportion to the offense.*

Christmas comes and goes. I stay on the coast for a month. In the new year, I return to the world.

I DREAMED ABOUT Janis once, in the first year after she died. She came to say good-bye, and to seek, one last time, my blessing: In the dream, I am backstage at a concert in a large auditorium. I can see neither the stage nor the audience, but I can hear Janis at her best, singing her heart out, backed by Full Tilt Boogie. When the song ends, the audience gives her a roof-raising ovation. She comes tripping down a ramp to where I am waiting, and I see in her face the same little-girl uncertainty that I have seen so many times in life. Despite the sustained applause from the auditorium, there is real concern in her voice when she asks me, "Did I do okay?"

I take her in my arms and hug her with all my strength. "You did great."

God bless, and Godspeed.

---

*At the time, I believed that Janis had misjudged the dose of heroin she could tolerate. When I later learned from Laura Joplin's *Love, Janis* that the heroin she took was unusually strong, and that others among her dealer's customers had died of overdoses in the same week, I saw that Janis's share of the responsibility for her misstep was smaller than I had imagined, and this made her fate seem all the more disproportionate.

Memories

"And Janis, I think with all of her blustering and shows of strength, was an enormously vulnerable human being. And I think that people responded to that, responded to the fact that here is somebody putting on a spectacular show of strength because they're really—the only strength there is will. The world really is—*is* more than this poor child can cope with. And all of the people that Janis had close to her were thick-skinned Jewish mothers. I mean you are a thick-skinned Jewish mother when it comes to road managing. You don't let anything go by without being there with a stern word and comforting hand. Albert, the same. Me, I'm a Jewish mother, with all the credentials."

—Paul Rothchild, record producer, Janis's *Pearl* album

"I think most people go through what Janis had to deal with, wanting to be loved and wanting to be accepted and wanting to have an impact, but she was so fierce about it, and it was so unhidden, that she just hit you like a ton of bricks. And I felt it then, and I felt it all 'til now. That something about her was just so intense, it cut right into your soul."

—**Margaret Moore, author's companion at Threadgill birthday party, Janis's high school reunion**

"She was a very decent person, a very vulnerable person, a person who really wanted to be loved, and was desperate to be loved and to have relationships with other people. And that's the thing that I remember most about it. And then as a second thought, I think, 'Wow, could she sing.'"

—**Bennett Glotzer, Grossman Glotzer Management**

"In the last year of her life, I saw her two times, I think, maybe more, but two times that I remember the conversation. . . . One was in her house in Larkspur, and she spoke of the fact that she could sing. She said 'I'm really doin' it, man. For the first time in my life, I believe that I can sing.' . . . She was really excited that she had finally found it, and that she had mastered something that had bothered her for her whole life, her whole singing life, anyway."

—**Milan Melvin, Janis's lover, 1967**

"A great singer, a really great singer, is someone that no matter what material they take, who wrote the material, it becomes them. They make it themselves. They make it, in some way, like part of their autobiographical statement. And Janis is like that so much. . . . And if she did 'Bobby McGee,' she did 'Bobby McGee' not because it's a good song, which it is, but because in some way there was some part of her life that it spoke of. And 'Piece of My Heart,' and 'Ball and Chain,' and 'Move Over,' and 'Try a Little Bit Harder.' And every song. 'Maybe,' and there's

a range of songs, but they were all, to her, she made them autobiographical. And that is like the essence of what to me makes a great singer."

—David Getz, Big Brother and the Holding Company

"She overcame so much. It's usually not reserved for the funky people to
make it. That's not part of their future, or part of their role. . . . They're
not into the showbiz part of it. They're into the soul part of it, the expression, the artistic part of it. And really the need to use the medium, they
have to, emotionally, need to sing. It's not like they do it because they
do it best and they can make money at it. They sing because they must
sing and it's the only way they can express themselves in a manner that
they can get satisfied."

—Nick Gravenites, singer, songwriter,
Albert Grossman's friend and confidant

"Of all the lead singers that I know, or have worked with, she was the
most workable singer. I mean she was a producer's dream, for me."

—Paul Rothchild

"I feel that she was coming into her own, emotionally, as a person, and
that the drug use was so incidental, that her death was such a filthy dirty
little trick."

—Seth Morgan, Janis's fiancé

"That's the last time I ever saw her, spent any time with her, sitting in
the Landmine—the Landmark—in the hotel room, thinking about how
incredibly sweet she was, or could be, how sensitive and what a terrific
warm, open, pulsating human being she was, and how torn down and
exhausted and wrecked and self-destructive she was at the same time.
Just thinking, 'God, I wish that she could find a balance,' you know,

because what she was going for was so much softer and sweeter than anything that came through in a public persona. And I think that public persona, while it was fascinating to watch, just wasn't all of who she was."

—Howard Hesseman, the Committee

"Let's just say that Janis was a great performer, 'cause above and beyond anything else, she was a great performer. She had musical skills, but her performance skills carried the day even if she had no throat, right? . . . It's part stage chops, it's part desperation, it's part 'I love you. I need to be loved so much I'll fucking implode if you don't fucking look at me.' It's like all that fucking stuff. And the thing about it is that she was so much smarter than the public record."

—Bob Neuwirth

"She was a force of nature. And, like all forces of nature . . . she was unpredictable and difficult to be around. She was extraordinarily attractive, in terms of being magnetic, and sometimes repellant. She had the ability to suck all the air out of the room, because she needed it all, and it was more important for her to breathe than for anybody else to, and at the same time, she had the ability to breathe life into a room, depending on whether she was ebbing or flowing."

—Alan Myerson, director, the Committee

"And she also liked being the center of attention, and she liked getting attention from people that she didn't know well, and brief sexual encounters with people who she knew would only do that because she was famous. And she liked that. That was part of the attraction of being famous, and part of the downfall of being famous."

—Lyndall Erb, Janis's roommate, 1970

———

"She was smart, funny, intelligent, warm, caring. She was not a doper, in my mind, despite what she died of. . . . She just didn't want to kill herself. She was not a suicidal person. What she was looking for, and I think found in Big Brother, and to a lesser extent in Full Tilt Boogie, was a core family of people who would accept her for what she is and allow her to be as outgoing and as communicative as she could possibly be."

—Mark Braunstein, Big Brother and Kozmic Blues equipment man

———

"Many people have asked me the question, do you think she did herself in. And I said 'Absolutely not.' There was no question—I mean, suicide—in my mind there was no question of her committing suicide. It had to be an accident. [The heroin] had to have been stronger than she expected. She was on too big a high. She was too happy with where her career was going, and her abilities. . . . It fuckin' near killed me, man. I just could not—that was the first, and stands out in my mind as the most affecting passing of anybody I ever knew, anybody I ever heard of. It still gives me weakness in the knees when I remember the moment. And I had this flash where she—I just got on my scooter [motorcycle] and I rode around Paris in tears, and at one point I felt her climb on the pillion seat, just like she had back in the old days, and give me this little hug and press her cheek against the back of my neck."

—Milan Melvin

———

"I was just devastated. I can't remember the highway, where I was. I might have been coming back from Woodstock. I don't remember. I remember pulling over, and just lighting up a joint. I put her record on. I just couldn't believe it. I was devastated. I was truly devastated. It really affected me. It broke my heart."

—John Fisher, Love Limousines, New York City

———

"Albert wasn't the kind of guy who cried a lot or became visibly hysterical. He was upset. He loved her. It was somebody that he loved a great deal that died. He didn't have any kids. Probably the closest thing he had to a child, for Christ's sake, was Janis."

—Bennett Glotzer

———

"[Albert's] energy and spirit were severely damaged when Janis died. As if he'd lost his alter ego. He adored Janis."

—Peter Yarrow, Peter, Paul and Mary

———

"All my life, I just wanted to be a beatnik. Meet all the heavies, get stoned, get laid, have a good time. That's all I ever wanted. Except I knew I had a good voice and I could always get a couple of beers off of it. All of a sudden someone threw me in this rock-n-roll band. They threw these musicians at me, man, and the sound was coming from behind. The bass was charging me. And I decided then and there that that was it. I never wanted to do anything else."

—Janis Joplin

NOTES

CHAPTER 1

Page 6 "I remember Janis took to you right away, man": Author interview with Sam
Andrew, October 18, 1973.

CHAPTER 2

Page 7 "I eat a persimmon": Robert Penn Warren, *All the King's Men*, Boston: Mariner
Books, 1996, 331.

Page 12 When whisperings of the Monterey Pop Festival reached Gleason's ears: Author
interview with Ralph J. Gleason, October 2, 1973.

*Page 13 "Big Brother and the Holding Company and Janis were on the Pop Festival be-
cause":* Author interview with Ralph J. Gleason, October 2, 1973.

Page 13 Five days before the festival began: Ralph J. Gleason, *San Francisco Chronicle*,
Sunday, June 11, 1967, *This World* magazine, 34.

Page 14 Altschuler said thanks but no thanks: Author interview with D. A. Pennebaker,
June 3, 1997.

Page 19 "Oh, groovy. A nice sound system at last": Monterey Pop, Monterey International
Pop Festival, Inc., 1968, D. A. Pennebaker, director.

Page 20 Denny, still nursing his wounds, has not yet arrived in Monterey: The Mamas &
the Papas: Straight Shooter (video), Rhino Home Video, 1988.

*Page 21 "It's a Mexican standoff, typical of the yawning gulf between L.A. and San
Francisco":* Rock Scully and David Dalton, *Living with the Dead*, Boston: Little,
Brown, 1996, 102–103.

CHAPTER 3

Page 22 The evening performances are sold out: Ralph J. Gleason, *San Francisco Chronicle*, June 11, 1967, *This World* magazine, 34.

Page 22 One girl has hitchhiked from Champaign, Illinois: Monterey Pop, D. A. Pennebaker, director.

Page 24 Over the course of the weekend: Ralph J. Gleason, *San Francisco Chronicle*, June 19, 1967, "On the Town" column.

Page 25 "So much of Monterey had nothing to do with logistics or planning": Bill Graham and Robert Greenfield, *Bill Graham Presents*, New York: Dell, 1992, 189, 193–194.

Page 28 "Sittin' down by my window / Just lookin' out at the rain": Willie Mae Thornton, "Ball and Chain."

Page 28 "Wow. Wow! That's really heavy!": Mama Cass, in *Monterey Pop*, D. A. Pennebaker, director.

Page 28 By the account of one insider, Julius refuses to discuss business: Author interview with San Francisco photographer Bob Seidemann, August 12, 1997.

Page 30 John L. Wasserman, film critic for the San Francisco Chronicle, *said in his review of* Dont Look Back: John L. Wasserman, *San Francisco Chronicle*, May 17, 1967.

Page 31 "Don't worry," Albert said: Author interview with D. A. Pennebaker, June 3, 1997.

Page 32 On Sunday morning, Chief Marinello sends home half the officers: Ralph J. Gleason, *San Francisco Chronicle*, June 21, 1967, "On the Town" column.

Page 33 A plan to have bagsful of the festival's signature pink orchids: Author interview with Peter Pilafian, September 16, 1997.

Page 34 Finally Shankar holds up his arms and the audience quiets: Ralph J. Gleason, *San Francisco Chronicle*, June 21, 1967, "On the Town" column.

Page 35 "The best time of all was Monterey": Janis Joplin, quoted in Laura Joplin, *Love, Janis*, New York: Villard, 1992, 241.

Page 35 They trash the same amp at every show: Ralph J. Gleason, *San Francisco Chronicle*, June 21, 1967, "On the Town" column.

Page 36 "I saw Owsley give him two of his little purple tabs": Author interview with Peter Pilafian, September 16, 1997.

Page 36 "I saw him take, literally, a handful of Owsley tabs": Author interview with Bob Seidemann, August 12, 1997.

Page 37 "I thought that [Monterey] just cut the whole scene wide open": Author interview with Peter Pilafian, September 16, 1997.

Page 37 "My idea of a good festival, the best festival of all time, was Monterey": Grace Slick, quoted in Graham and Greenfield, *Bill Graham Presents*, 189.

CHAPTER 4

Page 40 "The first annual Monterey International Pop Festival this weekend was a beautiful, warm, groovy affair": Ralph J. Gleason, *San Francisco Chronicle*, June 19, 1967, "On the Town" column.

Page 52 "I thought [Joe Val] was a really good steady guy, and a good musician": Author interview with Peter Berg, December 7, 1997.

CHAPTER 5

Page 55 Chet's out-of-hand dismissal of Shad's interest: Author interview with Sam Andrew, December 3, 1997.

Page 55 "I have a problem," she wrote: Janis Joplin, quoted in Laura Joplin, *Love, Janis*, 161–162, letter dated August 22, 1966. In this letter, and in others Laura quotes in her book, there is evidence that Janis would write a letter over several days and date it when she mailed it. In this case, Janis evidently began the letter at least a week before Big Brother left California for Chicago, where their gig at Mother Blues began on Tuesday, August 23.

Page 55 Paul gathered several musicians in a living room in Berkeley: Author interviews with Paul Rothchild, March 19, 1974, and Sam Andrew, July 27, 1997.

Page 56 In San Francisco, Paul Rothchild and I tried to recruit Janis Joplin for Elektra: Jac Holzman and Gavan Daws, *Follow the Music: The Life and High Times of Elektra Records in the Great Years of American Pop Music*, Santa Monica, Calif.: First Media, 1998, 157.

Page 56 In the letter to her parents, Janis expressed another doubt: Janis Joplin, quoted in Laura Joplin, *Love, Janis*, 162.

Page 56 Janis told the boys about Paul Rothchild's offer **through** *Taken aback by Peter's onslaught, Janis gave in:* Author interviews with David Getz, July 24, 1997, and Sam Andrew, December 3, 1997.

Page 57 At her next meeting with Paul Rothchild: Author interview with Paul Rothchild, March 19, 1974.

Page 57 She wrote her parents: Laura Joplin, *Love, Janis*, 162.

Page 59 Janis comes offstage, skipping and happy: Author interview with Ralph J. Gleason, October 2, 1973.

Page 60 "Big Brother was really a delight and Miss Joplin is a gas": Ralph J. Gleason, *San Francisco Chronicle*, Monday, September 18, 1967, "On the Town" column.

Page 60 Graham knows that realizing Big Brother's full potential: Graham and Greenfield, *Bill Graham Presents*, 205. In this book, Graham gave his reasons for passing Janis to Grossman: "I knew who Janis was. I knew she was not a sometime thing.

She needed full-time management or she would go astray. . . . And I couldn't give my life over to her. Because I felt that what I was doing was bigger and more important than dealing with one single artist."

Page 61 "At that period, there were only two people that Albert really wanted to work with": Author interview with Sally Grossman and Barry Feinstein, September 4, 1997.

Page 61 Linda was one of a few creative women: Author interview with Linda Gravenites, May 9, 1986.

Page 62 "If you want to stay in San Francisco and play around": Author interview with Linda Gravenites, May 9, 1986. Linda offered an additional reason why Janis, for her part, was willing to fire Julius: "Julius was such a prick sometimes. And Janis, of course, gets her back up very easily. So they were just bitching at each other constantly. And I think what happened was, Julius freaked out after the Monterey Pop Festival. It got too big for him to cope."

Page 63 More recently, Columbia has expressed interest: Author interview with Peter Albin, July 19, 1997.

Page 64 "I wouldn't say that either Jerry or Herb are really nasty people": Author interview with Bob Gordon, May 10, 1986.

Page 64 Bob represented Big Brother when they were asked to appear: Author interview with Bob Gordon, May 10, 1986.

Page 65 They ask Albert to guarantee that he will make them: Author interview with David Getz, July 24, 1997.

CHAPTER 6

Page 72 Invited to sit in with Junior Wells at the Blue Flame Lounge: Author interview with Nick Gravenites, December 7, 1973.

CHAPTER 7

Page 75 She and Dave Getz had been to a party in the city: Author interview with David Getz, July 24, 1997.

Page 85 "She was very compassionate": Author interview with Sam Andrew, July 27, 1997.

Page 88 "One day Nancy [later James's wife] and I took LSD together": Author interview with Bob Seidemann, August 12, 1997.

Page 90 One of the actors, Howard Hesseman, emigrated from Oregon to San Francisco for the jazz: Author interview with Howard Hesseman, August 8, 1997.

Page 91 "I would let her sing at the Coffee Gallery": Author interview with Howard Hesseman, August 8, 1997.

Page 93 "I just remember that when I actually heard her": Author interview with Howard Hesseman, August 8, 1997.

CHAPTER 8

Page 98 He met Janis in the Haight, on the street: Author interview with Mark Braunstein, September 10, 1997.

Page 99 "Before I was working with the band": Author interview with Mark Braunstein, September 10, 1997.

Page 101 "She could play the roles that men were playing really well": Author interview with Nick Gravenites, December 14, 1973.

Page 102 Except for Janis, who says it makes her think too much: Author interview with Linda Gravenites, May 9, 1986.

Page 102 With her boyfriend at the time: Author interview with Milan Melvin, October 5, 1997.

Page 102 Sam is a former speed freak as well: Author interview with Sam Andrew, July 19, 1997.

Page 102 At the Golden Bear: Author interviews with Sam Andrew, April 23, 1997, and David Getz, July 24, 1997.

Page 103 It rattles the band's confidence when: Laura Joplin, *Love, Janis*, 211.

CHAPTER 9

Page 110 "You were very distant": Author interview with Mark Braunstein, September 9, 1997.

Page 112 "There were women who turned her on": Author interview with Linda Gravenites, May 9, 1986.

Page 113 It was Debbie who received Janis through *Debbie tried to follow up on the idea:* Author interview with Debbie Green, April 3, 1998.

Page 114 On January 19, 1968, which is Janis's twenty-fifth birthday: Laura Joplin, *Love, Janis*, 214, letter dated January 31, 1968.

Page 115 After the gig, Janis doesn't fly back: Laura Joplin, *Love, Janis*, 215.

Page 115 The reason for Janis's restraint at Kaleidoscope: Author interview with Linda Gravenites, May 9, 1986.

Page 119 "Janis Joplin Is Climbing Fast in the Heady Rock Firmament": Robert Shelton, *New York Times*, February 19, 1968.

Page 120 We grab a couple of cabs and head uptown to the Black Rock: Laura Joplin, *Love, Janis*, 219, letter dated February 20, 1968, confirms the date of the signing.

Page 121 Meet Big Brother and the Holding Company: Albert B. Grossman Management press release pages.

CHAPTER 10

Page 127 "At first, [New York] seemed to have made us all crazy": Janis Joplin, quoted in Nat Hentoff, *The New York Times*, April 21, 1968, Sec. II.

Page 127 The other act on the bill is a new band: Author interview with Al Kooper, June 11, 1998.

Page 131 The Grande's manager, Russ Gibb: Goodman, *The Mansion on the Hill*, 160.

Page 131 When Albert listens to the recordings: Author interview with Sam Andrew, July 27, 1997.

Page 132 "For years, it was our particular lot not to rise to a given occasion": Author interview with Sam Andrew, July 27, 1997.

Page 133 The only conclusion that comes out of the meeting: Author interview with Sam Andrew, July 27, 1997.

Page 134 "I think fundamentally he didn't like Janis": Author interview with Sam Andrew, July 27, 1997.

Page 134 On the day we're filming, Janis arrives after the others: Studio scene and dialogue: *Comin' Home* (video), by Chris Hegedus and D. A. Pennebaker, 1991.

Page 135 "It was very hard to work with John Simon": Author interview with David Getz, July 24, 1997.

Page 138 "I always felt that the studio recording was stifling": Author interview with Peter Albin, July 19, 1997.

Page 138 A few people in New York who care about rock music: Graham and Greenfield, *Bill Graham Presents*, 229.

Page 138 Together, Graham and Monck have pulled off a miracle: Graham and Greenfield, 230–234.

Page 138 Big Brother headlines the opening night, with Albert King: Albert King was not related to the better-known B. B. King, but the two legendary blues guitarists came from the same part of Mississippi, where they were born two and a half years apart, Albert in 1923 and B.B. (Riley B. King) in 1925. B.B. wrote of Albert in his autobiography, "He wasn't my brother in blood, but he sure was my brother in Blues" (cascadeblues.org).

Page 139 The manager of the Anderson prints counterfeit tickets: Graham and Greenfield, *Bill Graham Presents*, 235.

Page 139 Among Graham's ushers, clad in an orange jumpsuit, is Robert Mapplethorpe: Patti Smith, *Just Kids*, New York: Ecco, 2010.

Page 140 Myra's greatest coup is arranging: Laura Joplin, *Love, Janis*, 221, letter dated April 4, 1968.

Page 141 For a guarantee of $6,000 against 50 percent of the gross over $12,000: Author's copy of Electric Factory contract.

Page 143 The next day, they're back in Columbia's Studio E: These titles, recorded in Studio E on April 1, 1968, are on Janis's posthumous CD *Farewell Song*. Columbia CK 37569.

Page 143 Backstage on opening night: Jazz & Pop magazine, May 1968, 34.

CHAPTER 11

Page 145 "We don't want to be connected with anti-anydamnthing": Scully and Dalton, *Living with the Dead*, 147.

Page 145 On Saturday, U.S. troops guard the Capitol Building: Theodore White, *The Making of the President 1968*, New York: Atheneum, 1969, 209.

Page 147 On Sunday, April 21, the **New York Times** *publishes an article:* Nat Hentoff, *The New York Times*, April 21, 1968, section II, 17, 19.

Page 149 "Janis was as together in the studio as anyone": Elliot Mazer, quoted in Laura Joplin, *Love, Janis*, 223–224.

Page 152 Howard Hesseman and Carl Gottlieb have made the acquaintance: Author interview with Howard Hesseman, August 8, 1997.

Page 153 By Howard's account, Jim took hold of Janis by the hair: Author interview with Howard Hesseman, August 8, 1997.

Page 153 Garry Goodrow's old lady, Annie: Author interview with Garry Goodrow, October 17, 1973, at which Annie was present.

Page 154 David Crosby, of the Byrds, has hung out with the drunk Morrison: David Crosby and Carl Gottlieb, *Long Time Gone: The Autobiography of David Crosby*, New York: Doubleday, 1988, 124–125.

Page 154 As Howard and Carl beat their retreat: Author interview with Howard Hesseman, August 8, 1997.

Page 156 At one point, Janis and Linda were lifted off their feet: Author interview with Linda Gravenites, May 9, 1986.

Page 157 South Dakota holds its primary: White, *The Making of the President 1968*, 182.

Page 157 In the piece that's new to me, the actors take a question: Author interview with Alan Myerson, September 27, 1997.

Page 161 His weekly **Letter from America** *for the BBC this week:* Alistair Cooke, *Letter from America*, June 7, 1968.

Page 162 He counseled Bobby against challenging Gene McCarthy: White, *The Making of the President 1968*, 163–164.

CHAPTER 12

Page 164 "John Simon and I talked in the last few years": Author interview with David Getz, July 24, 1997.

Page 167 Where Warner Brothers mogul Jack Warner used to eat in anonymity: Jean Stein, "West of Eden," *The New Yorker*, February 23/March 2, 1998 (double issue), 166–167.

Page 168 "dope, sex, and cheap thrills": It is my belief that the now better-known phrase "Drugs, sex, and rock and roll" did not come into use in the sixties. To accept that I am wrong, I will need to see the phrase in print, with a sixties dateline.

Page 170 "I couldn't possibly do that": Author interview with Bob Gordon, May 10, 1986.

Page 171 Threadgill and Wein have a friend: Author interview with Robert L. Jones, of George Wein's Festival Productions, June 3, 1997.

Page 171 Two years ago, the festival board almost rejected: Author interview with Robert L. Jones, June 3, 1997.

Page 172 This year's Newport program booklet: 1968 Newport Folk Festival program booklet, 17.

Page 172 This year, B. B. King is getting $1,000: Author's notes made at the time on Newport festival program; author interview with Robert L. Jones, June 3, 1997.

Page 173 At Newport, Janis and Geoff fall in together: Author interviews with Geoff Muldaur, May 5, 1997, and January 3, 1998.

Page 174 He responded positively to a suggestion by Grossman: Author conversation with Sally Grossman, July 2, 2014.

Page 174 He invited Joan to appear at the Gate of Horn: Joan Baez, *And a Voice to Sing With*, New York: Summit/Simon & Schuster, 1987, 58–61.

Page 175 Albert held out the lure of a recording contract: Baez, *And a Voice to Sing With*, 58, 61–62.

Page 176 Soon after Big Brother comes offstage: Author interview with Peter Albin, May 8, 1986.

Page 176 Albert says, "Something's just not happening": Author interview with Peter Albin, May 8, 1986.

CHAPTER 13

Page 178 "*I love those guys more than anybody else in the whole world*": Janis Joplin, quoted in David Dalton, *Piece of My Heart: A Portrait of Janis Joplin*, New York: Da Capo, 134–135.

Page 179 "*I think from Monterey on*": Author interview with David Getz, July 24, 1997.

Page 179 **When the others leave, Sam stays behind:** Author interview with Sam Andrew, October 18, 1973.

Page 181 **As we travel from city to city he helps her think:** Author interview with Sam Andrew, October 7, 1973.

Page 182 **It goes gold in three days:** Laura Joplin, *Love, Janis*, 237, letter dated September 28, 1968. Based on time and event references in the letter, much of it was written at least four to five days earlier.

Page 182 "*See, Albert deals in sensible things*": Author interview with Nick Gravenites, December 7, 1973.

Page 183 "*[Albert] doesn't direct me*": Janis Joplin, quoted in Laura Joplin, *Love, Janis*, 276.

Page 183 **Lip-readers interpret Daley's response:** Todd Gitlin, *The Sixties: Years of Hope, Days of Rage*, Toronto: Bantam Books, 1987, 334.

Page 183 **Three weeks earlier, in Miami Beach:** Norman Mailer, *Miami and the Siege of Chicago*, New York: Primus, 80.

Page 184 "*I always have a sense of history*": E-mail from Sam Andrew, April 2, 2011.

Page 187 **On an expedition to Beverly Hills:** Laura Joplin, *Love, Janis*, 227, undated letter.

Page 188 **In a letter home, Janis alerts her family:** Laura Joplin, *Love, Janis*, 238, letter dated September 28, 1968.

Page 189 **Where everyone in the band but Peter Albin:** Author interview with David Getz, July 24, 1997.

Page 191 **After the concert, the Joplins experience firsthand:** Laura Joplin, *Love, Janis*, 240–241.

CHAPTER 14

Page 199 "*It has to do with a certain self-abnegation*": Author interview with Nick Gravenites, December 7, 1973.

Page 200 "*I actually found Janis's Porsche for her*": Author interviews with Bob Gordon, May 10, 1986, and September 10, 1997.

Page 200 **We fly to Memphis two days ahead of the Stax-Volt gig:** Details of the Memphis rehearsal, party, and concert from Bill King, "Janis: Memphis Meltdown," 1995, unpublished; posted to allaboutjazz.com, October 2009; and Stanley Booth, "The Memphis Debut of the Janis Joplin Revue," *Rolling Stone*, February 1, 1969, 1, 4.

Page 201 We considered names for the new band: Laura Joplin, *Love, Janis*, 246.

Page 201 When Janis sees a poster for the Stax-Volt show: King, "Janis: Memphis Meltdown."

Page 201 Mark Braunstein and George Ostrow have worked with the equipment: Author interview with Mark Braunstein, September 7, 1997.

Page 204 Inferior men are rising to positions of power: Richard Wilhelm, *The I Ching, or Book of Changes*, English translation by Cary F. Baynes, Princeton, N.J.: Princeton University Press, 1967, 93–96.

Page 204 To everything there is a season: Book of Ecclesiastes; adaptation and music by Pete Seeger.

CHAPTER 15

Page 206 "I had never even heard of Janis Joplin": Author interview with Richard Kermode, January 25, 1974.

Page 209 Sam Andrew comes off the stage unsure: E-mail from Sam Andrew, January 3, 1999.

Page 209 "Miss Joplin has never been better": Michael Lydon, *The New York Times Magazine*, Sunday, February 23, 1969, section VI. The *Times* review of Janis's February 11 debut at Fillmore East is quoted in a sidebar to this piece.

Page 212 The writer is Michael Lydon, a Bay Area freelancer: The New York Times Magazine, February 23, 1969, 39.

Page 212 "Rumors had come from New York, where she debuted": Robb Baker, *Chicago Tribune*, March 9, 1969, A6.

Page 215 He shook my hand!: Laura Joplin, *Love, Janis*, 250.

Page 215 The latest edition of **Rolling Stone***:* Laura Joplin, *Love, Janis*, 246.

Page 217 "Lots of people don't want their stars to change": Author interview with Jon McIntire, May 8, 1986.

CHAPTER 16

Page 232 "Don't you know how happy we must be?": Tape recording by Bob Neuwirth, Albert Hall, April 21, 1969.

Page 233 I figure if you take an audience: Janis Joplin, quoted in Dalton, *Piece of My Heart*, 162–164.

Page 233 "Do you prefer it?": Tape recording by Bob Neuwirth, Albert Hall, April 21, 1969.

Page 234 "I'm so excited!": Tape recording by Bob Neuwirth, April 21, 1969.

Page 235 In Janis's suite, the presence of old friends: Account of events in Janis's room from author interview with Bob Seidemann, August 12, 1997.

CHAPTER 17

Page 238 Janis and Sam get word that Nancy Gurley: Author interviews with David Getz, July 24, 1997, and Sam Andrew, April 23, 1997.

Page 238 She will contribute to the legal fees: Author interview with Bob Gordon, May 10, 1986.

Page 243 "I felt the [new band] was constantly trying too hard": Author interview with Mark Braunstein, September 9, 1997.

Page 247 "Every now and then a guitarist will still come up to me": Author interview with Sam Andrew, July 27, 1997.

Page 248 Sam has known Albert longest: Author interview with Sam Andrew, October 18, 1973.

Page 248 Not long after this confrontation, on another evening at the Landmark: Paul Liberatore, *Marin Independent Journal,* July 14, 2006, interview with Sam Andrew.

Page 248 Walking across the patio by the pool: Author interview with Richard Kermode, January 25, 1974.

Page 251 "Janis was like this complete person": Author interview with Linda Gravenites, May 9, 1986.

Page 251 John Till is a Canadian who shares musical credentials: E-mail from John Till, March 26, 2004.

Page 252 Janis sings "To Love Somebody" and joins Cavett on the set: Video of talk segment from *The Dick Cavett Show,* July 18, 1969.

Page 253 From audience suggestions, an emotion is assigned: Author interviews with Garry Goodrow, October 17, 1973, and Howard Hesseman, August 8, 1997.

Page 253 Janis is assigned frustration, and Cavett love: Laura Joplin, *Love, Janis,* 256, is the source for the specific emotions.

CHAPTER 18

Page 259 "Here comes Peter Cottontail": Words and music by Steve Nelson and Jack Rollins, who also wrote "Rudolph, the Red-Nosed Reindeer."

Page 260 "The important thing that you've proven to the world": Max Yazgur, in *Woodstock: 3 Days of Peace & Music* (film), Warner Bros. Inc., 1970, Michael Wadleigh, director.

Page 260 "Woodstock, in all its mud and glory": Baez, *And a Voice to Sing With,* 165.

Page 260 "There was a vast relief today": Alistair Cooke, *The Guardian,* August 19, 1969.

Page 260 "Notwithstanding the personality": Quoted by Barnard L. Collier, "Tired Rock Fans Begin Exodus," *New York Times,* August 18, 1969.

Page 262 "But it was very East Coast, Woodstock": Graham and Greenfield, *Bill Graham Presents*, 282.

CHAPTER 19

Page 264 Somehow this bizarre exchange banishes John's doubts: Author interview with John Till, Clark Pierson, and Richard Bell, October 16, 1973.

Page 266 Carl keeps us amused in the green room: Author interview with Carl Gottlieb, August 7, 1997.

Page 268 We have got to get ourselves back to the Garden: "Woodstock," words and music by Joni Mitchell.

Page 268 "Tom Jones could've been a real heavyweight in the music biz": Janis Joplin, quoted in Dalton, *Piece of My Heart*, 64.

Page 272 Bobby connected with Michael the same day: Author interview with Bob Neuwirth, September 28, 1997.

Page 273 "Oh honey, I know how you feel, I know you feel that you're through": "Little Girl Blue," music by Richard Rodgers, lyrics by Lorenz Hart.

Page 274 "It was like a concentration camp for a day": Graham and Greenfield, *Bill Graham Presents*, 300.

Page 276 "With the Kozmic Blues Band, nobody gave it a chance": Author interview with Cornelius "Snooky" Flowers, October 20, 1997.

Page 277 "an excellent performance": Mike Jahn, "Janis Joplin Gives a Rousing Display of Blues and Rock," *New York Times*, December 20, 1969.

Page 280 "Heroin has some payoffs": Author interview with David Getz, July 24, 1997.

BRAZILIAN INTERLUDE

Page 283 Before she went to Carnival: Events in this paragraph from Laura Joplin, *Love, Janis*, 269–275, and author interview with Linda Gravenites, May 9, 1986.

Page 284 "When I came back from England": Author interview with Linda Gravenites, May 9, 1986.

CHAPTER 20

Page 286 Bobby goes to the Village to hear Ramblin' Jack Elliott through *newspaper headlines announcing the Kent State massacre:* Author interview with Bob Neuwirth, September 28, 1997.

Page 289 We hear Judy Collins sing "If I Had a Golden Thread," and a voice that may be Tom Hayden exhorting us: Author's recording of the demonstration on the National Mall, May 10, 1969.

Page 292 In the final days of the Kozmic Blues Band: Author interview with John Till, Clark Pierson, and Richard Bell, October 16, 1973.

Page 293 Clark is from Albert Lea, Minnesota: Author interview with Clark Pierson, John Till, and Richard Bell, October 16, 1973.

Page 295 Bennett Glotzer, who has been Albert's partner since: Author interview with Bennett Glotzer, August 11, 1997.

Page 296 During her set, a naked couple tried to make it onstage: Author interview with Peter Albin, September 15, 2011.

Page 296 Afterward, when Janis was leaving the hall: Author interview with Bennett Glotzer, August 11, 1997.

Page 298 As Jack tells the story: Author interview with Ramblin' Jack Elliott, July 25, 1997.

CHAPTER 21

Page 302 Janis has warned Dalton at the outset: Dalton, *Piece of My Heart*, 21–22, 24.

Page 305 "Something happened last year and I became a grownup": Dalton, *Piece of My Heart*, 185.

Page 308 "She knew what she wanted": Author interview with John Till, Clark Pierson, and Richard Bell, October 16, 1973.

CHAPTER 22

Page 316 It turns out that when Bill arrived in New York: Bill King, "Janis: Memphis Meltdown," 1995, unpublished; posted to allaboutjazz.com, October 2009, and e-mails to author, April 14 and 17, 2011.

Page 319 "Full Tilt Boogie, from what Janis was telling us": Author interview with Rock Scully, October 2, 1973.

Page 321 "The singer is only as good as the band": Dalton, *Piece of My Heart*, 233.

Page 324 "Everybody was just wiped, and pale": Author interview with Clark Pierson, Richard Bell, and John Till, October 16, 1973.

Page 324 "I've never seen Jerry drunk like he got drunk on that train": Scully and Dalton, *Living with the Dead*, Boston: Little, Brown, 1996, 197.

Page 327 "I had a corner room on the twenty-eighth floor": Author interview with John Till, Oct. 16, 1973.

Page 328 "The times that I went out with Full Tilt": Author interview with Lyndall Erb, October 18, 1997.

CHAPTER 23

Page 330 For Janis, Threadgill was a mentor and an inspiration: Laura Joplin, *Love, Janis*, 101–102.

Page 331 On a small stage in one corner of the lounge: Author interview with Margaret Moore, October 7, 1997.

Page 334 "Kenneth was as big a ham as Janis": Author interview with Margaret Moore, October 7, 1997.

Page 334 When the applause dies down: Author interview with Margaret Moore, October 7, 1997.

Page 335 "I just remember that she was just awesome": Author interview with Margaret Moore, October 7, 1997.

Page 336 I learn from Margaret that Janis told Julie she had to promise me: E-mail from Margaret Moore, July 15, 2011.

CHAPTER 24

Page 340 "I haven't had so much fun since the first year with Big Brother!": Janis Joplin, quoted in John Wasserman, *San Francisco Chronicle*, July 15, 1970, 47.

Page 343 "Grossman not only said his clients were artists, he believed it": Fred Goodman, *The Mansion on the Hill: Dylan, Young, Geffen, Springsteen, and the Head-on Collision of Rock and Commerce*, New York: Times Books, 1997, 273.

Page 344 When Janis shows an interest in the technical aspects: Laura Joplin, *Love, Janis*, 292.

Page 349 "That was when I first realized": Author interview with Margaret Moore, October 7, 1997.

Page 351 "Man, those people hurt me": Janis Joplin, quoted in Michael Lydon, *New York Times Magazine*, Sunday, February 23, 1969, section VI.

Page 352 Q: What do you remember most about Port Arthur?: Janis, Crawley Films/MCA Home Video, 1974, F. R. Crawley, executive producer.

Page 353 "That name was not supposed to reach the press": Janis Joplin, quoted in Laura Joplin, *Love, Janis*, 300.

Page 353 As Bob Neuwirth makes his way back to our table: Author interview with Bob Neuwirth, September 28, 1997.

Page 353 It's meant to be funny, but: Laura Joplin, *Love, Janis*, 296–297.

Page 354 On Saturday, Janis and Clark Pierson and David Dalton went to see: Dalton, *Piece of My Heart*, 136–139.

Page 354 Bound to continue her quest tonight: Author interview with Margaret Moore, October 7, 1997; Laura Joplin, *Love, Janis*, 301–302.

Page 355 "And I remember Janis was kind of tinkly and giggly": Author interview with Margaret Moore, October 7, 1997.

Page 355 "And she was foul-mouthin' him": Author interview with Bob Neuwirth, September 28, 1997.

CHAPTER 25

Page 357 Songs arrive by the bucketload, through *a manageable signal to work with:* Author interview with Fritz Richmond, November 27, 1997.

Page 358 In the first week, Janis and Paul Rothchild settle into a routine: Information on music submissions and Janis-Paul routine: author interview with Fritz Richmond, November 27, 1997.

Page 359 "Rothchild is . . . a little bit above the musicians": Author interview with Brad Campbell, October 11, 1973.

Page 364 Seth is surprised to learn that: Author interview with Seth Morgan, February 10, 1974.

Page 365 "I felt very out of place": Author interview with Seth Morgan, February 10, 1974.

CHAPTER 26

Page 374 Bennett Glotzer is here: Author interview with Bennett Glotzer, August 11, 1997.

Page 380 "Everybody continued to make that record with just a little bit more love": Author interview with Paul Rothchild, March 19, 1974.

Page 381 "It was amazing to watch Paul operate": E-mail from John Till, March 26, 2004.

Page 381 "That album's a miracle": Author interview with Bob Neuwirth, September 10, 2012.

Page 385 When I later learned from Laura Joplin's Love, Janis: pages 310–311.

MEMORIES

Page 386 "And Janis, I think with all of her blustering and shows of strength": Author interview with Paul Rothchild, March 19, 1974.

Page 386 "I think most people go through what Janis had to deal with": Author interview with Margaret Moore, October 7, 1997.

Page 387 "She was a very decent person, a very vulnerable person": Author interview with Bennett Glotzer, August 11, 1997.

Page 387 "In the last year of her life, I saw her two times": Author interview with Milan Melvin, October 5, 1997.

Page 387 "A great singer, a really great singer": Author interview with David Getz, July 24, 1997.

Page 388 "She overcame so much": Author interview with Nick Gravenites, December 14, 1973.

Page 388 "Of all the lead singers that I know": Author interview with Paul Rothchild, March 19, 1974.

Page 388 "I feel that she was coming into her own": Author interview with Seth Morgan, February 10, 1974.

Page 388 "That's the last time I ever saw her": Author interview with Howard Hesseman, August 8, 1997.

Page 389 "Let's just say that Janis was a great performer": Author interview with Bob Neuwirth, August 13, 1997.

Page 389 "She was a force of nature": Author interview with Alan Myerson, September 27, 1997.

Page 389 "And she also liked being the center of attention": Author interview with Lyndall Erb, October 18, 1997.

Page 390 "She was smart, funny, intelligent, warm, caring": Author interview with Mark Braunstein, September 9, 1997.

Page 390 "Many people have asked me the question": Author interview with Milan Melvin, October 5, 1997. Milan's guess was right that the heroin Janis took was unusually strong. Laura Joplin, in her biography of her sister, *Love, Janis*, was the first to report this fact (pages 310–311).

Page 390 "I was just devastated": Author interview with John Fisher, November 15, 1997.

Page 391 "Albert wasn't the kind of guy who cried a lot": Author interview with Bennett Glotzer, August 11, 1997.

Page 391 "[Albert's] energy and spirit were severely damaged when Janis died": Peter Yarrow, quoted in Goodman, *The Mansion on the Hill*, 108.

Page 391 "All my life, I just wanted to be a beatnik": Janis Joplin, quoted in Dalton, *Piece of My Heart*, 240–241, from a conversation he taped between Janis and Bonnie Bramlett aboard the Festival Express.

BIBLIOGRAPHY

INTERVIEWS

Taped interviews conducted by the author. In a few cases, notably with Sam Andrew, I followed up on the interviews through e-mails.

Members of Janis's Bands

Big Brother
Peter Albin
Sam Andrew
David Getz
Mark Braunstein—Equipment

Kozmic Blues Band
Sam Andrew
Brad Campbell
Terry Clements
Richard Kermode
John Till
Mark Braunstein—Equipment

Full Tilt Boogie
Richard Bell
Brad Campbell
Clark Pierson
John Till

Others

Barbara Carroll—widow of Bert Block, who was Albert Grossman's partner, 1968–1969

Ramblin' Jack Elliott—the one and only

Lyndall Erb—Janis's roommate, April–October 1970

Mimi Baez Fariña—Joan Baez's sister; wife of Richard Fariña

Barry Feinstein—photographer; *Monterey Pop* cameraman

John Fisher—Love Limousines, New York City

Ralph J. Gleason—*San Francisco Chronicle* music critic

Bennett Glotzer—Albert Grossman's partner, 1969–

Garry Goodrow—the Committee

Robert E. Gordon—attorney for Albert Grossman, Big Brother, Janis

Carl Gottlieb—the Committee; television writer

Bill Graham—rock promoter

Linda Gravenites—Janis's roommate, 1968–spring 1970; former wife of Nick Gravenites

Nick Gravenites—singer, songwriter, Albert Grossman's friend and confidant

Debbie Green—taught Joan Baez guitar; Cabale Creamery coffeehouse, Berkeley

Sally Grossman—widow of Albert Grossman

Howard Hesseman—the Committee

Robert L. Jones—George Wein Productions: Newport Folk Festivals

Jon McIntire—Grateful Dead management

Peter Melchior—Esalen Institute; Big Sur Folk Festivals

Milan Melvin—Janis's early lover in San Francisco; involved in underground FM radio in San Francisco

Seth Morgan—Janis's fiancé at the time of her death

Geoff Muldaur—Jim Kweskin Jug Band

Alan Myerson—director of the Committee

Bob Neuwirth—artist, musician, songwriter

D. A. Pennebaker—filmmaker: *Monterey Pop* and others

Fritz Richmond—author's Cambridge roommate, Charles River Valley Boys, Jim Kweskin Jug Band, Elektra Records engineer

Paul A. Rothchild—record producer: Doors, Janis's *Pearl* album, others

Rock Scully—Grateful Dead management

Bob Seidemann—San Francisco photographer; early friend of Big
Brother and the Holding Company

BOOKS

Baez, Joan, *And a Voice to Sing With*, New York: Summit/Simon & Schuster, 1987.

Crosby, David, and Carl Gottlieb, *Long Time Gone: The Autobiography of David Crosby*, New York: Doubleday, 1988.

Dalton, David, *Piece of My Heart: A Portrait of Janis Joplin*, New York: Da Capo, 1991.

Gleason, Ralph J., *The Jefferson Airplane and the San Francisco Sound*, New York: Ballantine, 1969.

Goodman, Fred, *The Mansion on the Hill: Dylan, Young, Geffen, Springsteen, and the Head-on Collision of Rock and Commerce*, New York: Times Books, 1997.

Graham, Bill, and Robert Greenfield, *Bill Graham Presents*, New York: Dell, 1993.

Grushkin, Paul, *The Art of Rock*, New York: Artabras, 1987.

Holzman, Jac, and Gavan Daws, *Follow the Music: The Life and High Times of Elektra Records in the Great Years of American Pop Music*, Santa Monica, Calif.: First Media, 1998.

Janis Joplin: A Performance Diary, Petaluma, Calif.: Acid Test Productions, 1997, includes ten essays by John Byrne Cooke.

Joplin, Laura, *Love, Janis*, New York: Villard, 1992.

Kooper, Al, *Backstage Passes and Backstabbing Bastards*, New York: Billboard Books, 1998.

Lemke, Gayle, and Jacaeber Kastor, *The Art of the Fillmore 1966–1971*, Petaluma, Calif.: Acid Test Productions, 1997.

Mailer, Norman, *Miami and the Siege of Chicago*, New York: Primus, Donald I. Fine, Inc.

Scully, Rock, and David Dalton, *Living with the Dead*, Boston: Little, Brown, 1996.

Von Schmidt, Eric, and Jim Rooney, *Baby, Let Me Follow You Down: The Illustrated Story of the Cambridge Folk Years*, Garden City, N.Y.: Anchor/Doubleday, 1979.

Whitburn, Joel, ed., *Billboard Top 1000 Singles 1955–96*, Milwaukee, Wis: Hal
    Leonard, 1997.
White, Theodore H., *The Making of the President 1968*, New York: Athe-
    neum, 1969.

FILMS

Comin' Home, by Chris Hegedus and D. A. Pennebaker, 1991.
Janis, Crawley Films/MCA Home Video, 1974, F. R. Crawley, executive pro-
    ducer.
The Mamas & the Papas: Straight Shooter, Rhino Home Video, RNVD 1931,
    1988.
Monterey Pop, The Complete Monterey Pop Festival, The Criterion Collec-
    tion, 1968, Lou Adler and John Phillips, producers; D. A. Pennebaker,
    director.
Woodstock: 3 Days of Peace & Music, Warner Bros. Inc., 1970, Michael Wad-
    leigh, director.

ABOUT THE AUTHOR

To TELL THE story of road-managing Janis Joplin, John Byrne Cooke draws on his experience as a musician and his skill as a writer. He played music from Cambridge, Massachusetts, to New York, Berkeley and Los Angeles. He recorded two albums before Janis made her first. He traveled with all three of Janis's bands, from 1967 until her untimely death in 1970. Cooke has written award-winning historical novels and a critically acclaimed book of nonfiction. As Laura Joplin's *Love, Janis*, is the only book that reveals Janis's life from within the perspective of her family, *On the Road with Janis Joplin* is the only book that tells the story of Janis's brief, spectacular career from inside her life on the rock-and-roll road.

In the folk music boom of the 1960s, John Byrne Cooke was a member of the Cambridge, Massachusetts, bluegrass band the Charles River Valley Boys. Joan Baez and Bob Dylan were among his friends and contemporaries. When rock and roll displaced folk music, John was in the right place at the right time. He was a member of D. A. Pennebaker's film crew at the Monterey Pop Festival in June 1967, where Janis and Jimi Hendrix became overnight sensations.

When Albert Grossman signed on a few months later to manage Janis and her band, Big Brother and the Holding Company, he hired John to road-manage them. When Janis left Big Brother in the fall of 1968, she asked John to stay with her as she formed her new group, the Kozmic Blues Band. John was with Janis and Kozmic Blues when they toured Europe in the spring of 1969, and at Woodstock in August.

Janis's 1970 tour with her last (and best) band, Full Tilt Boogie, included the famed Festival Express train trip across Canada. John was Janis's only companion when she went to Austin to celebrate her mentor Ken Threadgill's sixtieth birthday, and John was with her when she attended her tenth high school reunion in Port Arthur, Texas.

John Byrne Cooke is also an award-winning author of five previous books, a photographer, and an innovative filmmaker. He lives in Jackson Hole, Wyoming. Visit him online at johnbyrnecooke.com.

The author in his pointy-toed Beatles boots.